SAP PRESS e-books

Print or e-book, Kindle or iPad, workplace or airplane: Choose where and how to read your SAP PRESS books! You can now get all our titles as e-books, too:

▸ By download and online access
▸ For all popular devices
▸ And, of course, DRM-free

Convinced? Then go to **www.sap-press.com** and get your e-book today.

Getting Started with SAPUI5

 PRESS

SAP PRESS is a joint initiative of SAP and Galileo Press. The know-how offered by SAP specialists combined with the expertise of the Galileo Press publishing house offers the reader expert books in the field. SAP PRESS features first-hand information and expert advice, and provides useful skills for professional decision-making.

SAP PRESS offers a variety of books on technical and business-related topics for the SAP user. For further information, please visit our website:
www.sap-press.com.

Bönnen, Drees, Fischer, Heinz, Strothmann
OData and SAP NetWeaver Gateway
2014, 666 pp., hardcover
ISBN 978-1-59229-907-2

Dave Haseman, Ross Hightower
Mobile Development for SAP
2013, 617 pp., hardcover
ISBN 978-1-59229-448-0

Thorsten Schneider, Eric Westenberger, Hermann Gahm
ABAP Development for SAP HANA
2014, 609 pp., hardcover
ISBN 978-1-59229-859-4

James Wood, Shaan Parvaze
Web Dynpro ABAP: The Comprehensive Guide
2012, 784 pp., hardcover
ISBN 978-1-59229-416-9

Miroslav Antolovic

Getting Started with SAPUI5

Galileo Press

Bonn • Boston

Galileo Press is named after the Italian physicist, mathematician, and philosopher Galileo Galilei (1564–1642). He is known as one of the founders of modern science and an advocate of our contemporary, heliocentric worldview. His words *Eppur si muove* (And yet it moves) have become legendary. The Galileo Press logo depicts Jupiter orbited by the four Galilean moons, which were discovered by Galileo in 1610.

Editor Sarah Frazier
Acquisitions Editor Kelly Grace Weaver
German Edition Editor Kerstin Billen
Translation Lemoine International, Salt Lake City, UT
Copyeditor Melinda Rankin
Cover Design Graham Geary
Photo Credit iStockphoto.com/13633639/© AWSeebaran
Layout Design Vera Brauner
Production Kelly O'Callaghan
Typesetting Publishers' Design and Production Services, Inc.
Printed and bound in the United States of America, on paper from sustainable sources

ISBN 978-1-59229-969-0
© 2014 by Galileo Press Inc., Boston (MA)
1st edition 2014
1st German edition published 2014 by Galileo Press, Bonn, Germany

Library of Congress Cataloging-in-Publication Data
Antolovic, Miroslav.
Getting started with SAPUI5 / Miroslav Antolovic. — 1st edition.
pages cm
ISBN 978-1-59229-969-0 (print) — ISBN 1-59229-969-5 (print) — ISBN 978-1-59229-970-6 (e-book) —
ISBN 978-1-59229-971-3 (print and e-book) 1. SAP NetWeaver Gateway. 2. User interfaces (Computer systems)
3. Web site development. 4. HTML (Document markup language) I. Title.
QA76.76.S27A58 2014
006.7'4—dc23
2014018246

Contents at a Glance

1   HTML5 and CSS3   19

2   JavaScript   47

3   jQuery   85

4   Getting Started in SAPUI5   105

5   SAPUI5 Runtime Environment   149

6   SAPUI5 Controls   219

7   Development Example of an Application   283

8   SAP Gateway   353

9   SAP HANA   381

10 Mobile Applications   405

A   Further Sources of Information   451

B   The Author   453

Dear Reader,

Being a web developer is a lot like being an architect or structural engineer. Not only do they have to consider every brick, but also their weight, how they fit together, and the geography they sit on. However, building a structure with code on multiple platforms and devices might be even more difficult than building a brick and mortar structure! One missing brick, or in our less obvious case, one missing <div> element, and the whole thing could collapse. This book will help you to build safely and swiftly, while presenting you with options for creating sleek, uncluttered HTML5-based applications through the use of elements such as HTML5, CSS3, JavaScript, and the incredibly helpful jQuery library.

With the expertise of Miroslav Antolovic, you'll gain a greater understanding of how these individual elements function, how they fit together, and how to best use them to create the next-generation UIs for responsive SAP applications. I'm confident that with the help of this book, you'll approach your next project with an extensive toolbox of knowledge as you pursue your vision, brick-by-brick, <div>-by-<div>.

As always, we appreciate your business and welcome your feedback. What did you think about *Getting Started with SAPUI5*? Your comments and suggestions are the most useful tools to help us improve our books for you, the reader. We encourage you to visit our website at *www.sap-press.com* and share your feedback.

Sarah Frazier
Editor, SAP PRESS

Galileo Press
Boston, MA

sarah.frazier@galileo-press.com
www.sap-press.com

Contents

Introduction 13

1   HTML5 and CSS3 19

1.1   Introduction to HTML5 20
   1.1.1   Basic Framework of a Document 20
   1.1.2   Important Language Elements 25
1.2   Introduction to CSS 36
   1.2.1   General Structure 36
   1.2.2   Integrating CSS in HTML 37
   1.2.3   Selectors 41
   1.2.4   Example 44

2   JavaScript 47

2.1   Basic Principles 47
   2.1.1   Logging 48
   2.1.2   Positioning JavaScript Code 49
   2.1.3   Comments 50
   2.1.4   Functions 50
   2.1.5   Objects 53
2.2   Variables 56
2.3   Operators 60
   2.3.1   Arithmetic Operators 60
   2.3.2   Increment and Decrement Operators 60
   2.3.3   Assignment Operators 61
   2.3.4   Relational Operators 61
   2.3.5   The typeof Operator 62
   2.3.6   Logical Operators 62
2.4   Control Structures: Conditions and Loops 63
   2.4.1   The if Statement 63
   2.4.2   The switch Statement 65
   2.4.3   The for Loop 67

2.4.4   The while Loop   69

2.4.5   The do-while Loop   71

2.4.6   The for-in Loop   71

2.5   Document Object Model   73

2.5.1   The DOM Tree   74

2.5.2   Addressing Elements   74

2.5.3   DOM Manipulation   76

2.6   Events   81

3   jQuery   85

3.1   Basic Principles   85

3.2   Selectors and Events   86

3.2.1   Selectors   87

3.2.2   Events   91

3.3   DOM Manipulation   93

3.4   AJAX   97

4   Getting Started in SAPUI5   105

4.1   Installation of the SAPUI5 Library in SAP
       Business Suite   106

4.2   Setting Up the Development Environment   109

4.2.1   Installation Requirements   109

4.2.2   Installation   109

4.2.3   Updating the Components   114

4.3   SAPUI5 Development Scenarios   116

4.3.1   Development in the SAP NetWeaver
         Application Server ABAP   117

4.3.2   Creating Your Own Service   121

4.4   Model View Controller Architecture Pattern   125

4.4.1   Model   126

4.4.2   View   126

4.4.3   Controller   127

4.4.4   Interaction in Web Development   127

4.4.5   MVC in SAPUI5   127

4.5   First Example   131

5 SAPUI5 Runtime Environment 149

5.1	Initialization of the Application	150
	5.1.1 SAPUI5 Resources	151
	5.1.2 Controls	154
	5.1.3 SAPUI5 Theming	155
5.2	Data Binding Models	160
	5.2.1 JSON Model	162
	5.2.2 XML Model	169
	5.2.3 Resource Model	170
	5.2.4 OData Model	173
	5.2.5 Binding Options	175
5.3	Multilingual Applications	185
5.4	SAPUI5 Data Typing	191
	5.4.1 Integers	192
	5.4.2 Floating-Point Numbers	193
	5.4.3 Strings	193
	5.4.4 Boolean Variable	194
	5.4.5 Date	195
	5.4.6 Time	196
	5.4.7 Date and Time	196
	5.4.8 Formatter Classes	196
	5.4.9 Your Own Types	196
5.5	Layout Adaptation via Your Own CSS	199
	5.5.1 Adapting CSS	199
	5.5.2 Theme Designer	203
5.6	Communication with the SAP Backend	212

6 SAPUI5 Controls 219

6.1	API Reference	220
6.2	Common Controls (sap.ui.commons)	224
	6.2.1 Layout	225
	6.2.2 UI Controls	253
6.3	UX3 Controls (sap.ui.ux3)	273
6.4	Table Control (sap.ui.table)	275
6.5	Charts (sap.viz)	275

6.6   Controls for Mobile Applications 276
6.7   Suite Controls (sap.suite.) 276
6.8   Your Own Controls 278

7   Development Example of an Application 283

7.1   The UI Design 283
        7.1.1   Start Page 284
        7.1.2   Time Sheet 285
        7.1.3   Leave Request 286
        7.1.4   Employee Directory 287
        7.1.5   Travel Planning 287
        7.1.6   My Data 288
7.2   Implementation 289
        7.2.1   Basic Structure 290
        7.2.2   Employee Directory 296
        7.2.3   Travel Planning 302
        7.2.4   My Data 308
        7.2.5   Tasks 314
        7.2.6   Time Sheet 324
        7.2.7   Leave Request 340

8   SAP Gateway 353

8.1   Basic Principles of SAP Gateway 353
8.2   Installation 355
8.3   Configuration 356
8.4   Implementing OData Service 358
8.5   Consuming OData Service 375

9   SAP HANA 381

9.1   XS Engine 382
9.2   HANA Access 383
9.3   Implementation of the Sample Application 389

10 Mobile Applications 405

10.1 Installation 407
10.2 Introduction to SAPUI5 for Mobile 408
10.3 Developing Mobile Solutions with SAPUI5 409
    10.3.1 Page Layout of Mobile Applications 409
    10.3.2 Page Navigation 414
    10.3.3 Where Am I? 417
    10.3.4 SplitApp Control 418
    10.3.5 Events on Mobile Devices 419
10.4 Application Example 420
    10.4.1 Backend Implementation 420
    10.4.2 Frontend Implementation 428

Appendices 451

A Further Sources of Information 451
  A.1 Links 451
  A.2 SAP Notes 451
  A.3 Books 452
B The Author 453

Index 455

Introduction

I'm delighted that you're curious and want to rise to new challenges in SAP development. In this book, I invite you along on a tour through the world of SAPUI5 development. On this trip, you'll learn about SAPUI5 on multiple platforms and devices.

With SAP NetWeaver 7.4, you'll develop ABAP in Eclipse, and with SAP HANA, you'll face the challenge of learning new programming languages such as SQLScript, R, and L. With *UI development toolkit for HTML5*, referred to ahead as *SAPUI5*, you have now finally arrived in the world of web development. You could implement your first Internet-enabled SAP applications in SAP GUI with ABAP through Web Dynpro or BSP. SAPUI5, however, requires knowledge of HTML, CSS, and JavaScript, and you need to work in the Eclipse development environment.

Goal of this book

My personal "working title" for this book was—to borrow from Douglas Adams' *The Hitchhiker's Guide to the Galaxy—The Hitchhiker's Guide to SAPUI5*. I chose this working title because of what Adams put so aptly: "You're lonely. You're light years from home. You're having problems understanding the natives. DON'T PANIC, this is the book for you." In keeping with this idea, I would like to help you get started in this new world of SAPUI5 with this book. I neither can, nor want, to provide you with a complete compendium for HTML, CSS, JavaScript, JQuery, or SAPUI5. My claim in this book is in fact to teach you the basics of these individual elements so that you can find your way in this new world. If you have discovered your passion for this world as I did, you can extend your newly acquired knowledge by reading relevant specialist literature. A list of useful links and books appears in the appendix of this book.

Hitchhiker's Guide

Structure of This Book

SAPUI5 is a new user interface technology from SAP that is based on the open standards HTML5 and CSS3, the JavaScript scripting language, and the jQuery library.

HTML5   In **Chapter 1**, you'll learn the basics of Hypertext Markup Language (HTML) and cascading style sheets (CSS). You will be able to structure a web page with HTML, while using CSS to format the content structured by that HTML. This means that you can use CSS to design and position the created elements. Imagine a house, for example: You use HTML to define where the kitchen or the bathroom is located, and then you use CSS to create how these rooms look by defining, for example, the color of the walls or the flooring. As in a house, you then need to implement some technology so that, for example, the light goes on when you press the light switch. This technology is called JavaScript.

JavaScript   I will introduce you to JavaScript in **Chapter 2**. There, you will learn about the basic elements of the language. In addition to the variable definition, the operators, and the control structures, I will also discuss the Document Object Model (DOM). JavaScript can do more than just make the light switches work. Imagine an advertisement for a large Swedish furniture store; by using JavaScript and DOM, you can transform that kitchen into a second bedroom in just a few steps.

jQuery   **Chapter 3** will introduce you to jQuery as a JavaScript library. So that you don't have to reinvent the wheel every time, it is standard practice in JavaScript, as in all other programming languages, to access existing libraries. I will focus on jQuery within this introduction, because SAPUI5 is based on jQuery; you will be able to find your way around the SAPUI5 library better if you understand the jQuery syntax.

SAPUI5 library   With **Chapter 4**, you will learn about the SAPUI5 library. You will set up the development environment in Eclipse and become familiar with the various development scenarios. I will also show you the Model View Controller architecture pattern, which will assist in structuring larger applications.

Runtime   In **Chapter 5**, you will learn how to bind data to a control and deploy your application in multiple languages. Furthermore, I will show you how to customize the layout of an application to suit your needs and with which technology you can read or write data from the backend.

I will provide an overview of the SAPUI5 controls in **Chapter 6**. As the standard version already contains a very large number of controls, and the presentation of all controls would be beyond the scope of this book, I have restricted myself to some key examples. In this chapter, my main concern is that you develop a feel for the structure of the library and that you are able to search in the right place in the API documentation.

Controls

In **Chapter 7**, we will develop a sample application together in SAPUI5 for an employee portal with six areas. In this application, the employee can maintain his own worklist, record working times, create leave requests, and maintain his personal information. An employee directory, and the integration of Google Maps as a route planner, round off the range of services of the employee portal. We use many different controls in this application to illustrate the interaction of the individual components. Even if the application has become very large as a result, it still provides enough scope for your own developments and improvements after reading this book. A bonus extension feature of this chapter is provided online, and will allow you to explore the backend integration of the employee portal.

Sample application

In **Chapter 8**, you will create an Open Data Protocol (OData) service in SAP Gateway and consume it in your SAPUI5 application. SAP Gateway allows you easy and direct access to SAP backend services based on the standard Web protocol OData.

SAP Gateway

With **Chapter 9**, you will learn about the development of applications in SAPUI5 with SAP HANA. In this chapter, you will develop a sample application on the Extended Application Services Engine (XS Engine) in SAP HANA and access a HANA view from SAPUI5.

SAP HANA

Finally, **Chapter 10** deals specifically with the development of applications for mobile devices. In this chapter, you will learn about the *sap.m* library and the special features found in the development of mobile applications. As an exercise, in this chapter you will develop an approval app for the leave requests from the employee portal that you will have implemented in Chapter 7.

Mobile applications

At the end of this tour, you will have learned the essential points of SAPUI5 development on various platforms—an ABAP backend and SAP HANA—and on different devices.

The goal of this book is to equip you with the knowledge required in being able to make reasonable decisions for your enterprise, while having the ability to implement them in a project. I hope that I have succeeded in this goal and look forward to receiving your personal feedback on the book at *antolovic@bsc-solutions.com*.

Special icons   To indicate important information and to facilitate your work with this book, I used the following symbols:

[◾] Checklist

Boxes with this icon show you the requirements (for example, tools) for the following chapter.

[+] Tip

Boxes with this icon will give you recommendations for settings or tips from professional experience.

[!] Caution

Boxes with this icon contain important information about the topic under discussion. I also use this icon to warn you about potential sources of error.

> **Material to Download**
>
> At *www.sap-press.com/3565*, you'll find supplemental material, which will hopefully facilitate implementing the practice activities. The downloadable information includes:
>
> ▶ All larger listings, which I show in the individual chapters
> ▶ Full listings, which are presented only in abbreviated form in the individual chapters for space reasons
> ▶ Installation instructions

Acknowledgments

For a book as for a movie, the movie poster or cover includes the director (or the publisher) and the main character (the author, in our case), while you learn only in the end credits the number of people who were actually involved in this work. My personal "credits" follow.

First of all, I would like to thank my wife Sandra and my son Dejan. Writing a book requires a lot of time and, bearing in mind that I mostly only had time to do so in the evening, at night, and on weekends, my family had to show a great deal of understanding for this book project and do without a normal family life for nearly a year. Although only two years old, my son developed a very keen sense of time management during this period. He pretty much knew when it was time for a break ("Daddy, come here, please, let's play!"), but also when it was time to start working again ("Daddy, work!").

Aside from me, a great number of other people were involved in this book, and I would like to thank these people here. Special thanks must go to my colleagues from bsc solutions, who performed some of my daily tasks and helped me write some chapters. I would like to thank Stefan Huber for checking the source code, suggesting ideas for the employee portal, and assisting in the implementation of the sample applications. I would like to thank Johannes Kettenhofen for assisting in the implementation of the employee portal and the approval app and Benjamin Schneider for proofreading and improving how the text reads. With your ideas and suggestions for improvement, each one of you has contributed to getting the book into this final form.

However, where would a book be without a publisher? I would like to thank SAP PRESS for the trust placed in me and for the opportunity to write this book. I would like to extend a heartfelt thanks to the editors, Janina Schweitzer and Kerstin Billen. They supported me every step of the way, from the idea for the book to its publication, and provided advice and help at all times.

Miroslav Antolovic

> *"You cannot teach a man anything,*
> *you can only help him to find it within himself."*
> —*Galileo Galilei*

In this chapter, you'll learn the basics of web development. The first focus will be on Hypertext Markup Language (HTML), which is the basic component of web development.

1   HTML5 and CSS3

The basic language used to create websites is the Hypertext Markup Language (HTML). In this chapter, the basic syntax of HTML is presented. HTML is a formatting language for the structuring and semantic markup of content such as text, images, and hyperlinks in documents. Compared to HTML4, HTML in the fifth generation (HTML5) offers many new features, such as the integration of video, audio, local storage, and 3D graphics.

This book discusses only the most important language elements; a complete language reference can be found at *www.w3schools.com/*. The language is specified via the World Wide Web Consortium (W3C), and you can obtain information on their activities from their website at *www.w3.org*; the HTML-specific part can be found at *www.w3.org/html/*. The W3C also provides a validator for your HTML pages at *validator.w3.org/*.

W3C

Checklist	[⚑]
You will need the following for this chapter: ▶ A text editor such as Notepad or Notepad++ ▶ An installed browser You can download Notepad++ at *http://notepad-plus-plus.org/*. If you want to implement these examples directly in the SAPUI5 Eclipse plug-in, go to Chapter 4, and follow the installation instructions there.	

Each browser interprets an HTML page individually, depending on the rendering engine. For this reason, it's useful to test the pages you create in different browsers, while always focusing on the browser used throughout the company. Table 1.1 shows information for the main browsers.

Browser compatibility

Browser	Rendering Engine	Website
Firefox	Gecko	*www.mozilla.org*
Microsoft IE	Trident	*www.microsoft.com*
Chrome	WebKit	*www.google.com/chrome*
Safari	WebKit	*www.apple.com/safari*
Opera	Chromium	*www.opera.com*

Table 1.1 Rendering Engines

1.1   Introduction to HTML5

Tags

HTML is a pure definition language rather than a programming language. You use HTML to structure and format the content of the page to be displayed. The content of an HTML document consists of *HTML elements*; these are marked by *tags*. A start tag is indicated by angle brackets (<>), and an end tag is indicated by an additional forward slash (</>). Apart from a few exceptions, a complete descriptive sentence in HTML always sits between a start and an end tag.

HTML element

The validity area for the actual content of the HTML element is located within these two tags—for example:

```
<p>Text section in a paragraph</p>
```

The opening tag <p> signals to the browser that a section (p = paragraph) is to follow, and the validity area extends to the closing tag </p>. The text within the tags is displayed by the browser as text in *section* formatting.

1.1.1   Basic Framework of a Document

Structuring of the HTML document

An HTML document essentially consists of the following parts:

- ▶ Document type declaration
- ▶ Header area
- ▶ Document body

Listing 1.1 shows us these parts.

20

```
<!DOCTYPE html>
<html>
   <head>
      <meta charset="UTF-8">
      <title>First Page</title>
   </head>
   <body>
      <!--Page content -->
   </body>
</html>
```

Listing 1.1 Page body.html

The first line in this example is the document type declaration according to the HTML5 standard. Each HTML page is enclosed by the actual HTML tag:

HTML document type

```
<html> </html>
```

In the header area, `<head>...</head>`, for example, search engine–relevant meta information, the page title, and references to JavaScript or CSS files are declared.

Header area: <head> tag

Character Encoding
In this example, the character encoding `UTF-8` (`<meta charset="UTF-8">`) is used. If you omit this line, the browser does not display special characters correctly.

[!]

The actual content of the page now follows between the `<body>` tags. To display our first example in a browser, enter the HTML code from Listing 1.1 in a text editor and, within the `<body>` tags, add the statement

Document body – <body> tag

```
<p>Text section in a paragraph</p>
```

and save it under *First_page.html*. You should have now created a file as in Listing 1.2.

```
<!DOCTYPE html>
<html>
      <head>
         <meta charset="UTF-8">
         <title>First Page</title>
      </head>
      <body>
```

```
            <p>Text section in a paragraph</p>
        </body>
</html>
```

Listing 1.2 First_page.html

Open the file in the browser (see Figure 1.1).

Figure 1.1 First HTML Page

For the sake of clarity, only the area within the <body> tags are mapped in the following listings. It's best if you use Listing 1.1 as a template, add the mapped source text within the <body> tags to it, and save the page under a new name.

Structure of the SAPUI5 application

Let's take a look at the basic page of an SAPUI5 application as a sneak preview of the following chapter (see Listing 1.3).

```
<!DOCTYPE HTML>
<html>
<head>
<meta http-equiv="X-UA-Compatible" content="IE=edge">
<script src="resources/sap-ui-core.js"
        id="sap-ui-bootstrap"
        data-sap-ui-libs"sap.ui.commons"
        data-sap-ui-theme="sap_goldreflection" >
</script>
</head>
<body class="sapUiBody" role="application">
    <div id="content"></div>
</body>
</html>
```

Listing 1.3 Body of an SAPUI5 Page

To facilitate reading, use SAPUI5 in this book as an acronym for UI development toolkit for HTML5; strictly speaking, an HTML page created with UI development toolkit for HTML5 is what is meant when referring to an SAPUI5 page. The basic elements are included here as well:

- Document type declaration
- Header area
- Document body

HTML Document Types

The document type determines what markup language (in this case, HTML) you use in what version. The browser, for example, is based on this notation in order to process the page correctly and display it.

Document type

You're already familiar with the document type for HTML5:

HTML

```
<!DOCTYPE html>
```

The document type for HTML5 is simple. If you have worked with HTML in the past, then you also know the notation for HTML4:

```
<!DOCTYPE html PUBLIC "-//W3C//DTD HTML 4.01 //EN" "http://www.
w3.org/TR/html4/strict.dtd">
```

Document Type	[+]
Always use the HTML5 document type even if, strictly speaking, you do not use any HTML5 functions. Because HTML4 is integrated completely in HTML5, you can access all HTML4 functions with the HTML5 document type.	

Header Data of the Document

In the header area of the HTML document, you can record, among other things, the following data:

Header area

- Metadata such as the character encoding used
- Logical connections and links to other resources
- Style sheet definitions throughout a document
- Areas for JavaScript

If you look at the basic page of SAPUI5, you'll discover the following information in the header:

```
<head>
<meta http-equiv="X-UA-Compatible" content="IE=edge">
<script src="resources/sap-ui-core.js"
        id="sap-ui-bootstrap"
        data-sap-ui-libs="sap.ui.commons"
        data-sap-ui-theme="sap_goldreflection" >
</script>
</head>
```

Compatibility mode

The meta-attribute `X-UA-Compatible` in line 2 indicates the setting for the document compatibility mode in Internet Explorer. Here, the `edge` mode specifies that content is to be displayed in the highest mode available.

JavaScript

The path to a JavaScript library is specified in the next line:

```
<script src="resources/sap-ui-core.js...
```

A web page becomes dynamic and interactive with JavaScript. Although you format the page with HTML—you divide the page into sections with block capitals, for example—JavaScript ensures the interaction with the user. JavaScript is covered in Chapter 2, and the individual SAPUI5 libraries are discussed in detail in Chapter 4.

Document Body

Document body

The document body is defined within the `<body>` tags: `<body></body>`. The content of the page to be displayed is described in this area. As of HTML5, the `<body>` area can be further subdivided and thus logically structured. This is possible due to the tags `<section>`, `<header>`, and `<footer>`.

These elements have no visual effect; they are used only to separate the content of sections semantically. This is clear from the following example (Listing 1.4):

```
<body>
  <header>
  This is the header of a page
  </header>
  <section>
  This is a section
```

```
    </section>
    <footer>
    This is the footer
    </footer>
  </body>
```

Listing 1.4   Semantic_separation.html

Figure 1.2 shows the display in the browser.

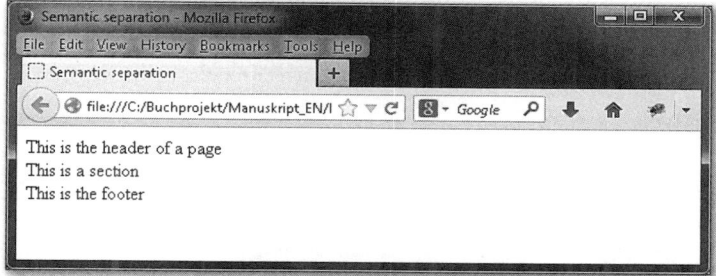

Figure 1.2   Semantic Separation

1.1.2   Important Language Elements

As you'll see later, you can create SAPUI5 pages without any knowledge of HTML. However, it is worth knowing the most common elements.

HTML language elements

Headings

The tag `<h[1-6]>` introduces a heading; the number in the tag stands for the level of the heading (Listing 1.5).

Headings tag

```
<body>
  <h1>This is heading 1</h1>
  <h2>This is heading 2</h2>
  <h3>This is heading 3</h3>
  <h4>This is heading 4</h4>
  <h5>This is heading 5</h5>
  <h6>This is heading 6</h6>
</body>
```

Listing 1.5   Headings.html

Figure 1.3 shows how the different headings are displayed in the browser.

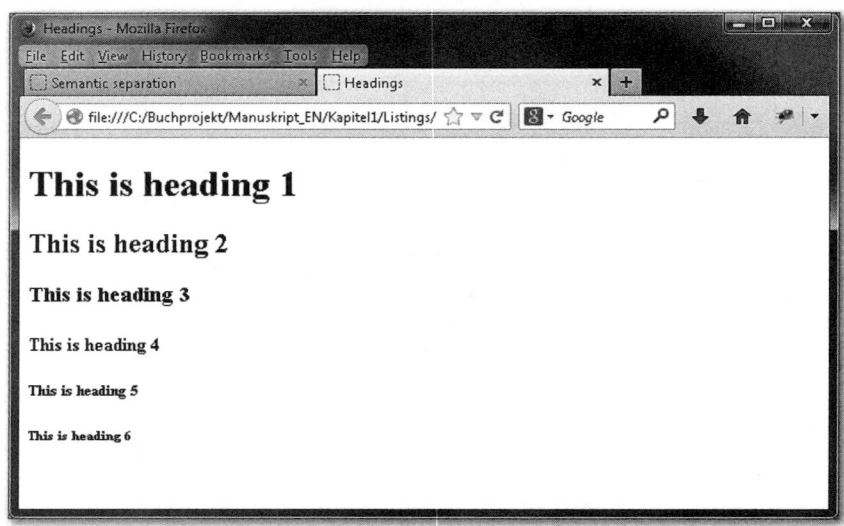

Figure 1.3 Headings in the Browser

Paragraph Types

HTML language
elements

You were already introduced to the text paragraph `<p>` at the beginning of this chapter. Other important language elements are shown in Table 1.2.

Language Element	HTML Tag
Line breaks	` `
Ordered lists	`<ol>`
Unordered lists	`<ul>`
List entries	`<li>`
Block quotes	`<blockquote>`
Horizontal lines	`<hr>`
General areas	`<div>`

Table 1.2 Language Elements in HTML

In the following example (see Listing 1.6), the individual elements are used in a page. (Lorem ipsum, which you will see in this example, is used by designers and graphic artists as dummy text. This text serves as a placeholder in the layout in order to get an impression of the finished document. You can generate any length of text in lorem ipsum at *www. loremipsum.de/index_e.html*.)

```
<body>
    <p>Lorem ipsum dolor sit amet, consetetur sadipscing
    elitr,<br>
  sed diam nonumy eirmod tempor invidunt ut labore
  et dolore magna aliquyam erat,<br>
  sed diam voluptua.
</p>
<p> At vero eos et accusam et justo duo dolores
    et ea rebum. Stet clita kasd gubergren,
    no sea takimata sanctus est
    Lorem ipsum dolor sit amet.
</p>
<ol>
    <li>First entry ordered list</li>
    <li>Second entry ordered list</li>
  </ol>
  <ul>
    <li>First entry unordered list</li>
    <li>Second entry unordered list</li>
  </ul>
  <hr>
  <blockquote>
    Lorem ipsum dolor sit amet,
    consetetur sadipscing elitr,
    sed diam nonumy eirmod tempor invidunt ut
    et dolore magna aliquyam erat.
  </blockquote>
</body>
```

Listing 1.6   Paragraph types.html

Figure 1.4 shows how the different paragraph types are displayed in the browser.

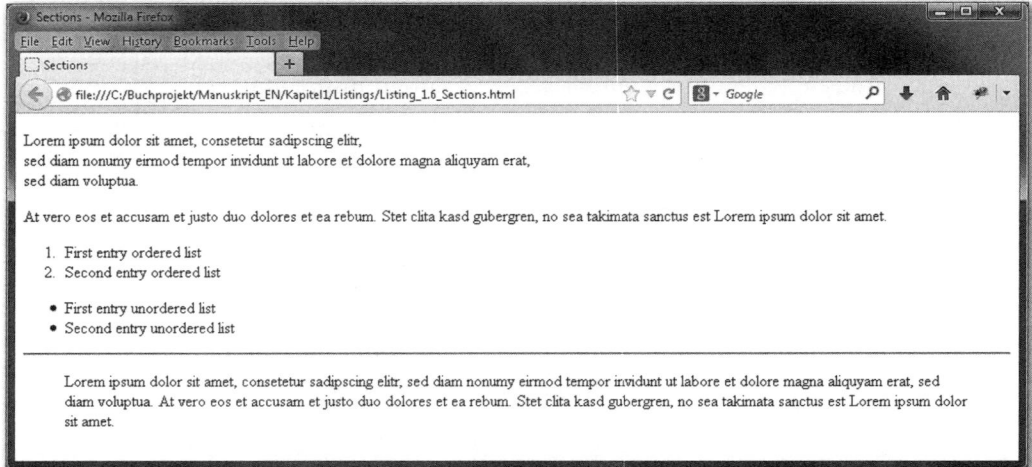

Figure 1.4 Paragraph Types

Areas

The language element `<div>` (div = division = area) is particularly suited to any content in a common area. Let's take another look at the basic listing of the SAPUI5 page:

```
<body class="sapUiBody" role="application">
    <div id="content"></div>
</body>
```

Here, you already see that the complete SAPUI5 page is displayed in a `<div>` container with `id="content"`. CSS technology, in particular, provides you with a very simple and effective means of arranging and formatting page areas with precise pixel values.

The example in Figure 1.5 shows two overlapping areas. This effect is achieved by the fact that, due to CSS, the first area is arranged in each case 100 px from the margin (`left:100px; top:100px;`) and the second area in each case is 50 px (`left:50px; top:50px;`) from the margin. You use `z-index` to arrange the elements in the desired depth (foreground or background). To make this easier to understand, the two areas are given different background colors (`background-color:green`, or `background-color:grey`; see Listing 1.7).

```
<body>
  <div style="position:absolute; width:300px;
    height:150px; left:100px; top:100px;
    z-index:2; border:1px solid #000000;
    background-color:green">
  Division in green, by z-index:2 in the foreground
  </div>
  <div style="position:absolute; width:300px;
      height:150px; left:50px; top:50px;
      z-index:1; border:1px solid #000000;
      background-color:grey">
  Division in grey, by z-index:1 in the background
  </div>
<body>
```

Listing 1.7 Areas.html

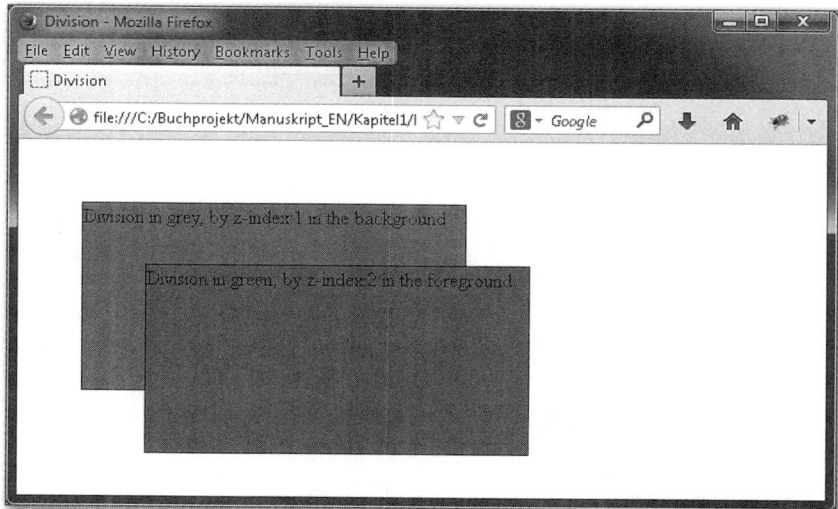

Figure 1.5   `<div>` Container Elements as Areas

Text Markups

You use text markups to assign special formatting to individual words **Text formatting** or passages of text. The most important language elements are shown in Table 1.3.

29

Text Markup	HTML Tag
Hyperlink	`<a>`
Bold	`<b>`
Italic	`<i>`
Highlighted	`<em>`

Table 1.3 Language Elements

You may have noticed immediately that no "underlined" tag is listed; underlined text should not be used because of the risk of confusion with hyperlinks.

Hyperlinks

References Hyperlinks in particular have ultimately made the World Wide Web what it is today. A hyperlink does not necessarily have to refer to another HTML page; you can reference any resource with hyperlinks:

▶ Link to another page:

```
<a href="http://www.sap.com">SAP-Homepage</a>
```

▶ Email link:

```
<a href="mailto:name@company.com">Email</a>
```

▶ Link to any resource:

```
<a href="Worksheet.xls" type="application/msexcel">Excel</a>
```

Anchor You can also use hyperlinks to navigate within a page. These *anchors* facilitate easier navigation within a page; the best-known example is a "back to top" link at the bottom of a long page.

```
<a href="#top">to top</a>
```

If you want to navigate to a specific chapter from within a page, assign an ID, and then reference this ID in the anchor tag, as shown in Listing 1.8.

```
<body>
  <a href="#Paragraph 1">Paragraph 1</a>
  <a href="#Paragraph 2">Paragraph 2</a>
  <h1 id="Paragraph 1">Paragraph 1</h1>
  <p>
```

```
<i>Lorem ipsum dolor sit amet, consetetur </i>
<b>sadipscing elitr, sed diam nonumy tempor</b>
<em>invidunt ut</em>
<i><b>labore et dolore magna aliquyam erat,</i></b>
sed diam voluptua. At vero eos et accusam et justo duo
dolores et ea rebum. Stet clita kasd gubergren,
no sea takimata sanctus est Lorem ipsum dolor
sit amet. Lorem ipsum dolor sit amet, consetetur
sadipscing elitr, sed diam nonumy eirmod tempor
invidunt ut labore et dolore magna aliquyam erat,
sed diam voluptua. At vero eos et accusam et justo
duo dolores et ea rebum. Stet clita kasd gubergren, no
sea takimata sanctus est Lorem ipsum dolor sit amet.
</p>
<h1 id="Paragraph 2">Paragraph 2</h1>
<p>
Lorem ipsum dolor sit amet, consetetur sadipscing
elitr, sed diam nonumy eirmod tempor invidunt ut
labore et dolore magna aliquyam erat, sed diam
voluptua.
</p>
<a href="#top">Top of page</a>
```

Listing 1.8 Text markup.html

Make sure that the text is long enough within sections 1 and 2 so you can see the effects of the anchor tags. If you now call the page in the browser (see Figure 1.6), you can navigate to the relevant section via the defined hyperlinks or navigate back to the top of the page using the "back to top" hyperlink within the displayed page.

Page navigation

You can now also figure out why the `<div>` element in the SAPUI5 page was assigned an ID:

ID attribute

```
<body class="sapUiBody" role="application">
    <div id="content"></div>
</body>
```

This ID enables the element to be addressed, and it can, for example, be addressed directly via JavaScript. This topic will be discussed in detail in the following chapters.

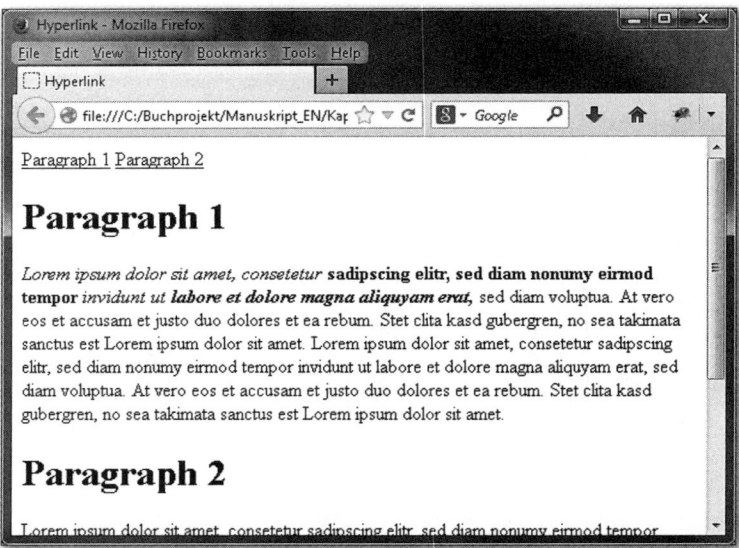

Figure 1.6 Anchor

Tables

To develop an SAP application, you need two main components: forms and tables.

Table definition
You define a table element using `<table>...</table>`, followed by the table header `<thead>...</thead>`, the table body `<tbody>...</tbody>`, the actual table row `<tr>`, and the content `<th>` for the header, as well as `<td>` for the content in the table body (see Listing 1.9).

```
<body>
  <table border="1">
    <thead>
      <tr>
        <th>Header Column 1</th>
        <th>Header Column 2</th>
        <th>Header Column 3</th>
      </tr>
    </thead>
    <tbody>
      <tr>
        <td>Cell Row 1</td>
        <td>Cell Row 1</td>
```

```
          <td>Cell Row 1</td>
        </tr>
        <tr>
          <td>Cell Row 2</td>
          <td>Cell Row 2</td>
          <td>Cell Row 2</td>
        </tr>
      </tbody>
   </table>
</body>
```

Listing 1.9 Tables.html

Figure 1.7 shows how the table is displayed in the browser. The table header is automatically displayed in bold by the browser, and each table cell is surrounded by a border.

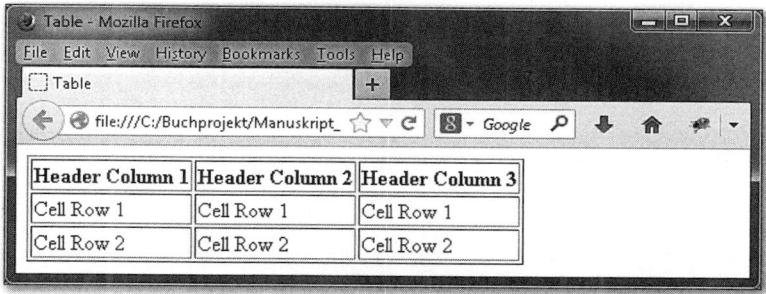

Figure 1.7 HTML Table

Forms

By using a form, you allow the user to interact with the application. Input templates are typical forms that you can process directly with JavaScript or, as in our case, send to the SAP backend for further processing. Typical forms on the web include login dialogs for protected areas or contact forms.

Interactive pages

You use `<form>`...`</form>` to define a form in HTML; the form contains, among other things, the following elements:

▶ Labels: `<label>`
▶ Input fields: `<input>`

- ▶ Text areas: `<textarea>`
- ▶ Selection lists: `<select>`
- ▶ Dropdown lists: `<datalist>`
- ▶ Radio buttons: `<input type="radio">`

You must define the `action` so that the form can accept the input, and thus you specify which URL should be called after sending.

POST/GET   By using the `method` attribute, you also specify how the browser is to send the data to the URL specified under `action`. The two possible methods are POST and GET. With GET, the browser attaches the form data to the specified URL in the form `/?form field-ID=[Value]&form field-ID=[Value]&...`, and with POST the parameters are provided via the standard input channel. In the following example, a form is provided for time recording, and when you click SEND it is sent via the GET method to a target server (see Listing 1.10).

```
<body>
<form method="get" action="http://targetserver">
<fieldset id="timesheet">
    <legend>Time Sheet</legend>
    <label for="name">Name</label>
    <input type="text" name="name">
  <br>
    <label for="task">Task</label>
    <select name="task" size="1">
    <option value"consulting">Consulting</option>
    <option value"development">Development</option>
    </select>
  <br>
    <label for="hour">Hour</label>
    <input type="number" name="Hour"
             min="0" max="8"
             id="hours">
  <br>
    <label for="desc">Description</label>
    <textarea name="desc" rows="3"></textarea>
  <br>
    <label for="billing">Billable</label>
```

```
    <input type="checkbox" name="billing" id="BILL">
  <br>
    <input type="submit" value="Submit">
</fieldset>
</form>
</body>
```

Listing 1.10 Form.html

Figure 1.8 shows how the form is displayed in the browser.

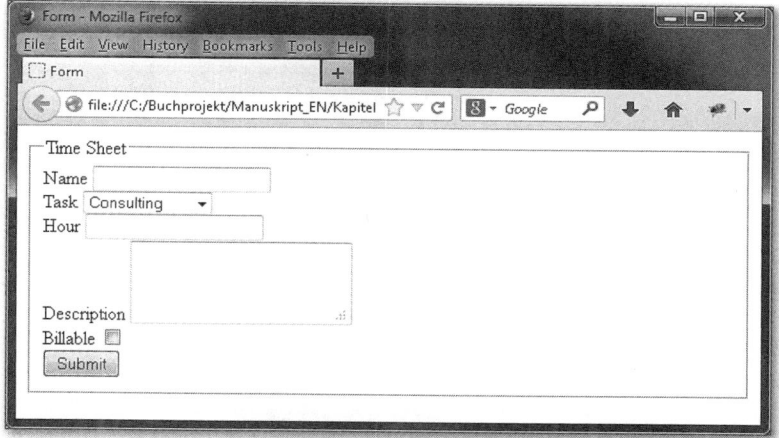

Figure 1.8 HTML Form

The GET method, in particular, is only suitable for transferring sensitive data to a limited extent, because the transferred data is displayed in plain text in the address bar of the browser.   **GET method**

Enter any data in the form, and click SUBMIT. Here, you can see two effects: On the one hand, you understandably receive an error message that the target server could not be found; on the other hand, you can read the data that was entered in the address bar of the browser, for example:

```
http://targetserver/?name=My+Name&task= Consulting&hours=8&des
c=entered+description
```

Server-based processing will be described in greater detail in Chapter 4.

1.2   Introduction to CSS

**Cascading
style sheets** Language elements and functions were the focus of the previous examples, but they were definitely not visually appealing. This is exactly why cascading style sheets (CSS) come into play.

[+] **Cascading Style Sheets**

CSS contains information about position, size, type of font, background colors, images, and much more. The content that is structured by HTML is formatted by cascading style sheets. This means that you use CSS to design and position the elements that were created.

1.2.1   General Structure

Selector The basic syntax of CSS is very simple. You define rules that consist of a selector and the declaration (see Figure 1.9).

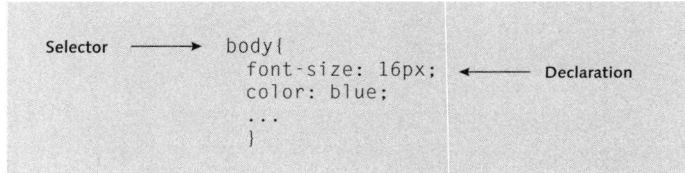

Figure 1.9   Basic Syntax

CSS declaration The selector determines to which HTML element the rule applies. The declaration is made in curly brackets. The first part of the declaration indicates the property (e.g., the font size) to be designed, and the second part determines the value that the property is to accept. In Figure 1.9, the CSS defines that a font size of 16 px and a blue font color are to be used in the <body> area.

[+] **CSS Syntax**

The basic CSS syntax is as follows:

```
Selector {
   characteristic: value;
   characteristic: value;
   ...
}
```

1.2.2 Integrating CSS in HTML

There are three options for integrating CSS in an HTML page (shown in Figure 1.10):

- ▶ Paged out to a separate file and included in the head area via hyperlink:

```
<link href="style.css" rel="stylesheet" />
```

- ▶ In the header area of the HTML document
- ▶ Inline at the relevant HTML tag in the HTML document

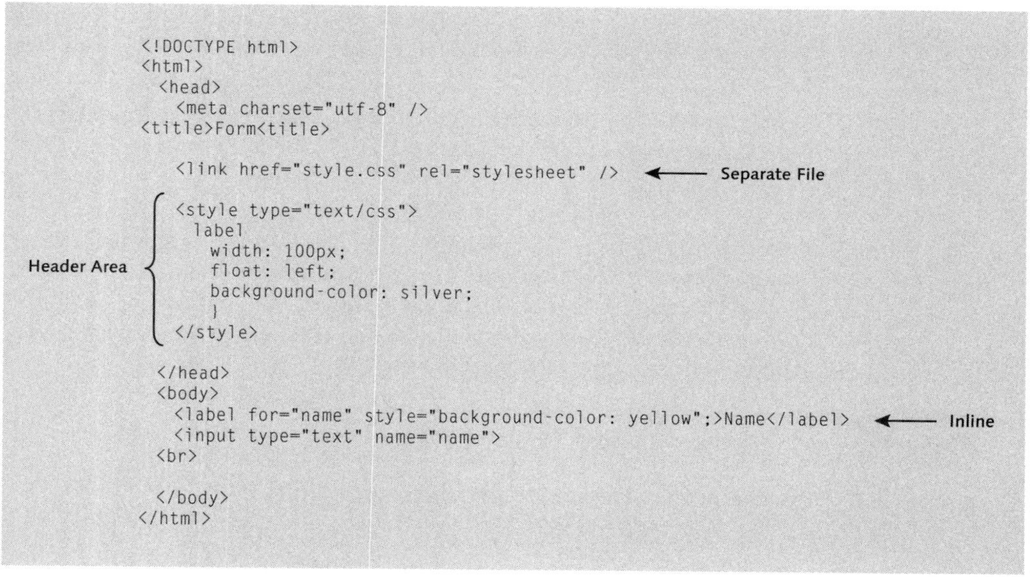

```
<!DOCTYPE html>
<html>
  <head>
    <meta charset="utf-8" />
<title>Form<title>

    <link href="style.css" rel="stylesheet" />          ◄──── Separate File

    <style type="text/css">
      label
        width: 100px;
        float: left;
        background-color: silver;
      }
    </style>

  </head>
  <body>
    <label for="name" style="background-color: yellow";>Name</label>   ◄──── Inline
    <input type="text" name="name">
  <br>

  </body>
</html>
```

Header Area {

Figure 1.10 Integrating CSS in HTML

What happens if you use all three options in one page and define a style for the same element in all three CSS definitions? In this case, the CSS hierarchy applies, which defines a sequence here. If all selectors are equal, the last defined rule applies; that is, the browser renders the page from top to bottom, and the last rule encountered when rendering is regarded as valid.

To illustrate the principle of "top trumps bottom," create a separate CSS file and save it as *style.css* in the same directory as the HTML page (see Listing 1.11).

```
label {
  width: 150px;
  float: left;
  background-color: black;
}
```

Listing 1.11 style.css

[+] **Path Specifications in HTML**

You should always use relative paths for the path specifications. This means that the current URL is the reference URL, and you continue to address relative to it.

If, for example, you store the CSS file in a *.css* subdirectory, the path specification changes to `href="css/style.css"`. If the file is located above the current URL, use `href="../style.css"` to reference the parent directory and to reference from there back to the file path.

Although you can specify absolute paths in HTML—for example, *http://networkcomputing.com/netdesign/1005part1a.html*—you should refrain from doing so in the SAP context. Once you transport your application from the development system to the production system, the server name changes, and your references no longer work properly.

Sequence Next, change Listing 1.11 as follows:

▶ In the header area, reference the separate file
  `<link href="style.css" rel="stylesheet" />` that you created in Listing 1.11.

▶ Add the same style definition in the header, and change only the statement
  `background-color: silver;`

▶ For the first label element, add the following inline statement:
  `style="background-color: yellow";`

This results in Listing 1.12.

```
<!DOCTYPE html>
<html>
  <head>
```

```
      <meta charset="UTF-8" />
      <title>Form</title>
      <link href="style.css" rel="stylesheet" />
      <style type="text/css">
        label {
            width: 100px;
            float: left;
            background-color: silver;
          }
      </style>
  </head>
<body>
<form method="get" action="http://targetserver">
  <fieldset id="timesheet">
  <legend>Time sheet</legend>
  <label for="name" style="background-color:
      yellow";>Name</label>
  <input type="text" name="name">
  <br>
  <label for="task">Task</label>
  <select name="task" size="1">
  <option value"consulting">Consulting</option>
  <option value"development">Development</option>
  </select>
  <input type="submit" value="Submit">
  </fieldset>
  </form>
</body>
</html>
```

Listing 1.12   Form_with_CSS.html

Due to the sequence description, expect the following:

▸ No black background for any element

▸ A yellow background for the first element

▸ A grey background for all other elements

To illustrate the situation better, also activate the web developer tools (in Firefox, for example, they can be accessed in the menu under EXTRAS • WEB DEVELOPER • TOOLS; these tools can be accessed via the [F12] function key in most browsers), and call the page (see Figure 1.11).

Web developer tools

39

Call hierarchy   On the one hand, the browser displays the expected result; on the other hand, you can see via the web tools how the individual CSS statements are overwritten in the sequence described. However, if you now call the external file according to the header definition, the last element is displayed in black (see Figure 1.12).

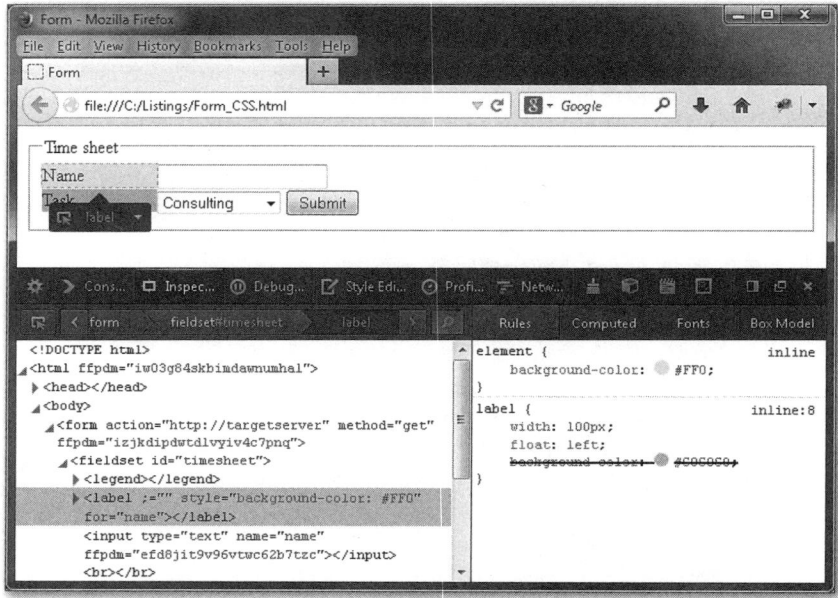

Figure 1.11   CSS Call Hierarchy

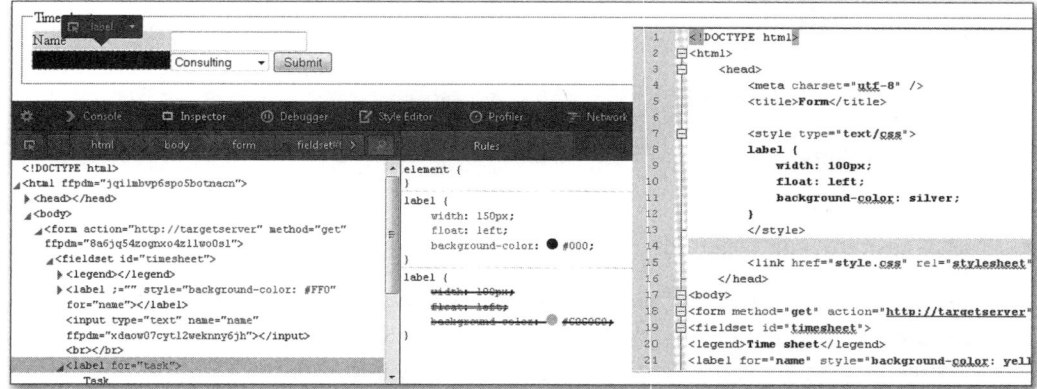

Figure 1.12   CSS Call Hierarchy (2)

The next rule in the CSS hierarchy is the specificity rule, which is related to the chosen selector. For this reason, this will first be presented in the various selectors.

1.2.3 Selectors

You use the *selector* to determine to which HTML elements the format definition should apply. CSS provides several options here:

CSS selector

▶ **Universal selector**
The universal selector is indicated by an asterisk (*) and is thus valid for all elements:

```
*{characteristic: value;}
```

▶ **Type selector**
You use the type selector to address the explicitly named element, such as the label element in Listing 1.12:

```
label {characteristic: value;}
```

▶ **ID selector**
You do not address any element initially with the ID selector; this statement is valid for all elements with the relevant ID:

```
#main {characteristic: value;}
<p id="main">Paragraph</p>
```

▶ **Class selector**
You address all elements with the relevant class attribute by using the class selector:

```
.Navigation { characteristic: value;}
<p class="Navigation">Paragraph</p>
```

▶ **Descendant selector**
You can define nestings with the descendant selector, and assign the property to an element only if it is found inside another element:

```
p i{characteristic: value;}
```

In this example, the CSS statement is valid for the `<i>` element only if it is within a `<p>` element.

Specificity The second rule of the CSS hierarchy, the rule of specificity, applies to the selectors. This rule states that specific selectors overwrite general selectors. The more specifically a rule describes an element in your selector, the higher it is weighted. The weighting is carried out according to a predefined point system. In this system, a numerical series of four digits are assigned to each rule definition:

► Level a = style attribute: highest specificity

► Level b = number of ID attributes

► Level c = number of other attributes and pseudoclasses

► Level d = number of element names and pseudoelements

This results in a number according to the schema:

► Level a = thousands position

► Level b = hundreds position

► Level c = tens position

► Level d = ones position

Example The p selector therefore results in a specificity of 0001 (style = 0, ID = 0, class = 0, element = 1). The Navigation class selector results in a value of 0010 (style = 0, ID = 0, class = 1, element = 0). With this rule, the HTML element is displayed with the style definition that has the highest value.

As an example, create the HTML document *CSS_hierarchy.html* with the source code from Listing 1.13.

```
<!DOCTYPE html>
<html>
  <head>
    <meta charset="UTF-8" />
    <title>CSS Hierarchy</title>
    <style type="text/css">
    p {
      background-color: green;
    }
    p.yellow {
      background-color: yellow;
    }
    p#red {
```

```
      background-color: red;
    }
    </style>
  </head>
<body>
<p class="yellow" id="red">
Lorem ipsum dolor sit amet, consectetur adipisici elit,
sed eiusmod tempor incidunt ut labore et dolore magna
aliqua. Ut enim ad minim veniam, quis nostrud exercitation
ullamco laboris nisi ut aliquid ex ea commodi consequat.
</p>
</body>
</html>
```

Listing 1.13   CSS Hierarchy

What result do you expect? Now calculate the specificity on the basis of the previously discussed rule (see Table 1.4).

Rule calculation

Selector	a-b-c-d (Specificity)	Result
p	0-0-0-1	0001
p.yellow	0-0-1-1	0011
P#red	0-1-0-1	0101

Table 1.4   Calculating CSS Specificity

Per the results, the section should be displayed with a red background. Call the page in the browser and check the result (see Figure 1.13).

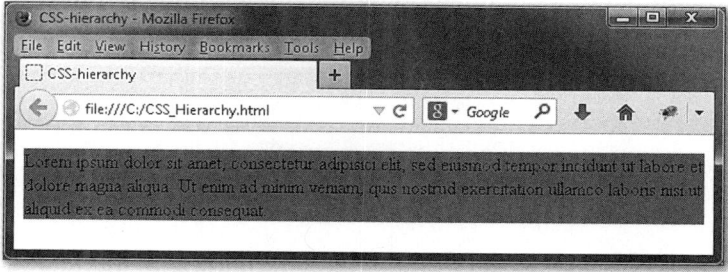

Figure 1.13   CSS Hierarchy

As expected, the section is displayed with a red background. You will find the exact rule definition on the W3C home page at *www.w3.org/TR/ CSS21/cascade.html#specificity*.

1.2.4 Example

A complete CSS language reference would be beyond the scope of this book; for a complete listing, see *www.w3schools.com*. The abridged Listing 1.14 (you can download the complete listing from the web page for the book) illustrates how to design attractive pages very easily.

```
<!DOCTYPE html>
<html>
<head>
  <meta charset="UTF-8" />
  <title>CSS Demo</title>
  <style>
  body {
    font-family: Arial, Helvetica, sans-serif;
   }
  label {
    margin: 10px; display: inline-block; width: 150px;
   }
  input {
    margin-left: 10px; border-radius: 4px;
   }
  #Site {
    background-image:
    -moz-linear-gradient(top, lightblue, white);
    background-image:
    -webkit-linear-gradient(left, lightblue, white);
    box-shadow: 5px 5px 5px #333333;
    -webkit-box-shadow: 5px 5px 5px #333333;
    padding: 20px; height: 100px; width: 500px;
   }
  </style>
</head>
<body>
  <div id="Site">
    <div id="Form">
      <label>Input field</label>
```

```
          <input type="text">
          <button class="button" type="button">Submit
          </button>
        </div>
      </div>
  </body>
</html>
```

Listing 1.14   CSS_demo.html

Figure 1.14 shows the result displayed in the Firefox browser.

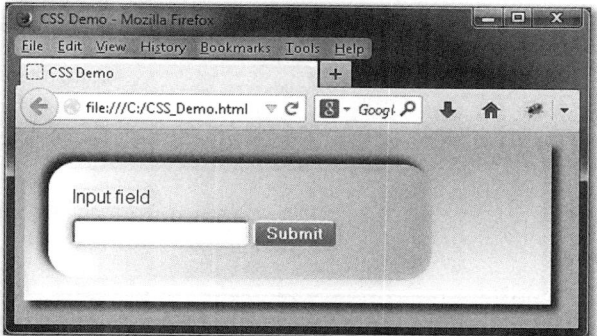

Figure 1.14   CSS Demo

In this example, the differences between the various browsers are shown very clearly. For the CSS3 attributes in particular, you must specify browser-specific (or more precisely, rendering engine–specific) statements to some extent. In our example, specific CSS statements are defined for Mozilla and Chrome:

```
background-image:-moz-linear-gradient(…)
background-image:-webkit-linear-gradient(…)
```

The entry moz applies for Mozilla and webkit for Chrome (see Table 1.1). If in doubt, you must consult the relevant developer network of the browser manufacturer. For Mozilla, you will find the MDN at *https://developer.mozilla.org/*. In the category CSS and Mozilla Enhancements, you will find the relevant commands, which are shown in Figure 1.15.

Mozilla Developer Network (MDN)

Figure 1.15   Mozilla Developer Network (MDN)

In this chapter, you'll learn about the basic language elements of JavaScript. With JavaScript, you can implement user interactions, change page content dynamically, or generate it at runtime. SAPUI5 is based on JavaScript.

2 JavaScript

JavaScript is a scripting language that was originally developed for dynamic HTML in web browsers; it was also known as DHTML (dynamic HTML). With JavaScript, it was possible to "breathe new life" into previously static websites; it enabled a developer to, for example, evaluate user interactions and change content dynamically. SAPUI5 is based on JavaScript, and we'd like to show you the basics of this scripting language in this chapter.

Checklist	[■]
You will need the following for this chapter:	
▶ A text editor such as Notepad or Notepad++	
▶ An installed browser	
If you want to implement these examples directly in the SAPUI5 Eclipse plug-in, read Chapter 4, and follow the installation instructions there.	

2.1 Basic Principles

JavaScript, which was developed by Brendan Eich, was presented for the first time in 1995 by Netscape as part of Netscape Navigator 2.0. For licensing reasons, Microsoft published its own version (called JScript) in response. This action sparked a "browser war" that continues to this day; the differences between the individual browsers when they interpret JavaScript are striking.

History

In 1997, the language was standardized by the European organization ECMA; since that time the language has officially been called ECMAScript.

Standardization

Strictly speaking, JavaScript and JScript are special ECMAScript implementations, but the term *JavaScript* is still used in common parlance. Due to the acquisition of Sun Microsystems, JavaScript is now one of Oracle's brands.

Developer tools

Because you are getting into web development with JavaScript, you'll need a developer's standard tools:

► A console for displaying errors/logs

► A debugger

Fortunately, the developer tools are already integrated in the new browsers; Table 2.1 contains the relevant key combinations for calling the tools.

Browser	Keyboard
Firefox	`F12`
Microsoft IE	`F12`
Chrome	`F12`
Safari	`Ctrl` + `Alt` + `i`
Opera	`Ctrl` + `Alt` + `i`

Table 2.1 Developer Tools

2.1.1 Logging

Logging

The command `console.log()` is useful in writing intermediate results or errors to the console and then looking at them in the developer tools. Listing 2.1 illustrates this, and Figure 2.1 shows the console output in the browser.

```
<!DOCTYPE html>
<html>
  <head>
    <meta charset="UTF-8">
    <title>Paragraph Types</title>
  </head>
<body>
  <h1>First JavaScript</h1>
    <script type="text/javascript">
      console.log("I was called");
```

```
        </script>
    </body>
</html>
```

Listing 2.1 Console.html

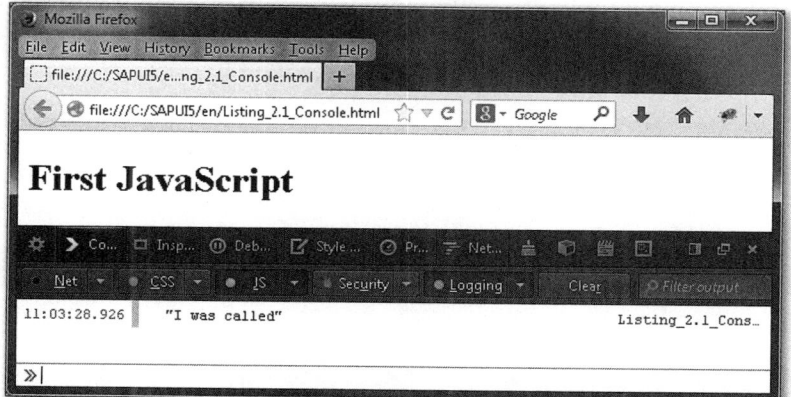

Figure 2.1 Console Output

Alternatively, you can use the `alert` command to display a dialog box. **Alerts**
However, we'd advise against using this option, because you could easily
overlook a point before going live and quickly annoy the user with too
many dialog boxes in live operation.

2.1.2   Positioning JavaScript Code

JavaScript is not an executable file by itself; it must be embedded in an
HTML page. Basically, you can integrate the JavaScript code in the same
manner as CSS:

▶ As a separate file and reference in the header:

```
<script src="script.js" type="text/javascript"></script>
```

▶ Within the header area:

```
<script type="text/javascript"></script>
```

▶ Within the `<body>` area:

```
<script type="text/javascript"></script>
```

The actual JavaScript code is stored within the `<script>` tags. Multiple JavaScript commands are separated by a semicolon, and functions are enclosed within curly brackets (`{ }`).

2.1.3 Comments

Single-line comments are enclosed within two forward slashes at the beginning, and multiline comments are enclosed within `/*...*/`:

```
// Single-line comment
/* Multi-line comment, with two
   lines in this example*/
```

2.1.4 Functions

Functions are defined with the keyword `function`, followed by a function name and brackets; the actual function is enclosed within curly brackets:

```
function func() {
    // actual function
};
```

This function can be called by its name—`func` in this example:

```
<script type="text/javascript">
    func();
</script>
```

In the following example, you add a button to the web page with which you call the function for the `onclick()` event or trigger the function call directly when you load the page via the `onload()` event (in Section 2.6, we'll discuss event processing in greater detail). This results in the complete Listing 2.2.

```
<!DOCTYPE html>
<html>
  <head>
    <meta charset="UTF-8">
    <script type="text/javascript">
      function button(){
            // Call function
            alert("Button pressed");
      };
```

```
    function loaded(){
         alert("Page loaded");
         console.log("Page loaded");
    };
         /* Two entries are generated
         in the console */
         console.log("First entry");
         console.log("Second entry");
    </script>
</head>
<body onload="loaded()">
  <button type="button" onclick="button()">
    Call function
  </button>
</body>
</html>
```

Listing 2.2 Basic Syntax

After loading the page, the first dialog box is displayed with the note "Page loaded," and after clicking on the button the second dialog box is displayed with the note "Button pressed."

Digging more deeply into the flow logic of JavaScript, if you look at the console output for this example, it is immediately obvious that the two entries—"First entry" and "Second entry"—are displayed first and are only then followed by the note "Page loaded" (see Figure 2.2).

Flow logic

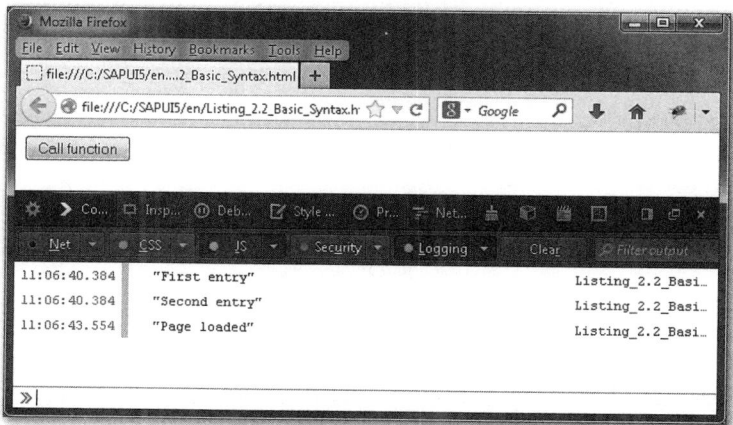

Figure 2.2 Flow Sequence

This effect is due to the fact that the browser processes an HTML page from top to bottom, and the `onload()` event is triggered only after the page is loaded.

[!]

Function and Variable Names
Certain keywords may not be used as functions or variable names. These include, among others: ▶ switch ▶ case ▶ break ▶ if ▶ else ▶ for ▶ function ▶ try ▶ catch

Transfer Values

Return   In the previous examples, the functions still do not have any defined interfaces. They have neither provided the function with input values—the arguments—nor have they received a return value from the function. Arguments are provided for the function in parentheses, and return values are indicated by the keyword `return`. You accept the `return` value in turn via a variable by assigning the result of the function to the variable. The general syntax is:

```
var Value = function();
```

In Listing 2.3, there is a function for multiplying two numbers provided.

```
<!DOCTYPE html>
<html>
<head>
<meta charset="UTF-8">
<script type="text/javascript">
function button(){
    // Call function
    var output = multiply(5,5);
```

```
      // Output
      alert(output);
   };

// Multiplication function
function multiply(a,b){
      var y = a * b;
      return y;
   };

</script>
</head>
<body >
   <button type="button" onclick="button()">
     Call function
   </button>
</body>
</html>
```

Listing 2.3 Functions.html

2.1.5 Objects

JavaScript is an object-oriented language, and each element of a web page is treated as an object. This means that you have, for example, the `window` object that represents the actual browser window. The window in turn has certain properties, such as its size. In addition, each object comprises specific methods. The `window` object uses the `alert()` method, for example, with which you are already familiar. Strictly speaking, in order to call the `alert` method you would have to write the window object `alert window. alert(output);`. Due to the special role of the `window` object, however, you can omit the object in this case and call the method directly.

Object

You create an object by using the keyword `new`, followed by the *Object Constructor* `Object();` or by literals `{}`. The Constructor is generally capitalized. Although this is not absolutely necessary, it has prevailed as a universal naming convention.

Constructor

```
var oObject = new Object();
```

or

```
var oObject {
   Characteristic1 : "Value1",
   Characteristic2 : "Value2"
   Method: function() {
   ...
   },
   };
```

Predefined objects   In addition to the `window` object, there are other predefined objects, such as `Date`, `Math`, `String`, or `Array`. By calling the Constructor, you create an object instance and can thus access the implemented methods. You can, for example, use the method `getDate()` or `getMonth()` to access the predefined `Date` object on the current date or month:

```
var oDate = new Date();
var sDate = oDate.getDate();
var sMonth = oDate.getMonth();
```

> **[+]**   **Current Month**
>
> JavaScript starts with 0 for the months. If you want to determine the current month, you must always add the value 1:
>
> `var sMonth = (oDate.getMonth() + 1);`

Dot notation   You access the relevant properties or methods of an object via the dot notation. As was shown in the preceding example, you use `oDate.get-Date()` to access the `getDate` method of the `Date` object.

You have already encountered this dot notation with `console.log()`, although you did not create an explicit object instance. In JavaScript, there are specific objects with a certain special role, such as the `window` object (see Section 2.5) or the `console` object. You can access these objects directly without having to create an instance.

> **[+]**   **Call by Reference**
>
> If you transfer a variable to a function, it is transferred as a copy to the function, and changes made to the variable within the function have no effect outside the function (Call by Value). For objects, the reference of the object is transferred, rather than the copy of the object. If you change object properties within a function, the object is also changed outside the function (Call by Reference).

How do you access the object in an object method anyway? Let's assume you have defined the following object and want to implement a function that displays `Characteristic2` in an `alert` dialog box:

```
var oObject {
  Characteristic1 : "Value1",
  Characteristic2 : "Value2"
}
```

You use the keyword `this` to access the context object within an object function. In our example, the function would be implemented as follows:

this

```
var oObject {
    Characteristic1 : "Value1",
    Characteristic2 : "Value2",
        outputCharacteristic2: function() {
            alert("Characteristic2 is" + this.Characteristic2);
    }
}
```

JSON   [+]

The abbreviated form { key : value, ... : ...} from the previous example is called JSON (pronounced like "Jason"), JavaScript Object Notation.

In ABAP, you've become used to the fact that an object instance contains the methods and attributes of its class. In JavaScript, you can freely extend each object and add your own properties and functions. This is because JavaScript regards the object as a type of container in which you can place any objects. In Chapter 3, you'll discover that the variable declaration in JavaScript follows the same principle (see the explanation of loose typing in Section 2.2).

Even if objects may still seem confusing at the moment, you will be working in SAPUI5 almost solely with objects and will get used to this notation very quickly. To test your understanding, Listing 2.4 illustrates a piece of source code for displaying a dropdown list in an SAPUI5 page.

Example in SAPUI5

```
// Listbox
var oListBox = new sap.ui.commons.ListBox("Days",
  {items : [
    new sap.ui.core.ListItem("Mon",
              { text : "Monday" }),
```

```
new sap.ui.core.ListItem("Tues",
            { text : "Tuesday" }),
    // etc.
        ]});

// Dropdown Listbox
var oDropBox = new sap.ui.commons.DropdownBox("DropBox",
    {
            "association:listBox"      : oListBox
    });
```

Listing 2.4 Example of a Dropdown Box in SAPUI5

As you can see in Figure 2.3, the weekdays are written in JSON notation as an entry in a listbox and are linked to the dropdown list as selection options.

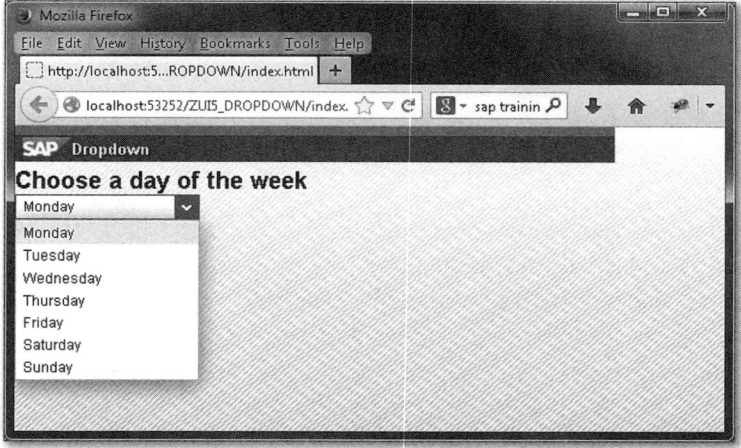

Figure 2.3 Dropdown List in SAPUI5

2.2   Variables

Dynamic typing The variable declaration in particular is unfamiliar at first for ABAP developers, because JavaScript is dynamically typed. This means that the variable type is determined only by the runtime. Unfortunately, this variable does not then retain the type in JavaScript; instead, it always adopts the type that is actually in use by the runtime. In ABAP, many are used to always assigning a fixed type to a variable—for example:

```
data: variable type sy-date.
```

A variable in JavaScript could be compared most closely to a field symbol type any in ABAP, where any in JavaScript can be simply anything: any variable or any object instance. The statement for a variable declaration in JavaScript is very simple:

```
var variable = 123;
```

With this statement, you create a variable of type integer. If you want to create a variable of type string, the statement changes as follows:

```
var variable = "123";
```

Due to this dynamically typed behavior, you can assign several types in the course of a script to a single variable. Strictly speaking, you can also omit the keyword var; thus, the following statement is also syntactically correct:

```
variable = "123";
```

The omission of the var keyword also has another effect: If you omit it within a function, the variable will be globally visible as a result. Variables that are declared outside functions are already global by definition.

Visibility

Variable Nomenclature

[+]

For reasons of clarity, readability, and maintainability, it is recommended that you always use the keyword var and introduce a type of Hungarian notation (see *http://en.wikipedia.org/wiki/Hungarian_notation*) —for example:

```
var sVar = "Text";          // string
var iVar = 123;             // integer
var fVar = 12.34;           // float
var oObject = new Object(); // object
```

JavaScript differentiates between uppercase and lowercase; the statements sVar and sVAR would create two different variables in JavaScript!

Dynamic typing, also known as *loose typing*, can lead to unfathomable side effects. Let's assume you declare two variables:

Loose typing

```
var iVar = 10;
var sVar = "10";
```

You then perform the following operation:

```
var result = iVar + sVar;
```

The interpreter now cannot clearly decide whether you want to perform a string concatenation or a calculation. When in doubt, JavaScript interprets the variable as a string. In this example, the result would be a string concatenation: 1010. To avoid this pitfall, you can use the parseInt function to force a conversion in integer. The following code would produce a result of 20.

```
var iVar = 10;
var sVar = "10";
var result = iVar + parseInt(sVar);
```

In the following listing, a form field is added to Listing 2.2 and displays the result with the onclick() event of the button in an alert dialog box.

```html
<!DOCTYPE html>
<html>
  <head>
    <script>
    function display(){
      var oName = document.getElementById("day");
      alert(oName.value);
    }
    </script>
  </head>
  <body>
    <form>
    Tag: <input type="day" name="day" id="day">
    <button type="button" onclick="display()">
        Send
    </button>
    </form>
  </body>
</html>
```

Listing 2.5 Variables.html

Execute the example in the browser. If you enter "Monday" in the form field, for example, and click on SEND, the value *Monday* is then displayed in a dialog box (see Figure 2.4).

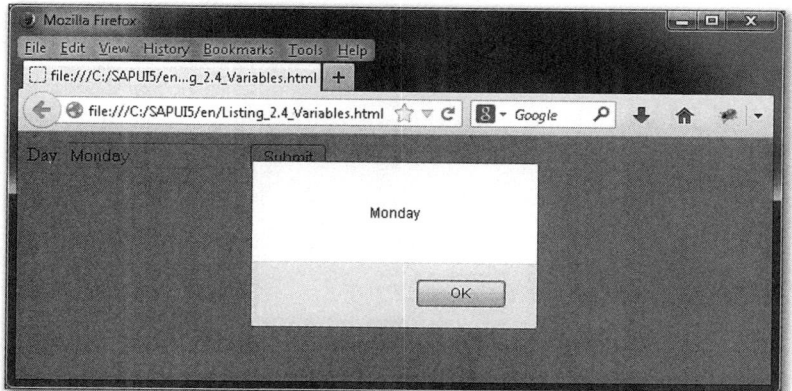

Figure 2.4 Variables

The access `document.getElementById` to the DOM (Document Object Model) element that is used here is discussed in detail in Section 2.5.

Special Values for Variables

You usually assign a value directly to a variable in JavaScript. If you define only the variable, JavaScript uses `undefined` as the initial variable value.

undefined

If you want to know whether a variable is empty, you must query the value `zero` in JavaScript. The value `zero` specifies that the variable is initial.

zero

In JavaScript, the *Boolean values* are implemented as `true` and `false`.

Boolean values

The value `NaN` stands for *Not a Number*; this value is always assigned to a variable if an integer operation could not be performed. You can query this state with the integrated function `isNaN()`. The following would display `true` as a result:

NaN

```
var iVar = parseInt("XX");
var sBool = isNaN(iVar);
alert(sBool);
```

2.3 Operators

JavaScript supports a wide variety of operators. In this section, we'll categorize some of these operators and discuss their use.

2.3.1 Arithmetic Operators

The arithmetic operators listed in Table 2.2 are defined as in ABAP.

Arithmetic Operation	Sign
Addition	+
Subtraction	–
Multiplication	*
Division	/

Table 2.2 Arithmetic Operators

String concatenation

The + operator is used in JavaScript in addition to the string concatenation, which corresponds to the ABAP command CONCATENATE. Alternatively, you can use the concat() method of the JavaScript object String.

```
var firstname = "Linda";
var lastname = "Walker";
var Name = firstname.concat(lastname);
```

or

```
var Name = "Linda" + "Walker";
```

2.3.2 Increment and Decrement Operators

To increase or decrease a variable by a value of 1, the abbreviated forms Variable++ and Variable-- are available in JavaScript. The following example returns a value of 2:

```
var iNumber = 1;
iNumber++; // Equal to iNumber = iNumber + 1;
alert(iNumber);
```

2.3.3   Assignment Operators

The assignment operators are defined as in ABAP. If, for example, you
want to increase a variable by a value of 10, you can write the following:

```
iNumber = iNumber + 10;
```

However, there are also abbreviated forms for these operators in JavaS-
cript, unlike in ABAP. Thus, you can also express the previous statement
in the following abbreviated form:

Abbreviated form

```
iNumber += 10;
```

2.3.4   Relational Operators

Relational operators are used mostly with numeric values. These com-
parisons are possible even with strings. Here, the ranking of individual
signs (which sign is "greater" than another) is determined according to
the ASCII code of the relevant sign. Table 2.3 provides an overview.

Operator	Description
==	Equal to
===	Strictly equal to
!=	Not equal to
!==	Strictly not equal to
>	Greater than
<	Less than
>=	Greater than or equal to
<=	Less than or equal to

Table 2.3   Relational Operators

The distinction between *equal to* and *strictly equal to* is surprising for a
start. Due to the dynamic typing, a type conversion takes place during a
relational operation, and you cannot be sure whether the two variables
are really equal or if they became equal due to the automatic conversion.
If you want to exclude this effect, use the "strictly equal to" operator:

Type conversion

```
alert("1" == 1);     // true
alert("1" === 1);    // false
```

2.3.5 The typeof Operator

You can use `typeof` to determine the type of variable. You will obtain one of the following values:

- ▶ undefined
- ▶ boolean
- ▶ function
- ▶ number
- ▶ object
- ▶ string

The `typeof` operator is particularly suited for checking whether a variable is defined at all due to its `undefined` return value.

2.3.6 Logical Operators

if query
In most cases, you link multiple conditions to a logical query, particularly with `if` statements (see Section 2.4.1). If you want to query whether a particular person is already an adult but still under 60 years of age, for example, you would have to implement two nested `if` queries, as shown in Listing 2.6.

```
if (Age >= 18) {
  if (Age < 60) {
    // Both conditions apply
  }
}
```

Listing 2.6 Nested if Query

Operators
The AND operator (&&) and the OR operator (||) are available for these links in JavaScript. If you want to reverse a condition, the negation operator (!) is available (see Table 2.4).

Operator	JavaScript	ABAP
AND	&&	and
OR	||	or
Negation	!	is not

Table 2.4 Logical Operators

In our example, this results in the following:

```
if ((Age >= 18) && (Age < 60)) {
  // Both conditions apply
}
```

2.4 Control Structures: Conditions and Loops

Next we will deal with conditions, such as `if` and `switch` statements, and loops, such as `for` and `while`.

2.4.1 The if Statement

The basic syntax for an `if` statement is:

```
if (condition) {
    // true;
} else {
    // false;
};
```

The condition in an `if` query must be a *Boolean variable* and can take on either `true` or `false`.

Conditional Operator   **[+]**

An `if-else` query has an abbreviated form with the conditional operator:
```
(condition) ? true : false;
```
This is equal to:
```
if (condition) {
    // true;
} else {
    // false;
};
```
To facilitate the readability of the source code, it is recommended that you refrain from using this abbreviated form, at least at the outset.

---

if control structure In Listing 2.7, you add an `if` control structure to Listing 2.5.

```html
<!DOCTYPE html>
<html>
  <head>
    <script>
        function display(){
            var oName = document.getElementById("day");
            if (oName.value == 'Monday') {
                alert("Garfield says: I hate Mondays!");
            } else {
                alert("At least it's not Monday");
            };
        };
    </script>
  </head>
  <body>
    <form>
      Tag: <input type="day" name="day" id="day">
      <button type="button" onclick="display()">
          Submit
      </button>
    </form>
  </body>
</html>
```

Listing 2.7 IF_statement.html

The result of Listing 2.7 in the browser is shown in Figure 2.5.

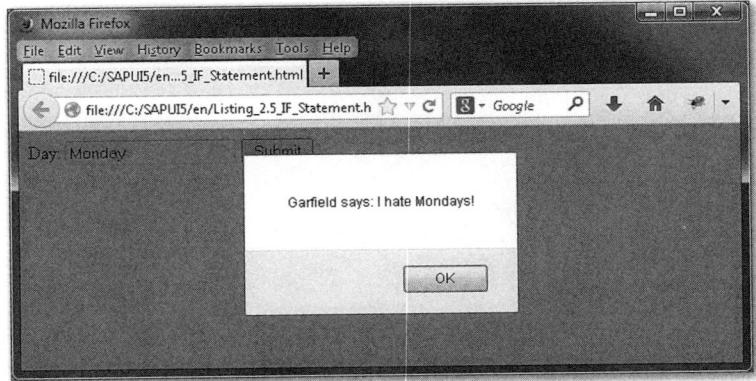

Figure 2.5 if Control Structure

2.4.2 The switch Statement

As you saw in Section 2.4.1, an `if` statement for variables with more than two possible values due to nestings can quickly become unclear. For this reason, a `switch` statement should be used in cases in which a variable can take more than two values.

The basic syntax for a `switch` statement is shown in Listing 2.8.   Syntax

```
switch (condition) {
    case Value1:[Code];
        break;
    case Value2: [Code];
        break;
    default: [Code];
};
```

Listing 2.8   switch Statement

Let's use Listing 2.5 again as a template and generate a different output in each case for the different days (see Listing 2.9).

```
<!DOCTYPE html>
<html>
  <head>
    <script>
    function display(){
    var oName = document.getElementById("day");

    switch (oName.value) {
        case "Monday":
            alert("Garfield says: I hate Mondays!");
            break;
        case "Tuesday":
            alert("At least it's not Monday");
            break;
        case "Wednesday":
            alert("Better known as hump day");
            break;
        case "Thursday":
            alert("Almost Friday");
            break;
        case "Friday":
            alert("It is Friday");
```

```
            break;
        default:
            alert("Weekend...!");
        };
    };
    </script>
  </head>
  <body>
    <form>
      Tag: <input type="day" name="day" id="day">
      <button type="button" onclick="display()">
              Submit
      </button>
    </form>
  </body>
</html>
```

Listing 2.9 switch_statement.html

Execute the example in the browser (see Figure 2.6). Depending on the day you entered, the relevant text is output after you click the SEND button.

Figure 2.6 switch Statement

break From the perspective of an ABAP developer, the break statement is certainly unusual. In JavaScript, a switch statement is used merely as a jump label, and the complete source code is executed after the first true condition. If, for example, you were to remove all break statements in Listing 2.9 and enter them in the form field Thursday, the output would be a sequence of dialog boxes with the content "Almost Friday," "It is Friday," and "Weekend...!". The `break` statement ensures that the `switch` statement is exited after processing the true condition.

2.4.3   The for Loop

The `for` loop is always used when the number of loop passes has been determined in advance. The number of loop passes are controlled by a variable that is usually incremented with each loop pass by the value 1 using the increment operator (see Section 2.3.2), until the test condition is reached. The basic syntax for a `for` loop is:

Syntax

```
for ( [index variable] ; [check condition] ; [variable
operator] ){
    // Loop body
}
```

In most cases, an integer variable is incremented by the value 1 with `for` loops:

```
for (i = 0; i < 10; i++){
// Loop body
};
```

In this example, the loop passes ten times. The first part of the statement (i = 0) defines an `integer` variable, which is also called an *index variable*. The second part of the statement (i < 10) is the *check condition*. If this condition is met, the loop is exited. The third part of the statement (i++) increments the index variable by a value of 1 by using the already known increment operator.

Index variable

In order to be able to provide a better illustration of the effect of the loop, you will no longer produce the output with the `alert` dialog box in the following examples; instead, you will write it directly in the HTML page (see Listing 2.10). The technique of DOM manipulation will be discussed, in detail, in Section 2.5.

```
<!DOCTYPE html>
<html>
  <head>
    <script>
    function load(){
```

```
      var oContent = document.getElementById("content");
      var sOutput  = " ";
            for ( var i = 1; i < 10; i++){
            sOutput = sOutput + i + "<br>";
            };
      oContent.innerHTML = sOutput;
      oContent.innerHTML += "Players. And the coach?";
      };
   </script>
 </head>
 <body onload="load()">
    <p> A baseball team consists of...</p>
    <div id="content">
      <!-- Output from JavaScript -->
    </div>
 </body>
</html>
```

Listing 2.10   for_loop.html

The for loop ensures that the numbers 1 to 9 are written in the `<div>` area with the ID content. Execute the example in the browser and check the result (see Figure 2.7).

Figure 2.7   The for Loop

2.4.4   The while Loop

In contrast to the `for` loop, the number of loop passes does not have to   Syntax
be specified in advance for the `while` loop. Only the test condition is
defined, which is set within the loop. The basic syntax is:

```
while ([check condition]){
// Loop body
};
```

The preceding example can be mapped with a `while` loop as follows:

```
while (i < 10){
   i++;
}
```

In Listing 2.11, you use the `while` loop to specify the team's strength,
depending on the selected sport.

```html
<!DOCTYPE html>
<html>
  <head>
  <meta charset="UTF-8" />
   <script>
   function get(){
     var oSport = document.getElementById("sport");
     var sOutput  = " ";
     var oContent = document.getElementById("content");
     var sDone = false;
     var iCount = 1;

     while (!sDone){
      sOutput = sOutput + iCount + "<br>";
      switch (oSport.value) {
        case "Baseball":
            if (iCount == 9) {
             sDone = true;
            }
        break;
        case "Icehockey":
            if (iCount == 6) {
             sDone = true;
            }
        break;
        };
```

69

```
        iCount++;
      };
    oContent.innerHTML = sOutput;
    oContent.innerHTML += " Players. And the coach?";
    };
  </script>
</head>
<body>
<form>
  <label for="sport">Team size</label>
  <select name="sport" id="sport" size="1">
    <option value"Baseball">Baseball</option>
    <option value"Icehockey">Hockey</option>
  </select>
  <button type="button" onclick="get()">
        Submit
  </button>
  <br>
</form>
<div id="content">
  <!-- Output from JavaScript -->
</div>
</body>
</html>
```

Listing 2.11 While_loop.html

If you execute this example in the browser and click on the SUBMIT button, the team of the selected sport is displayed (see Figure 2.8).

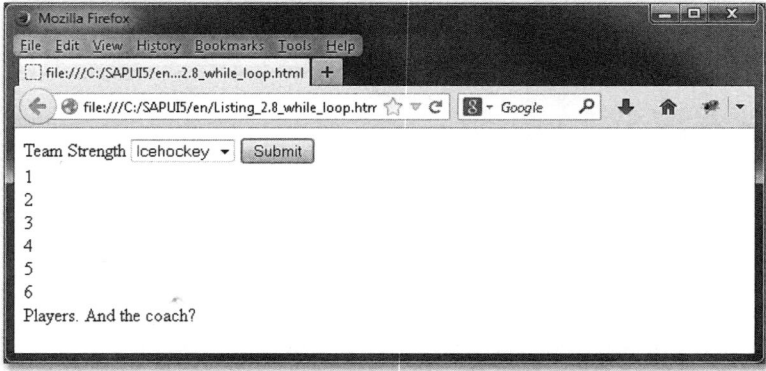

Figure 2.8 while Loop

2.4.5   The do-while Loop

With the `do-while` loop, in contrast to the `while` loop, the test condition to terminate the loop is performed only at the end of the loop. The general syntax is

```
do{
// Loop body
} while ([check condition]);
```

With a `do-while` loop, the preceding example would look like this:

```
do{
  i++;
} while (i < 10);
```

2.4.6   The for-in Loop

The `for-in` loop is particularly useful, if, for example, you want to go through all of the properties of an object (see Listing 2.12).

```
<!DOCTYPE html>
<html>
  <head>
  <meta charset="UTF-8" />
  <script type="text/javascript">
    function get(){

    var oSport = document.getElementById("sport");
    var sOutput  = " ";
    var oContent = document.getElementById("content");

    for (i in oSport){
      sOutput += (i + ":" + oSport[i] + "<br>");
    }
    oContent.innerHTML = sOutput;
    };
  </script>
  </head>
  <body>
    <form>
      <label for="sport">Object</label>
      <select name="sport" id="sport" size="1">
          <option value"baseball">Baseball</option>
```

71

```
        <option value"icehockey">Hockey</option>
    </select>
    <button type="button" onclick="get()">
          Submit
    </button>
    <br>
  </form>
  <div id="content">
      <!-- Output from JavaScript -->
  </div>
  </body>
</html>
```

Listing 2.12   for_in loop.html

The entire DOM is displayed in this example, as illustrated in Figure 2.9.

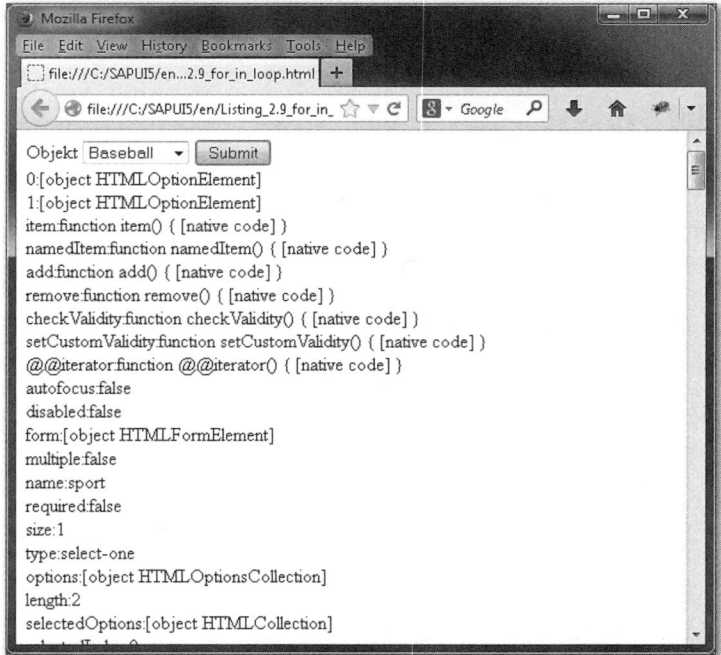

Figure 2.9   for-in Loop

2.5   Document Object Model

The Document Object Model (DOM) is a specification defined by W3C for accessing HTML documents. The DOM represents the web page in a tree structure (see Figure 2.10). The three basic objects in the DOM are the screen, window, and document.

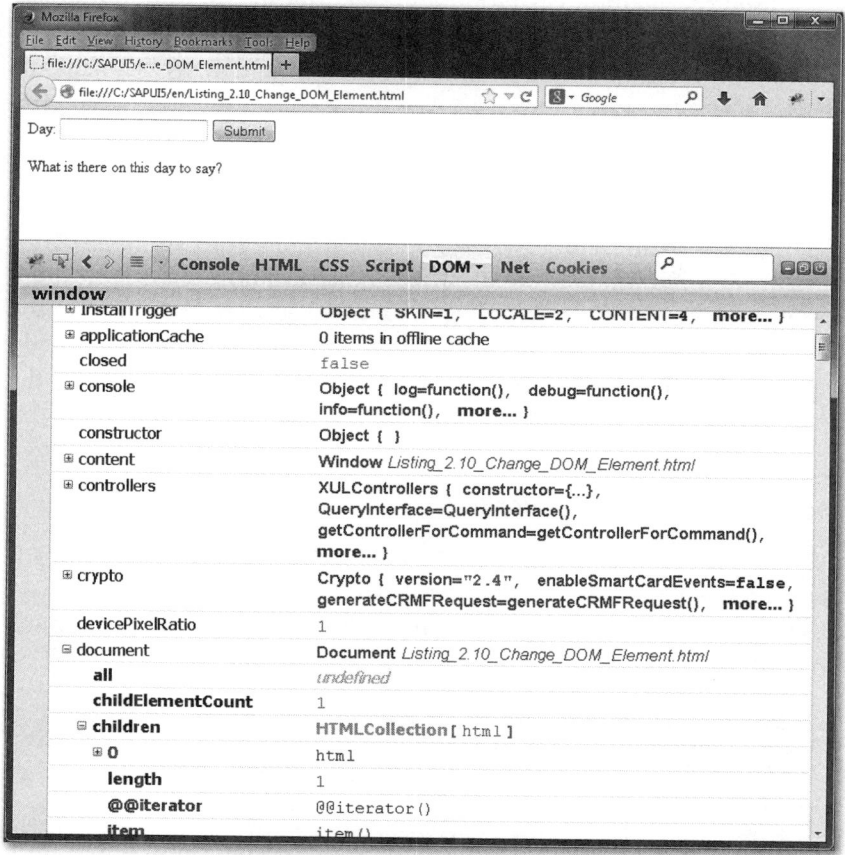

Figure 2.10 Document Object Model

The screen object represents the screen; you can use this object to determine, for example, the height and width of the screen.   **Screen object**

The actual browser window is represented by the window object. In the preceding section, you already used a method of the window object: the   **Window object** alert() method. Due to the special role of the window object, you can omit the window statement; the exact syntax of the statement is window. alert().

Document object

The web page displayed in the browser window is represented by the document object. You can use this object to access all components of the displayed web page. You are also already familiar with this object and have used the method document.getElementById() to read the object reference of a specific element. The DOM defines how these individual elements of a web page are linked to each other and maps the elements in an object hierarchy—the DOM tree.

2.5.1 The DOM Tree

DOM structure

Each HTML element in a web page becomes a *node* in the DOM tree, in which the HTML tags are known as *elements* and the actual content between the start tag and end tag are known as a *text node*. Due to the hierarchical mapping, the superordinate elements are known as *parent objects*, subordinate elements are known as *children*, and elements of the same rank are known as *siblings*.

2.5.2 Addressing Elements

Array

In the preceding examples, you have addressed the relevant elements with document.getElementById(), and when you use the method getElementsByTagName() an *array* is returned with all objects that were found for the specified type.

[+]

Digression: Arrays

An array is an object implemented in JavaScript that is comparable to the internal tables in ABAP. An array is generated by the following statement:

```
var oArray = new Array(); //Constructor
```

You can now write any values in the array object by using the following index:

```
oArray[0] = "First entry";
oArray[1] = "Second entry";
```

You can use the same index to read the values again, and the following statement would have "Second entry" as its output:

```
alert(oArray[1]);
```

Due to the representation of the web page as a DOM tree, you can address each element by using the `childNodes` array. The options listed in Table 2.5 are available for this step.

Property	Description
firstChild	First child node
childNodes[]	Child node [array]
lastChild	Last child node
nextSibling	Next node at the same level
previousSibling	Previous node at the same level
parentNode	Parent node

Table 2.5   DOM Properties of an Element

Figure 2.11 shows the properties of the DOM tree.

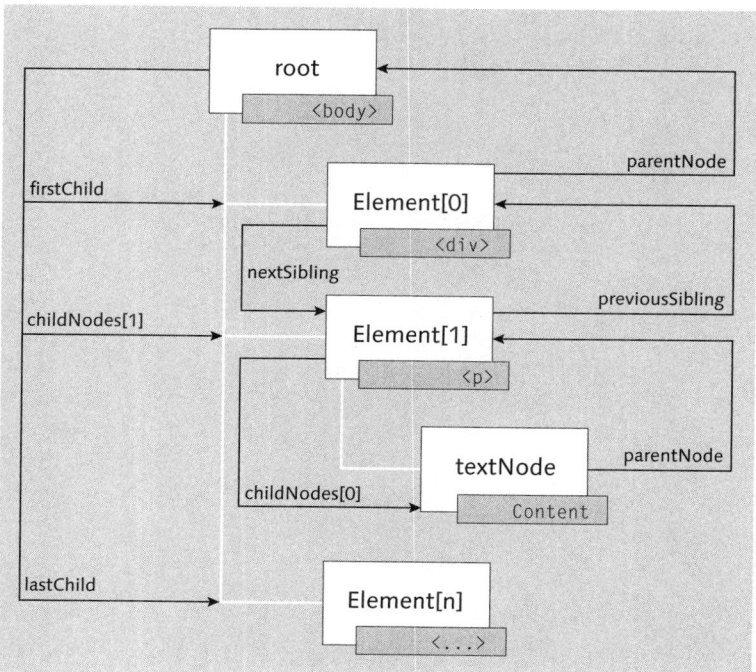

Figure 2.11   DOM Tree Properties

[!] **The Pitfalls of the Browser**

In theory, it sounds very simple to address certain elements by the `childNodes` array. In reality, some browsers interpret blank characters or line breaks as elements; this shifts the position of these elements in the array to an unpredictable and particularly browser-dependent point.

For this reason, you should always work with IDs, and address the desired element with `document.getElementById()`.

2.5.3 DOM Manipulation

Changing object

You cannot only access the DOM in read-only mode, but also change properties, move existing objects, add new objects, and even delete objects.

innerHTML

As you have already seen in the preceding examples, you can use the property `innerHTML` to add any HTML code at a particular point. In Listing 2.13, you change Listing 2.9 so that the output no longer appears in the `alert` dialog box, but is displayed directly on the web page.

```
<!DOCTYPE html>
<html>
<head>
<meta charset="UTF-8" />
<script type="text/javascript">
function display(){
  var oName = document.getElementById("day");
  var oOutput = document.getElementById("output");

  switch (oName.value) {
  case "Monday":
    oOutput.innerHTML ="Garfield says: I hate Mondays!";
    break;
  case "Tuesday":
    oOutput.innerHTML="At least it's not Monday";
    break;
  case "Wednesday":
    oOutput.innerHTML="Better known as hump day";
    break;
  case "Thursday":
```

```
      oOutput.innerHTML="Almost Friday";
      break;
    case "Friday":
      oOutput.innerHTML="It is Friday";
      break;
    default:
      oOutput.innerHTML="Weekend...!";
    };
  };
</script>
</head>
<body>
  <form>
    Tag: <input type="day" name="day" id="day">
    <button type="button" onclick="display()">
          Submit
    </button>
  </form>
<p>What is there on this day to say?
    <div id="output"></div>
</p>
</body>
</html>
```

Listing 2.13   Changing_DOM_element.html

You can use the DOM to change the properties of each element. However, what properties are available? Here, it is easiest if you install an add-on in your browser to display the DOM tree; for Firefox, try the add-on *Firebug*, which you can download under EXTRAS • ADD-ONS. If you start Firebug after installation and reload the page, you can display the entire DOM tree of the web page in the DOM tab (see Figure 2.12).

Firebug

You can then navigate through the tree. You can find the properties of an element by choosing the path DOCUMENT • BODY • CHILDNODES • [ELE-MENT]. You can use JavaScript to change all the properties listed there. If, for example, you would like to change the font color, you have to change the property `style.color`; for the background color you would have to change the property `style.backgroundColor`.

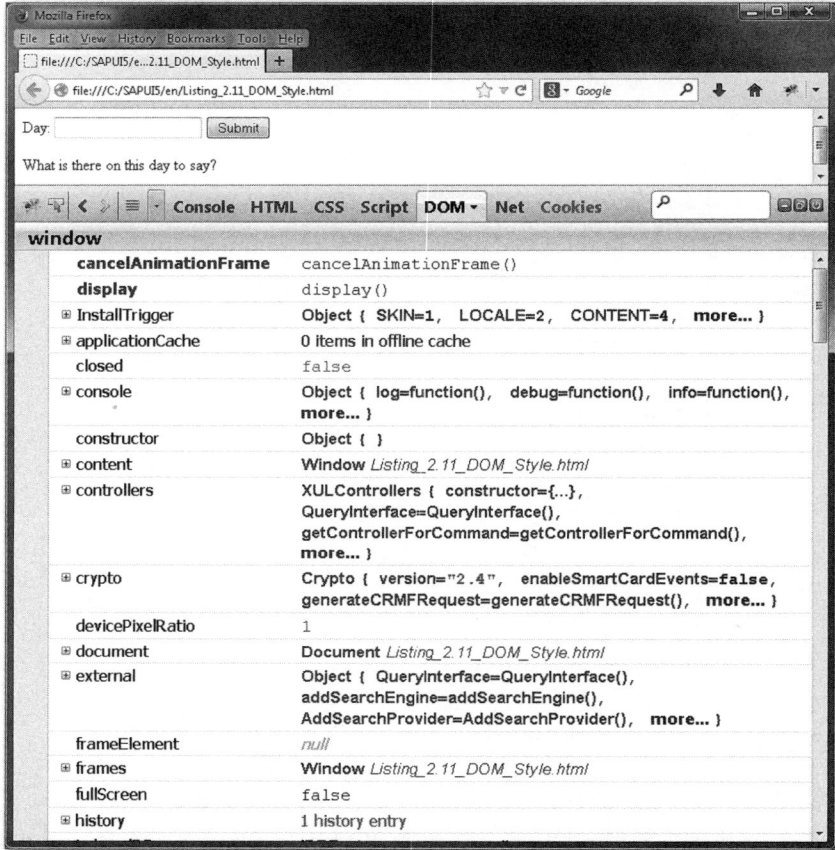

Figure 2.12 DOM in Firebug

The search in the DOM tree is a bit tedious, of course; at this point, it's only important that you develop an understanding of the structure of the DOM tree. Under the relevant Developer Network pages, you will find detailed documentation on the DOM, including a reference. For example, see *https://developer.mozilla.org/en/docs/DOM*.

Enhancements   In Listing 2.14, you enhance Listing 2.13 so that the font for the output "Weekend...!" is displayed in red and the background is displayed in yellow. To do this, you enhance the `default` branch of the `switch` statement in Listing 2.14 by adding two aforementioned commands to it:

```
default:
    oOutput.style.color="red";
    oOutput.style.backgroundColor="yellow";
    oOutput.innerHTML="Weekend...!";
  };
```

Listing 2.14 DOM_style.html

If you now execute this example in your browser and enter "Saturday," the text is displayed in red with a yellow background (see Figure 2.13).

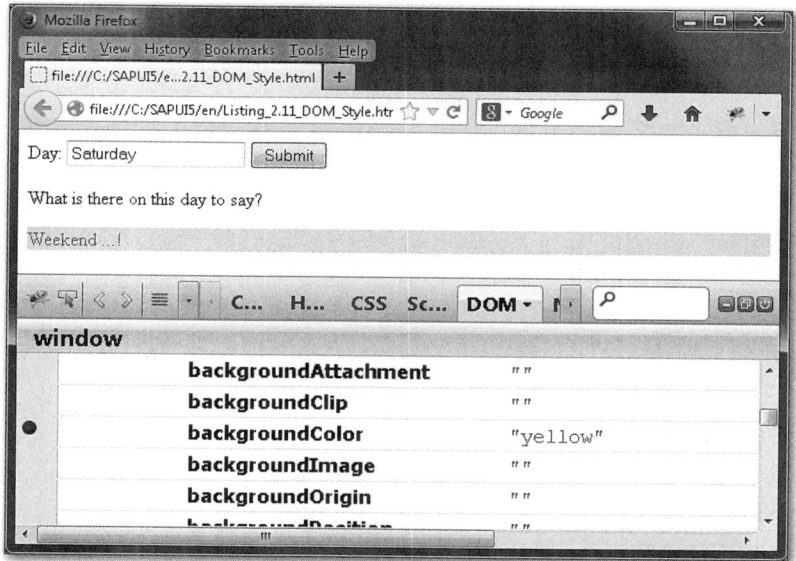

Figure 2.13 Style Change due to DOM Manipulation

Because you can change CSS attributes at runtime, it's also possible, for example, to design animations without much effort. In the example from Listing 2.15, the HTML5 logo (image source: *www. w3.org/html/logo/ downloads/HTML5_sticker.png*) appears from the right.

CSS at runtime

```
<!DOCTYPE html>
<html>
<head>
<title>Fly!</title>
```

```
<meta charset="UTF-8" />
<script type="text/javascript">

function init(){
  set(-300)
  animate()
}

function animate(){
  if (get()>0)
    set(0)
  if (get()<0){
    set(get() + 3)
    setTimeout("animate()", 30)
  }
}

function get(){
  return parseInt(
  document.getElementById("logo").style.left)
}

function set(n){
  document.getElementById("logo").style.left = n+"px"
}

</script>
</head>
<body onLoad="init()">
  <div STYLE="position:relative" ID="logo" >
    <IMG SRC="HTML5_sticker.png">
  </div>
</body>
</html>
```

Listing 2.15 Animated_logo.html

If you execute this example in the browser, the image moves slowly from the right side into the browser window (see Figure 2.14).

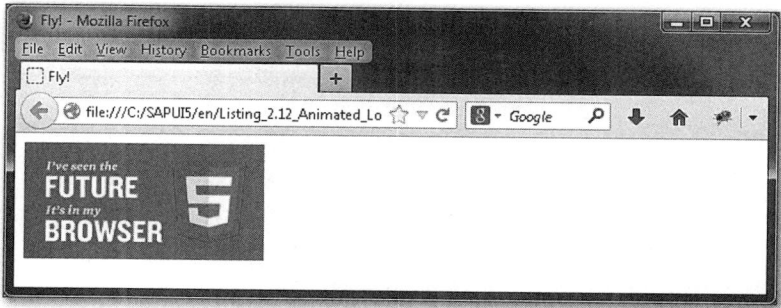

Figure 2.14 Animated Logo

By the same principle you followed to change element attributes, you can add elements (appendChild();), copy elements (cloneNode();), or remove elements (removeChild();).

Adding elements

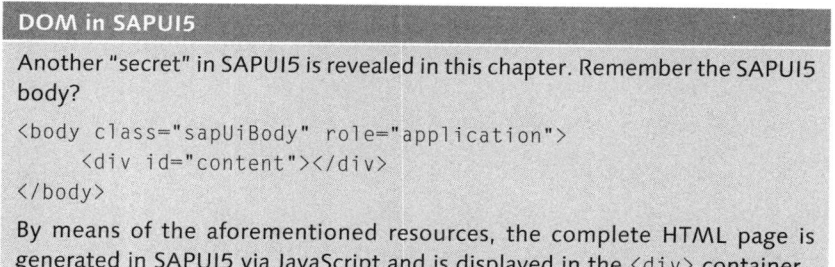

DOM in SAPUI5 [+]

Another "secret" in SAPUI5 is revealed in this chapter. Remember the SAPUI5 body?

```
<body class="sapUiBody" role="application">
    <div id="content"></div>
</body>
```

By means of the aforementioned resources, the complete HTML page is generated in SAPUI5 via JavaScript and is displayed in the <div> container.

2.6   Events

In Section 2.1.4, you already learned about the *events* onclick() and onload() and defined an *event handler* for these events. The event model determines how the browser handles the relevant event.

Unfortunately, the browser manufacturers also couldn't decide on a standard for this point. As in most cases, Internet Explorer also occupies a special role here; it implements the W3C standard as of version 9.0. Because of that, the differences between IE and Firefox, Chrome, or Safari have been reduced, but they definitely still exist. If you are developing for older versions of Internet Explorer, you must access the Internet

W3C standard

Explorer–specific event object. You'll find further information on this topic at *http://msdn.microsoft.com*, the Microsoft Developer Network.

Event model The best known standard method is probably the hyperlink. If the user clicks on a hyperlink, the browser responds to the event `click` of the link object. You do not need to do anything as a developer for these default actions; they are already implemented in the browser. It is nevertheless important to understand that it also involves an event, because you can explicitly prevent these default actions.

Return value To this end, you must implement a return value in the event handler via the keyword `return`. This ensures that the default action is prevented in the browser, and you can implement your own logic—for example, in this default action:

```
<a href="link.html" onclick="return false;">
```

Event handler The following list provides an overview of the most important event handlers:

- ▶ `onabort` (when terminated)
- ▶ `onblur` (when exiting)
- ▶ `onchange` (when changed)
- ▶ `onclick` (when clicking)
- ▶ `ondblclick` (when double-clicking)
- ▶ `onerror` (in the event of an error)
- ▶ `onfocus` (when activating)
- ▶ `onkeydown` (when a key is pressed)
- ▶ `onkeypress` (when a key is pressed and held down)
- ▶ `onkeyup` (when a key is released)
- ▶ `onload` (when loading a file)
- ▶ `onmousedown` (when a mouse button is pressed)
- ▶ `onmousemove` (when moving a mouse further)
- ▶ `onmouseout` (when exiting the element with the mouse)
- ▶ `onmouseout` (when moving over the element with the mouse)
- ▶ `onmouseup` (when the mouse button is released)

- ▸ onreset (when resetting the form)
- ▸ onselect (when selecting text)
- ▸ onsubmit (when submitting the form)
- ▸ onunload (when exiting the file)

In the W3C standard version, you use the method addEventListener()   **addEventListener()**
to define an *event listener*, and you can thus register one or more events
on any object. The method expects three arguments:

- ▸ The name of the event as a string: for example, mouseover
- ▸ The function to be called without parentheses
- ▸ Control of the event flow

In the following example, you change Listing 2.13 so that the style changes
are made for the mouseover event. Listing 2.16 was shortened for clarity.

```
<script type="text/javascript">
function display(){
  var oName = document.getElementById("day");
  var oOutput = document.getElementById("output");

    oOutput.addEventListener(
            'mouseover',
            highlight,
            false
    );
    oOutput.addEventListener(
            'mouseout',
            init,
            false
    );

  switch (oName.value) {
  case "Monday":
    oOutput.nodeValue="Garfield says: I hate Mondays!";
    break;
    // shortened, cf. Listing 2.13
  };
}

function highlight() {
```

```
    var oOutput = document.getElementById("output");
    oOutput.style.color="red";
    oOutput.style.backgroundColor="yellow";
  }

function init() {
    var oOutput = document.getElementById("output");
    oOutput.style.color="black";
    oOutput.style.backgroundColor="white";
  }
</script>
    // shortened, cf. Listing 2.13
```

Listing 2.16 Event_listener.html

If you execute this example in your browser and move over the text with the mouse, the text is displayed in red with a yellow background (see Figure 2.15).

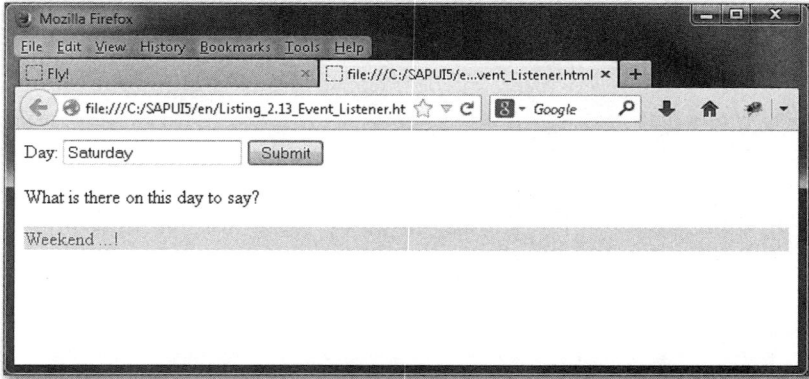

Figure 2.15 Style Change with Mouseover

In this chapter, we introduce the JavaScript library jQuery;
SAPUI5 is based on this library.

3   jQuery

Let's imagine that you have to develop an ABAP program without being able to access existing classes, methods, and function modules. Native development in JavaScript is similarly time consuming. Fortunately, there are JavaScript libraries that make life much easier for developers.

Checklist	[+]
You will need the following for this chapter:	
▶ A text editor such as Notepad or Notepad++	
▶ An installed browser	
▶ The current jQuery library, which you will find at *http://jquery.com/download/*	

If you want to implement these examples directly in the SAPUI5 Eclipse plug-in, read Chapter 4, and follow the installation instructions.

3.1   Basic Principles

Although there are many JavaScript libraries and frameworks, we will focus on jQuery in this book. In keeping with jQuery's motto, "write less, do more," this library saves you a lot of time spent on typing. jQuery was developed in 2008 by John Resig and has been developed continuously ever since.

jQuery

Before you can use the jQuery library, you must download it and integrate it into your web pages.

Download the library at *http://jquery.com/download/*; it's best if you use the non-compressed version for test purposes. This is because all blank characters were removed in the compressed version, which minimizes

Download

the space required and the loading times, but also makes everything unreadable. On the other hand, you should use the compressed version in live operation, because it will reduce the loading times of the web page.

Save the file in the same directory as your web pages. In order to be able to subsequently integrate new versions more easily into your web pages, it's best to rename the file *jquery.js*. Integrate the file in the header area of your pages, as shown in Listing 3.1.

```
<!DOCTYPE html>
<html>
  <head>
    <meta charset="UTF-8">
      <script type="text/javascript"
              src="jquery.js"
      </script>
  </head>
```

Listing 3.1 jQuery.html

The jQuery library contains the following:

▶ Element selection

▶ DOM functions

▶ Animations and effects, plus interface elements with jQuery UI

▶ AJAX functions

In the course of this chapter, you'll gain insight into the aforementioned areas; however, it's not a complete jQuery language reference, but only a brief introduction to the topic. We want to convey only the basic syntax of jQuery to you so that you will understand the syntax of the SAPUI5 library better as a result. You'll find the complete jQuery reference at *http://api.jquery.com/*.

3.2   Selectors and Events

As noted in the introduction, the jQuery library provides a variety of functions. In this section, we'll introduce the jQuery-specific selectors and show you how to link a jQuery function to an event.

3.2.1 Selectors

After you have integrated the library in your page, the question arises as to how you can access the functions that are provided. The basic construct for accessing the functions is the factory function $(). You can use this factory function to very conveniently access any objects, where the jQuery object is not only a simple instance of this object, but also acts as a wrapper and equips the object with new functions.

Factory function

As discussed in the previous chapter, the browser loads the page line-by-line; thus a function may be executed before the library has been fully loaded. For this reason, the ready function is implemented in jQuery, and you should ensure that you always implement your functions within this ready function when using jQuery. This function ultimately sets an event listener to the event DOMContentLoaded and ensures that the function is executed only after the page has been completely loaded.

Ready function

This results in the content of Listing 3.2 as the body of the page.

```
<!DOCTYPE html>
<html>
  <head>
    <meta charset="UTF-8">
      <script type="text/javascript"
              src="jquery.js"
      </script>
      <script type="text/javascript">
        $(document).ready(function() {
              // Implementation
        });
      </script>
  </head>
  <body>
    <!-- Content -->
  </body>
</html>
```

Listing 3.2 jQuery_body.html

You can now insert your implementation within the $(document).ready function. You can address the HTML elements in jQuery by selector, similar to the CSS selectors. In Table 3.1, you will find a comparison of CSS and jQuery selectors.

CSS	jQuery
`element { ... }`	`$("element");`
`#id`	`$("#id");`
`.class`	`$(".class");`

Table 3.1 Selectors in jQuery

Other selectors In addition to these selectors, which you already know from Chapter 1, there are jQuery-specific selectors, such as the `:header` selector for selecting all headings. In Listing 3.9, you use the `hasAttribute` selector `$("p[id]")`. This filter selector is especially suitable for selecting all elements with a particular property. `$("p[id]")` means, in this context, "Select all p elements with an ID." You will find complete documentation at *http://api.jquery.com/category/selectors/jquery-selector-extensions/*.

In Listing 3.3, the paragraph is selected with the ID `para`, and the jQuery function `animate()` is used. (You will find the complete API documentation at *http://api.jquery.com/animate/*.)

```
<!DOCTYPE html>
<html>
  <head>
  <meta charset="UTF-8">
  <title>Animation</title>
  <style>
      p {
         background-color    : light-gray;
         width               : 100px;
         border              : 1px solid black;
      }
  </style>
  <script type="text/javascript"
          src="jquery.js">
  </script>
  <script type="text/javascript">
    $(document).ready(function() {
          $( "#para" ).animate({
              width        : "70%",
```

```
                opacity      : 0.4,
                marginLeft   : "0.6in",
                fontSize     : "3em",
                borderWidth  : "10px"
        }, 1500 );
    });
  </script>
</head>
  <body>
      <p id="para">Paragraph</p>
  </body>
</html>
```

Listing 3.3 jQuery_animation.html

When you execute this example in the browser, the paragraph increases in size until it occupies 70% of the width of the browser window (see Figure 3.1).

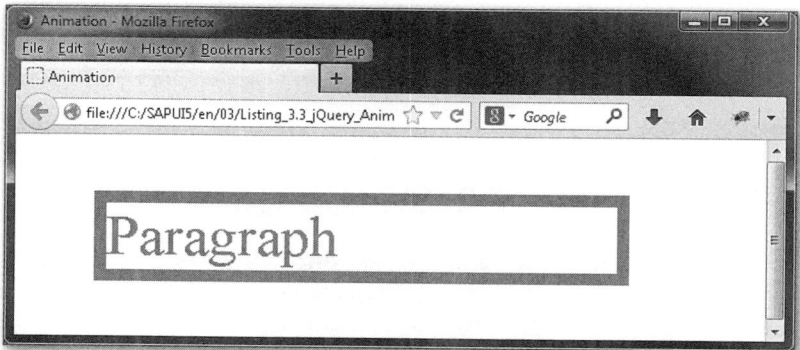

Figure 3.1 Animation with jQuery

However, what happens if the transferred element is not unique? Let's assume that Listing 3.3 had two sections, and you addressed them via the HTML tag rather than the ID. In this case, jQuery would create a list of objects and process all objects in a loop (see Listing 3.4).

Node list

```
<!DOCTYPE html>
<html>
  <head>
  <meta charset="UTF-8">
```

```
<title>Animation</title>
<style>
    p {
        background-color  : light-gray;
        width             : 100px;
        border            : 1px solid black;
    }
</style>
<script type="text/javascript">
    $(document).ready(function() {
        $("p").animate({
            width       : "70%",
            opacity     : 0.4,
            marginLeft  : "0.6in",
            fontSize    : "3em",
            borderWidth : "10px"
        }, 1500 );
    });
</script>
</head>
    <body>
        <p>First paragraph</p>
        <p>Second paragraph</p>
    </body>
</html>
```

Listing 3.4 Animation of Two Paragraphs

As a result, both paragraphs will have gradually increased in size until they have reached the width of 70% of the browser window.

Most functions in jQuery are structured so that each function returns a jQuery object again. As a result, you can chain these jQuery objects together using the dot notation:

```
$().method1().method2();
```

In Listing 3.5, you combine three methods. After you load the page, the animation is started, then the elements are hidden via the fadeOut function, and they are displayed again with the fadeIn function.

```
<!DOCTYPE html>
<html>
```

```
<head>
<meta charset="UTF-8">
<title>Animation</title>
  <style>
      p {
        width: 100px;
        border: 1px solid black;
      }
  </style>
  <script type="text/javascript"
        src="jquery.js">
  </script>
  <script type="text/javascript">
  $(document).ready(function() {
        $( "p" ).animate({
            width       : "60%",
            opacity     : 0.4,
            marginLeft  : "0.6in",
            fontSize    : "3em",
            borderWidth : "10px"
        }, 1500 ).fadeOut(1000).fadeIn(100);
      });
  </script>
</head>
  <body>
    <p>First paragraph</p>
    <p>Second paragraph</p>
    <div></div>
  </body>
</html>
```

Listing 3.5 jQuery Method Chaining

3.2.2   Events

Our previous examples were executed immediately after loading the
page. Although this is useful, you still usually register the function for
an event. jQuery supports all common events that you already learned
about in Chapter 2. To bind a function to an event, you use the factory
function again with the relevant event in the dot notation:

```
$().mouseover(handler);
```

In Listing 3.6, the background color of a `<div>` element changes when you move your mouse over it.

```html
<!DOCTYPE html>
<html>
<head>
  <meta charset="UTF-8" />
  <title>Event</title>
    <script type="text/javascript"
            src="jquery.js">
    </script>
  <style>
    .gray {
        background-color: gray
    }
    .l_gray {
        background-color: lightgray
    }
    .border {
        width: 90px;
        height: 90px;
        border: 5px solid black
    }
    .noborder {
        width: 100px;
        height: 100px;
        border: none
    }
  </style>
  <script type="text/javascript">
    $(document).ready(function() {
        $("#box1").mouseover(function() {
            $(this).removeClass("gray");
            $(this).addClass("l_gray");
            });

    $("#box1").mouseout(function() {
        $("#box1").removeClass("l_gray");
            $("#box1").addClass("gray");
            });
        });
  </script>
</head>
```

```
<body>
    <div id="box1" class="gray border"></div>
</body>
</html>
```

Listing 3.6 jQuery_event.html

An overview of the most important functions are provided ahead: **Event functions**

▶ .bind: Bind handler to event

▶ .on: Bind handler to event

▶ .blur: Event when an element loses its focus

▶ .click: Click with the mouse button

▶ .dbclick: Double-click with the mouse button

▶ .hover: Mouse pointer moves over an element

▶ .mousemove: Mouse pointer moves in an element

▶ .keypress: A keyboard key is pressed

▶ .keyup: A keyboard key is released

▶ .change: A form field is changed

Since jQuery version 1.7, the .on method has been the preferred method for binding an event handler; the .bind method was used for this purpose in earlier versions.

The complete list of events can be found at *http://api.jquery.com/category/events/*.

3.3   DOM Manipulation

You already learned about DOM manipulation in Chapter 2. jQuery also supports you here in the implementation of the DOM functions and adds useful additional functions to them.

Let's take the example of our listing from Chapter 2, from which we have adjusted the style via DOM manipulation (see Listing 2.13).

```
var oName = document.getElementById("day");
var oOutput = document.getElementById("output");
```

```
    oOutput.style.color="red";
    oOutput.style.backgroundColor="yellow";
    oOutput.innerHTML="Weekend...!";
```

Listing 3.7 Style Adjustment

**Web page with
its own style**

In Listing 3.8, we create the same web page, but this time we create it with jQuery.

```html
<!DOCTYPE html>
<html>
  <head>
    <meta charset="UTF-8" />
    <title>Event</title>
    <script type="text/javascript"
        src="jquery.js">
    </script>

<script type="text/javascript">
  $(document).ready(function() {
  $("#button").click(function() {

  switch ($("#day").val()) {
  case "Monday":
      $("#output").text("Garfield says: I hate Mondays!");
        break;
  case "Tuesday":
      $("#output").text("At least it's not Monday");
        break;
  case "Wednesday":
      $("#output").text("Better known as hump day");
        break;
  case "Thursday":
      $("#output").text("Almost Friday");
        break;
  case "Friday":
      $("#output").text("It is Friday");
        break;
  default:
      $("#output").text("Weekend...!").css(
                        {  color: "red",
                           backgroundColor:"yellow"
                        });
```

```
      };
    });
  });
</script>
</head>
<body>
  <form>
    Day: <input type="day" name="day" id="day">
        <button type="button" id="button">Submit</button>
  </form>
<p>What is there on this day to say?
  <div id="output"></div>
</p>
</body>
```

Listing 3.8 jQuery: DOM Manipulation

As you can see, you can manage completely with jQuery without variables, and the functions are much more readable and can be called (almost) intuitively, compared to `document.getElementById`.

The difference becomes much clearer if you want to add a new DOM node rather than change an existing DOM node. jQuery provides the following simple methods for this purpose:

jQuery DOM functions

- ▶ `.after()`: Appends the content after the element
- ▶ `.append()`: Appends the content at the end of the element
- ▶ `.appendTo()`: Appends the content at the end of the element
- ▶ `.insertAfter()`: Inserts the content in the element
- ▶ `.insertBefore()`: Inserts the content before the element
- ▶ `.prepend()`: Prepends the content to the beginning of the element
- ▶ `.prependTo()`: Prepends the content to the beginning of the element
- ▶ `.remove()`: Removes the element
- ▶ `.wrap`: Wraps the elements with the defined HTML structure
- ▶ `.addClass`: Adds the elements to the specified class
- ▶ `.removeClass`: Removes the transferred CSS class
- ▶ `.css`: Sets the CSS property

You will find the complete list of functions at *http://api.jquery.com/category/manipulation/*.

If, for example, in Listing 3.8 you want the `<div>` element to be generated only at runtime, you simply have to add the following line:

```
$("p").after("<div id='output'></div>");
```

After each p element (there is only one p element in our example), one `<div>` element with the ID output is generated as a result. In Listing 3.9, you create a new section and color all elements with an ID.

```
<!DOCTYPE html>
<html>
<head>
<meta charset="UTF-8" />
<title>jQuery - DOM Manipulation</title>
<style type="text/css">
  .bgr {
    background-color: gray;
  }
</style>
<script type="text/javascript"
  src="jquery.js">
</script>

<script type="text/javascript">
  $(document).ready(function() {
  $("#btn1").click(function() {
      $("#p2").after('<p id="p3">New</p>');
  });

  $("#btn2").click(function() {
      $("p[id]").wrapAll('<div class="bgr"></div>');
  });

  });
</script>
</head>
<body>
  <button type="button" id="btn1">
      Insert (.after)
  </button>
```

```
<button type="button" id="btn2">
    Wrap (.wrapAll)
</button>

<p id="p1">First paragraph</p>
<p id="p2">Second paragraph</p>

</body>
</html>
```

Listing 3.9 jquery_DOM2.html

Figure 3.2 shows the DOM manipulation displayed in the browser.

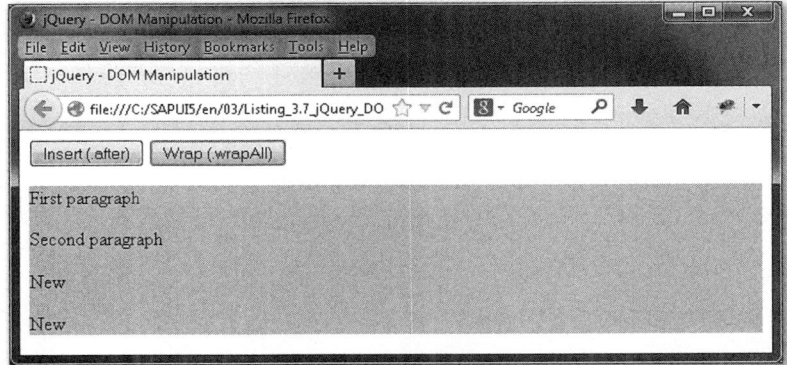

Figure 3.2 DOM Manipulation with jQuery

3.4   AJAX

Our previous examples were completely loaded from the local hard disk and displayed in the browser. Once you want to implement some dynamics in your web page, however, you'll need an option for reloading parts of a page or, depending on user interaction, for submitting a request to the web server without constantly having to reload the whole page. This is exactly where AJAX (Asynchronous JavaScript and XML) comes into play.

AJAX allows asynchronous data transfer between the browser and the server backend: in our case, an SAP NetWeaver Application Server for

Asynchronous data transfer

ABAP (SAP NetWeaver AS ABAP). This enables you to perform HTTP requests while the HTML page is displayed, as you can see in Figure 3.3.

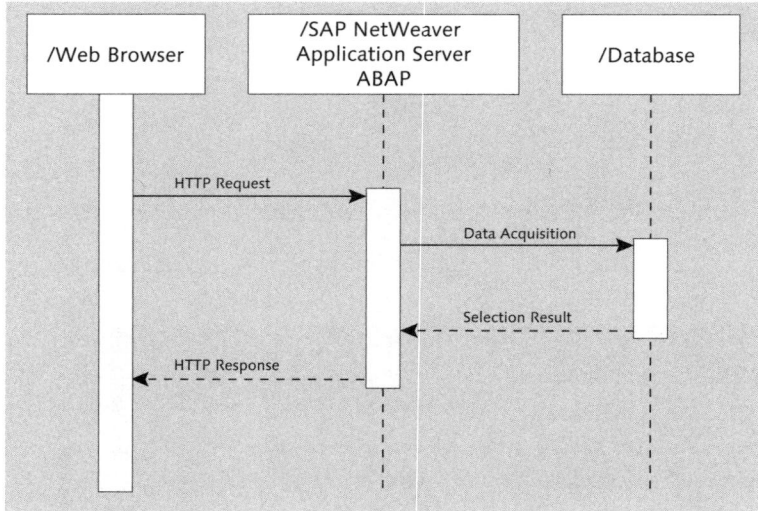

Figure 3.3 AJAX

AJAX is not limited to the XML format, even if the name seems to suggest this initially. Generally speaking, when we talk about AJAX technology, we mean the reloading of page fragments or any information from the server at runtime. The request does not have to take place asynchronously either, because you can also design the AJAX call to be synchronous. Thus, you can transfer synchronous or asynchronous XML, pure text, or JSON formats from the server to the web browser via AJAX. The AJAX request takes place in four steps:

1. Create AJAX object

2. Define server connection

3. Query data from the server

4. Receive the response from the server

Step 1: Creating object

First, you have to create an object that undertakes the HTTP request and receives the response from the server. In JavaScript, this is implemented in the object XMLHttpRequest (the complete API documentation can be found at *https://developer.mozilla.org/en-US/docs/Web/API/XMLHttpRequest*):

```
var oRequest = new XMLHttpRequest();
```

In the next step, you establish the connection to the backend; to do so, you use the `open()` method of the `XMLHttpRequest` object, as Listing 3.10 illustrates.

Step 2: Establishing server connection

```
oRequest.open(
    http-Method (GET, POST, PUT, DELETE)
    URL  (URL from Backend)
    Request-Method (Asynchronous true or false, optional)
    User (user name, optional)
    Password (password, optional)
);
```

Listing 3.10 XML HTTP Request

You should only choose `false` (synchronous processing) for the request method if a response for further processing is necessary; this is very often the case with forms, for example. If, however, you send different requests to the server to create the whole page but the various data is independent, you should always select `true` (asynchronous processing) as the request method. As a result, the system does not wait for the response from the server but continues to execute the script.

Synchronous/ asynchronous

How do you determine that the request has been completed? The attribute `readyState` is implemented in the AJAX object for this purpose. You can use this attribute to determine whether the request has been processed by the server and returned to the browser. This attribute can assume the values listed in Table 3.2.

readyState attribute

readyState	Explanation
0	Not initialized
1	Initialized
2	Contacted
3	Data stream from the backend is loaded
4	Completed

Table 3.2 Statuses of readyState

Callback Now you don't have to do anything other than implement a callback function that queries the value of the attribute. You can use the event handler `onreadystatechange` for this purpose:

```
oRequest.onreadystatechange = function() {
  if (oRequest.readyState == 4) {
  }
};
```

Step 3: Sending data to the server You then use the `send()` method to send the data to the server:

```
oRequest.send();
```

POST/GET The arguments of the `send()` method depend on the selected HTTP method. With `POST`, you do not have to transfer any further arguments. With `GET`, the method expects the key value pair as transfer parameters `Key1=Value1&Key2=Value2` in the URL (see Section 1.1).

The `GET` method plays only a very minor role in SAP web development because these arguments are attached in plain text to the browser URL and thus can be made visible at any time in the browser history. In addition, you can also store this URL as a browser favorite and, therefore, save the transferred password permanently in plain text. For these reasons, especially in the SAP context, the `POST` method has established itself as the method of choice.

Step 4: Processing data In the final step, you can process the received data. Two attributes are crucial: the *HTTP status code* and the actual *response*.

[+] **HTTP Status Codes**

The HTTP status code is returned by each server upon an HTTP request. The best known status code is probably 404 (resource not found). These status codes are transferred by a three-digit number, and based on the first digit you can see which category is involved:

1XX: Information

2XX: Successful request

3XX: Redirecting

4XX: Client-side error

5XX: Server-side error

Depending on the selected data format, the response is located in another attribute; you will find a detailed listing in Table 3.3.

Response

Data Type	Attribute
Text data	responseText
HTML	responseText
JavaScript	responseText
JSON	responseText
JSONP (JSONP means "JSON with Padding" and represents an enhancement for the JSON format)	responseText
XML	responseXML

Table 3.3 Response Attribute

The AJAX() object was implemented in jQuery and provides some help functions that facilitate an AJAX request to a server. In addition to the AJAX() object, particularly useful functions are implemented directly in the jQuery object. You can, for example, execute an AJAX call directly via $.get() (see Listing 3.11).

AJAX with jQuery

```
$.AJAX({
    url: "http://<server>:<port>/path/"
    success: function(result){
    // Implementation
    }
});

$.get("http://<server>:<port>/path/", function(result) {
    //Implementation
}
});
```

Listing 3.11 AJAX with jQuery

The complete API documentation can be found at *http://api. jquery.com/ jQuery.AJAX/*.

In the next example, you'll read the weekdays from a local file. Create a file with the content in Listing 3.12 for this purpose and save it as *day.json*:

```
{
  "Mon": "Monday",
  "Tue": "Tuesday",
  "Wed": "Wednesday",
  "Thur": "Thursday",
  "Fri": "Friday",
  "Sat": "Saturday",
  "Sun": "Sunday"
}
```

Listing 3.12   day.json

Create a file called *AJAX.html* with the code in Listing 3.13 and save it in the same directory as *day.json*.

```
<!DOCTYPE html>
<html>
  <head>
    <meta charset="UTF-8" />
    <title>jQuery AJAX</title>
    <script src="jquery.js"></script>

    <script>
     $(document).ready(function() {
         $("#get").click(function() {
         $.getJSON("day.json", function(data) {
         $.each(data, function(i, val){
         $('<li>' + val + '</li>').appendTo('#output');
           });
          });
         });
       });
    </script>
</head>
  <body>
    <h3>jQuery AJAX</h3>
    <button type="button" id="get">JSON</button>
    <p>
        Weekdays
        <ul id="output"></ul>
    </p>
```

```
    </body>
</html>
```

Listing 3.13 AJAX.html

After you click on the JSON button, the file is read, and the result is displayed as a list (see Figure 3.4).

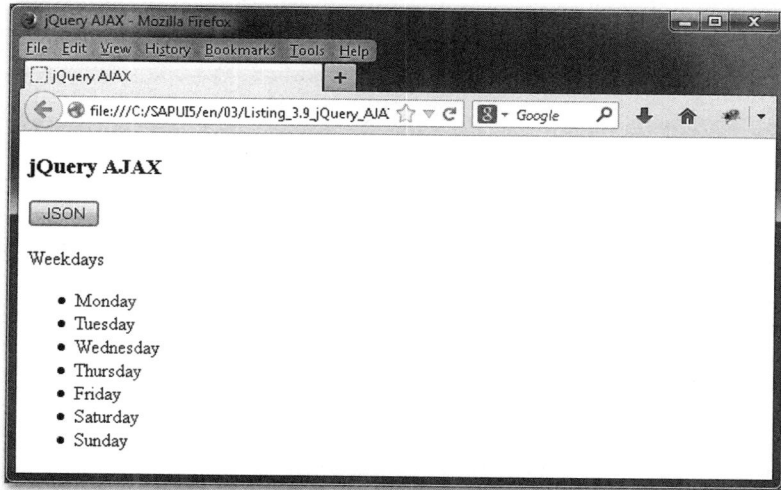

Figure 3.4 AJAX with jQuery

In this chapter, you will learn about the SAP NetWeaver Application Server ABAP. You will install the SAPUI5 library and set up the development environment.

4   Getting Started in SAPUI5

In this chapter, you will learn the basics of web development on the SAP NetWeaver Application Server ABAP (SAP NetWeaver AS ABAP). This chapter will show you how to install the SAPUI5 library on the backend and how to set up the development environment on the frontend.

Checklist	[✓]
You will need the following for this chapter: ▶ S user for SAP Service Marketplace ▶ Access to an ERP system and to an SAP Solution Manager system	

For the development of applications in SAPUI5, you need two pieces:

▶ An installed SAPUI5 library in the SAP backend

▶ A development environment set up on the frontend PC

If you have no SAP backend system, you can also deploy your applications on a local web server such as an Apache HTTPD server (as a download from the home page *www.apache.org*). If you have no access to SAP Service Marketplace, you can download the required SAPUI5 files at *https://tools.hana.ondemand.com/*.

Local web server

For the initial exercise, it is also sufficient to install only Eclipse and the SAPUI5 frontend tools. With this method, you can use the preview feature in Eclipse and display the result there. In this case, you can skip Section 4.1 and proceed directly to Section 4.2. You do not need the two components ABAP in Eclipse and SAPUI5 Team Provider for these local developments.

First, we will deal with the installation of the SAPUI5 library on the ABAP stack of the SAP system.

4.1 Installation of the SAPUI5 Library in SAP Business Suite

Downloading the components

SAPUI5 is integrated as an add-on in SAP Business Suite. The installation packages are available in the SAP Software Download Center (*http://service. sap.com/swdc*) under INSTALLATIONS AND UPGRADES • A-Z INDEX • N • UI ADD-ON FOR NETWEAVER • <RELEVANT EHP/ERP RELEASE> • INSTALLATION. The associated support packages are available under SUPPORT PACKAGES AND PATCHES • A-Z INDEX • N • UI ADD-ON FOR NETWEAVER • <RELEVANT EHP/ERP RELEASE>.

Start the Maintenance Optimizer in SAP Solution Manager and select UI ADD-ON 1.0 FOR NW (Figure 4.1) as the product version.

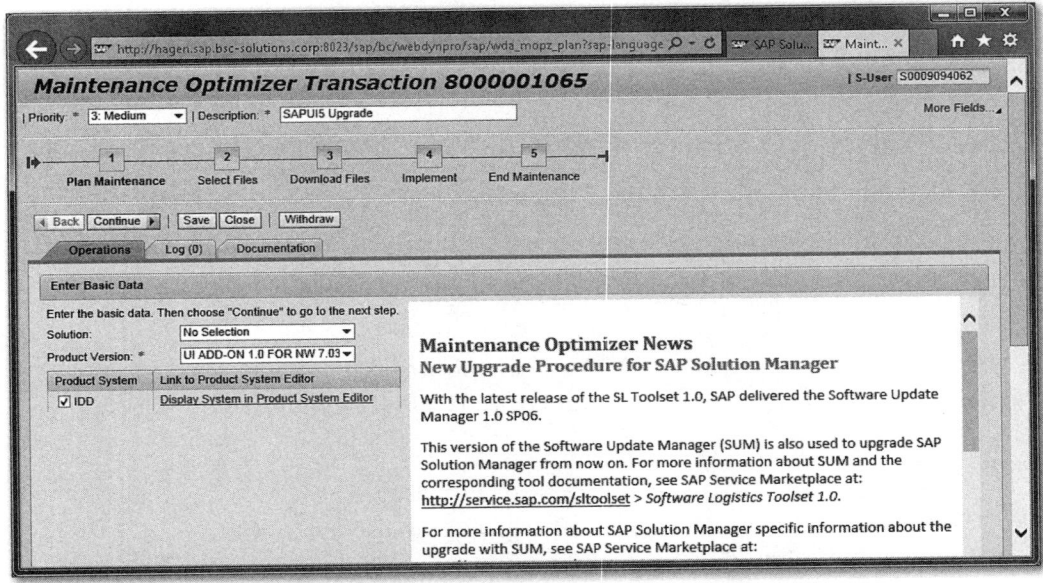

Figure 4.1 Maintenance Optimizer in SAP Solution Manager

Download the calculated support packages and the stack XML. Then unpack the support packages into the EPS directory and install the packages with the SAP Add-On Installation Tool (Transaction SAINT), or perform an update (Transaction SPAM). For detailed installation instructions, see SAP Note 1747308 (Installation Guide: UI Development Toolkit for HTML5 [SAPUI5]).

Installation

You can check whether the installation was successful by calling the URL *http://<HOST NAME>:<SERVICE>/sap/public/bc/ui5_ui5*, in which you replace <HOST NAME> and <SERVICE> with the values of your SAP system. The system should then display the UI Development Toolkit for HTML5 (see Figure 4.2).

UI Development Toolkit for HTML5

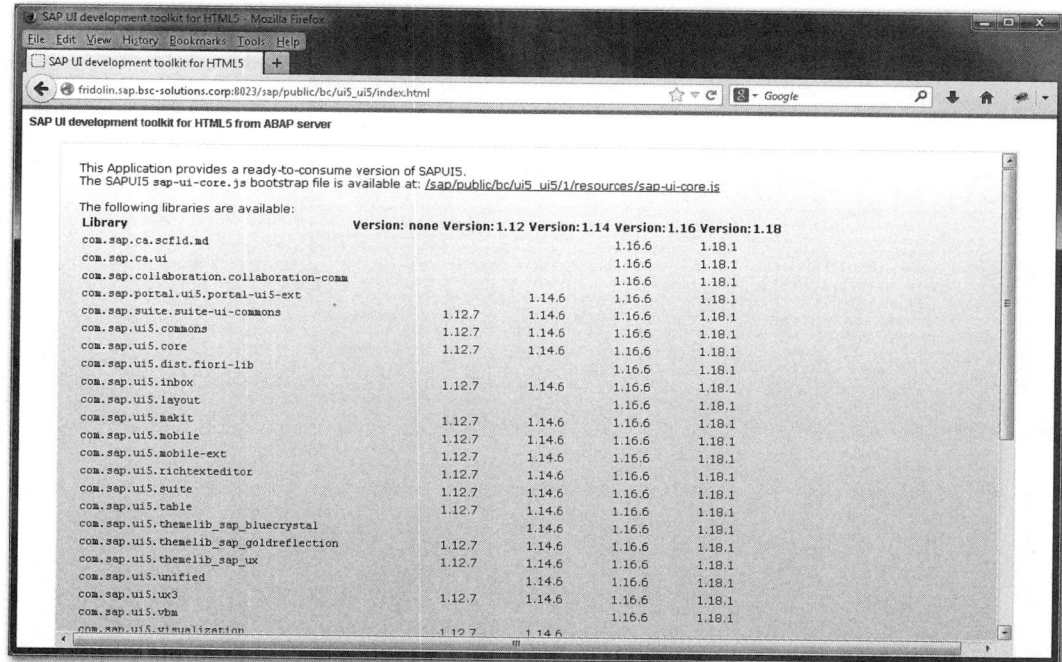

Figure 4.2 Development Toolkit for HTML5

If you obtain a different result, check whether the relevant service is active. To do so, call Transaction SICF, and activate the service *default_host/sap/public/bc/ui5_ui5/* if necessary (see Figure 4.3).

Activating ICF service

The examples shown in this book are based on Version SAPUI5 1.00 SP6, current at the time of writing. Use the *Product Availability Matrix* (PAM), which is available at *http://service.sap.com/pam*, to check the current supported version and install it.

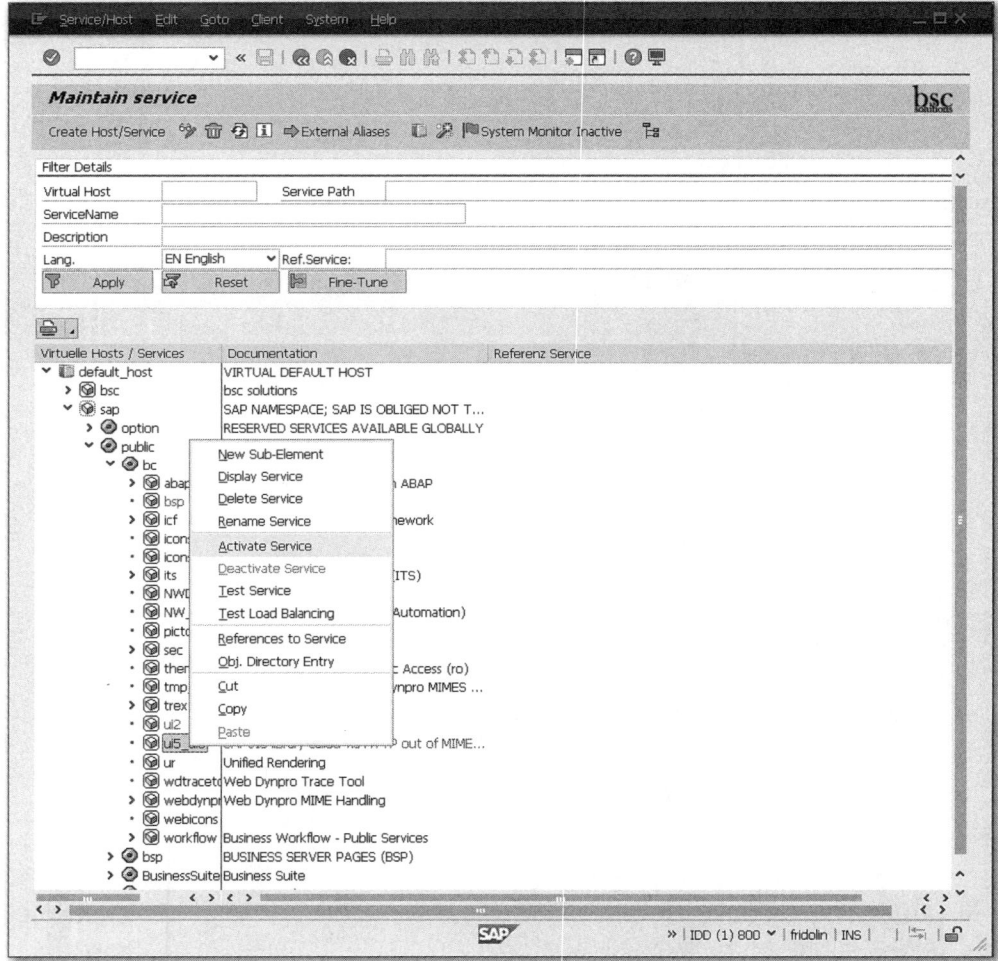

Figure 4.3 Activating Service

After the successful installation of the backend component, we will now deal with the installation of the SAPUI5 frontend tools.

4.2 Setting Up the Development Environment

The UI development tools are part of the SAPUI5 library. They include a number of Eclipse-based tools and editors that can assist you in the development of SAPUI5 applications. The SAPUI5 Team Provider functions can aid you in checking the applications developed in Eclipse in an ABAP backend system. The Team Provider has been available since version 7.0.2. For older SAP releases use the program /UI5/UI5_REPOSITORY_LOAD instead.

Eclipse

4.2.1 Installation Requirements

The developer tools for SAPUI5 must be installed separately as an Eclipse plug-in. Before you install Eclipse, check whether the installed Java Runtime version is at least Version JRE 1.6 and, if necessary, perform an update of the Java Runtime Environment before the installation. Choose START • CONTROL PANEL • PROGRAMS • JAVA to open the Java Control Panel. When you click the INFO button, the system displays the relevant JRE version. If the version is lower than Version 1.6, perform an update of the JRE version.

JRE

4.2.2 Installation

SAPUI5 supports the Eclipse Versions Indigo 3.7, Juno 3.8, and Juno 4.2. The current version, Juno 4.2, will be installed ahead. Always use the current version supported by SAP.

First, download Eclipse IDE for Java EE Developers at *www.eclipse.org/downloads*. Because SAPUI5 Team Provider works only with the 32-bit version, download the 32-bit version. After unpacking the zip file, you can start Eclipse directly by double-clicking *eclipse.exe*; Eclipse runs in the working memory and thus does not have to be installed. You can install the additional components in the Eclipse user interface by following the menu path HELP • INSTALL NEW SOFTWARE (see Figure 4.4).

Eclipse IDE for Java EE developers

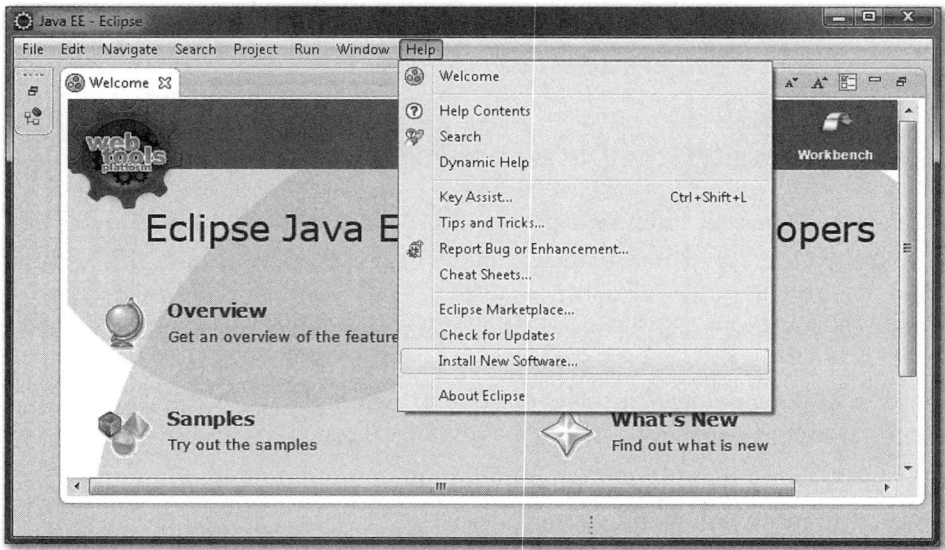

Figure 4.4 Installing Plug-In Components

First, install the required standard plug-ins and then the SAPUI5 tools.

Standard Plug-Ins

First, install the EMF – Eclipse Modeling Framework.

Start the Installation Wizard via the menu path HELP • INSTALL NEW SOFT-WARE; under WORK WITH, enter the update page for your Eclipse version (in our example in Figure 4.5). From the list in the middle of the screen, select the option EMF – ECLIPSE MODELING FRAMEWORK, and click NEXT to confirm your selection.

Component selection

On the next screen, you will see the components that are installed in this step. Confirm your selection by choosing NEXT, accept the license agreement on the next screen, and start the installation by choosing FINISH. For some components, the system displays a warning that you are installing software that contains unsigned content. Confirm the corresponding dialog box by clicking OK (see Figure 4.6), and proceed with the installation.

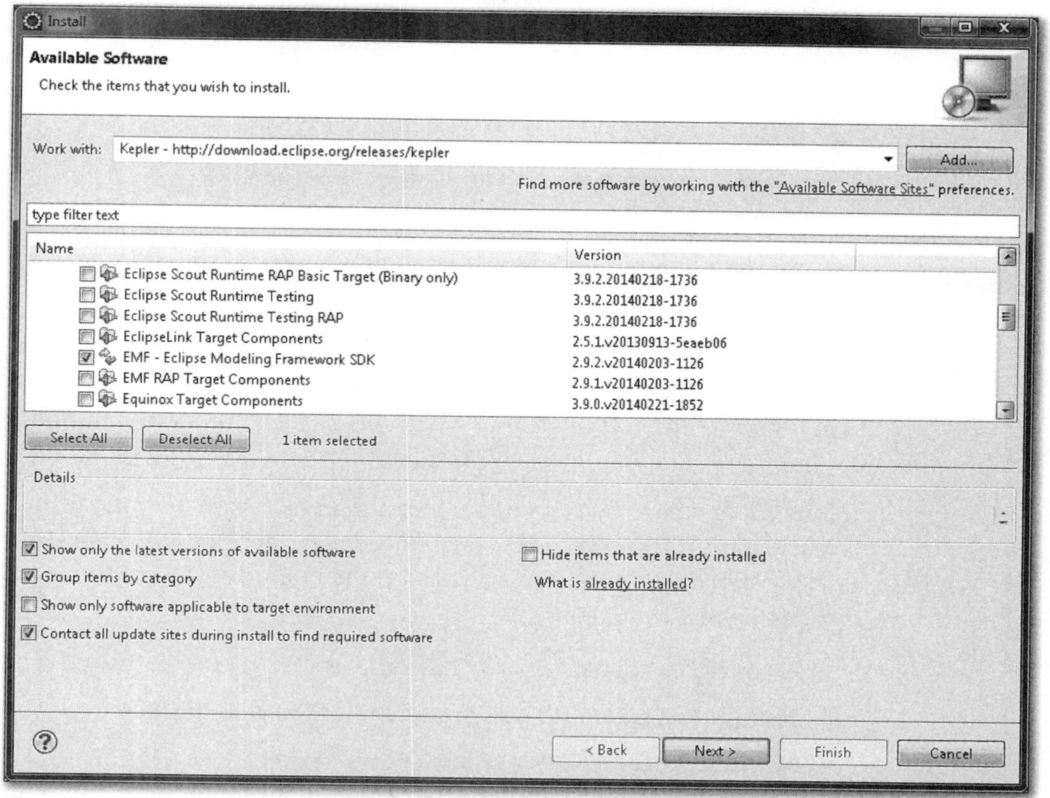

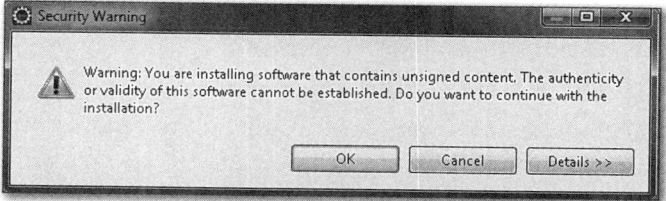

Figure 4.5   Selecting the EMF: Eclipse Modeling Framework

Figure 4.6   Security Warning

After the installation, you are prompted to restart Eclipse. Confirm this dialog box by clicking YES (see Figure 4.7).

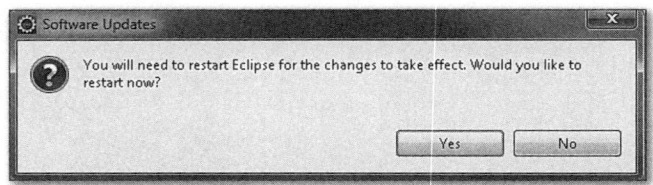

Figure 4.7 Restarting Eclipse

Necessary plug-ins

Next, you have to install additional standard plug-ins; the ABAP in Eclipse plug-in requires several standard plug-ins, and you will need to install these packages. The list provided here is applicable to the ABAP in Eclipse 2.16 version; check which installation requirements apply to your version in the SAP Notes specified ahead.

Start the Installation Wizard via the menu path HELP • INSTALL NEW SOFTWARE; under WORK WITH, enter the update page of your Eclipse installation (in this example, the Juno update page at *http://download. eclipse.org/releases/juno*). From the list in the middle of the screen, select the following components:

▶ ECLIPSERT TARGET PLATFORM COMPONENTS • JETTY TARGET COMPONENTS

▶ MODELING • EMF—ECLIPSE MODELING FRAMEWORK SDK

▶ MODELING • EMF COMPARE SDK

▶ MODELING • EMF VALIDATION FRAMEWORK SDK

▶ MODELING • EMF MODEL QUERY SDK

▶ MODELING • EMF MODEL TRANSACTION

▶ MODELING • GRAPHITI SDK (INCUBATION)

Follow the Installation Wizard in the same manner as you did for the installation of the EMF. After restarting Eclipse, you can proceed with the installation of the SAPUI5 tools.

SAPUI5 Tools

SAPUI5 components

After you have installed the necessary standard components, you can then install the SAPUI5 tools. For development, you need the following three components, which you install in the following sequence:

- ABAP in Eclipse
- SAPUI5 Tools IDE Plugin
- SAPUI5 Team Prov IDE

First, download the two necessary SAPUI5 components SAPUI5 Tools IDE Plugin 1.00 and SAPUI5 Team Prov IDE 1.00 from SAP Service Marketplace. The files are available in SAP Service Marketplace under Support Packages and Patches • A-Z Index • N • UI Add-On for NetWeaver • <relevant EHP / ERP release>. Add the current version of the two components to your download basket by clicking Add to Download Basket. For the SAPUI5 Team Provider, you will also need the plug-in for ABAP in Eclipse 2.16. The easiest way to find this is to look in the SAP Software Download Center for "ABAP in Eclipse." Add this file to your download basket. Then, download the three zip files through the SAP Download Manager.

After you have downloaded the files from SAP Service Marketplace, you can install them in Eclipse. Because the SAPUI5 tools were stored locally on your hard drive, you must manually include them in the Installation Wizard. Next to the Work with input field, click on the Add button; choose Archive in the following dialog box to select the path to the downloaded zip file (see Figure 4.8).

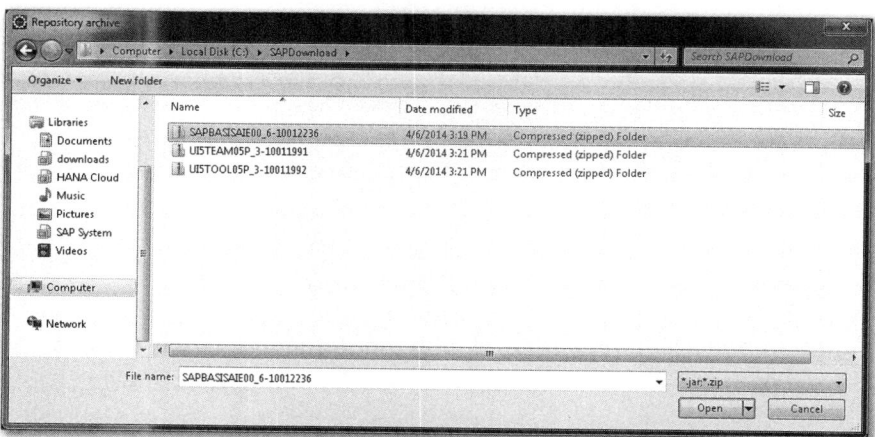

Figure 4.8 Selecting SAPUI5 Tools

Choose OK to confirm your selection (see Figure 4.9).

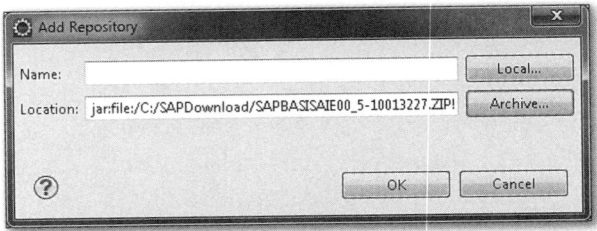

Figure 4.9 Installing SAPUI5 Components

Follow the Installation Wizard again, as described previously, and repeat the process for the two remaining components. This completes the installation of Eclipse IDE for Java EE developers.

The current version, SAPUI5 1.00 SP06, requires Version 2.16 of ABAP in Eclipse. To know which versions you have to install, see the following SAP Notes:

► Note 1747308 (Installation Guide: UI Development Toolkit for HTML5 [SAPUI5])

► Note 1718399 (ABAP developer tools for SAP NetWeaver)

4.2.3   Updating the Components

Installed components

We recommend that you update the Eclipse component Eclipse IDE for Java EE Developer. This component contains the code completion that can cause the application to crash in lower versions. To update a component, call the overview of installed components via the menu path HELP • ABOUT ECLIPSE (see Figure 4.10).

By clicking INSTALLATION DETAILS, you can display the versions of installed components (see Figure 4.11).

Updating the installed components

To perform an update, select the relevant component and click REFRESH. The system now displays a dialog box with the available updates. Confirm the installation by clicking NEXT, accept the license agreement, and click INSTALL to start the installation.

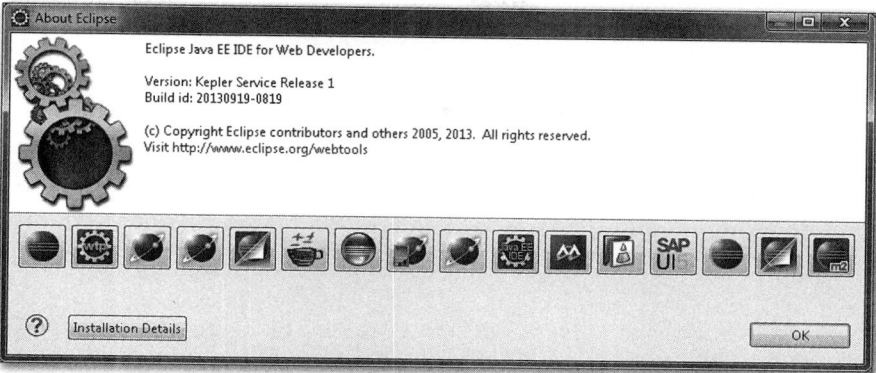

Figure 4.10　About Eclipse

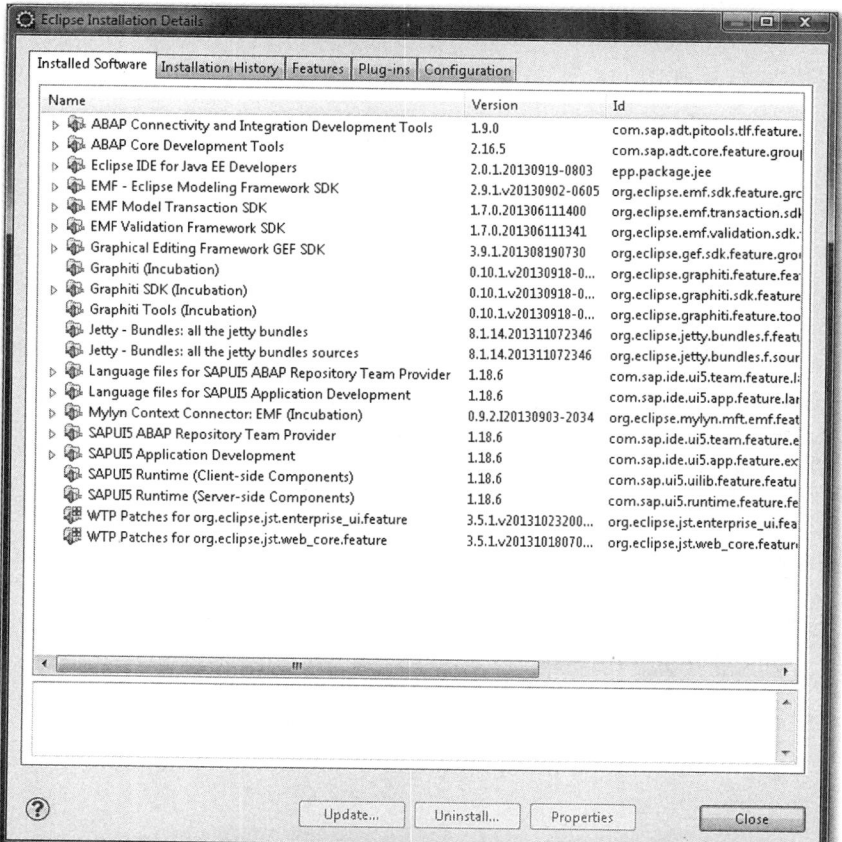

Figure 4.11　Installed Components

Before we create our first SAPUI5 page, let's explain the possible development scenarios you might face and the communication between the browser and the SAP backend in more detail. You will then learn about the Model View Controller (MVC) architecture pattern, and at that point you will be very well prepared to start developing applications in SAPUI5.

4.3   SAPUI5 Development Scenarios

Platforms   SAPUI5 offers many advantages—but also some disadvantages—compared to classic SAP GUI applications. Due to the fact that SAP refers to the standards HTML5, CSS3, AJAX, and the widely used jQuery library for the SAPUI5 library, SAPUI5 can be used to develop fast and flexible applications that can be ported easily to other platforms. SAPUI5 applications are already running today on a variety of platforms:

- ► SAP Cloud
- ► Sybase Unwired Platform
- ► SAP HANA XS
- ► SAP NetWeaver AS ABAP
- ► SAP NetWeaver AS JAVA
- ► Certain open source platforms

HTML is "understood" by almost every modern device, and so you can develop applications for desktop PCs, tablets, or smartphones without any major effort.

Eclipse   Another important advantage is that the development takes place in Eclipse, and so, from a developer perspective, it is no longer necessary to switch between different development environments because any development can take place centrally on one platform. It is now also possible to develop ABAP in Eclipse, as of SAP NetWeaver 7.4.

Corporate design and style guide   CSS3 enables the user interfaces to be easily adapted to the needs of a company—for example, in terms of the corporate design. It is precisely this flexibility that is often perceived as a disadvantage among users.

An SAP GUI always looks more or less the same, whereas CSS gives the developer the opportunity to give free rein to his creativity and his design ideas: Each page can be given a personal touch very quickly. Due to this "uncontrolled proliferation," however, the user has to reorient himself on each page. Therefore, you should define a uniform corporate design prior to the development of SAPUI5 pages and establish a style guide that is valid throughout the company.

The only disadvantage, but one which is often serious, is performance. Although this speed disadvantage can be minimized, an HTML page is nevertheless usually rendered more slowly than an SAP GUI application.

In Chapter 9, we will introduce development in the cloud or on SAP HANA. The main part of this book deals with development in SAP Business Suite.

4.3.1 Development in the SAP NetWeaver Application Server ABAP

The main development scenario is the development of desktop applications using an SAP NetWeaver AS ABAP backend. Before we focus on the implementation of the first SAPUI5 application, we must look at the question of how the ABAP server receives and processes requests from the Internet.

Our previous examples from the introductory chapters were executed from the local hard disk. In the SAP context, the data comes from an SAP system and must be displayed in the frontend browser. When you call up a web page, the requested page is retrieved by a server and then rendered and displayed in your browser. In the SAP context, this web server is SAP NetWeaver AS and is part of SAP NetWeaver Stack.

SAP NetWeaver Application Server ABAP

How is this browser request processed on SAP NetWeaver AS? SAP NetWeaver AS provides the infrastructure for developing and deploying web applications. It receives the HTTP requests, processes them, and returns the result in the HTTP response. Figure 4.12 illustrates this *roundtrip*.

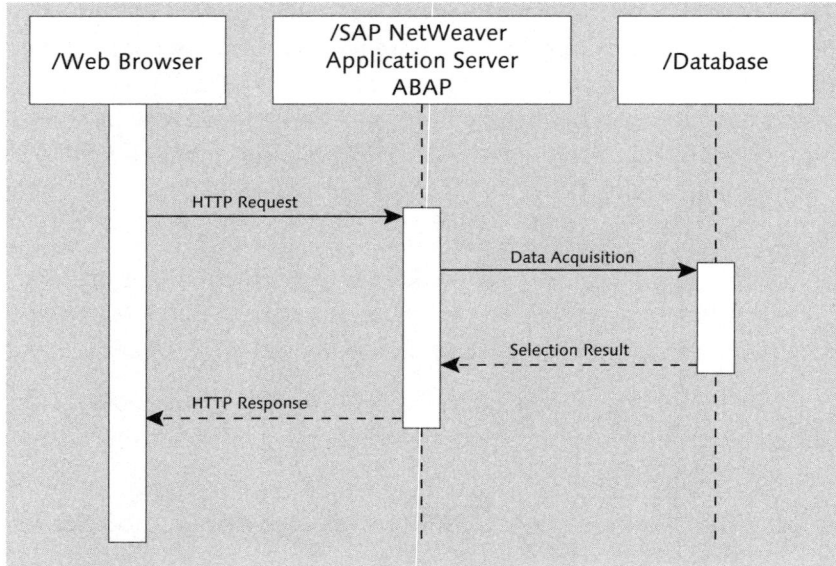

Figure 4.12 SAP NetWeaver Application Server ABAP

Internet
Communication
Manager

The Internet Communication Manager (ICM) ensures communication between SAP NetWeaver AS and the Web browser (see Figure 4.13). Strictly speaking, this does not involve a pure HTTP communication component, but the ICM contains the TCP/IP basic functions; thus, SMTP communication with SAP NetWeaver AS is possible in addition to pure HTTP/HTTPS communication. The ICM is a separate service within SAP NetWeaver AS and is started and monitored by the dispatcher.

HTTP request

The HTTP request is received by the ICM. The task handler starts the ICF controller; this is implemented as a function module, HTTP_DIS-PATCH_REQUEST. The ICF controller creates an object of the class CL_HTTP_SERVER (server control block). This object contains all necessary information from the client/server roundtrip. The actual HTTP request handler is determined based on the URL, and the request is forwarded to the handler. The authentication with respect to the SAP system takes place in the handler. If the authentication has been successful, the request is forwarded to the application by calling the method HANDLE_REQUEST.

The application processes the request, and the result is returned to the application in the HTTP response.

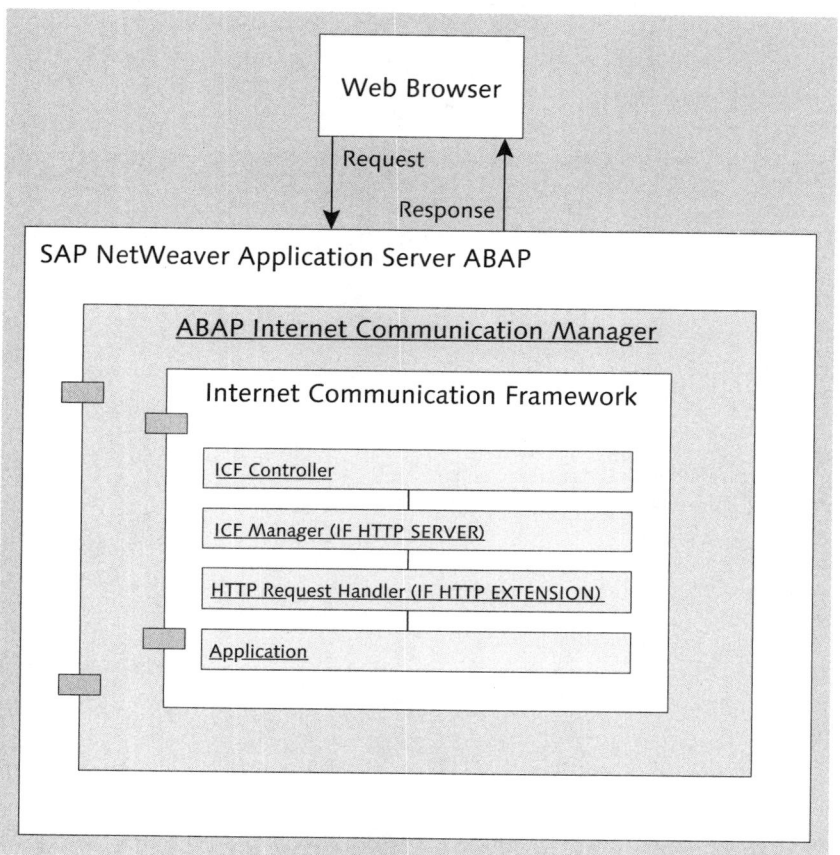

Figure 4.13 ICM: Internet Communication Manager

If you have previously dealt with web development within the SAP system (Web Dynpro or BSP), this function was provided by the relevant runtime environment, and as a developer you did not have to worry about how the ICF worked. During the generation of the Web Dynpro application, the relevant URL was written in the administrative data, and the Web Dynpro application was accessible via this

Port information

URL. If you now write your own applications, the questions arises as to how SAP NetWeaver AS can be accessed externally—that is, from the Internet. The answer to this question is in Transaction SICF. Call Transaction SICF and execute it with the default settings. Figure 4.14 shows the necessary information, found via the menu path GOTO • PORT INFORMATION.

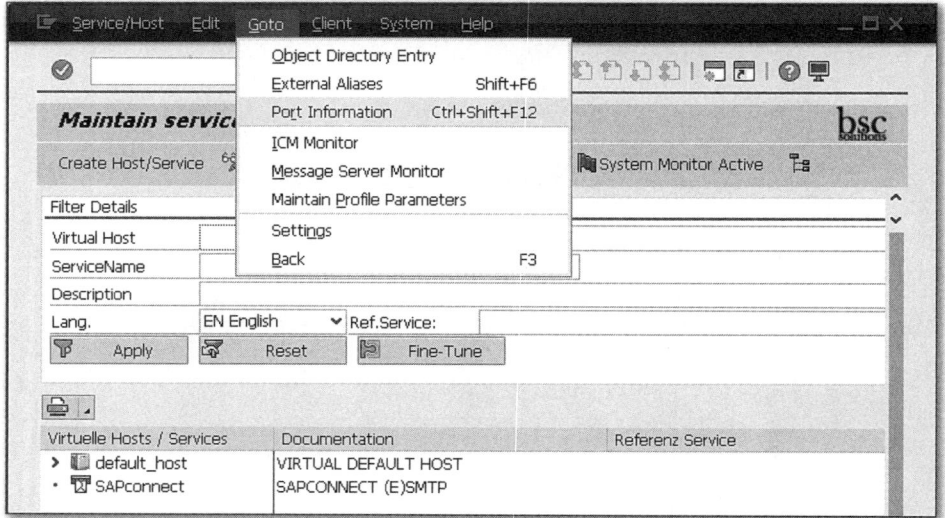

Figure 4.14 Transaction SICF

ICF path   In the dialog box, you will find the host name on the one hand and, on the other hand, the service (port) of the relevant system. The URL consists of *http(s)://<HOST NAME>:<SERVICE>/* and the remainder of the URL from the relevant ICF path (see Figure 4.15).

The path selected in Figure 4.15 is accessible from the URL *http://<HOST NAME>:<SERVICE>/sap/public/bc/ui5_ui5/*, in which you have to replace <HOST NAME> and <SERVICE> with the corresponding values of the SAP system. The SAP UI Development Toolkit is concealed behind this path.

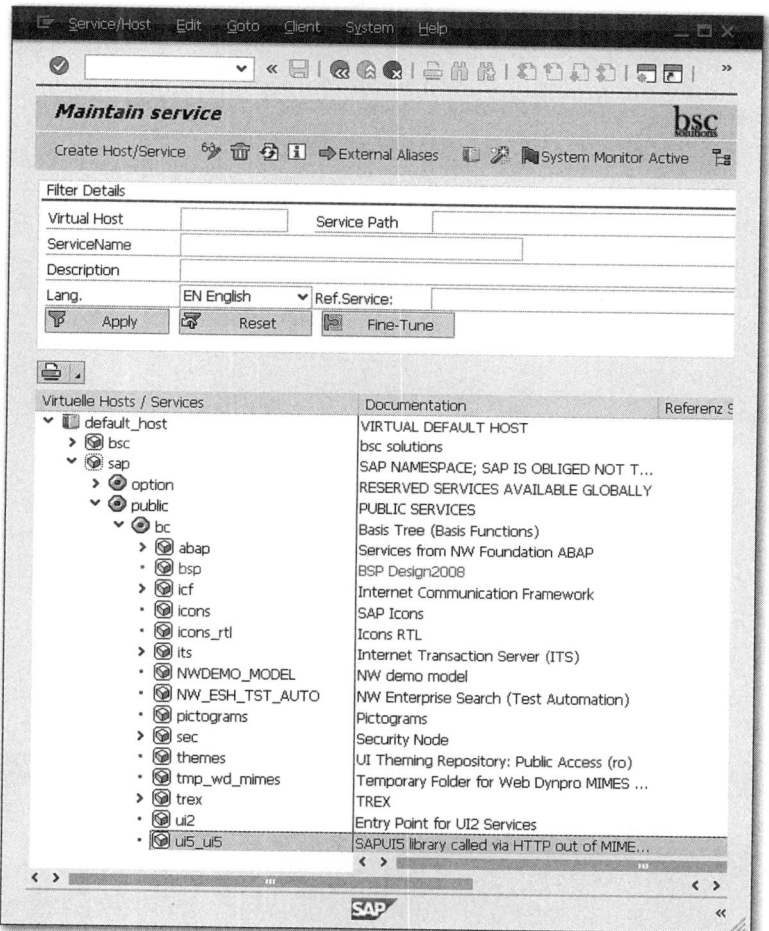

Figure 4.15 ICF Path

4.3.2 Creating Your Own Service

Now let's create our own service and test it. To do so, call Transaction SE24, create the class ZUI5_HTTP_HANDLER in it, and implement the interface IF_HTTP_EXTENSION (see Figure 4.16).

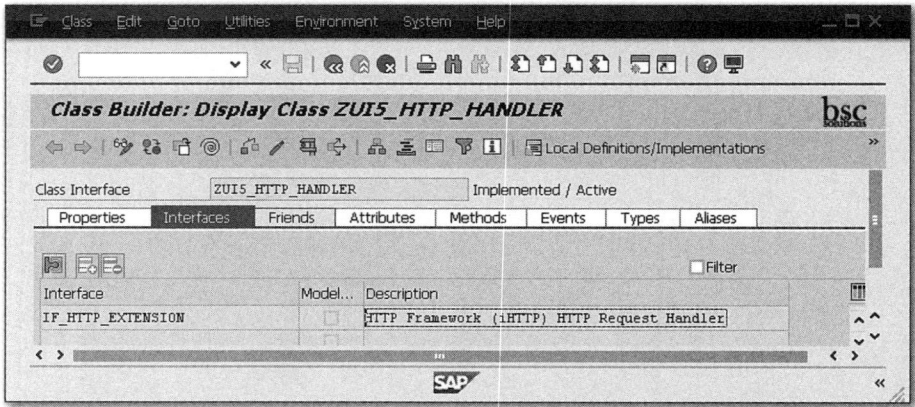

Figure 4.16 HTTP Handler Class

Method HANDLE_ REQUEST The interface implements the method HANDLE_REQUEST; this is executed during a request to the corresponding ICF node. At the moment, we want to set only the HTTP status; we will extend this handler successively throughout this book (see Figure 4.17). In the method HANDLE_REQUEST, add the following line of code to the class ZUI5_HTTP_HANDLER:

```
server->response->set_status( code = 200 reason = 'OK' ).
```

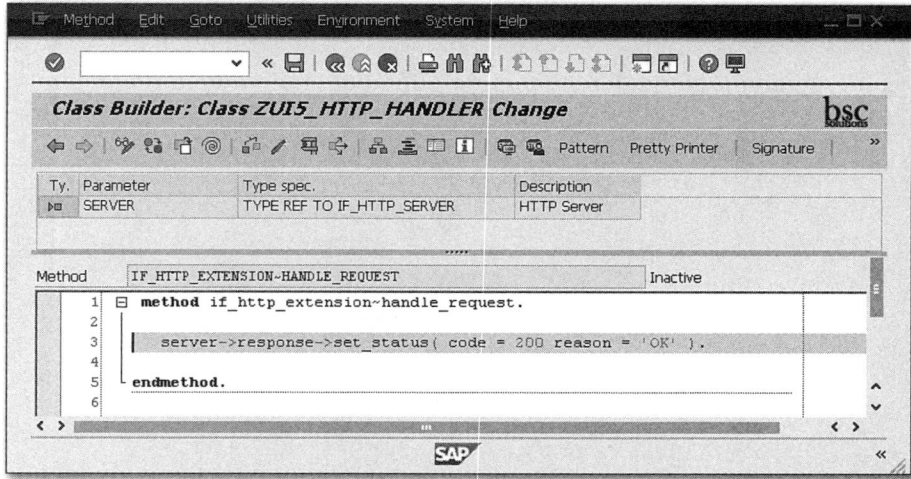

Figure 4.17 Method HANDLE_REQUEST

Save and activate the class. To be able to test the service better, set an external breakpoint in the line you entered. (Note that a session breakpoint has no effect at this point!)

Next, create an ICF node in Transaction SICF. In this example, create the node directly under the default_host node. Select the node, and use the context menu to select the entry NEW SUB-ELEMENT (see Figure 4.18).

Creating service

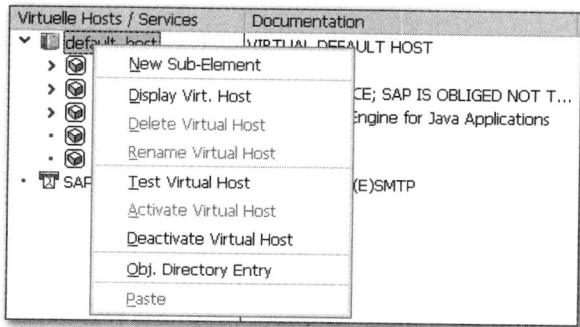

Figure 4.18 Creating the ICF Service

Enter a name ("ui5" is used in our example for Figure 4.19), and select the option INDEPENDENT SERVICE.

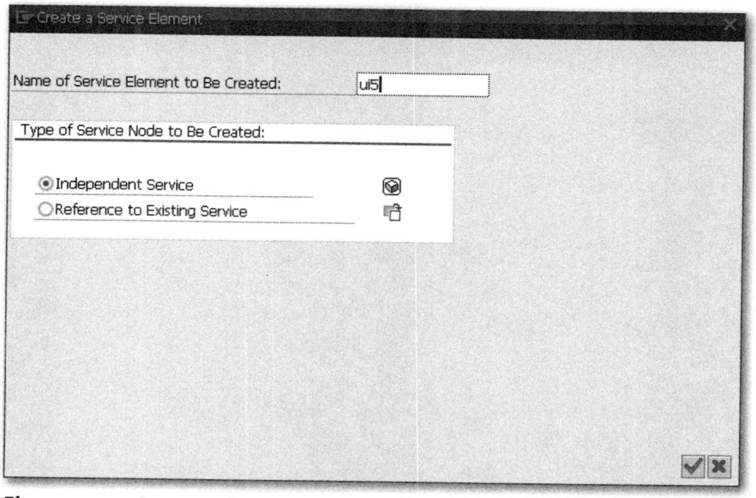

Service name

Figure 4.19 Creating the Service

HTTP handler

On the next screen, enter a description; in the HANDLER LIST tab, enter the previously created class ZUI5_HTTP_HANDLER (see Figure 4.20).

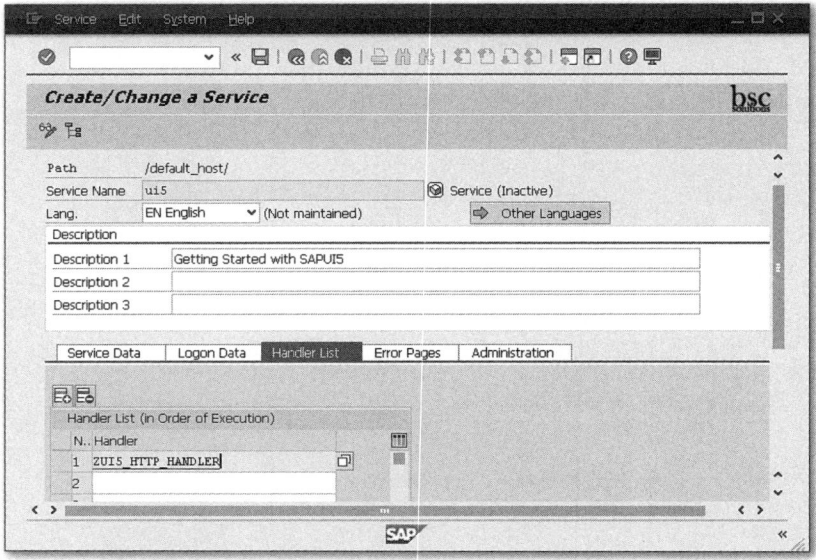

Figure 4.20 HTTP Handler for Service

Activating service

Save the service and exit the maintenance screen via BACK. Finally, you have to activate the service. Position the cursor on the created service, and select ACTIVATE SERVICE in the context menu (see Figure 4.21).

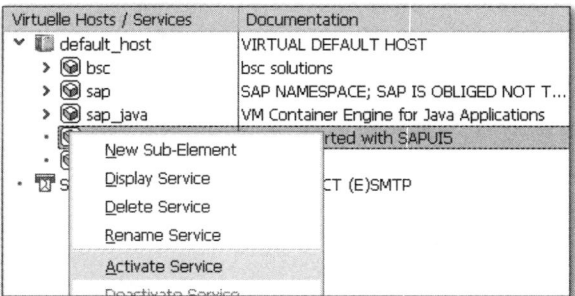

Figure 4.21 Activating the Service

Start your browser and enter the URL according to the schema *http://<HOST NAME>:<SERVICE>/ui5/*, in which you enter the host name and the service of your SAP system. If the service is accessible, the system displays a dialog box in which you have to enter your SAP user name and password for the system. After logging in successfully, the call stops at the external breakpoint that was set (see Figure 4.22).

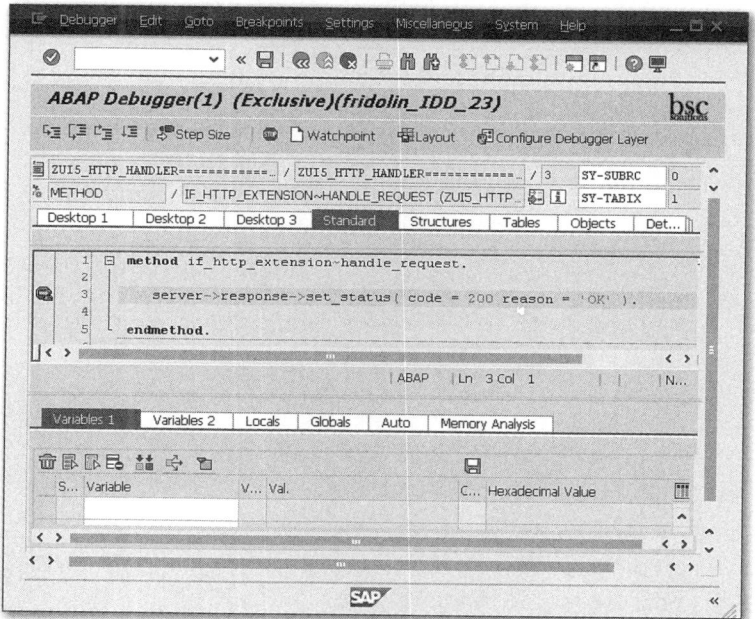

Figure 4.22 HTTP Handler in the Debugger

4.4　Model View Controller Architecture Pattern

The Model View Controller architecture pattern structures the software development in the three units Model, View, and Controller. This separation enables the individual components to be more easily extended, replaced, or reused. Figure 4.23 shows this architecture pattern.

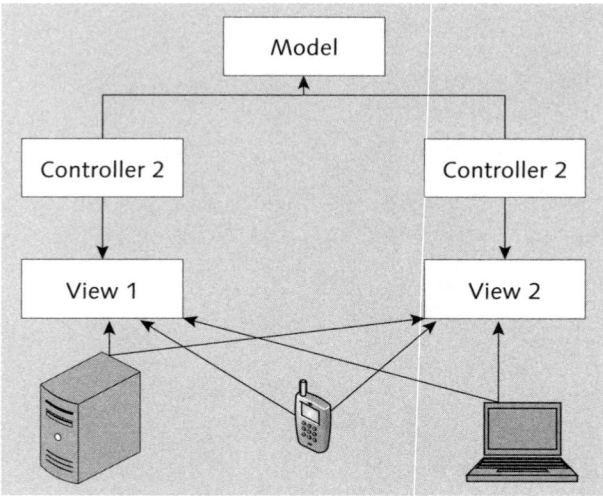

Figure 4.23 Model View Controller Architecture Pattern

This separation enables, for example, two different devices to use the same model; in that case, the view is implemented once for the desktop application and once for the mobile device.

4.4.1 Model

Publisher

The Model represents data model layer and provides the application data. It also represents and coordinates access to the database. In addition, the Model often includes the associated business logic. The relevant data is provided by the Model; for this reason, the Model is also often called the *Publisher*.

4.4.2 View

The presentation layer is responsible for the display on the device. The View receives the user actions, but does not process them; it forwards them to the Controller instead.

4.4.3 Controller

The Controller manages one or more Views, receives user actions from them, and analyzes them. There is one Controller for each View. If a data change occurs during a user action, the Controller performs the communication with the Model (see Figure 4.24).

4.4.4 Interaction in Web Development

For web applications, the MVC pattern includes the server and the browser and is thus slightly more complex than the classic MVC pattern. The browser displays the View as a graphical element, and the Controller is mostly JavaScript code and processes the user actions and forwards them to the Model if necessary.

MVC pattern

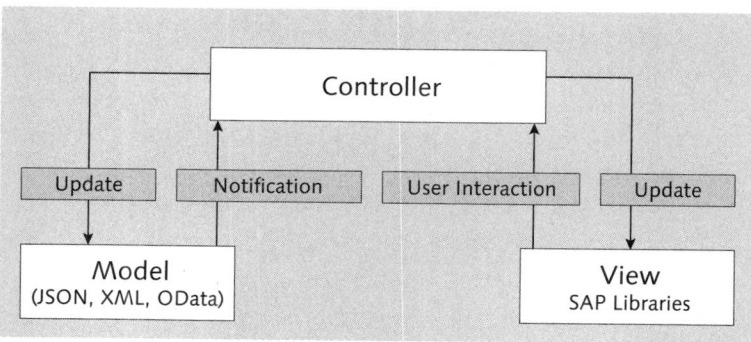

Figure 4.24 MVC Architecture Pattern

4.4.5 MVC in SAPUI5

The MVC is an integral part of the SAPUI5 development. When creating an SAPUI5 application project, you have to decide whether you want to create the page according to the MVC pattern. To create a new project in Eclipse, choose the menu path FILE • NEW • PROJECT, and a wizard for creating a new project will open (see Figure 4.25). In the wizard, select SAPUI5 APPLICATION DEVELOPMENT • APPLICATION PROJECT, and click NEXT to confirm your selection.

Creating an SAPUI5 project

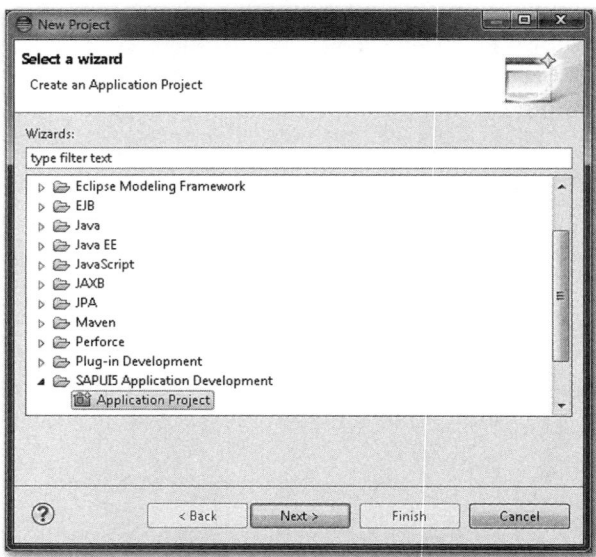

Figure 4.25 SAPUI5 Application Project

On the next screen, if you select the option CREATE AN INITIAL VIEW, the project is created in the MVC pattern (see Figure 4.26).

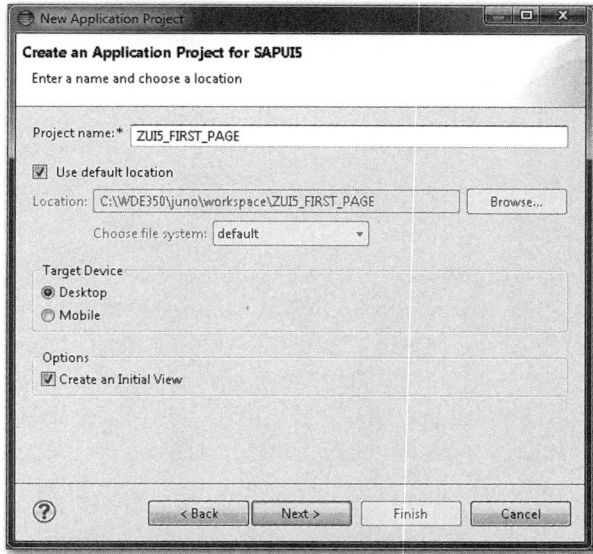

Figure 4.26 SAPUI5 Project According to the MVC Pattern

If you select this option, you will be prompted on the next screen to specify what development paradigm you want to use (see Figure 4.27). You use the development paradigm to define the format in which the view is to be implemented. You can choose from among the following options:

▶ XML: SAP.UI.CORE.MVC.XMLVIEW

▶ JAVASCRIPT: SAP.UI.CORE.MVC.JSVIEW

▶ JSON: SAP.UI.CORE.MVC.JSONVIEW

▶ HTML: SAP.UI.CORE.MVC.HTMLVIEW

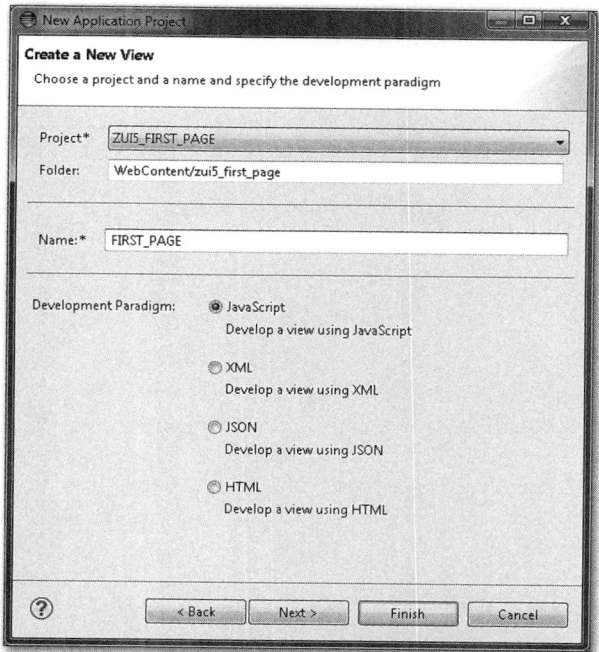

Figure 4.27 Selecting the Development Paradigm

Depending on the selection, the development environment generates a corresponding body of the page. If you decide on the HTML development paradigm, the wizard generates the template from Listing 4.1.

```
<template data-controller-name="html.HTML">
</template>
```

Listing 4.1 SAPUI5 body: HTML View

129

XML view

If you decide on the XML development paradigm, the body is generated from Listing 4.2.

```
<core:View xmlns:core="sap.ui.core" xmlns:mvc="sap.ui.core.
mvc" xmlns="sap.ui.commons"
                                    controllerName="xml.
XML" xmlns:html="http://www.w3.org/1999/xhtml">

</core:View>
```

Listing 4.2 SAPUI5 Body: XML View

JavaScript view

The most frequently used development paradigm is JavaScript (see Listing 4.3). All of the examples in this book are based on this paradigm.

```
sap.ui.jsview("js.JS", {

/** Specifies the Controller belonging to this View.
* In the case that it is not implemented, or that "null" is
returned, this View does not have a Controller.
* @memberOf js.JS
*/
getControllerName : function() {
      return "js.JS";
},

/** Is initially called once after the Controller has been
instantiated. It is where the UI is constructed.
* Because the Controller is given to this method, its
event handlers can be attached right away.
* @memberOf js.JS
*/
createContent : function(oController) {

}

});
```

Listing 4.3 SAPUI5 Body: JavaScript View

JSON view

If you decide on the JSON development paradigm, a page body is created according to Listing 4.4.

```
{
"Type":"sap.ui.core.mvc.JSONView",
"controllerName":"json.JSON",
"content": [{

}]
}
```

Listing 4.4 SAPUI5 Body: JSON View

In addition to the appropriate page body, a Controller file is also created; it already includes four predefined events:

▶ onInit (during the initialization)

▶ onBeforeRendering (before rendering the page)

▶ onAfterRendering (after rendering the page)

▶ onExit (when the controller is destroyed, such as when closing the page)

However, what does this separation mean? Due to the strict use of the MVC pattern, you can also implement individual Views as fragments and very easily reuse them in other pages. All events of the page are handled in the relevant Controller file, and the response to an event does not have to be painstakingly adjusted in several places if a change has been made. The two files *View* and *Controller* form a loose unit, and you should create a separate Controller for each View. Even though this is not absolutely necessary, this separation makes it easier to replace a View and its corresponding Controller.

It is now time to put the theory into practice. To conclude this chapter, you will now create your first two SAPUI5 applications: one without the MVC architecture pattern and one according to the MVC pattern.

4.5   First Example

We will start with a page that is not created according to the MVC pattern. In this case, choose the menu path FILE • NEW • PROJECT in Eclipse. In the Project Wizard, select SAPUI5 APPLICATION DEVELOPMENT • APPLICATION PROJECT, and click NEXT. Then give the project a suitable name

SAPUI5 without
MVC

131

(ZUI5_WO MVC in this example), select DESKTOP as the target device, remove the checkmark in front of the option CREATE AN INITIAL VIEW if necessary—the project will not be created according to the MVC pattern as a result—and choose FINISH. In Eclipse, a project is now created with the following structure (see Figure 4.28):

❶ Libraries

❷ Content

❸ Bootstrap

❹ Application

❺ UI area

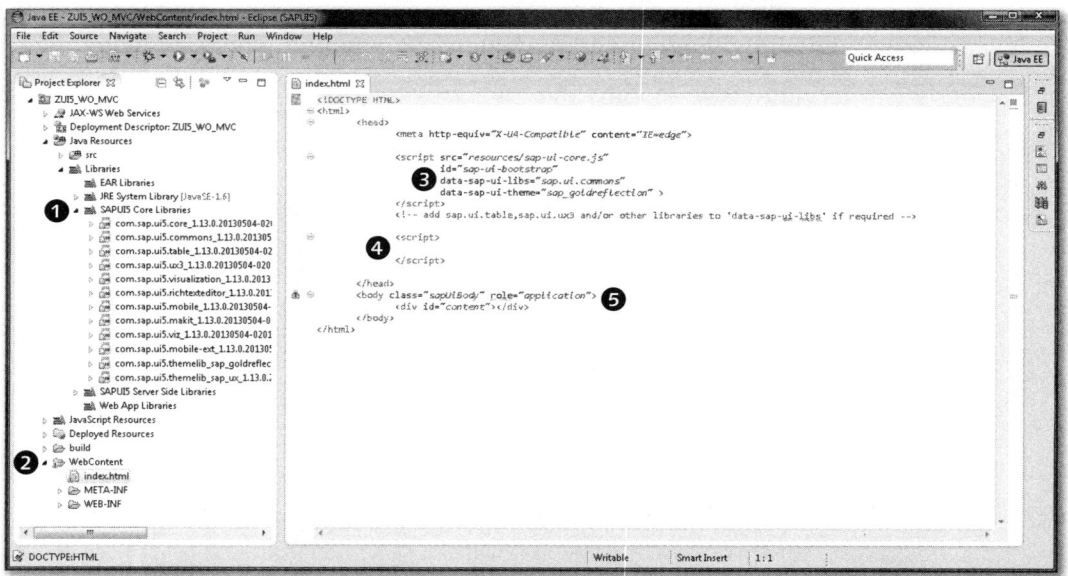

Figure 4.28 SAPUI5 Project Without MVC Pattern

We will discuss the individual areas in greater detail in the next chapter. It's enough right now to know that in this scenario, without MVC, you implement your application in the second script block (referred to in Figure 4.28 as APPLICATION).

In this simple case, we want to implement a button that displays an alert dialog box once it is clicked. To do so, first open the API documentation, which is located in the backend under *http://<HOST NAME>:<SERVICE>/sap/public/bc/ui5_ui5/demokit/* or, as of Version 1.18, under *http://<HOST NAME>: <SERVICE>/sap/bc/ui5_demokit/*, in which you replace <HOST NAME> and <SERVICE> with the values of your SAP system. Alternatively, you can also find the Demo Kit on the Internet at *https://sapui5.netweaver.ondemand.com/sdk/*.

In the Demo Kit, switch to the API REFERENCE area, and look for the appropriate control for a simple button (`sap.ui.commons.Button`) as shown in Figure 4.29.

API reference

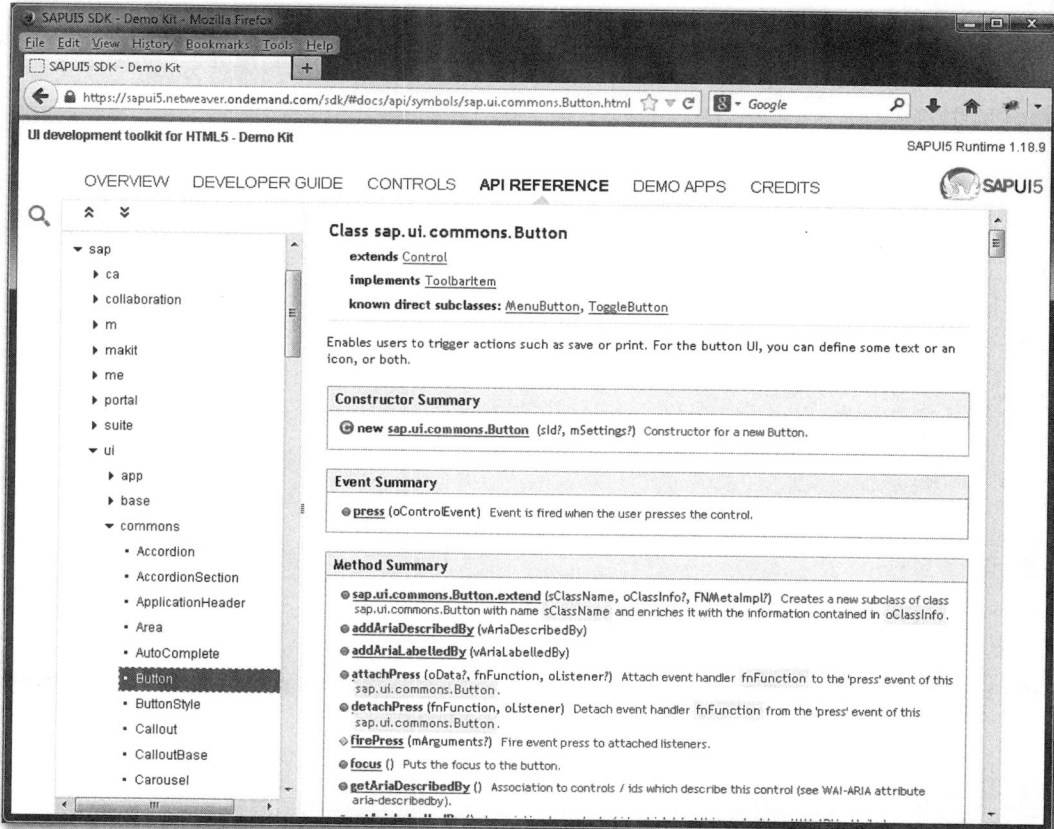

Figure 4.29 Button Control in SAPUI5

Constructor
function

After selecting the relevant control, the constructor function and (if available) the events and the available methods for this control are displayed in the in the right-hand area. Click on the constructor function, and the possible parameters are displayed (see Figure 4.30).

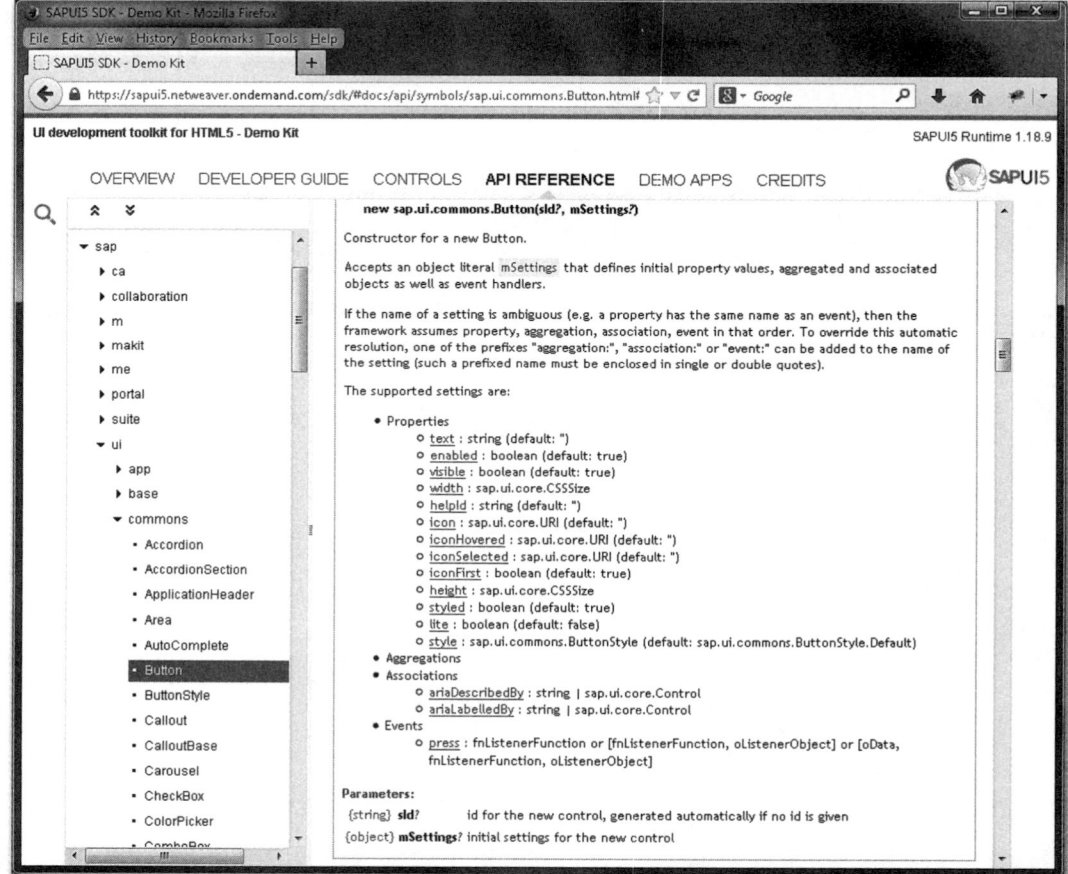

Figure 4.30 The sap.ui.commons.Button Constructor

Code completion

Once you are familiar with the SAPUI5 library, you can omit the API documentation completely. The documentation is also displayed in Eclipse via the key combination Ctrl + space bar . When you double-click the appropriate line, the relevant code pattern is inserted (see Figure 4.31).

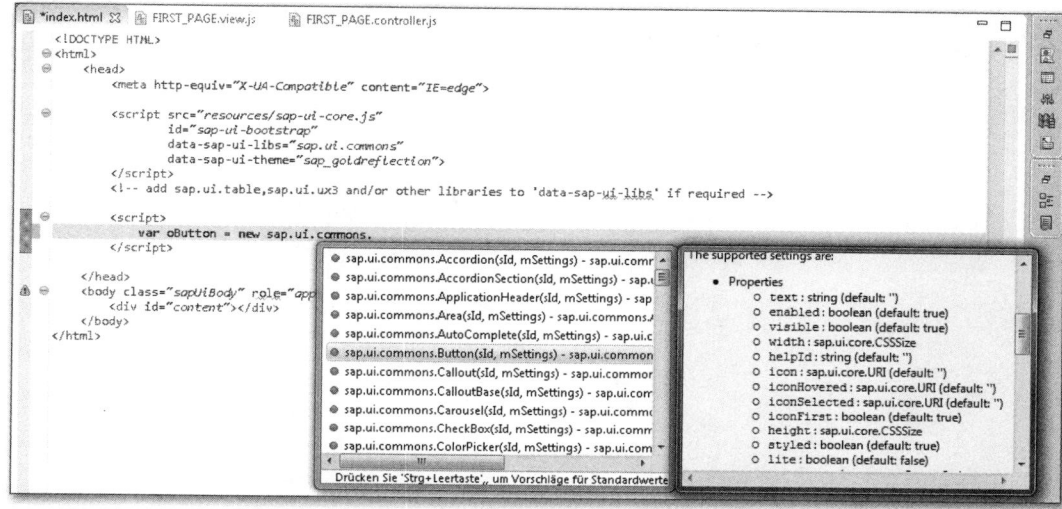

Figure 4.31 Documentation of SAPUI5 Classes in Eclipse

For our simple example, we require only a text and an event listener for the event `press`. For our button, this results in the content of Listing 4.5.

```
var oButton = new sap.ui.commons.Button({
                    text  : "Click me",
                    press : handleButtonClicked
             });
```

Listing 4.5 Button

From the button event `press`, we have registered the event listener `handleButtonClicked`; this function should only display an `alert` dialog box (see Listing 4.6).

Event listener

```
function handleButtonClicked() {
     alert("Pressed");
};
```

Listing 4.6 Event Handler

Finally, we must transfer our application to the UI area so that it can also be displayed. Here, we achieve this by using the `placeAt` function from the class `sap.ui.core.Control` (see Figure 4.32).

135

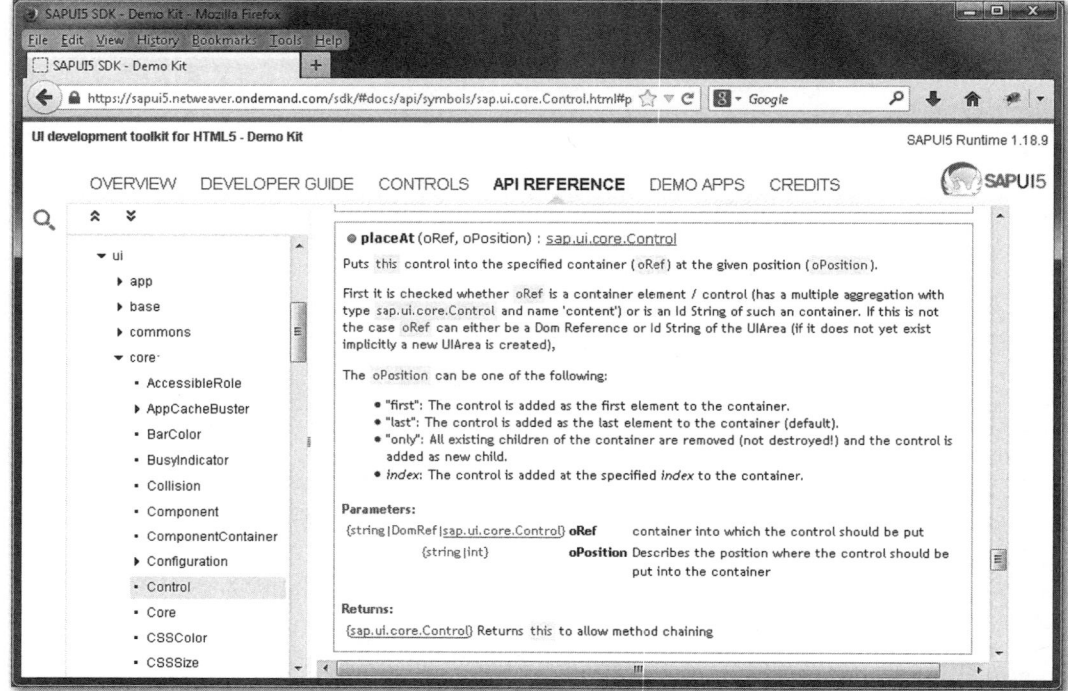

Figure 4.32 placeAt Function

placeAt function
For the `placeAt` function, make sure that you have to specify the name for the `<div>` element from the `<body>` area (see Listing 4.7, content).

```
<!DOCTYPE HTML>
<html>
    <head>
        <meta http-equiv="X-UA-Compatible" content="IE=edge">

        <script src="resources/sap-ui-core.js"
                id="sap-ui-bootstrap"
                data-sap-ui-libs="sap.ui.commons"
                data-sap-ui-theme="sap_goldreflection">
        </script>

        <script>
            var oButton = new sap.ui.commons.Button({
                    text  : "Click me",
                    press : handleButtonClicked
```

```
        });

    function handleButtonClicked() {
            alert("Pressed");
        };

        oButton.placeAt("content");
    </script>

  </head>
    <body class="sapUiBody" role="application">
        <div id="content"></div>
    </body>
</html>
```

Listing 4.7 Button in SAPUI5

Save the application and look at the result in the preview function. To do so, choose the context menu option Execute As • Preview of Web Application in the project. In the middle part, a new tab opens with an integrated web browser in which the page is displayed. You can now click the button, and the relevant `alert` message "Pressed" should be displayed (see Figure 4.33).

Preview function

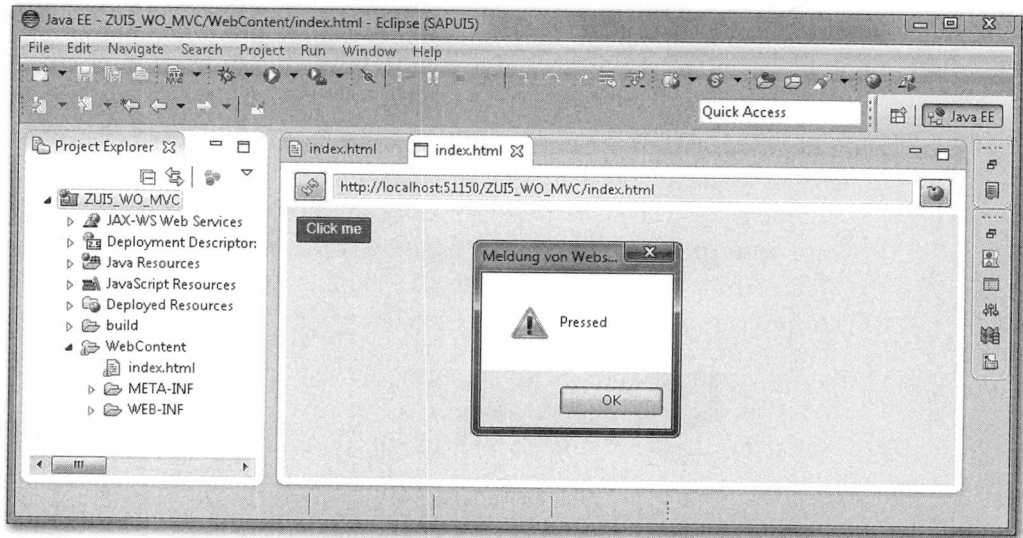

Figure 4.33 Preview of First Sample Application Example

Congratulations, you have just implemented your first SAPUI5 application!

About the general notation: We have already declared the necessary attributes and properties in the constructor with the JSON notation in this example. Of course, you can also call the constructor when it's empty and then use the relevant GET and SET methods of the control. Listing 4.8 illustrates both these options.

```
// JSON Notation
    var oButton = new sap.ui.commons.Button({
            text  : "Click me",
            press : handleButtonClicked
        });

// Alternatively: getter and setter functions
    var oButton = new sap.ui.commons.Button();
    oButton.setText("Click me");
    oButton.attachPress(handleButtonClicked);
```

Listing 4.8 Alternative Notation

Ultimately, you have to decide which notation you prefer; both types of notation have advantages and disadvantages. Particularly in the initial phase, it is recommended that you use the getter and setter, because the source code is easier to read as a result; the JSON-type notation quickly becomes confusing due to the many parentheses.

Let's create this example again—this time according to the MVC pattern.

Create the SAPUI5 application project ZUI5_WITH_MVC, select the CREATE AN INITIAL VIEW checkbox, and click NEXT to confirm your selection. On the next screen, you have to specify a name for the View and decide on a development paradigm (see Figure 4.34). Specify "main" as the View Name, and select JAVASCRIPT as the Development Paradigm. Click FINISH to confirm your entries.

Now, on the left side of the Explorer, navigate to ZUI5_WITH_MVC • WEBCONTENT • zui5_with_mvc. Here, you will find three files for the actual HTML page ❶, the View ❷, and the Controller ❸ (see Figure 4.35).

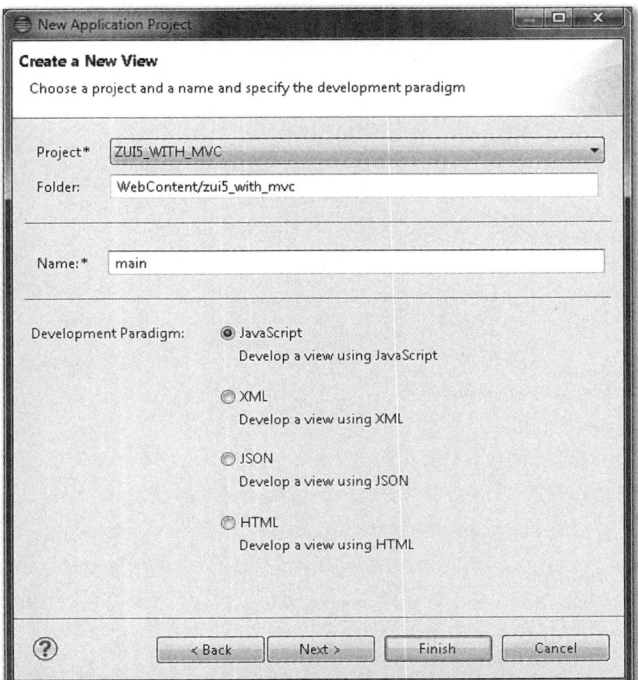

Figure 4.34 Creating View

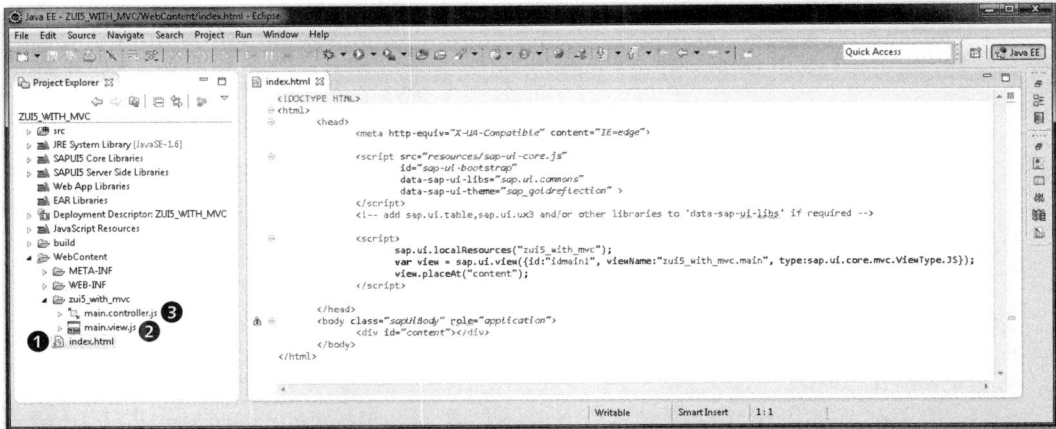

Figure 4.35 The Created Files of an SAPUI5 Application

Because you have selected the MVC pattern, the appropriate script is already generated automatically in the *index.html* file (see Listing 4.9).

```
<script>
    sap.ui.localResources("zui5_with_mvc");
        var view = sap.ui.view({
                    id        :"idmain1",
                    viewName :"zui5_with_mvc.main",
                    type      :sap.ui.core.mvc.ViewType.JS
            });
        view.placeAt("content");
/script>
```

Listing 4.9 Generated Script to Call the View

View In the View file (*main.view.js*), the function `createContent` is created automatically. Within this function, you define the corresponding UI elements. The four standard events are created in the Controller, as described previously. In our example, you also have to implement the function `handleButtonClicked`. Figure 4.36 illustrates the difference between these two development approaches.

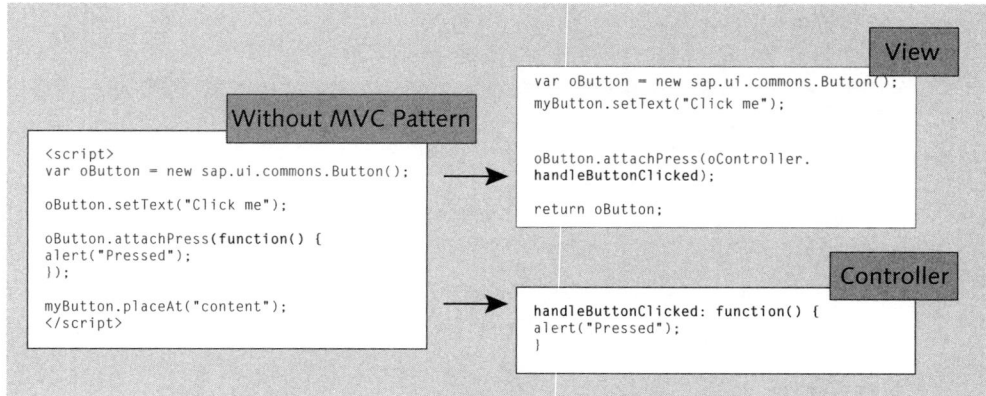

Figure 4.36 Comparison: with MVC and without MVC

To complete the MVC example, enhance the View (*main.view.js* file) within the `createContent` function by adding the source text from Listing 4.10.

```
createContent : function(oController) {

var oButton = new sap.ui.commons.Button();
    oButton.setText("Click me");
    oButton.attachPress(oController.handleButtonClicked);
return oButton;

}
```

Listing 4.10 view.js

In our example without MVC, you added the button with the `placeAt` function to the actual UI page. In the MVC pattern, you no longer have to do this, because you return the finished page definition as the `return` value from the `createContent` function instead.

In the Controller, you have only to include the function `handleBut-tonClicked` for the event `press`. In the Controller (*main.controller.js* file), below the generated functions, add the following:

Controller

```
handleButtonClicked: function() {
    alert("Pressed");
}
```

Save the two files via the DISK icon (you can save all changed files at once with the MULTIPLE DISK icon). In this example, the HTML page (*index.html* file) does not have to be changed. Check your results by viewing the page in the preview; it should correspond to the result in Figure 4.33.

Umlauts may not be displayed properly. Here, in the `<head>` area, add the already well-known `<meta charset="UTF-8">`, which sets the character encoding to `UTF-8`.

You have just implemented your first SAPUI5 application according to the MVC pattern! All that remains now is to check in the created page in the ABAP backend. This task is also very easy, thanks to the support provided by the SAPUI5 Team Provider. In the Project Explorer, open the context menu of the project and choose TEAM • SHARE PROJECT (see Figure 4.37).

SAPUI5 Team Provider

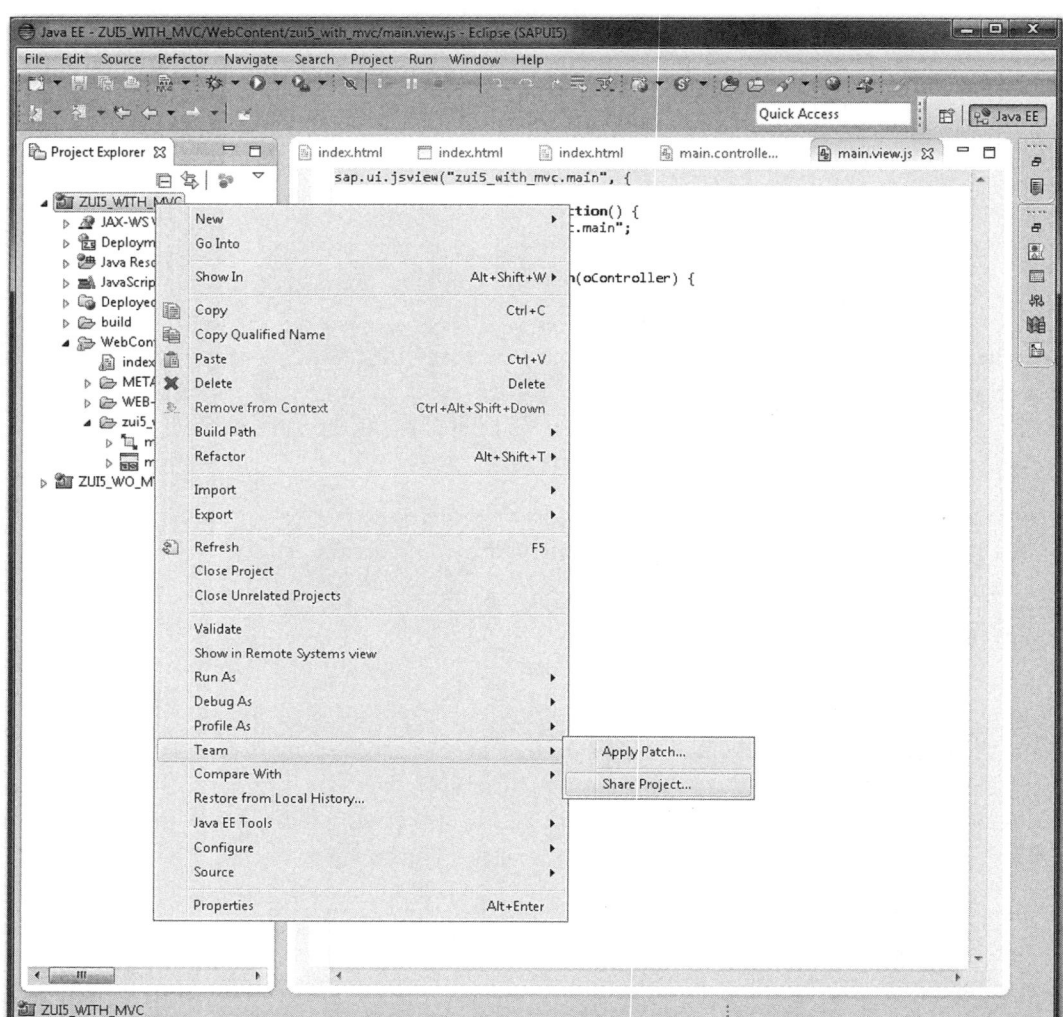

Figure 4.37 Sharing Projects

In the wizard, select SAPUI5 ABAP REPOSITORY, and click NEXT (see Figure 4.38). The Team Provider has been available since version 7.02. For SAP releases use the program /UI5.UI5_REPOSITORY_LOAD instead.

System selection Next to the CONNECTION field on the next screen, click BROWSE, select the desired system, and click OK (see Figure 4.39). The SAPUI5 Team Provider obtains the information from the SAP GUI installation.

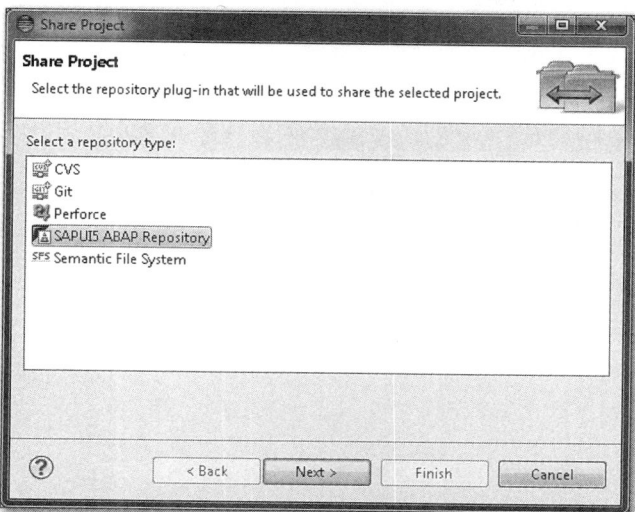

Figure 4.38 SAPUI5 ABAP Repository

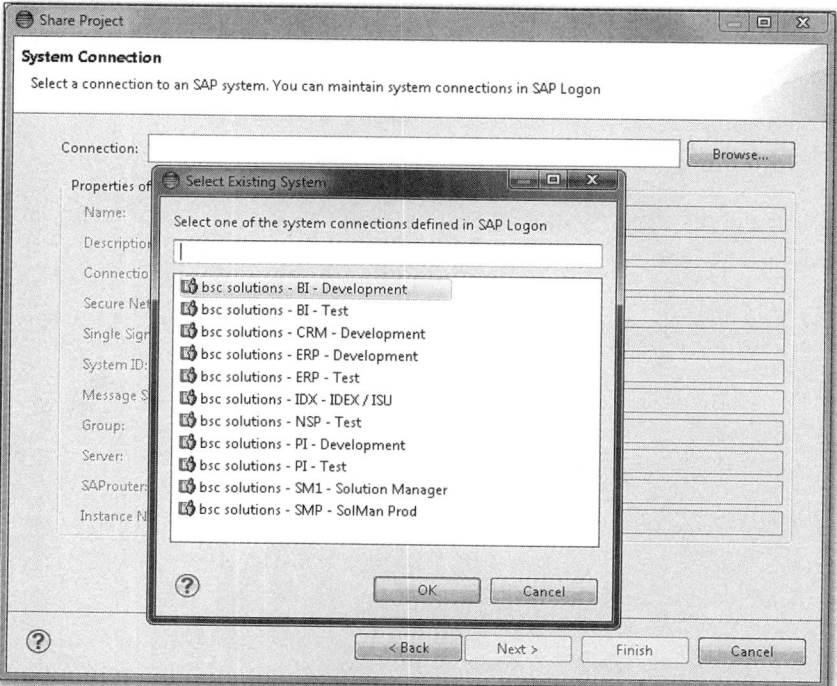

Figure 4.39 System Selection

The system data is transferred in the wizard (see Figure 4.40). Click NEXT to confirm your selection.

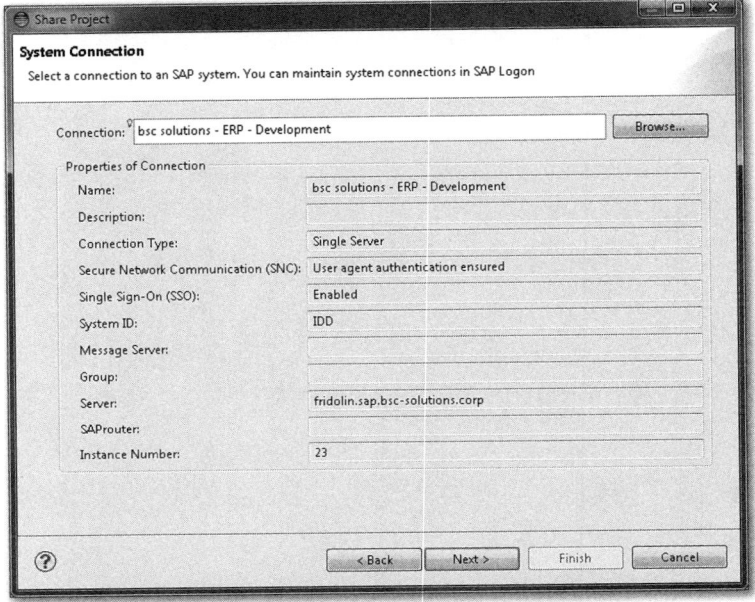

Figure 4.40 Selecting the SAP System

On the next screen, enter the logon data for the relevant system, and click NEXT (see Figure 4.41).

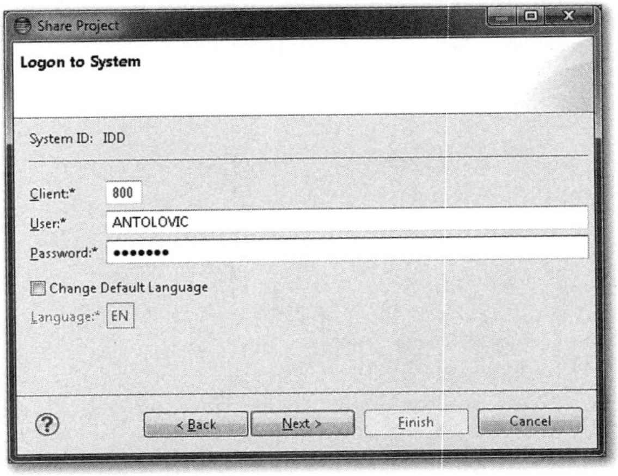

Figure 4.41 Logon Data

On the next screen, enter a NAME, a DESCRIPTION for the BSP page, and   Local object
a PACKAGE (as in this example, $TMP for local object), and click NEXT to
confirm your entries (see Figure 4.42).

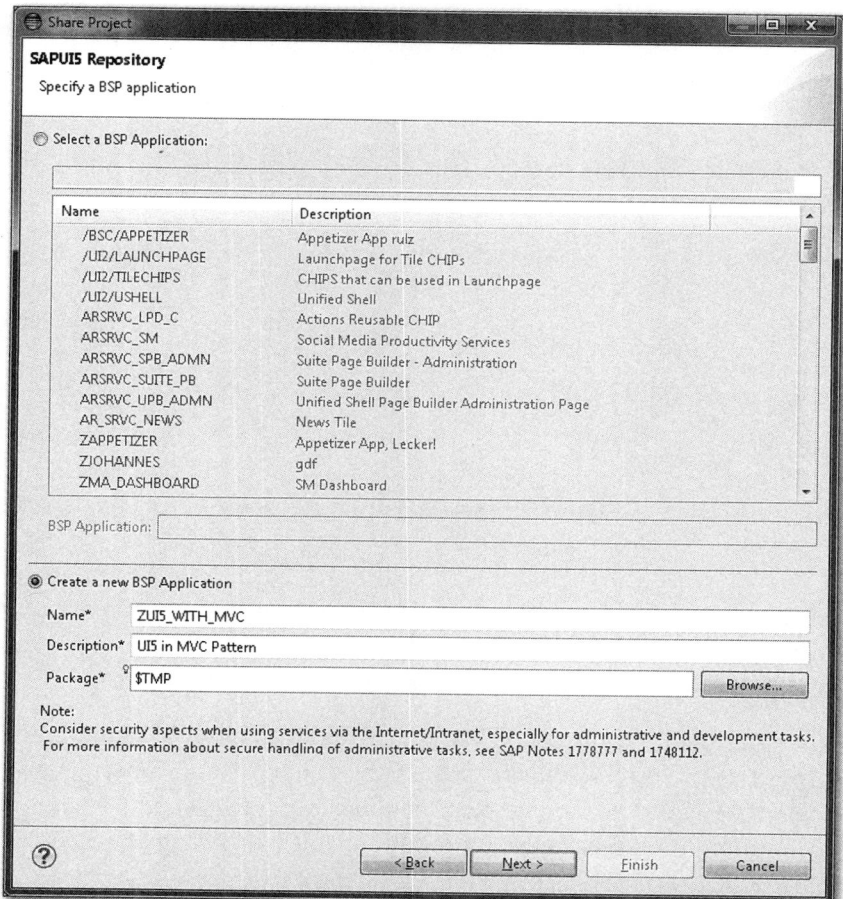

Figure 4.42 Creating a BSP Application

For local developments (package $TMP), you do not have to specify any
transport request on the next screen. For transportable objects, select
either an existing transport request or create a new transport request
(see Figure 4.43).

145

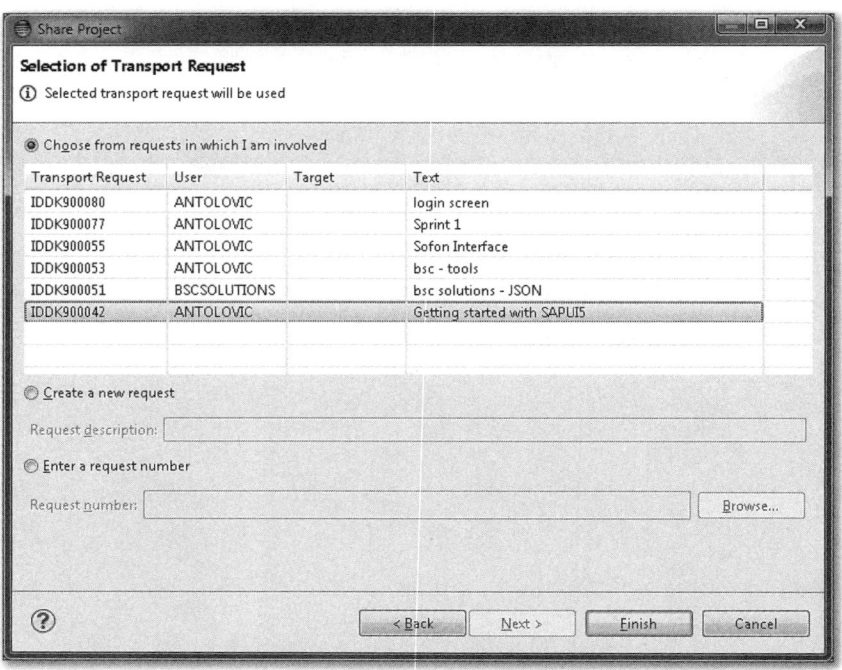

Figure 4.43 Selecting a Transport Request

System connection

Click FINISH to confirm your selection. Eclipse now establishes a connection to the SAP system, and the system ID, user name, language, and BSP page name are displayed in square brackets in the Project Explorer.

You can now check in the files in the SAP backend. To do so, go to the project again in the Explorer and, in the context menu, select TEAM • SUBMIT. A dialog box will appear in which you can select the resources to be submitted (see Figure 4.44). By default, the system transfers all objects that were changed since the last check-in.

Click FINISH to confirm your selection. Two essential components are now created in the backend. A service is created in the ICF under the path */sap/bc/ui5_ui5/sap/<BSP application name>/*, and a BSP application is generated, which contains the SAPUI5 page.

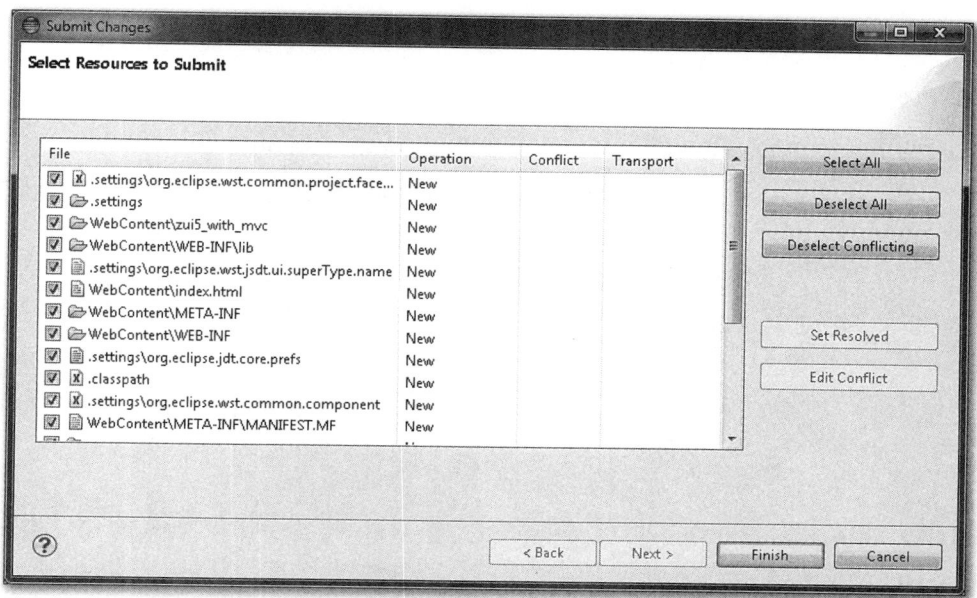

Figure 4.44 Selecting Resources to be Submitted

If the library version in your Eclipse version does not match the version in the SAP backend, you will receive a relevant warning message (see Figure 4.45).

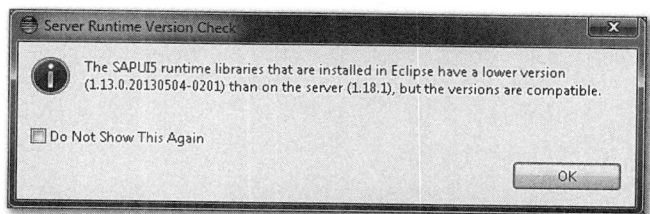

Figure 4.45 Version Check

In this case, you should test your application thoroughly on the SAP server and harmonize the two versions via a corresponding upgrade.

After uploading to the SAP backend, the application is accessible via the URL *http://<HOST NAME>:<SERVICE>/sap/bc/ui5_ui5/sap/<BSP application*

name>/. After logging on to the system, you should obtain the result displayed in Figure 4.46.

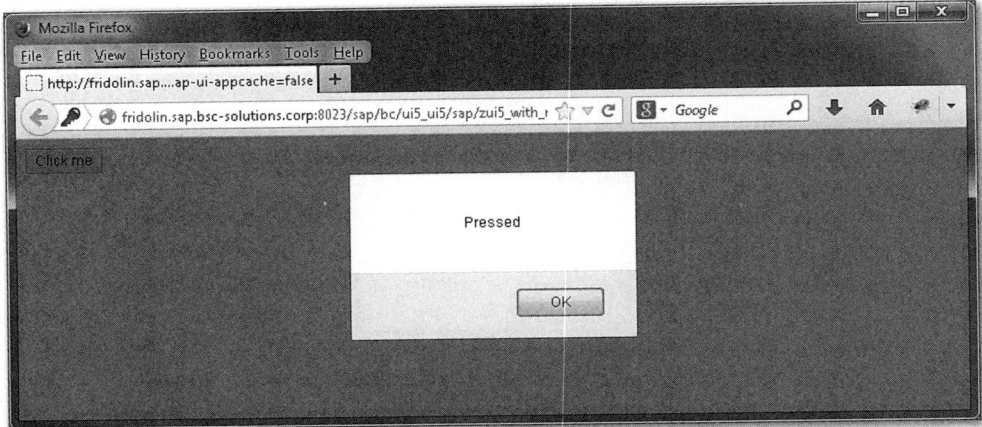

Figure 4.46 First SAPUI5 Application in the SAP Backend

Congratulations, you have just called your first SAPUI5 application in the SAP backend!

In Chapter 5, we'll discuss the most important components and controls of the SAPUI5 library in detail.

In this chapter, you will learn about the SAPUI5 bootstrap. You will discover how to bind data to a control and what options you have when communicating with the SAP backend.

5   SAPUI5 Runtime Environment

You created your first SAPUI5 applications at the end of Chapter 4, but you still require some more information. On the one hand, you may have heard the term *bootstrap* but you may not know what it means; on the other hand, it's probably still difficult for you to navigate the API documentation right now. In this chapter, we will introduce the basic elements of the SAPUI5 Runtime Environment (RTE); these include the topics of *bootstrapping*, *data binding*, and *theming*. The Runtime Environment ensures that application programs run on appropriate operating systems and that the software modules can be reused. In Chapter 6, the SAPUI5 library with the available UI controls will be presented.

RTE

Unfortunately, this is a catch-22 situation, you can't be given an example of *data binding* without referring to UI controls, which you won't learn about until the next chapter. At the same time, you can't be given any good examples of UI controls if you haven't dealt with *data binding*. Don't worry if you still don't understand everything fully in this chapter; everything will become clearer once you have read Chapter 6.

Checklist	[⌂]
You will need the following for this chapter: ▶ An installed and configured Eclipse development environment ▶ Access to an ERP system with an installed SAPUI5 library	

5.1   Initialization of the Application

The SAPUI5 library is a JavaScript library. You have to embed the library in your HTML document so that you can access the available functions and methods during development. You learned about embedding external JavaScript libraries in Chapter 3; Listing 5.1 can refresh your memory.

```
<!DOCTYPE html>
<html>
  <head>
    <meta charset="UTF-8">
      <script type="text/javascript"
               src="jquery.js"
      </script>
  </head>
```

Listing 5.1   Embedding External JavaScript Libraries

By comparison, let's take a look in Listing 5.2 at the *index.html* file of an SAPUI5 application.

```
<!DOCTYPE HTML>
  <html>
    <head>
      <script type="text/javascript"
              src="resources/sap-ui-core.js"
              id="sap-ui-bootstrap"
              data-sap-ui-libs="sap.ui.commons"
              data-sap-ui-theme="sap_goldreflection">
      </script>
```

Listing 5.2   Bootstrap of an SAPUI5 Application

As you can see from this example, you embed the SAPUI5 library just like any other external JavaScript library. In an SAPUI5 application, the first part is called the *bootstrap*; this is followed by the application in a separate script area and the UI area within the <body> tags (see Figure 5.1).

Bootstrap   Within the bootstrap, you specify the desired JavaScript resource in the attribute src, the required UI libraries in data-sap-ui-libs, and the desired page design in the attribute data-sap-ui-theme.

```
<!DOCTYPE HTML>
<html>
  <head>
    <meta http-equiv="X-UA-Compatible" content="IE=edge">

    <script src="resources/sap-ui-core.js"
            id="sap-ui-bootstrap"
            data-sap-ui-libs="sap.ui.commons"
            data-sap-ui-theme="sap_goldreflection">
    </script>

    <script>
            sap.ui.localResources("ui");
            var view = sap.ui.view({
                    id:"idappl1",
                    viewName:"ui.appl",
                    type:sap.ui.core.mvc.ViewType.JS
                    });
            view.placeAt("content");
    </script>

  </head>
<body class="sapUiBody" role="application">
    <div id="content"></div>
  </body>
</html>
```

- } Bootstrap
- } Application
- } UI Area

Figure 5.1 Index Page of an SAPUI5 Application

This gives rise to some questions: What is the menu path to the JavaScript resources? What are the various libraries? What themes are available, and how can you change them? These questions will be answered in the course of this chapter.

5.1.1 SAPUI5 Resources

Remember Chapter 3? In that chapter, you had the option of using the packed or unpacked version of the jQuery libraries for performance reasons. SAP has gone one step further: SAPUI5 is divided into several JavaScript and UI libraries. In the UI libraries, you should embed only those resources that you need for the development of the application (see Figure 5.2).

SAPUI5 libraries

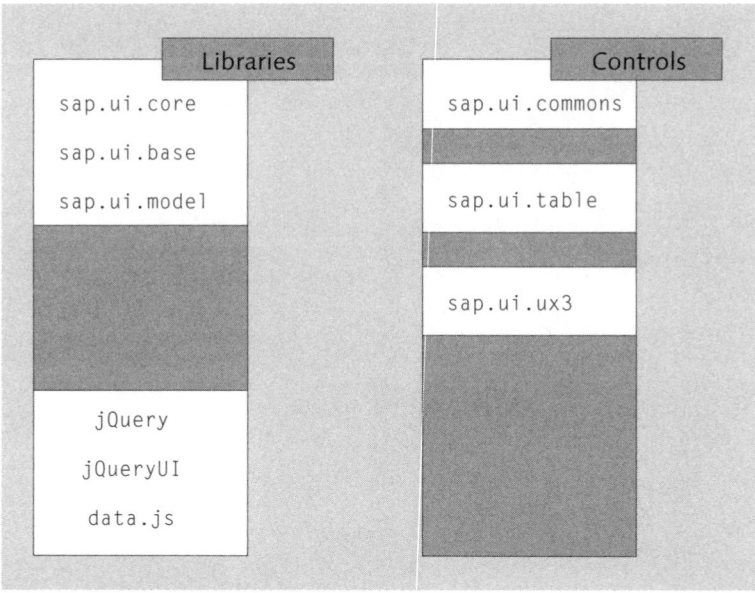

Figure 5.2 SAPUI5 Architecture

SAPUI5 provides various JavaScript libraries depending on the use case, and *sap-ui-core.js* is the most frequently used library.

Resource file

For the sake of completeness, all available resources are listed in Table 5.1. Because these resources are special cases that you rarely use, we won't discuss them any further at this point.

Resource	Description
sap-ui-core.js	Default resource; already contains the jQuery plug-in and jQuery UI plug-in (jQuery.sap.*). The required files are loaded dynamically via XMLHttpRequests (XHRs).
sap-ui-core-lean.js	Similar to the *sap-ui-core.js* library; however, only jQuery and a few SAPUI5 components are loaded immediately. The other components are dynamically reloaded at runtime.
sap-ui-core-all.js	Contains all the resources of the SAPUI5 library. Although this reduces the reloading of necessary components, it increases the initial load time.

Table 5.1 SAPUI5 Resources

Resource	Description
sap/ui/core/library-preload.js	Similar to the *sap-ui-core-all.js* resource; however, the individual components are only parsed as required.
sap-ui5.js	This file contains all JavaScript modules, including `sap.ui.core`, `sap.ui.commons`, `sap.ui.table`, and `sap.ui.ux3`.
sap-ui-custom*.js	Reserved namespace for customer developments.

Table 5.1 SAPUI5 Resources (Cont.)

To embed resources in your application, you must determine the relevant path on the server. Use the URL *http://<HOST NAME>:<SERVICE>/sap/public/bc/ui5_ui5/* to open the SAPUI5 Development Toolkit in your SAP system (see Figure 5.3).

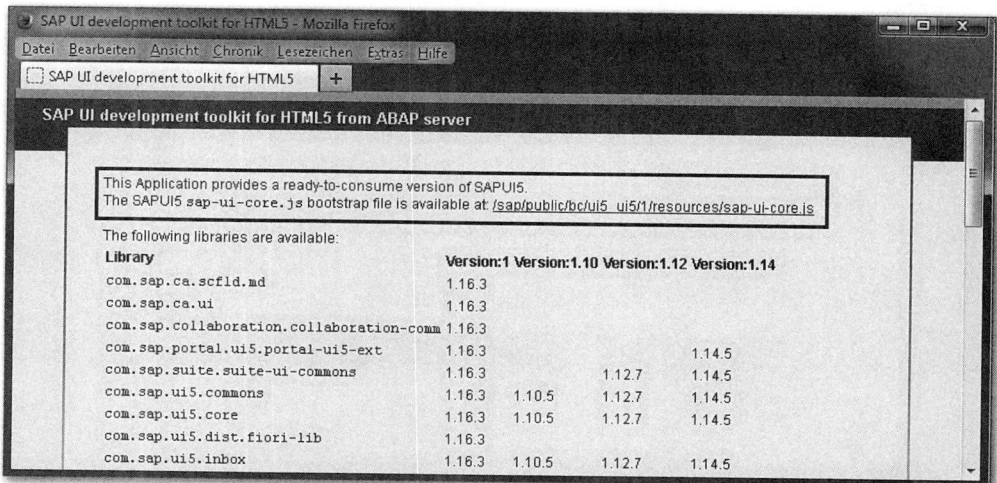

Figure 5.3 SAPUI5 Development Toolkit

In the upper part, you will find the path to the resources, which you enter in the bootstrap of your application. In the middle area, you will find the installed SAPUI5 versions. The latest version is Version 1; for the bootstrap, this results in the path */sap/public/bc/ui5_ui5/1/resources/sap-ui-core.js*. If you would like to test your application with an older version, you have to adjust the version number in the bootstrap. If you

Runtime version

test your application with Version 1.14.5, for example, the relevant path in the bootstrap is */sap/public/bc/ui5_ui5/***1.14***/resources/sap-ui-core.js* (see Figure 5.3). You can use the key combination Ctrl + Alt + Shift + P to determine the runtime version of any SAPUI5 application (see Figure 5.4). The runtime version display is particularly useful for troubleshooting, because the loaded modules are displayed and you can also switch directly to debug mode.

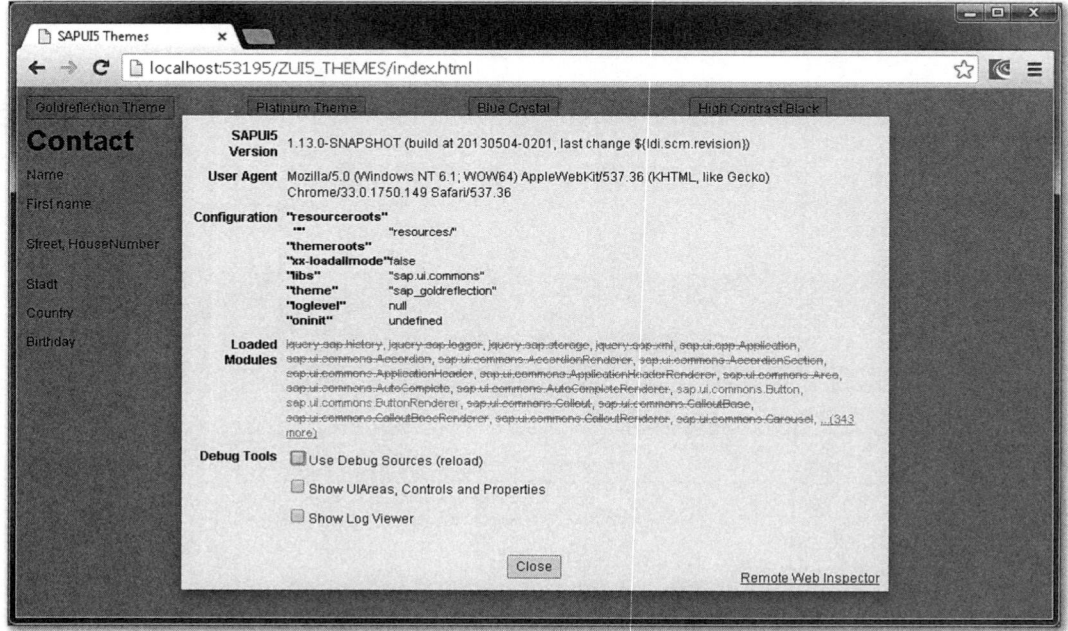

Figure 5.4 Determining Runtime Version

5.1.2 Controls

Namespace

The UI controls are divided into several thematically related classes known as namespaces. Each of these classes is in turn divided into further subclasses and belongs to its own library. The library *sap.ui.table*, for example, is responsible for the display of table controls.

Library in the bootstrap

Depending on the controls used in your application, you have to embed the relevant library in the bootstrap. If you would like to embed table controls, for example, the bootstrap changes as shown in Listing 5.3.

```
<script src="resources/sap-ui-core.js"
        id="sap-ui-bootstrap"
        data-sap-ui-libs="sap.ui.commons, sap.ui.table"
        data-sap-ui-theme="sap_goldreflection" >
</script>
```

Listing 5.3 Bootstrap with sap.ui.table

If you forget to embed the necessary libraries in the bootstrap, the system displays the relevant error message "sap.ui.table is undefined" in the console of the browser development tool, as Figure 5.5 illustrates.

Undefined error message

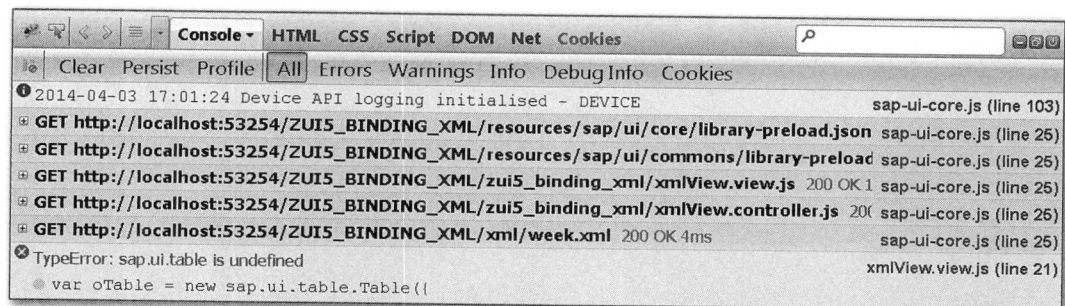

Figure 5.5 TypeError: sap.ui.table is undefined

The controls are the subject of Chapter 6; however, you can work in this chapter with the API reference and also reproduce the illustrated examples based on the API reference.

5.1.3 SAPUI5 Theming

In addition to the various JavaScript resources and UI libraries, various themes are also delivered in the standard system, which you define in the bootstrap and which can change the page design.

Themes

Currently, the following themes are provided in the standard system:

▶ Gold Reflection (sap_goldreflection)

▶ Platinum (sap_platinum)

▶ Blue Crystal (sap_bluecrystal)

▶ High Contrast Black (sap_hcb)

▶ SAP Mobile Visual Identity (`sap_mvi`; only available for mobile applications)

In Section 5.5, you will learn how to create your own theme or change individual elements with your own CSS.

Changing Theme

To enable you to look at the themes, you'll implement a page with which you can switch between themes at the touch of a button.

Even as a personal advocate of the MVC architecture pattern, let's refrain from using it in the following examples for the sake of clarity. In Chapter 7, you'll implement your first slightly larger application, and you will implement that application according to the MVC pattern.

Example

Create the SAPUI5 application project ZUI5_THEMES in Eclipse, and refrain from creating the Initial View file. In addition to the buttons, also implement a small form so that you can see the differences between the themes more easily.

In Listing 5.4, you implement four buttons, each of which calls a function when it is clicked.

```
var oButton_sg = new new sap.ui.commons.Button({
    text : "Goldreflection Theme",
    press : sap_goldreflection,
});
```

Listing 5.4 Button for Changing Theme

You'll use this statement to create a UI control of type *button* and you'll trigger the event `sap_goldreflection` when you click on the button. Next, you have to process the button events and switch the theme; to switch the theme, use the method `applyTheme` from the core component. For this example, doing this results in the content of Listing 5.5.

```
<!DOCTYPE HTML>
<html>
<head>
<TITLE>Themes in SAPUI5</TITLE>
<meta charset="UTF-8">
<meta http-equiv="X-UA-Compatible" content="IE=edge">
<script src="resources/sap-ui-core.js" id="sap-ui-bootstrap"
```

```
      data-sap-ui-libs="sap.ui.commons"
      data-sap-ui-theme="sap_goldreflection">
  </script>
  <script>
  // Layout
      var oMatrix = new sap.ui.commons.layout.MatrixLayout({
          layoutFixed : true,
          width : '800px',
          columns : 4,
          widths : [ '200px', '200px', '200px', '200px', ]
      });

  // Buttons for switching themes
      var oButton_sg = new sap.ui.commons.Button();
      oButton_sg.setText("Goldreflection Theme");
      oButton_sg.attachPress(sap_goldreflection);

      var oButton_sp = new sap.ui.commons.Button();
      oButton_sp.setText("Platinum Theme");
      oButton_sp.attachPress(sap_platinum);

      var oButton_sb = new sap.ui.commons.Button();
      oButton_sb.setText("Blue Crystal");
      oButton_sb.attachPress(sap_bluecrystal);

      var oButton_sh = new sap.ui.commons.Button();
      oButton_sh.setText("High Contrast Black");
      oButton_sh.attachPress(sap_hcb);

      oMatrix.createRow(oButton_sg, oButton_sp,
                        oButton_sb, oButton_sh);
  // Small form for better clarity of theme
  // Page content heading and a small form
      var oCell = new sap.ui.commons.layout.MatrixLayoutCell({
          colSpan : 4
      });
      var oTV = new sap.ui.commons.TextView({
          text : 'Contact',
          vdesign : sap.ui.commons.TextViewDesign.H1
      });
      oCell.addContent(oTV);
      oMatrix.createRow(oCell);
```

```
    var oLabel = new sap.ui.commons.Label({
        text : 'Name'
    });
    var oTF = new sap.ui.commons.TextField({
        editable : false,
        value : 'Doe',
        width : '200px'
    });
    oLabel.setLabelFor(oTF);
    oMatrix.createRow(oLabel, oTF);
// ... abbreviated ...
    oMatrix.placeAt("content");
// Functions
    function sap_goldreflection() {
        sap.ui.getCore().applyTheme("sap_goldreflection");
    };
    function sap_platinum() {
        sap.ui.getCore().applyTheme("sap_platinum");
    };
    function sap_bluecrystal() {
        sap.ui.getCore().applyTheme("sap_bluecrystal");
    };
    function sap_hcb() {
        sap.ui.getCore().applyTheme("sap_hcb");
    };
</script>
</head>
<body class="sapUiBody" role="application">
    <div id="content"></div>
</body>
</html>
```

Listing 5.5 Switching the Theme

Uploading project   Save your changes and upload the project to the SAP backend. In the context menu of the project, choose the menu path TEAM • SHARE PROJECT, and then create the BSP page ZUI5_THEMES as a local object. Upload the content to the SAP backend via the context menu TEAM • SUBMIT. After uploading successfully, start your application in the browser via the URL *http://<HOST NAME>:<PORT>/sap/bc/ui5_ui5/sap/zui5_themes/*, in which you replace the host name and port with the relevant values of your SAP backend. After calling the page, you can use the buttons to switch between the individual themes. In this book, you mostly use the Blue Crystal theme shown in Figure 5.6. Try out the themes to see which theme you like best.

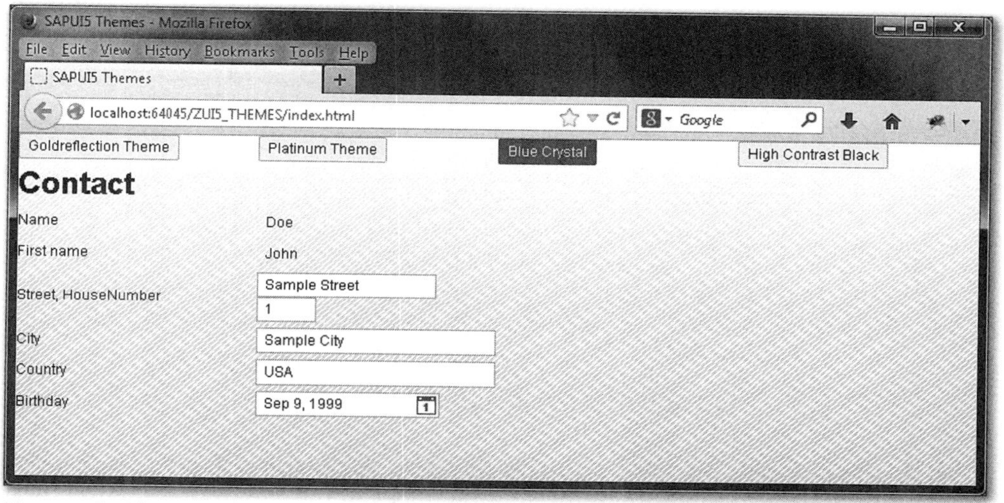

Figure 5.6 Blue Crystal Theme

As a small exercise, you can now change the preceding example so that all button events are controlled via the same function. For this purpose, assign an ID to each button, and register the same function in each button, as illustrated in Listing 5.6.

```
var oButton_sg = new sap.ui.commons.Button("GOLD");
oButton_sg.setText("Goldreflection Theme");
oButton_sg.attachPress(
        function(oEvent){changeTheme(oEvent);}
        );
```

Listing 5.6 Same Event for All Buttons

Implement a `switch` statement in the function according to the pattern shown in Listing 5.7.

```
changeTheme : function(oEvent) {
var sTheme = oEvent.getSource().getId();
switch(sTheme)
  {
```

```
    case "GOLD":
      sTheme = "sap_goldreflection";
      break;
// etc.
  }
  sap.ui.getCore().applyTheme(sTheme);
},
```

Listing 5.7   Event Processing

You will find the complete solution (ZUI5_SAMPLESOLUTION_THEM-ING) in the downloadable content of this book. Now that you've learned about all the elements of the bootstrap, we'll cover the options SAPUI5 provides for binding data to a UI element.

5.2   Data Binding Models

Through interaction with the SAP system, the particular challenge for an SAPUI5 application is to display data from the backend and, if possible, to communicate to the backend and keep in sync changes in the frontend due to user interactions. For this purpose, SAPUI5 provides various *data binding* options. In the object-oriented world, this is known as the mapping of data (for example, in XML or in JSON) to objects or the representation of data by objects. Data binding is a technique that links two data or information sources together in order to keep them in sync. Bidirectional binding also automatically updates the application data in the associated model when data is changed (for example, due to user input).

Data binding is always required in the SAPUI5 context if, for example, you want to display data from the SAP backend in a relevant control. This includes, for example, tables or dropdown fields, as shown in Figure 5.7.

SAPUI5 supports four data binding patterns:

▶ JSON model

▶ XML model

▶ Resource model

▶ OData model

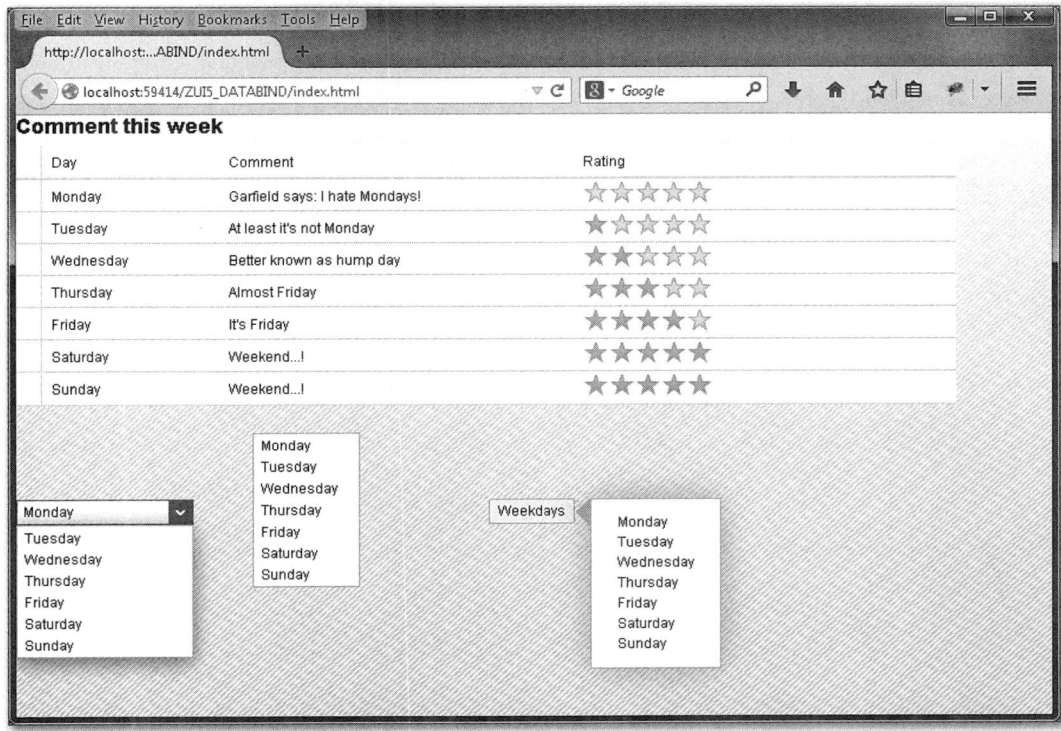

Figure 5.7 Examples of Controls with Data Binding

Regardless of the pattern you use, the data binding principle is always the same:

1. Data definition
2. Create an instance of the data binding model
3. Bind a model to the UI control

The data definition can take place either locally or from an SAP system. Depending on the selected data model, generate a corresponding model, load the data into the model, and bind it to the UI control. A few peculiarities arise for each data model, which will be discussed now in greater detail.

5.2.1 JSON Model

JSON
You have already learned about the JSON format in the previous chapters. To enable you to use the relevant model, you first need to create an instance of the JSON Model:

```
var oModel = new sap.ui.model.json.JSONModel();
```

Next, you bind the data source to the model; <URL> is a placeholder for the path to the JSON file:

```
oModel.loadData("<URL>");
```

You can now bind the data from the model to a UI control—for example, to a table control:

```
oTable.setModel(oModel);
oTable.bindRows("<Path in JSON>");
```

Relative path
specifications
The path in JSON is composed according to its attributes; in Listing 5.8, you see a menu for calendar week 43.

```
{
Week:{
    name: "CW43",
    info: {
            Motto: "Thai Weeks",
            SetMeal: 2
            },
    Weekdays: [{
      name: "Monday",
      SetMeal1: "Chicken with noodles",
      SetMeal2: "Bami goreng"
          },{
      name: "Tuesday",
      ...
    }]
  }
}
```

Listing 5.8 JSON Example

If you would like to know, for example, how much ordinary food was offered this week, the path would be */Week/info/Ordinary food*. If you already set the context to "Week" in data binding, this results in the relative path */info/Ordinary food*.

Create a local JSON file with information about the weekdays and bind it to a table control. In Eclipse, create the project ZUI5_JSON without an Initial View, and use the context menu to create a new folder in the *WebContent* directory as shown in Figure 5.8.

Example using JSON

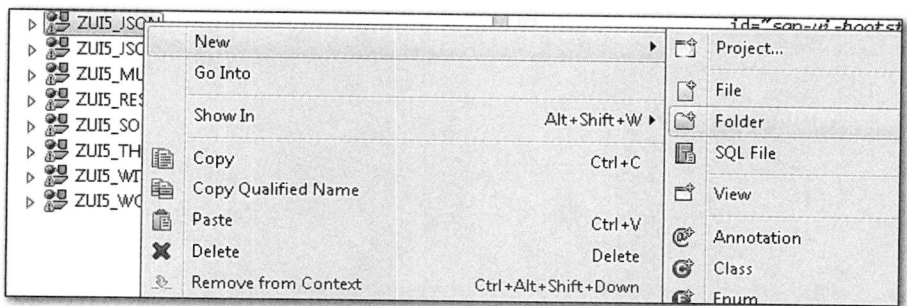

Figure 5.8 Creating a New Folder

Name the folder "json" and click FINISH (see Figure 5.9).

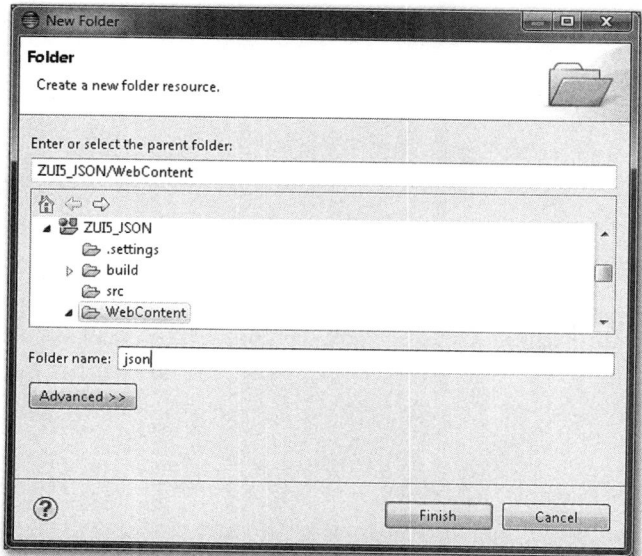

Figure 5.9 Creating the json Folder

Next, use the context menu to create a file within the new *json* folder (see Figure 5.10).

In the following dialog box, name the file "week.json," and then click FINISH. In the *WebContent* directory, you should see the path JSON • WEEK.JSON, as shown in Figure 5.11.

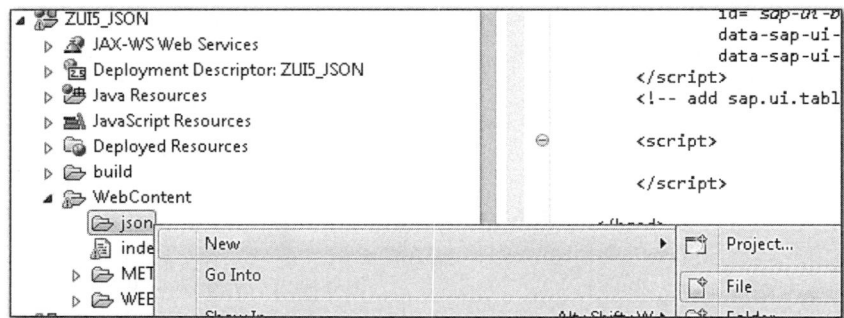

Figure 5.10 Creating a File

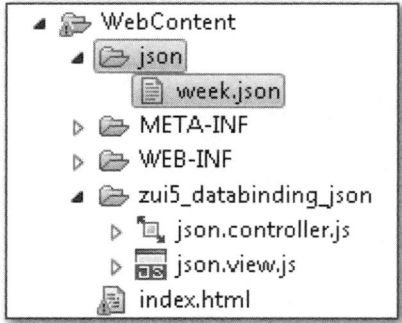

Figure 5.11 Path to the JSON File

Insert the following in the JSON file from Listing 5.9 (let's show an abridged version here for the sake of clarity; you can download the complete listing from the book's web page).

```
{
    "week": [
        {
            "we_day": "Monday",
```

```
                "we_comment": "Garfield says: I hate Mondays!",
                "we_rating": 0
            },
            {
                "we_day": "Tuesday",
                "we_comment": "At least it's not Monday",
                "we_rating": 1
            }
// etc.
    ]
}
```

Listing 5.9 week.json

To bind the JSON file to the table control, do the following:

JSON binding

► Create an instance of the JSON model

► Read a file in the model

► Bind the model to the columns of the table control

Next, create a table control within the View and bind the JSON file to the control (see Listing 5.10). This listing was shortened for clarity; you can download the complete listing from the book's web page. Remember to specify the table library in the bootstrap (*sap.ui.table*).

```
<!DOCTYPE HTML>
<html>
    <head>
        <TITLE>JSON-Databinding</TITLE>
        <meta charset="UTF-8">
        <meta http-equiv="X-UA-Compatible" content="IE=edge">
    <script src="resources/sap-ui-core.js"
            id="sap-ui-bootstrap"
            data-sap-ui-libs="sap.ui.commons, sap.ui.table"
            data-sap-ui-theme="sap_bluecrystal">
    </script>
    <script>
// Create instance of JSON model
    var oModel = new sap.ui.model.json.JSONModel();
// Load JSON in model
    oModel.loadData("json/week.json");
```

```
//Create instance of table control
 var oTable = new sap.ui.table.Table({
    title: "Comment this week",
    visibleRowCount: 7,
    firstVisibleRow: 0
});

    //First column "Day"
    oTable.addColumn(new sap.ui.table.Column({
        label: new sap.ui.commons.Label({text: "day"}),
        template: new
        sap.ui.commons.TextView().bindProperty(
                            "text", "we_day"),
        width: "150px"
    }));
    //Second column "Comment"
    oTable.addColumn(new sap.ui.table.Column({
        label: new sap.ui.commons.Label(
            {text: "Comment"}),
            template: new
            sap.ui.commons.TextView().bindProperty(
                            "Text", "we_comment"),
            width: "300px"
    }));

// abbreviated

    //Bind model to table control
    oTable.setModel(oModel);
    oTable.bindRows("/week");

    oTable.placeAt("content");
</script>
</head>
<body class="sapUiBody" role="application">
    <div id="content"></div>
</body>
</html>
```

Listing 5.10 JSON Data Binding

Note in this example that for the `RatingIndicator` control, you have to convert the value from JSON to the `float` format.

Now, check in the project in the SAP backend, or view the result in the Eclipse preview (see Figure 5.12).

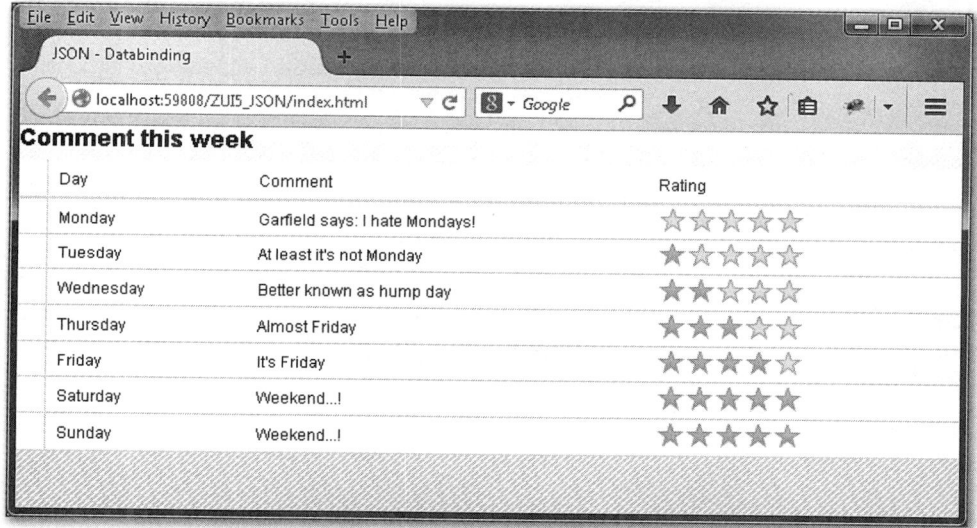

Figure 5.12 Data Binding with JSON

As you can see, the information from JSON is "bound" via the data binding to the corresponding columns and rows of the table and is displayed. The most common errors when binding are:

▸ An incorrect path specification

▸ Uppercase and lowercase issues (JavaScript is case sensitive!)

▸ Invalid JSON format

In the event of an error, first check the JSON via the web console (see Figure 5.13) and compare the path as well as the uppercase and lowercase characters against your implementation.

JSON Validator   If you can't find an error here, then check whether a valid JSON is involved in the transfer. Under *www.jsonlint.com*, you will find a validator that will indicate the relevant point in JSON in the event of an error.

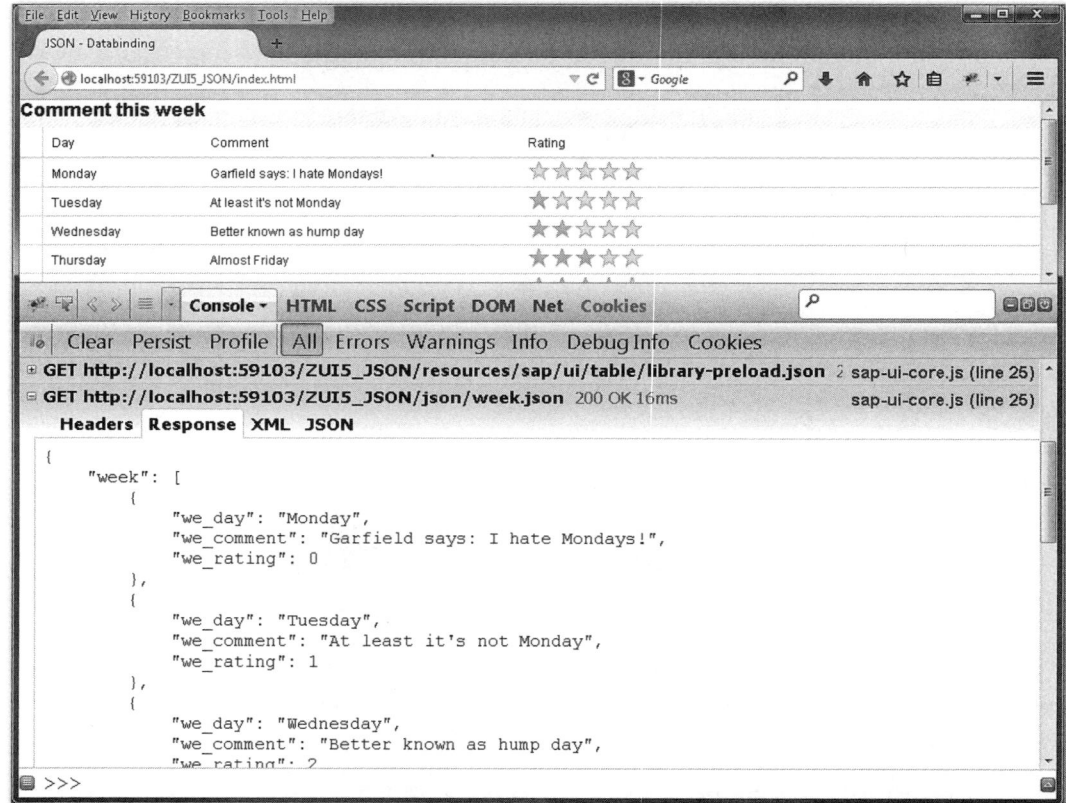

Figure 5.13   JSON in the Web Console

You can also view the binding in the Document Object Model. In the example in Figure 5.14, you will find the values bound to the control under the path OTABLE • MBINDINGINFOS • ROWS • BINDING • OLIST.

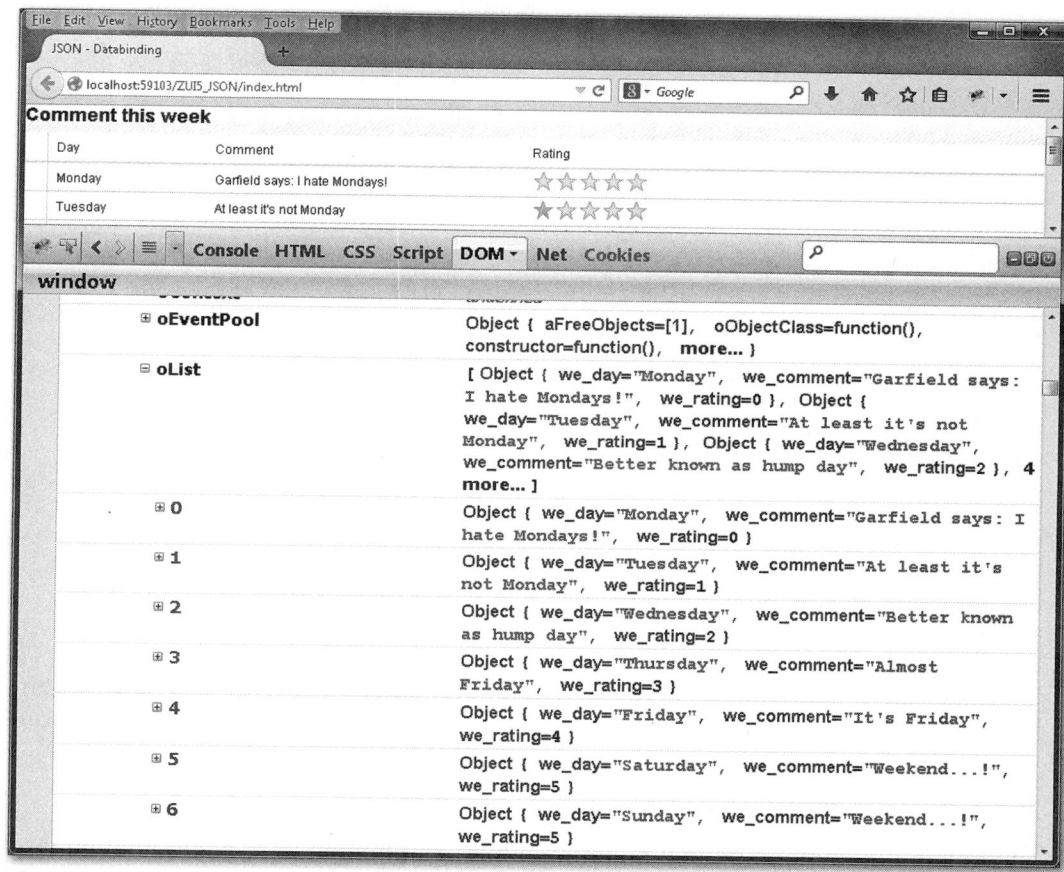

Figure 5.14 DOM

5.2.2 XML Model

You can use the XML Model almost analogous to the JSON Model. There XML binding are only two differences: First, the file must be an XML file; second, you must omit the root node of the XML file for the data binding path. You create the instance for the model via the following statement:

```
var oModel = new sap.ui.model.xml.XMLModel();
```

Let's assume that you would like to read the information from the XML file in Listing 5.11; this is in the *xml\week.xml* directory.

```
<week>
<days>
.....<day>Monday</day>
.....<comment>Garfield says: I hate Mondays!</comment>
.....<rating>0</rating>
</days>
...
```

Listing 5.11 XML with Information About the Weekdays

Creating instance

Similar to the previous JSON example, create an instance of the XML Model and use the `loadData` method to load it in the model:

```
var oModel = new sap.ui.model.xml.XMLModel();
oModel.loadData("xml/week.xml");
```

In contrast to JSON, you have to omit the `root` node—`<week>` in this example—when actually binding the XML Model. For the binding, this results in the following:

```
oTable.setModel(oModel);
oTable.bindRows("/days/");
```

Example

As a small exercise, now create the project ZUI5_BINDING_XML. In the *WebContent* directory, create an *xml* folder with a *week.xml* file, and insert the XML according to the schema from Listing 5.11 (you can download the complete XML file from the book's web page).

Create an XML Model instead of the JSON Model, read the XML into the model, and then bind it to a table control. Make sure that you omit the `root` node when binding.

5.2.3 Resource Model

Multilingual capability

The Resource Model is used as a kind of adapter to manage several thematically related sources. This is helpful if, for example, you would like to create and manage texts in a language-dependent manner. You create the instance according to the following schema:

```
this.oLangu = new sap.ui.model.resource.ResourceModel(
{ bundleUrl : "translations/translation.properties",
  "bundleLocale":"en"});
```

The attribute `bundleURL` specifies the path to the relevant directory, and `bundleLocale` specifies the language. In this example, this indicates that the language files were created under the path TRANSLATIONS with the name *translation[LANGUAGE].properties*. Note that the files must have the extension *.properties*. The *.properties* file itself is created according to the key value schema.

Bind the model under an ID — i18n in this example — to the Core Model:

```
sap.ui.getCore().setModel(this.oLangu, "i18n");
```

Usually, internationalization is abbreviated to the numeronym *i18n* because there are 18 letters between the "i" and the "n" in the word *internationalization*. In your UI controls, you can now bind the model under the ID i18n to the displayed text:

i18n

```
var oText = new sap.ui.commons.TextView(
{"text":"{i18n>[TEXT-ID]})
```

To illustrate the Resource Model, create a new project, ZUI5_RESOURCE. Under the *WebContent* directory, create a *translations* folder in which you create the two files *translation_de.properties* and *translation_en.properties*:

Example

```
BUKRS = Buchungskreis
MD = Stammdaten
```

The *translation_en.properties* file contains the following English terms:

```
BUKRS = Company Code
MD = Master Data
```

For the language files, note that the ID has to be the same in all *.properties* files. Of course, you can work with the typical SAP text-001, text-002, and so on at this point, but this is on a more readable form for this example. This also has the advantage in the source code that you can subsequently see from the ID BUKRS what is in this field. With the numbered version, you always have to consult the *.properties* file if in doubt.

Load the relevant *.properties* file, depending on the language, by creating an instance of the Resource Model and binding this model under an ID (in Listing 5.12, this is i18n) to the Core Model.

```
this.oLangu = new sap.ui.model.resource.ResourceModel(
    {bundleUrl : "translations/translation.properties",
    "bundleLocale":"en"});
sap.ui.getCore().setModel(this.oLangu, "i18n");
},
```

Listing 5.12   Resource Model

In this example, the texts are displayed in English; if you set `"bundleLocale":"de"`, the texts are displayed in German. In this example, you bind the language-dependent texts to two Text Views. This results in the complete Listing 5.13.

```
this.oLangu = new sap.ui.model.resource.ResourceModel({
    bundleUrl : "translations/translation.properties",
    "bundleLocale":"en"
    });

    sap.ui.getCore().setModel(this.oLangu, "i18n");
// Layout
var oMatrix = new sap.ui.commons.layout.MatrixLayout({
        layoutFixed : true,
        width : '400px',
        columns : 2,
        widths : ['200px', '200px',] });

var oText = new sap.ui.commons.TextView(
        { "text":"{i18n>BUKRS}" });
var oText2 = new sap.ui.commons.TextView(
        { "text":"{i18n>MD}" });

oMatrix.createRow(oText, oText2); oMatrix.placeAt("content");
```

Listing 5.13   Resource Binding

Determining language dynamically In this example, the language is hard-coded. Because the logon language in the SAP backend is saved in the URL parameter `sap-ui-language`, you can use this parameter to read the language. This results in Listing 5.14.

```
var sLangu = function(){
        var sPageURL = window.location.search.substring(1);
        var sURLVariables = sPageURL.split('&');
        for (var i = 0; i < sURLVariables.length; i++)
        {
```

```
        var sParameterName = sURLVariables[i].split('=');
         if (sParameterName[0] == 'sap-ui-language')
         {
           return sParameterName[1];
         }
     }
};

this.oLangu = new sap.ui.model.resource.ResourceModel(
  {bundleUrl : "translations/translation.properties",
   "bundleLocale":sLangu});
...
```

Listing 5.14 Language Change Based on the Logon Language

Depending on the SAP logon language, this reads the relevant *.properties* file and binds it to the model.

Fortunately, this function is already included in the core component, so that you can use the statement:

```
var sLangu =
        sap.ui.getCore().getConfiguration().getLanguage();
```

to determine the relevant language.

For large applications, it is sometimes difficult to keep the individual *.properties* files in sync. Section 5.3 will show you how to provide an application in several languages by using the translation tools.

5.2.4 OData Model

Open Data Protocol (OData) is a protocol that is published by Microsoft. The protocol is based on HTTP and builds on the older protocols Open Database Connectivity (ODBC) and Java Database Connectivity (JDBC). OData has been implemented primarily for the CRUD operations (Create, Read, Update, and Delete).

Open Data Protocol

As in the preceding examples, you must first create an instance of the OData Model:

```
var oModel = new sap.ui.model.odata.ODataModel(<URL>);
```

173

odata.org   Under *www.odata.org*, you will find examples of the OData Services. If, for example, you call the service *http://services.odata.org/V3/OData/OData.svc/*, an XML file with the metadata of this service is displayed (see Figure 5.15).

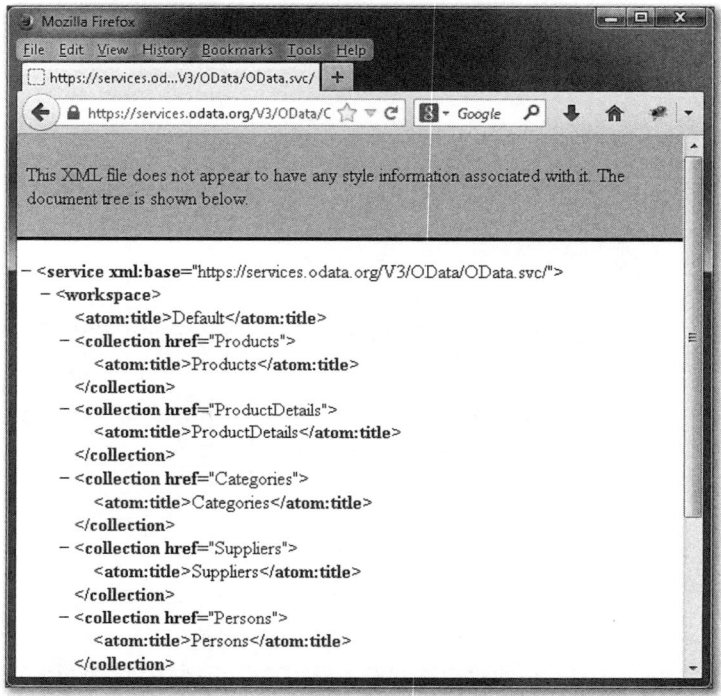

Figure 5.15   OData Service Example

Here, each XML node represents a path; for this service, there is /Products, which you can bind to a control:

```
oTable.bindRows({ path: "/Products });
```

SAP Gateway   SAP provides OData services with SAP Gateway; in Chapter 6, you will implement an example in which you use an OData service of the SAP Gateway.

You have now learned about the four models JSON, XML, Resource, and OData, with which you can bind data to a model depending on the input format of the data stream. The only question that remains concerns *what*, or *in which form*, you can bind the data to a UI control.

5.2.5 Binding Options

After the model has been created, you can assign the model to the core element or specific controls with the `setModel` method.

What happens now if you have bound two models, one bound to the core element and one to the Control or to the View? The relevant model for a control is the element which is located nearest to the `root` (UI area; DOM). If no model is found along this path, the model that is located in the core element will be used.

```
//Model at Core
sap.ui.getCore().setModel(oModel);

//Model at UI level
var oMainArea = sap.ui.getCore().getUIArea("main");
oMainArea.setModel(oModel);

//Model on a control
var oTable = sap.ui.getCore().byId("table");
oTable.setModel(oModel);
```

SAPUI5 provides three binding options:

▶ Property binding

▶ Aggregation binding

▶ Element binding

Property Binding

Most properties of a control can be bound to a model via *property binding*. There are three options for binding objects from the model to the property of the control: within curly brackets in the constructor, via the `bindProperty` method, or via the path.

Property Binding

▶ Curly brackets:
```
var oControl = new sap.ui.commons.TextView({
  controlProperty: "{modelProperty}"
});
```

175

- `bindProperty` method:
  ```
  oControl.bindProperty(
      "controlProperty", "modelProperty");
  ```
- Path:
  ```
  var oControl = new sap.ui.commons.TextView({
    controlProperty: { path: "modelProperty" }
  });
  ```

Aggregation Binding

Aggregation binding

With *aggregation binding*, you bind a collection of values to a control element. This control element serves as a kind of *data container* and represents a template of the data to be displayed (for example, line type). You can then bind this *template* to a multiline UI element (for example, a table; see Figure 5.16).

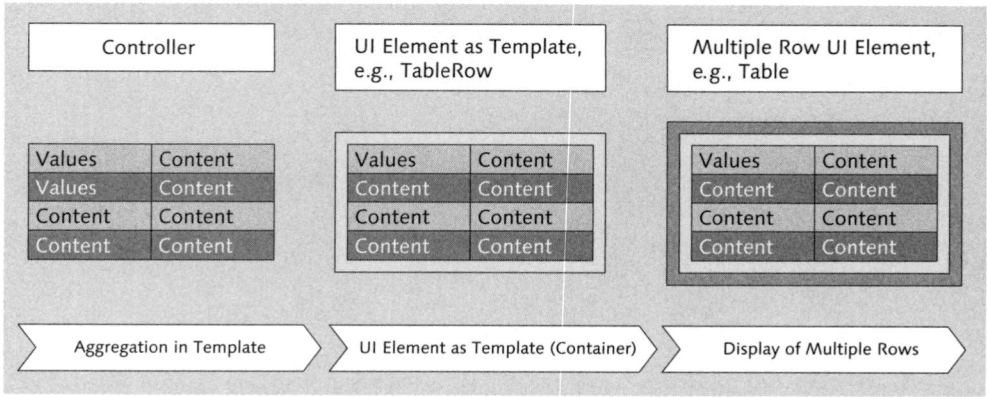

Figure 5.16 Aggregation Binding

Example

If you would like to display a ComboBox, this consists of multiple entries. Bind the aggregate to a ListItem that serves as a template for the actual ComboBox (see Listing 5.15).

```
var oItemTemplate = new sap.ui.core.ListItem({
        text: "{aggrProperty}"
      });
```

```
var oComboBox = new sap.ui.commons.ComboBox({
  items: { path:"/modelAggregation",
          template: oItemTemplate }
});
```

Listing 5.15 Aggregation Binding

Most multiline UI controls also provide a relevant `bindAggregation` method:

```
oComboBox.bindAggregation(
  "items",
  "/modelAggregation", oItemTemplate );
```

To understand this effect better, you will create a page for which an error log is to be displayed. Because you cannot know how many errors will be transferred in the log during the implementation, you must bind the collection to a UI template control via aggregation binding, and display it via a `RowRepeater` control.

In Eclipse, create the project ZUI5_AGGR_BIND and, below its *WebContent* folder, create the *log* folder containing the *error.json* file with the content shown in Listing 5.16. This listing was shortened for clarity; you can download the complete listing from the book's web page.

```
{ "data" : [
    {
      "index": "0",
      "level": "Success",
      "description": "Performance is good"
    },
    {
      "index": "1",
      "level": "Warning",
      "description": "Service not available."
    }
  ]}
```

Listing 5.16 error.json

Create an instance of a JSON Model, load the file in the model, and bind the data to a `RowRepeater` control (see Listing 5.17).

```
<script>
  // Create instance of JSON Model
  var oModel = new sap.ui.model.json.JSONModel();
  // Load JSON in Model
  oModel.loadData("log/error.json");
  // Bind Model to core
  sap.ui.getCore().setModel(oModel);
  // Create template of message type
  var oRowTemplate = new sap.ui.commons.Message(
                  {   text: "{description}",
                      type: "{level}"
  });

  // Create RowRepeater and bind message template
  var oRowRepeater = new sap.ui.commons.RowRepeater();
  oRowRepeater.bindRows("/data", oRowTemplate);
  oRowRepeater.placeAt("content");

</script>
</head>
<body class="sapUiBody" role="application">
    <div id="content"></div>
</body>
</html>
```

Listing 5.17   Aggregation Binding

Execute this example either in the preview function or in the ABAP back-end after uploading it. As you can see in Figure 5.17, the entire error log is displayed due to the aggregation binding.

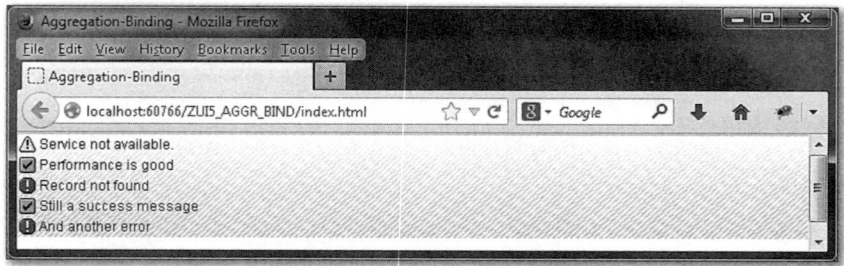

Figure 5.17   Aggregation Binding

Element Binding

Element binding enables an element to be bound to an object in the
Model, which, in turn, represents the context for the relative binding
to a control. You need this parent–child binding whenever you want to
display a detailed list for selected header information (for example, purchase orders and the associated purchase order items; see Figure 5.18).

Element Binding

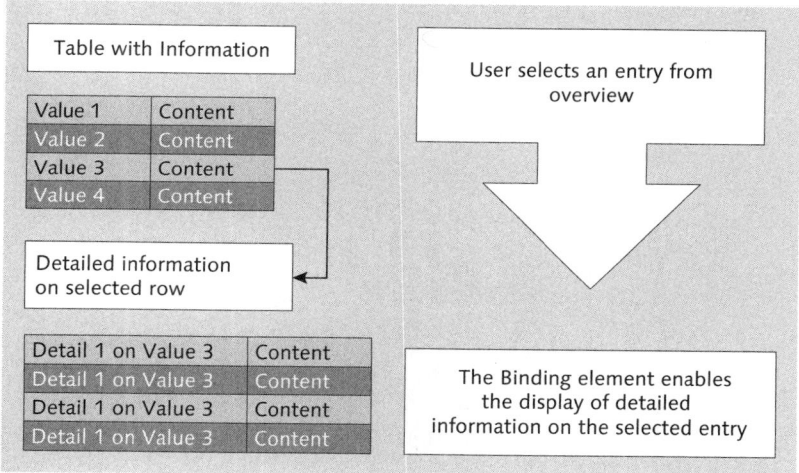

Figure 5.18 Element Binding for Drill-Down Functions

In the following example, you create an admittedly somewhat simple
menu with the various ordinary food items per day. You then read the
file, and display the weekdays along with the number of ordinary food
items. If you select an entry from the table, the meals of the relevant day
are displayed in the table below.

Example

Create the project ZUI5_BIND_ELEM, and below its *WebContent* folder
create the *json* folder containing the *menu.json* file with the content from
Listing 5.18 (abridged; you can download the complete listing from the
book's web page).

```
{
    "weekdays": [
        {
            "day": "Monday",
            "no_meals": "2",
```

```
                "id": "1"
        },
        {

            "day": "Tuesday",
            "no_meals": "3",
            "id": "2"

        }
    ],
    "meals": [
        {
            "MealNo": "1",
            "dayId": "1",
            "items": "Burger with french fries"
        },
        {

            "MealNo": "2",
            "dayId": "1",
            "items": "French fries with Burger"

        },
        {

            "MealNo": "3",
            "dayId": "2",
            "items": "French fries"

        }
    ]
}
```

Listing 5.18 Menu.json

Listing 5.19 is created for the actual page. This listing was shortened for clarity; you can download the complete listing from the book's web page.

```
<script>
var oModel = new sap.ui.model.json.JSONModel();
oModel.loadData("json/menu.json");
sap.ui.getCore().setModel(oModel);

// Table with weekdays
var oTable = new sap.ui.table.Table({
    width           : "100%",
    title           : "Weekdays",
    visibleRowCount : 5,
    selectionMode   : sap.ui.table.SelectionMode.Single,
```

```
        editable        : false
});

oTable.addColumn(new sap.ui.table.Column({
    label: new sap.ui.commons.Label({text: "ID"}),
    template: new sap.ui.commons.TextField({value:"{id}"}),
    visible: false
}));
oTable.addColumn(new sap.ui.table.Column({
    label: new sap.ui.commons.Label({text: "Weekday"}),
    template: new sap.ui.commons.TextField({value:"{day}"})
}));

oTable.bindRows("/weekdays");
oTable.placeAt("master");

// Display of meals
var oTable2 = new sap.ui.table.Table({
    title           : "Meals",
    visibleRowCount : 3,
    width           : "100%",
    selectionMode   : sap.ui.table.SelectionMode.Single,
    editable        : false
});

oTable2.addColumn(new sap.ui.table.Column({
  template: new sap.ui.commons.TextField({value:"{dayId}"}),
  visible: false
}));

oTable2.addColumn(new sap.ui.table.Column({
  label: new sap.ui.commons.Label({text: "Description"}),
  template: new sap.ui.commons.TextField({value:"{items}"})
}));
oTable2.bindRows("/meals");
oTable2.placeAt("slave");

oTable.attachRowSelectionChange(function(oEvent){
// Read binding context of main table
    var selectedRowContext =
                    oEvent.getParameter("rowContext");
    var selectedClientId =
            oModel.getProperty("id", selectedRowContext);
```

```
// Filter meals depending on context
var listBinding = oTable2.getBinding();
var oFilter = new sap.ui.model.Filter(
                "dayId",
                sap.ui.model.FilterOperator.EQ,
                selectedClientId);
  listBinding.filter([oFilter]);
});

</script>
</head>
  <body class="sapUiBody" role="application">
    <div id="master"></div>
    <div id="slave"></div>
  </body>
</html>
```

Listing 5.19 Menu by Element Binding

If you execute this example in the browser and select an entry in the upper table, the meals of the selected day are displayed in the table below (see Figure 5.19).

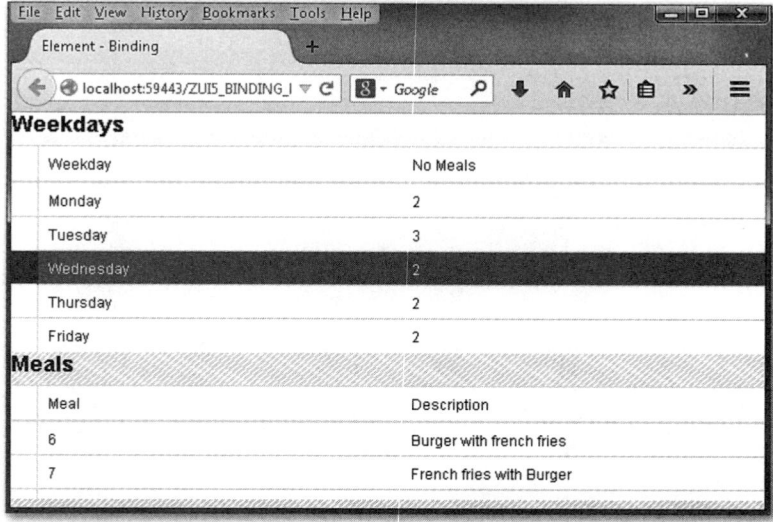

Figure 5.19 Element Binding

Named Binding

In SAPUI5, it is possible to bind multiple models to one element. You achieve this *named binding* by assigning an ID to each model (see Listing 5.20). You can use this ID to access the model in a targeted manner.

Named binding

```
var oModel = new sap.ui.model.json.JSONModel();
oModel.loadData("<URL>");
sap.ui.getCore().setModel(oModel, "Model ID");

// Binding
    // Property Binding
        oText.bindValue("Model ID>/[PATH]");
    // Aggregation Binding
        oListItem.bindProperty("text", "Model ID>[PATH] ");
        oComboBox.bindItems("Model ID>/[PATH] ", oListItem);
```
Listing 5.20 *Model with ID*

You already encountered this principle in Section 5.2.3. You stored the model there under the ID i18n:

```
sap.ui.getCore().setModel(this.oLangu, "i18n");
```

With the extended data binding syntax, you can not only assign the path or the property of a model, but also specify format functions, type functions, sorting, or filters when binding due to this special syntax (see Listing 5.21).

Extended data binding

```
// Extended data binding as property
  {
    path: "path/model/property",
    formatter: funcCallback,
    type: oType
  }
// Extended data binding as aggregation
  {
    path: "path/model/aggregation",
    template: oTemplate,
    sorter: oSorter
  {
```
Listing 5.21 *Extended Data Binding*

In the application example in Chapter 7, you will use the extended data binding syntax to convert the date fields directly into a readable format when binding.

In the previous examples, you always bound an element to a UI control. The *complex binding* enhancement also enables multiple values to be bound to a UI element. Complex binding is still in the experimental stage, and so you must declare it explicitly in the bootstrap (see Listing 5.22).

```
<script src="resources/sap-ui-core.js"
  id="sap-ui-bootstrap"
  data-sap-ui-libs="sap.ui.commons"
  data-sap-ui-theme="sap_bluecrystal"
  data-sap-ui-xx-bindingSyntax = "complex">
</script>
```

Listing 5.22 Bootstrap Complex Binding

As a result, it's possible to bind multiple elements to a UI control (see Listing 5.23).

```
<script>
  // Create instance of JSON Model
  var oModel = new sap.ui.model.json.JSONModel();

  // Create JSON
  oModel.setJSON(
      '{ "data": [{"TITLE": "Mr.",'+
      '"FNAME": "John", "LNAME": "Doe"},' +
      '{"TITLE": "Mrs.", "FNAME": "Jane",  '+
      '"LNAME": "Doe"}]}');
  // Bind model to core
    sap.ui.getCore().setModel(oModel);

  // Complex binding
    var oItemTemplate = new sap.ui.core.ListItem("name",
      {text: "{TITLE} {FNAME} {LNAME}"}
    );

    var oComboBox = new sap.ui.commons.ComboBox(
      {items: {path: "/data",
```

```
          template: oItemTemplate}}
    );

    oComboBox.placeAt("content");
  </script>
```

Listing 5.23 Complex Binding

As you can see in Figure 5.20, several items of information are displayed in a control as a result.

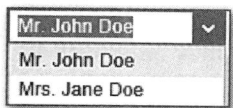

Figure 5.20 Multiple Elements in a Control

5.3 Multilingual Applications

In Section 5.2.3, you learned about the Resource Model, which you can use to bind multiple *.properties* files to a model and thus provide an application in multiple languages. Managing these *.properties* files can quickly become very complex for large applications; therefore, it's better to use the translation tools in the SAP backend.

In order to be able to use this function, new translation object types are required in the SAP system; implement SAP Note 1686090 in your system.   **SAP Note**

For translating in the SAP backend, the *.properties* file must meet certain conditions:

▸ The file must contain a unique GUID (Globally Unique Identifier).

▸ Each text must be provided with a text type and text length.

You can generate the GUID with the ABAP program /UI5/TEXT_FILE_   **Generating GUID**
GEN_TRANS_KEY; this program generates a GUID as a translation key (see Figure 5.21).

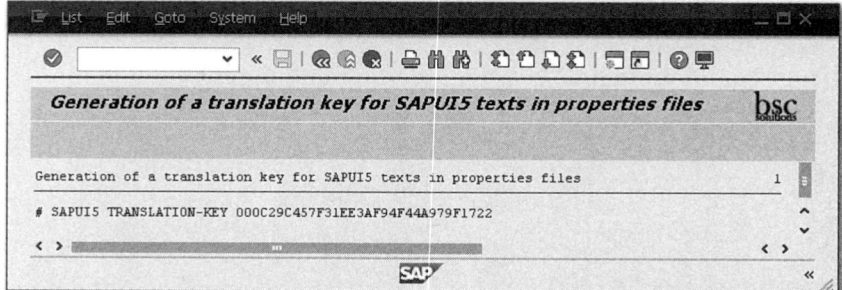

Figure 5.21 Generated GUID

The text types listed in Table 5.2 are available up to a length of 120 characters.

Text type	Description
XACT	Access
XALT	Alternative text
XBCB	Breadcrumb step
XBLI	Listing
XBUT	Button text
XCAP	Caption
XCEL	Cell
XCKL	Checkbox
XCOL	Table column headings
XCRD	Tab page
XDAT	Navigation text
XFLD	Label
XFRM	Box
XGLS	Term
XGRP	Group title
XHED	Heading
XLGD	Legend
XLNK	Hyperlink

Table 5.2 Text Types up to a Length of 120 Characters

Text type	Description
XLOG	Log entry
XLST	List box entry
XMEN	Menu
XMIT	Menu entry
XMSG	Message text
XRBL	Radio button
XRMP	Roadmap step
XROW	Heading of the table row
XSEL	Selection text
XTBS	Tab page text
XTIT	Table heading
XTND	Tree node
XTOL	Tooltip
XTXT	General text

Table 5.2 Text Types up to a Length of 120 Characters (Cont.)

The text types listed in Table 5.3 are available for texts with a length in excess of 120 characters.

Text type	Description
YACT	Access
YBLI	Listing
YDEF	Definition
YDES	Description
YEXP	Explanation
YFAA	FAQ answer
YFAQ	FAQ
YGLS	Glossary
YINF	Information
YINS	Statement

Table 5.3 Text Types for a Text Length in Excess of 120 Characters

Text type	Description
YLOG	Log entry
YMSE	Error message
YMSG	Message text
YMSI	Information (message)
YMSW	Warning message
YTEC	Technical long text
YTIC	Ticker
YTXT	General text

Table 5.3 Text Types for a Text Length in Excess of 120 Characters (Cont.)

You can use NOTR to indicate texts that are not to be translated, which is comparable to the pseudocomment #EC NOTEXT in ABAP.

Maximum length   As in ABAP, you can specify the maximum length of the text element after the text type. The maximum length should be adjusted according to the given UI design so that there are no unnecessary line breaks on the page after the translation. The *.properties* file for the example from Section 5.2.3 would then look like Listing 5.24.

```
# SAPUI5 TRANSLATION KEY 000C29C457F31EE3AF94F44A979F1722
#XTXT,20
BUKRS = Company Code
#XTXT,20
MD = Master Data
```

Listing 5.24 .properties File

It's important at this point that you write the texts in the language in which you also uploaded the resources to the SAP backend (the default system language).

Create, for example, the project ZUI5_ABAP_TRANS in Eclipse in a manner similar to the procedure in Section 5.2.3. Then use the program /UI5/TEXT_FILE_GEN_TRANS_KEY to generate a GUID, and in the *translations* folder create the *translation.properties* file with the content from Listing 5.24. Note that you do not have to include any language identifier in the file name at this time. You can copy the *index.html* file from the example in Section 5.2.3. Upload the project to the SAP backend.

After uploading successfully, call Transaction SE63 (initial screen for translating). Navigate to the selection of object types via the menu path TRANSLATION • ABAP OBJECTS • SHORT TEXTS. Translation

Under object type U5, you will find the SAPUI5 text elements, which are shown in Figure 5.22.

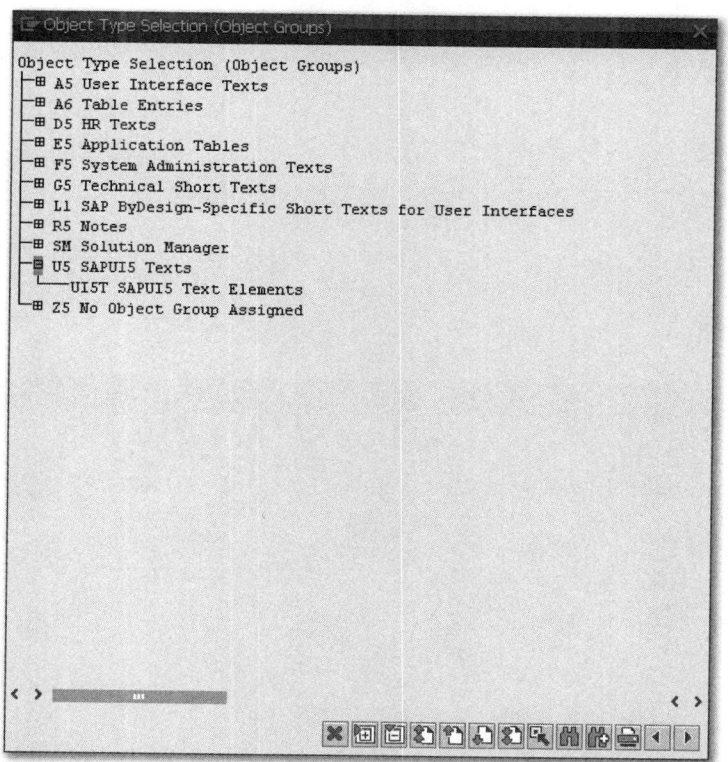

Figure 5.22 SAPUI5 Text Elements

Enter the generated GUID in OBJECT NAME, and select the source language (ENUS in this example) and the desired target language (DEDE in this example; see Figure 5.23). Selecting
translation object

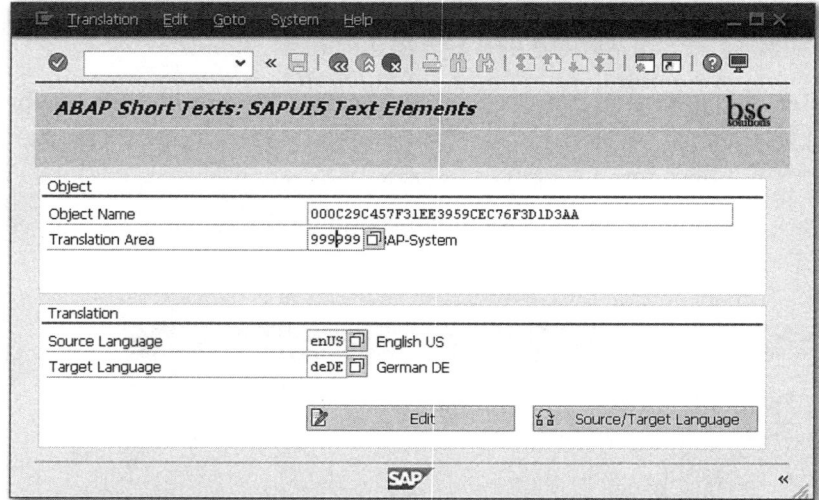

Figure 5.23   Selecting the Translation Object

Click EDIT. All translation-relevant texts are displayed as a result (see Figure 5.24).

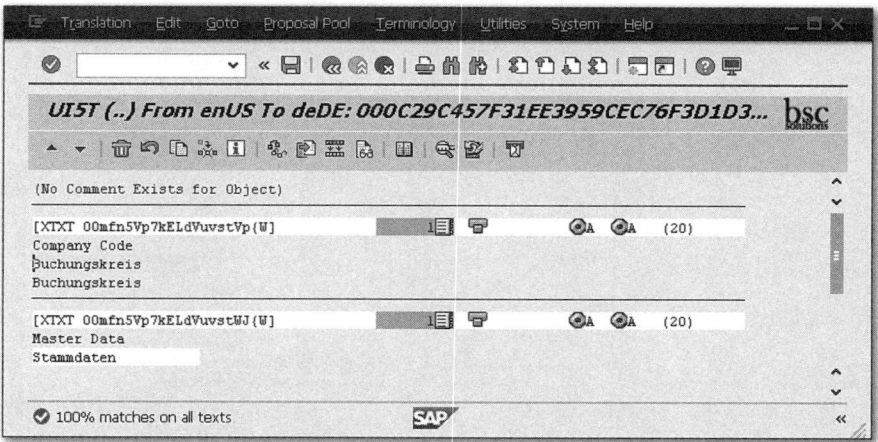

Figure 5.24   Translation

Translate the displayed texts, and save the translations as default texts. If you now call the application, the texts are displayed depending on the logon language (see Figure 5.25).

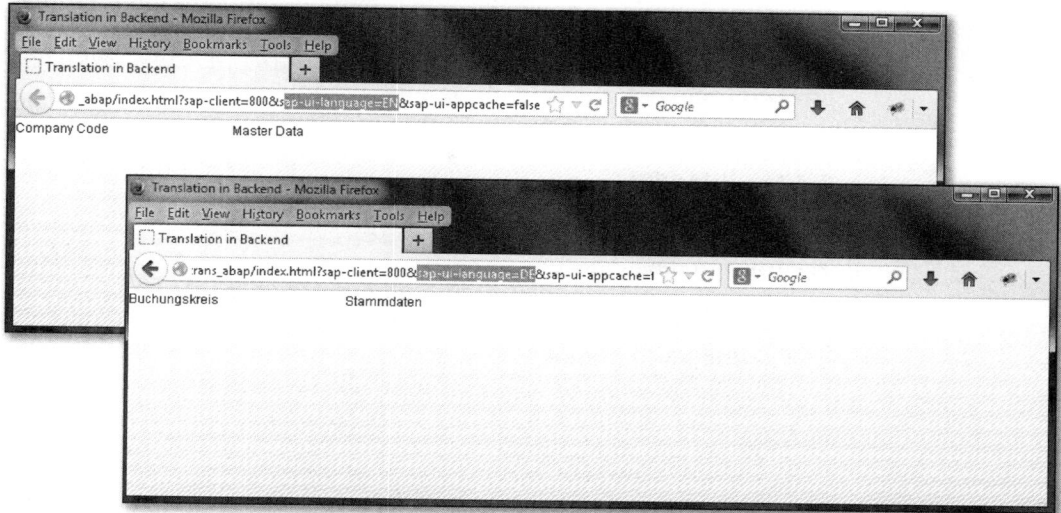

Figure 5.25 Language-Dependent Display

The translation in the backend has two major advantages: First, you have   **Advantages**
to maintain only one *.properties* file, and thus there is no risk of forgetting
texts; second, previously translated texts are displayed as default values
for the translation in the SAP backend.

5.4   SAPUI5 Data Typing

In SAPUI5, you can specify the data type for the object in the model   **Data type**
when binding. Thus, the transferred values are automatically converted
into the desired format by the runtime environment.

The following data types are provided by the SAPUI5 runtime environment:

▶ sap.ui.model.type.Integer

▶ sap.ui.model.type.Float

▶ sap.ui.model.type.String

▶ sap.ui.model.type.Boolean

▶ sap.ui.model.type.Date

▶ sap.ui.model.type.Time

▶ sap.ui.model.type.DateTime

Conversion error

If the conversion is not possible, the error `sap.ui. model.FormatException` (format error) or the error `sap.ui. model.ParseException` (parse error) is triggered.

5.4.1 Integers

Integer data type

Integers are represented via the data type `sap.ui.model.type.Integer`. The value in the model must be a number, and, depending on the bound property of the UI element, it is converted as follows:

Conversion

► **Floating-point number**
The value is rounded down via the `Math.floor` function.

► **Integer**
There is no conversion.

► **String**
The value is formatted according to the specified pattern.

The initialization is performed with the statement:

```
var oInt = new sap.ui.model.type.Integer();
```

Formatting

As a formatting option, all options of the class `sap.ui.core.format.NumberFormat` are available:

► `minIntegerDigits`: Minimum number of integer digits

► `maxIntegerDigits`: Maximum number of integer digits

► `minFractionDigits`: Minimum number of fractional digits

► `maxFractionDigits`: Maximum number of fractional digits

► `groupingEnabled`: Enable grouping

► `groupingSeparator`: Group separator (if `groupingEnabled: true`)

► `decimalSeparator`: Decimal separator used

► `plusSign`: Plus sign used

► `minusSign`: Minus sign used

Example

Listing 5.25 shows an example of the `Integer` data type.

```
oInt = new sap.ui.model.type.Integer({
        minIntegerDigits: 1,
```

```
        maxIntegerDigits: 99,
        minFractionDigits: 0,
        maxFractionDigits: 0,
        groupingEnabled: false,
        groupingSeparator: ",",
        decimalSeparator: "."
});
```

Listing 5.25 Example: Integer Data Type with Formatting Specifications

5.4.2 Floating-Point Numbers

Floating-point numbers are represented via the data type `sap.ui.model.`   **Float data type**
`type.float`. The value in the model must be a number, and, depending
on the bound property of the UI element, it is converted as follows:

▶ **Floating-point number**   **Conversion**
There is no conversion.

▶ **Integer**
The value is rounded down via the `Math.floor` function.

▶ **String**
The value is formatted according to the specified pattern.

The initialization is performed with the statement:

```
var oFloat = new sap.ui.model.type.Float();
```

Here, you also have all the options of the class `sap.ui.core.format.`   **Formatting**
`NumberFormat` as formatting options.

5.4.3 Strings

Strings are represented via the data type `sap.ui.model.type.String`.   **String data type**
The value in the model must be a `string`, and, depending on the bound
property of the UI element, it is converted as follows:

▶ **String**   **Conversion**
There is no conversion.

▶ **Integer/floating-point number**
The string is parsed accordingly.

▶ **Boolean**
true and "X" are interpreted as true, and false and " " (space) are interpreted as false.

The initialization is performed with the statement:

```
var oString = new sap.ui.model.type.String();
```

Formatting The following options are available as a parameter:

▶ maxLength: Maximum length of the string.

▶ startsWith: A valid string must start with this prefix; it is case sensitive.

▶ startsWithIgnoreCase: A valid string must start with this prefix; it is not case sensitive.

▶ endsWith: A valid string must end with this suffix; it is case sensitive.

▶ endsWithIgnoreCase: A valid string must end with this suffix; it is case sensitive.

▶ contains: This infix must occur within the string.

▶ equals: Only this value is allowed.

▶ search: A regular expression; the parsed string must result in true.

5.4.4 Boolean Variable

Boolean data type The Boolean variables are represented by the data type sap.ui.model.type.Boolean. The value in the model must be a string, and, depending on the bound property of the UI element, it is converted as follows:

Conversion ▶ **Boolean**
There is no conversion.

▶ **String**
true and "X" are interpreted as true, and false and " " (space) are interpreted as false.

The initialization is performed with the statement:

```
var oBool = new sap.ui.model.type.Boolean();
```

5.4.5 Date

A date is represented by the data type `sap.ui.model.type.Date`. The value in the model must correspond to formatting in the Locale Data Markup Language (LDML). You will find an exact description of the format on the home page of the Unicode Consortium, *http://unicode.org*, under Unicode Locales (CLDR) • LDML Specification (see Figure 5.26).

Date data type

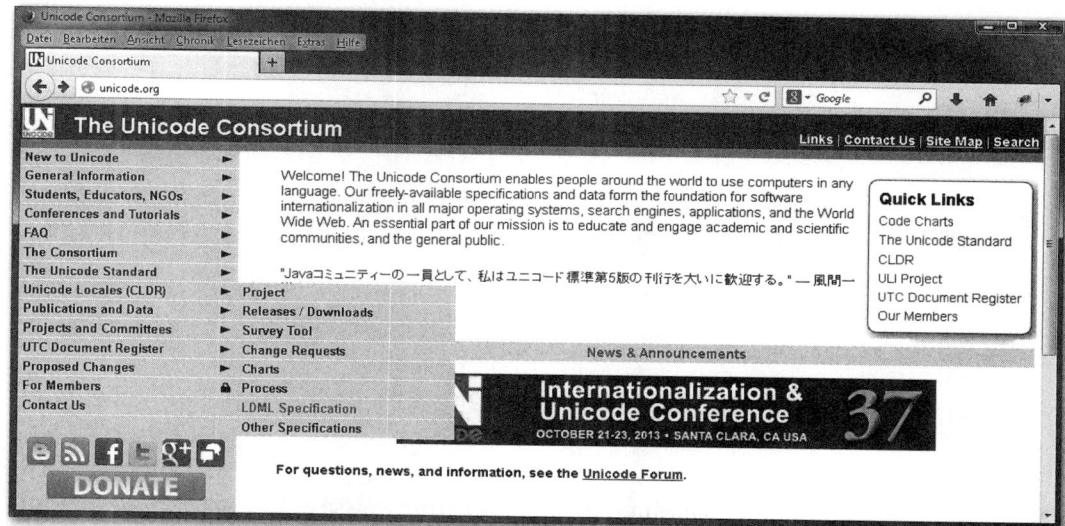

Figure 5.26 LDML Specification

When specifying the output format, you can use either a format in LDML or the predefined formats `short`, `medium`, `long`, or `full`.

The initialization is performed with the statement:

```
var oDate = new sap.ui.model.type.Date();
```

If, for example, the input format is `Timestamp`, and you would like to have the English format MM.DD.YYYY, the complete statement would be as follows:

Conversion

```
oDate = new sap.ui.model.type.Date(
        {source: {pattern: "timestamp"},
         pattern: "mm.dd.yyyy"});
```

In Chapter 7, you will use this typing to convert dates in the internal SAP format YYYYMMDD to the more readable format MM.DD.YYYY.

5.4.6 Time

Time data type
A time is represented by the data type `sap.ui.model.type.Time`; the values must be stated, like the date, in LDML format.

The initialization is performed with the statement:

```
var oTime = new sap.ui.model.type.Time();
```

5.4.7 Date and Time

DateTime data type
A DateTime specification is represented by the data type `sap.ui.model.type.DateTime`; the values must be stated in LDML format in this case also.

The initialization is performed with the statement:

```
var oTime = new sap.ui.model.type.DateTime();
```

5.4.8 Formatter Classes

All previous examples of SAPUI5 data typing were used with a corresponding data binding; the formatter classes can also be used without a corresponding binding. Two formatter classes are currently available:

▶ `sap.ui.core.format.DateFormat`: This class formats a string into a JavaScript Date object and vice versa.

▶ `sap.ui.core.format.NumberFormat`: This class formats a string into a number and vice versa.

5.4.9 Your Own Types

In SAPUI5, you can also define your own types and use them as a formatting or check function in a UI element. In the following example, you have a field in which you must enter a password and, after entering it, you want to check whether it is at least eight characters long and consists of letters and numbers. In this case, you would implement your own type function and add it to the corresponding password field (see Listing 5.26).

```
<script>
  // Own typing function
  sap.ui.model.SimpleType.extend("my.pass.check", {
    formatValue : function(oValue) {
      return oValue;
    },
    parseValue : function(oValue) {
      return oValue;
    },
    validateValue : function(oValue) {
    // Only as test: write value in Console
    console.log(oValue);
    if
      (!/^(?=.*\d)(?=.*[a-zA-Z])[0-9a-zA-Z]{8,16}$/.
                  test(oValue)) {
    throw new sap.ui.model.ValidateException(
          "Password: At least
eight characters, letters and numbers");
    } else {
    throw new sap.ui.model.ValidateException(
          "Password valid");
    }
  }
});
// Model
  var oModel = new sap.ui.model.json.JSONModel({
    pwd : ""
  });
  sap.ui.getCore().setModel(oModel);

  var oText = new sap.ui.commons.PasswordField({
    value : {
        path : "/pwd",
        type : new my.pass.check()
    }
  });

  oText.placeAt("content");

  // Event Listener
  sap.ui.getCore().attachValidationError(function(ex) {
    alert(ex.getParameter("exception").message);
  });
```

```
</script>

</head>
<body class="sapUiBody" role="application">
  <div id="content"></div>
</body>
</html>
```

Listing 5.26 Your Own Type Definition

Of course, you would never write a real password field in the console; we have only entered this in the example so that you can understand it better. In Figure 5.27, you see the result in the browser.

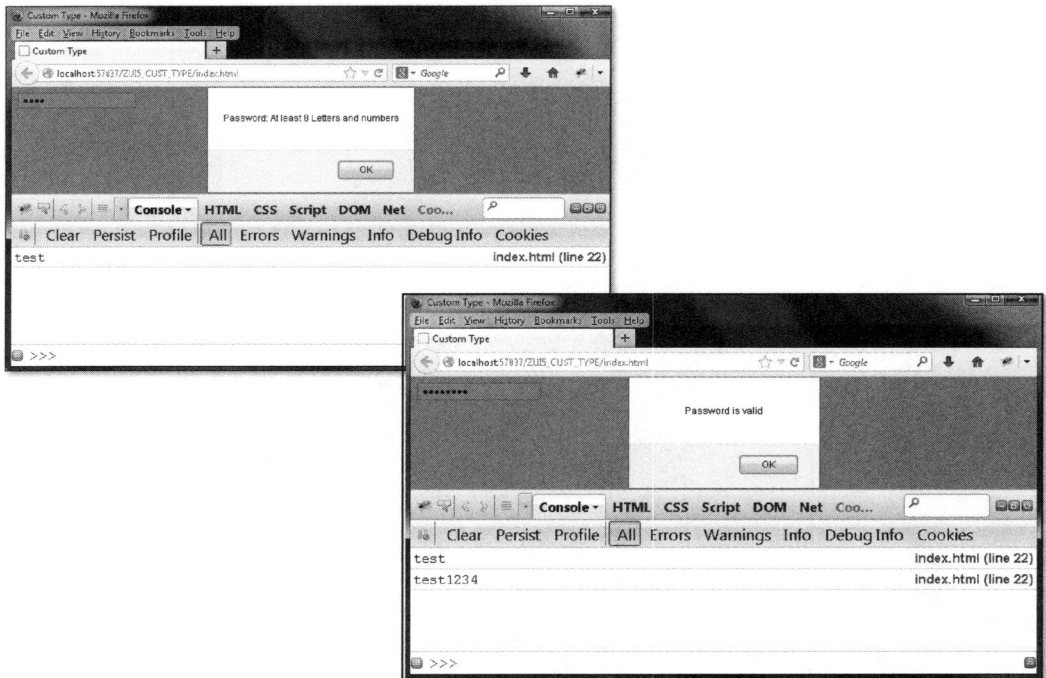

Figure 5.27 Your Own Type Definition

5.5   Layout Adaptation via Your Own CSS

You encountered the standard themes of SAPUI5 at the beginning of this chapter. The SAPUI5 themes are based on CSS and CSS parameters; a CSS file is always used for each control library (*library.css*). The CSS parameters are controlled via the style sheet language LESS. LESS is a JavaScript library that adds dynamic behavior to the CSS. For more information on LESS, see *www.lesscss.org*.

You will find the *library.css* file in the directory of the relevant theme—for example:

sapui5/resources/sap/ui/commons/themes/sap_bluecrystal/library.css.

To adapt the styling of an SAPUI5 application, you always have two options:

Adapting layout

▶ Provide individual UI elements with their own CSS

▶ Create a new theme using the Theme Designer

5.5.1   Adapting CSS

If you want to adapt individual items only, the easiest way to do so is with your own style definitions. You can generally change the style for an element, or use the `addStyleClass` method to assign your own style definitions to individual elements in a targeted manner.

First, you have to find out which CSS classes describe the UI element. The easiest way to do so is with the relevant developer tools of the browser. In Figure 5.28, you can see that the button refers to the style information for the font color and the background color of the class `.sapUiBtnS. sapUiBtnNorm.sapUiBtnStd`.

Browser tools

If you now want to change the background color of the button, you can override the corresponding class with your own style definition.

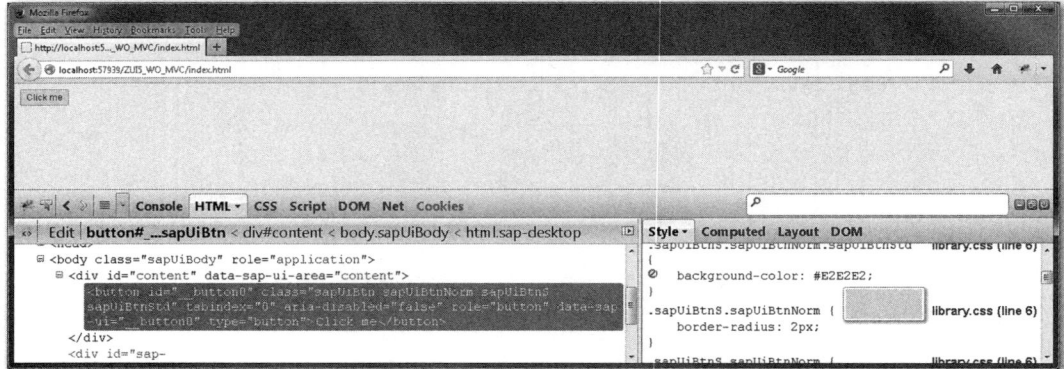

Figure 5.28 CSS Classes in SAPUI5

Changing
background color

In the following example, you change the background color of the button to the typical SAP gold; the hex value for this is #F0AB00. For the sake of clarity, we will omit the MVC pattern in this example. In Eclipse, create an SAPUI5 application project ZUI5_OWN_CSS, deselect the checkmark for CREATE AN INITIAL VIEW, and add two buttons to the page (see Listing 5.27).

```
<script>
// Layout
var oMatrix = new sap.ui.commons.layout.MatrixLayout({
    layoutFixed : true,
    width : '800px',
    columns : 2,
    widths : [ '200px', '200px' ]
});

// Two Buttons
    var oButton_1 = new sap.ui.commons.Button();
    oButton_1.setText("First Button");

    var oButton_2 = new sap.ui.commons.Button();
    oButton_2.setText("Second Button");
  // Bind button to layout
    oMatrix.createRow(oButton_1, oButton_2);
  // Bind layout to page
    oMatrix.placeAt("content");
</script>
```

Listing 5.27 index.html

This results in a page with two buttons. Add your style definition after the bootstrap; this is where you change the background color to SAP gold (see Listing 5.1).

Style definition

```
<style>
.sapUiBtnS.sapUiBtnNorm.sapUiBtnStd {
  background-color: #F0AB00;
  }
</style>
```

Listing 5.28 Button Definition in SAP Gold

The preview function of Eclipse does not always consider your own style definitions correctly; however, you can open the page in your standard browser by clicking the button OPEN IN EXTERNAL BROWSER. As a result, you'll see the page with two gold buttons (see Listing 5.29).

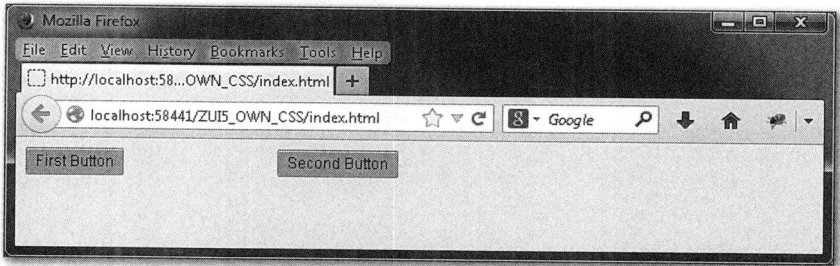

Figure 5.29 Buttons in SAP Gold

In this example, you'll see the disadvantage of this method: every UI element with this CSS class now has a gold background color. You usually want to represent individual elements in a different manner, and so the addStyleClass method is more appropriate in this case. Starting from the previous example, change the style definition as follows:

Disadvantage

```
<style>
.goldBackground { background-color: #F0AB00; }
</style>
```

Then assign one of the two buttons via the addStyleClass method to your own class (goldBackground in this example):

addStyleClass method

```
oButton_1.addStyleClass("goldBackground ");
```

If you now test this example in the browser, you will notice that both buttons are still displayed in gray. Where does this effect come from? As explained in Chapter 1, not only the sequence, but also the specificity of a CSS statement, plays a part in the rule calculation (specific before unspecific). Because the default statement is more specific than your own class, the default statement "wins," so to speak. If you view the page with the developer tools, you will see that your own class has been overwritten by the SAPUI5 class (see Figure 5.30).

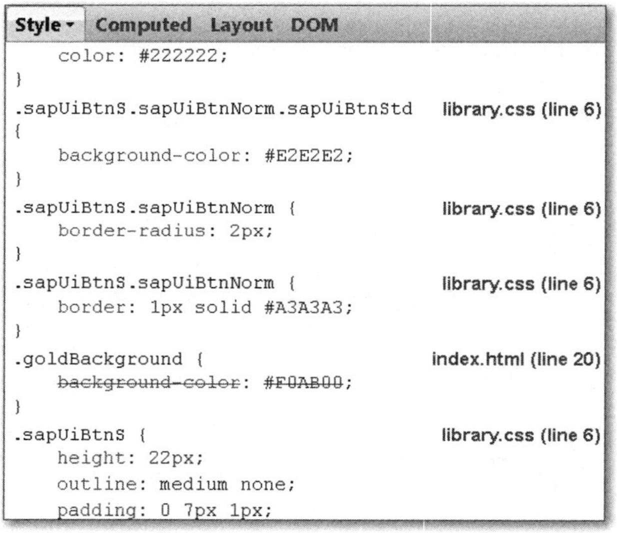

Figure 5.30 CSS Sequence

ID selector   You can solve this problem by, for example, using an ID selector instead of the class selector. To do this, change the CSS as in Listing 5.29.

```
<style>
#goldButton {
    background-color: #F0AB00;
}
</style>
```

Listing 5.29 CSS with ID Selector

Assign this ID to one of the two buttons:

```
var oButton_1 = new sap.ui.commons.Button("goldButton");
```

By using the ID selector, the expected result will be shown in the browser (see Figure 5.31).

However, it would be very time-consuming to adapt a whole layout according to this method. Fortunately, since Service Pack 4 the SAPUI5 library has provided the Theme Designer—used to adapt the basic settings of a theme in a graphical interface.

Theme Designer

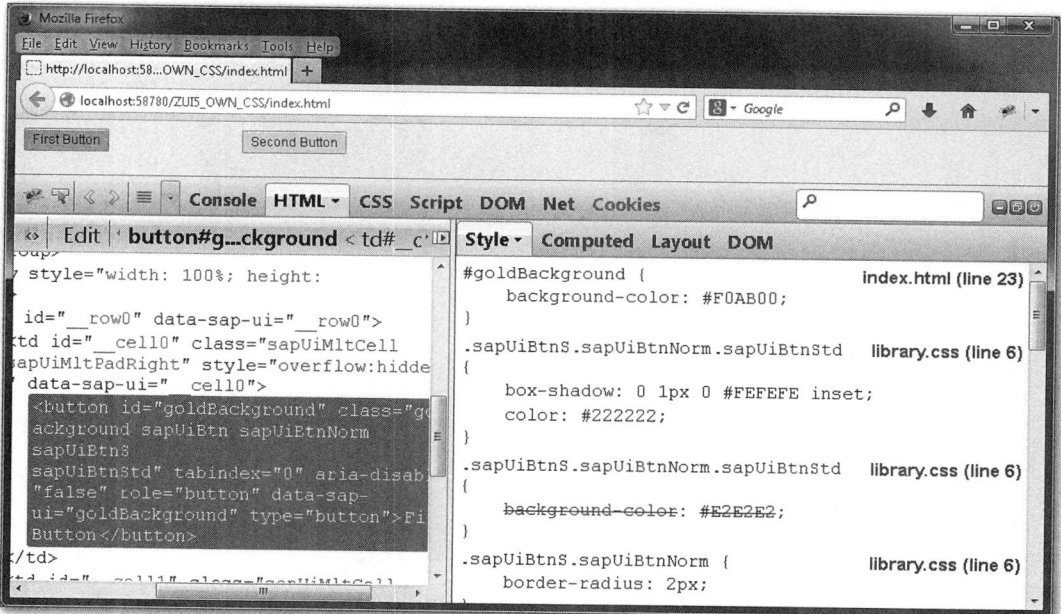

Figure 5.31 CSS with the ID Selector

5.5.2 Theme Designer

You can use the Theme Designer to create separate themes and embed them into your page. In order to use the Theme Designer, the following two services must be active (Transaction SICF):

ICF services

▸ /sap/public/bc/themes
▸ /sap/bc/theming

You also need authorizations for the authorization object /UI5/THEME:

Authorization object

▶ Authorization object: /UI5/THEME

▶ Theming: Theme Name: * (all themes)

▶ Activity: 02 (change)

You start the Theme Designer via Transaction /UI5/THEME_DESIGNER (see Figure 5.32).

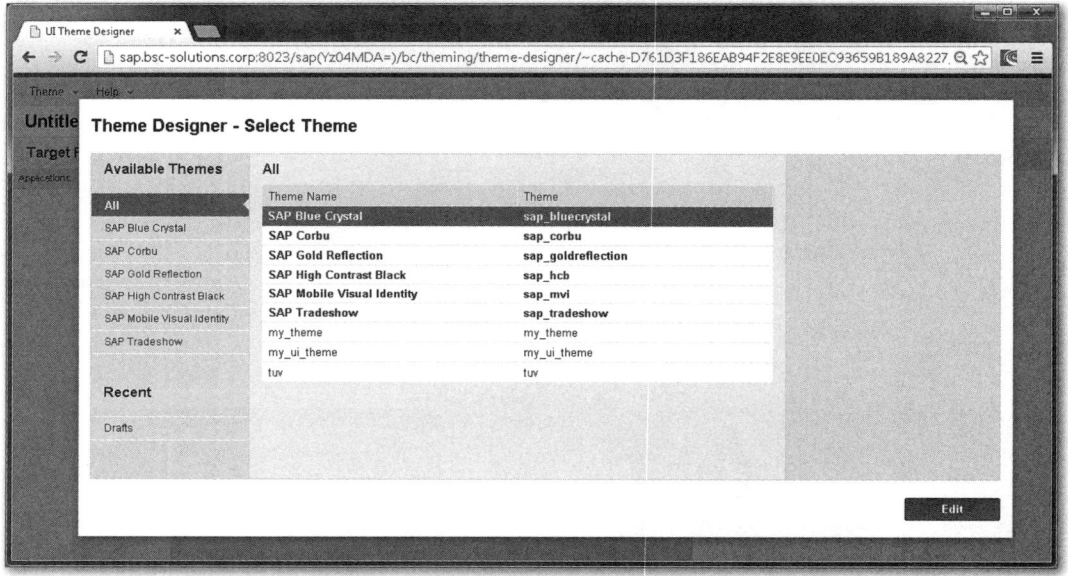

Figure 5.32 Theme Designer in SAPUI5

After you start the transaction, a window opens in which you select a theme (see Figure 5.33). You can either take an existing SAP theme as a basis for your own theme, or you can select an already created theme to which you want to make changes.

For now, select the Blue Crystal theme as a basis for your own theme. Select the theme, and click EDIT. On the next screen, assign a name to your theme; "my_theme" in our example. In the middle part of the window, you can use the link UI5 CONTROL PREVIEWS to select UI elements that are displayed in the preview in the middle of the screen. Thus, you can assess your theme changes directly and adjust them if necessary.

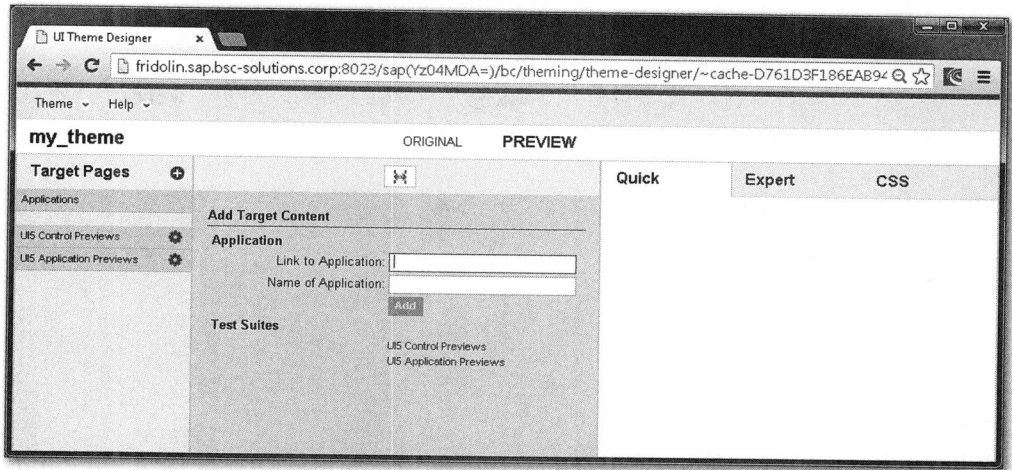

Figure 5.33 Selecting Elements

For the preview, it's best if you select SHELL from the UX3CONTROLS control set, because many UI elements are already displayed there. We will select a UI element from each category and consider the changes to the various UI elements.

Preview function

For our simple example, it's sufficient to select the subset BUTTON under the control set SIMPLECONTROLS (see Figure 5.34).

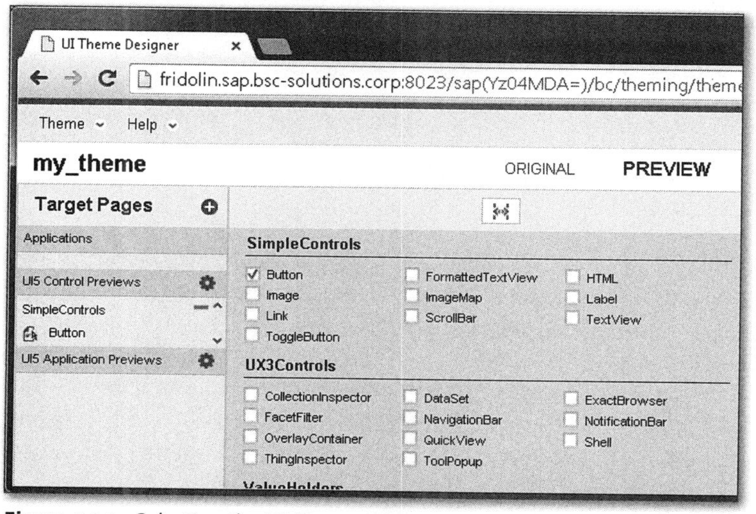

Figure 5.34 Selecting the UI Element Button

Next, select the element BUTTON on the left-hand side of the screen. A page with many different buttons is displayed in the middle area of the preview function as a result. The style options of the Theme Designer are displayed on the right-hand side of the screen (see Figure 5.35).

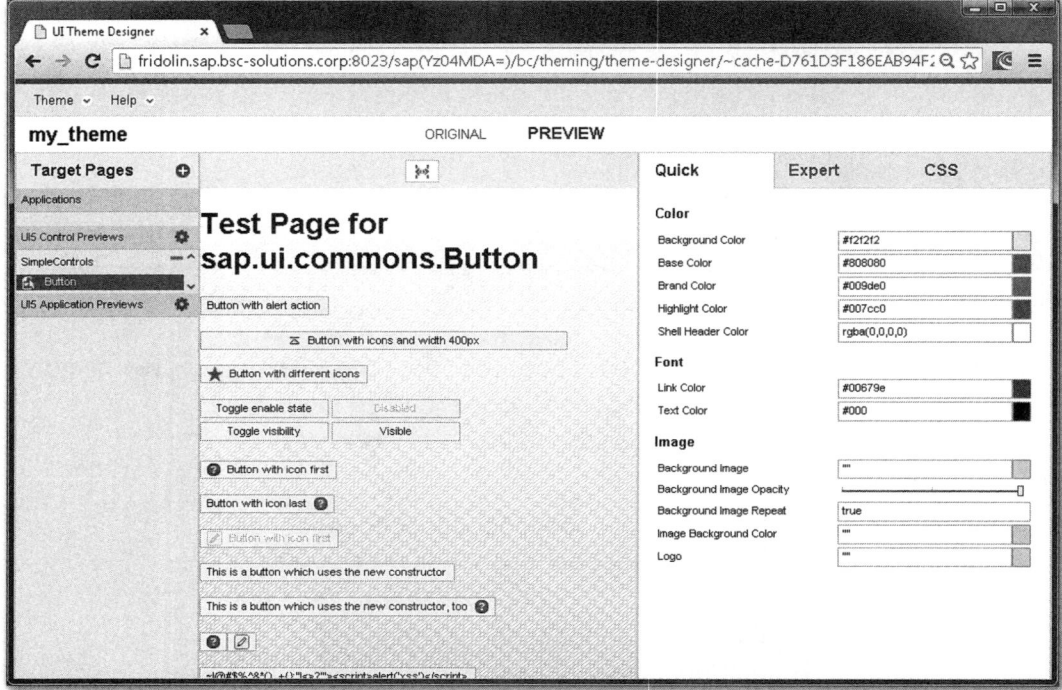

Figure 5.35 Style Options

On the right-hand side of the screen, you can choose between the options QUICK, EXPERT, and CSS.

In the QUICK option, the individual selection options are displayed in a legible and orderly form; for EXPERT, you see a larger selection of changeable CSS statements to some extent; and under CSS, you can implement your own CSS statements.

For our example, we would like to change the background color to a rich red (see Figure 5.36). The color may be a bit blinding, but you'll recognize the change more easily as a result. To do this, select the colored square on the right side after the BACKGROUND COLOR field, and a Color Picker will open in which you can set the background to red (#FF0000).

Click OK to confirm your selection, and the result is displayed directly in the preview. Next, let's add color to the buttons again and enlarge something at the same time. To do this, switch to the CSS tab, and insert the CSS from Listing 5.30.

```
.sapUiBtnS.sapUiBtnNorm.sapUiBtnStd {
    background-color: #F0AB00;
    height: 60 px;
    font-family: Comic Sans MS;
    font-size: medium;
}
```

Listing 5.30 Custom CSS in the Theme Designer

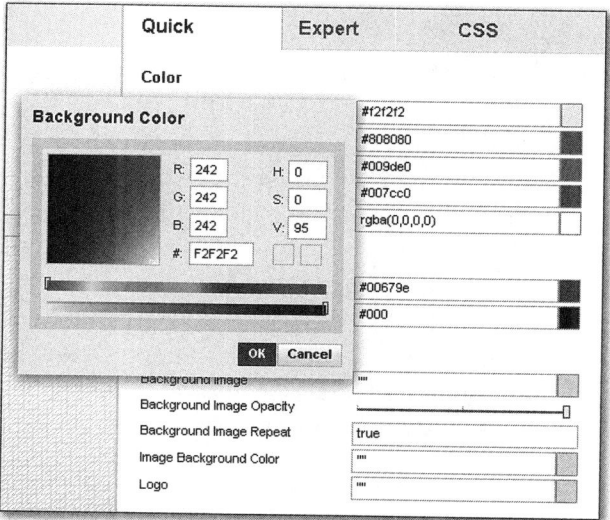

Figure 5.36 Changing the Background Color

The change is displayed directly in the preview function here also (see Figure 5.37).

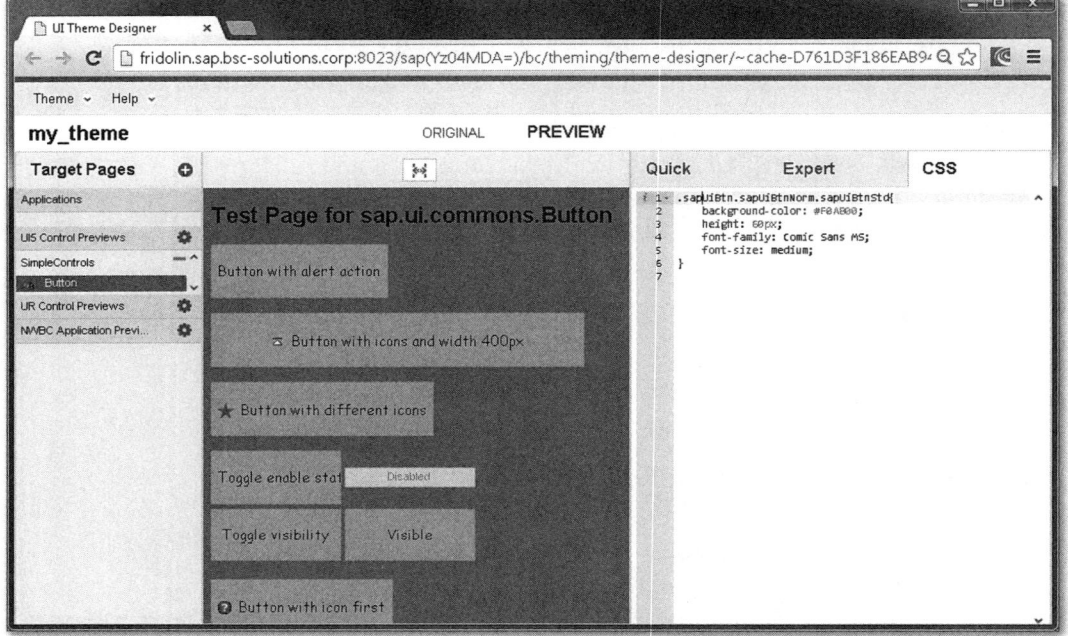

Figure 5.37 Theme with Custom CSS

Publishing theme

After you have made all the desired changes, you must first save the theme and then publish it. To do this, follow the menu path THEME • SAVE DESIGN; you'll receive a success message indicating that the theme was saved. After you have saved the theme, you can publish it by following the menu path THEME • PUBLISH. In the dialog box in Figure 5.38, you can change the name and the ID of the theme. In our example, leave the values unchanged and choose PUBLISH. From a technical perspective, the theme is now deployed in the MIME Repository of the SAP backend.

In order to embed the theme in your application, you must export it from the SAP backend. To do this, call Transaction /UI5/THEME_TOOL. All customer themes are displayed in this transaction. Select the previously created theme MY_THEME, and save it to your hard disk by double-clicking DOWNLOAD (see Figure 5.39).

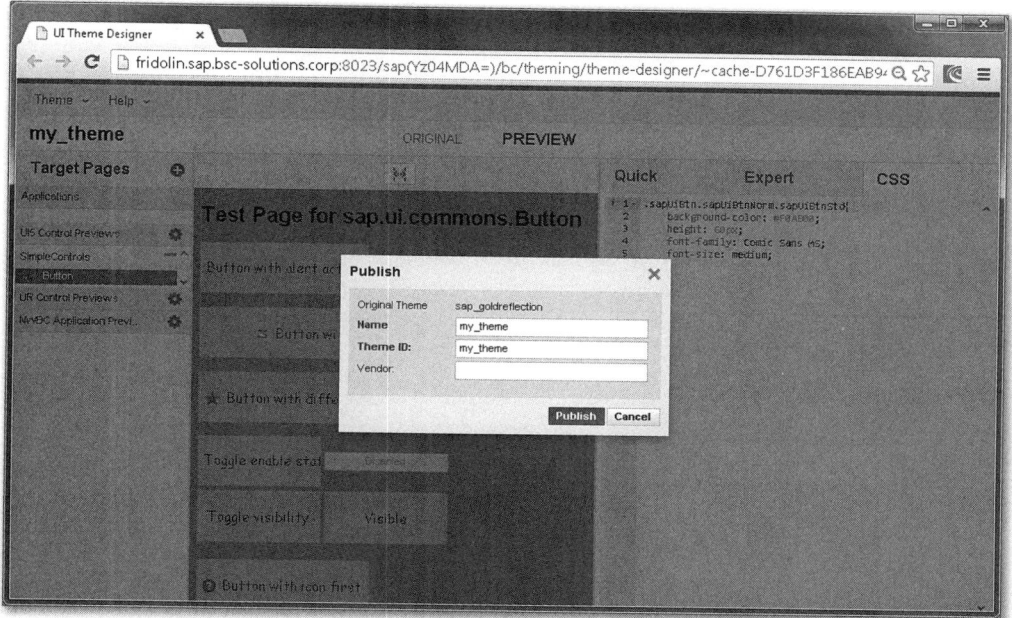

Figure 5.38 Publishing the Theme

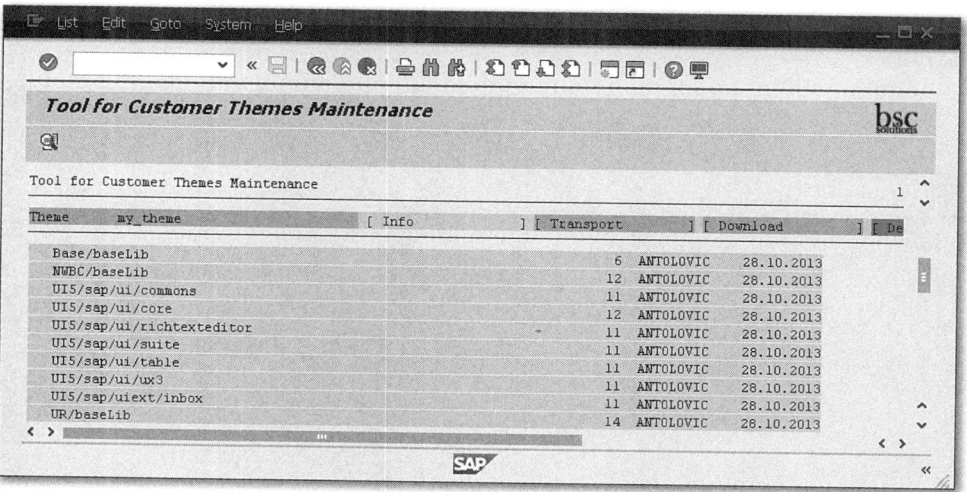

Figure 5.39 Downloading the Theme

After unpacking on the local hard disk, depending on the selected basis theme, the directory structure will look something like Figure 5.40.

209

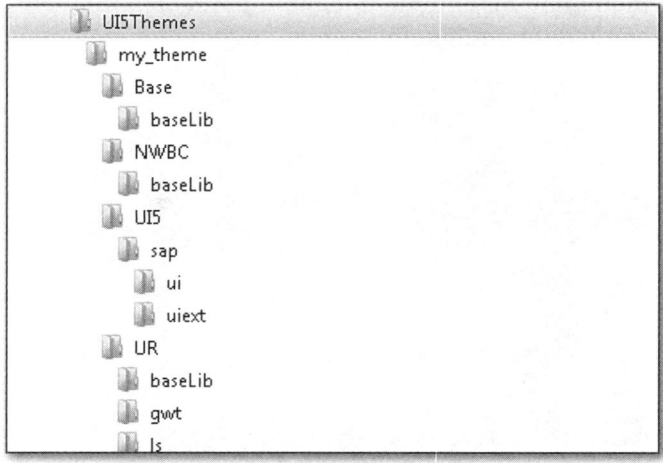

Figure 5.40 Directory Structure of the Theme

This is because the Theme Designer is also used for Web Dynpro or NWBC applications. In our application, we're interested only in the UI5 directory.

Below the *WebContent* folder in your Eclipse project, create a *resources* folder, and save everything from your theme under the UI5 folder there (see Figure 5.41). The easiest way to do this is via drag and drop.

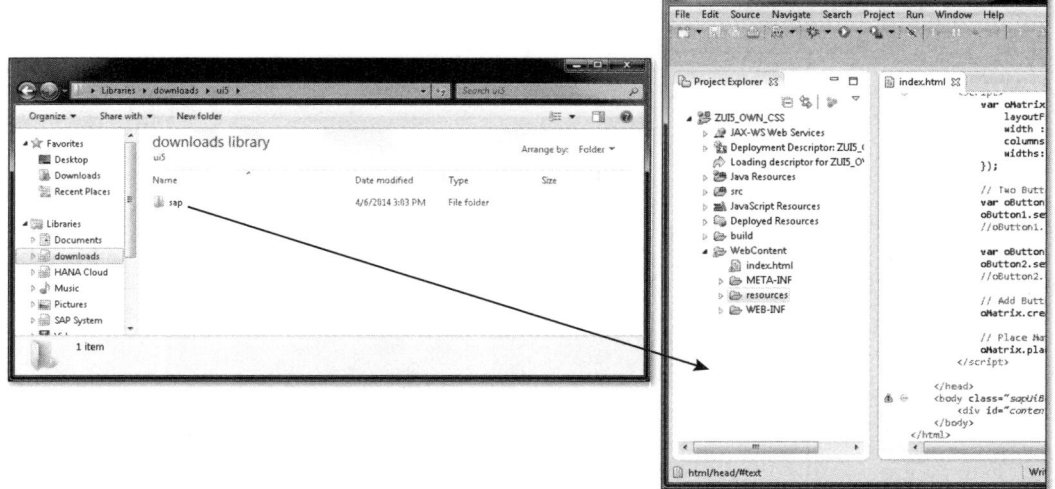

Figure 5.41 Inserting the Theme via Drag and Drop

In the following dialog box, select COPY FILES AND FOLDERS, and click OK (see Figure 5.42).

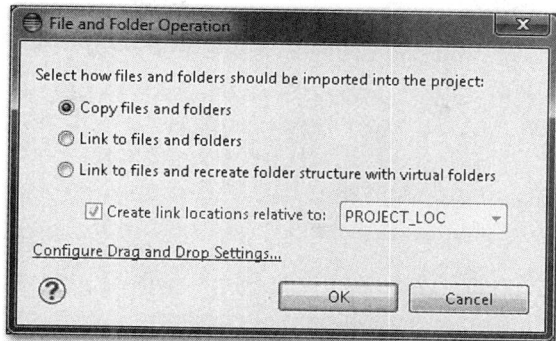

Figure 5.42 Copying CSS Files

You can now embed the theme in the bootstrap under its assigned name (my_theme in our example).

```
<script src="resources/sap-ui-core.js" id="sap-ui-bootstrap"
    data-sap-ui-libs="sap.ui.commons"
    data-sap-ui-theme="my_theme">
</script>
```

Listing 5.31 Embedding Your Own Theme in the Bootstrap

The result of our example (shown in Figure 5.43) may not be beautiful, but it is original!

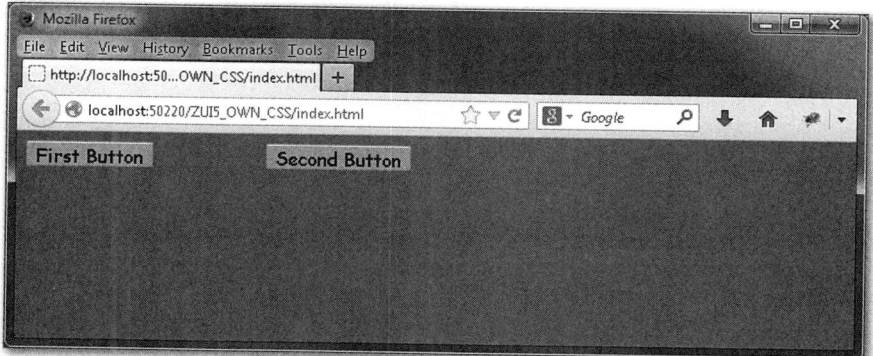

Figure 5.43 Your Own CSS

5.6   Communication with the SAP Backend

AJAX   All of the data from the previous examples came from a local file. However, you normally want to read the data in an SAP system and display
it in your SAPUI5 application. You have already encountered the AJAX
technique for sending an HTTP request to a web server in the preceding
chapters. You also use this technique when communicating with SAP
NetWeaver AS ABAP. The HTTP data stream returned by the SAP server
can use the familiar formats JSON, XML, or OData. Figure 5.44 shows a
schematic diagram of the communication with SAP NetWeaver AS ABAP.

Example   To send a request to the SAP backend, specify the path to the ICF node
in the loadData method of the corresponding model.

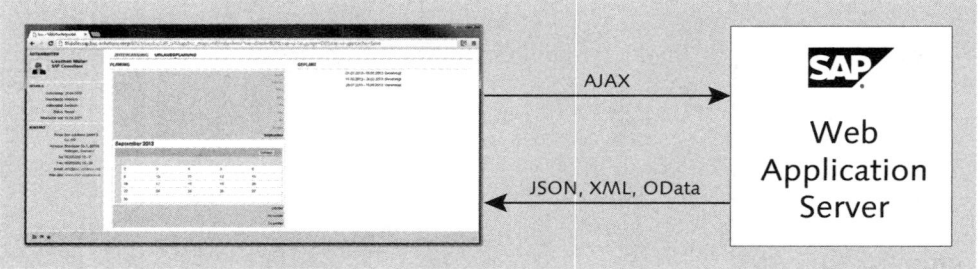

Figure 5.44   Communication with SAP NetWeaver Application Server ABAP

In the previous chapter, you created the ICF node DEFAULT_HOST/UI5/ and
implemented your own HTTP handler, ZUI5_HTTP_HANDLER. To implement a request for this service in SAPUI5, proceed according to the same
pattern as for local requests (omit the node default_host for the URL):

```
oModel = new sap.ui.model.json.JSONModel();
oModel.loadData("/ui5/");
```

In order to test the service, copy the example from Listing 5.10 to a new
project, ZUI5_JSON_SAP, and change only the line:

```
oModel.loadData("json/week.json");
```

to

```
oModel.loadData("/ui5");
```

Upload the project to your SAP backend under the name ZUI5_JSON_SAP, and set an external breakpoint in the method `HANDLE_REQUEST` of your HTTP handler (`ZUI5_HTTP_HANDLER` in our example). Start your application via the URL *http://<HOST NAME>:<SERVICE>/sap/bc/ui5_ui5/sap/zui5_json_sap/*. As a result, the application stops at the external breakpoint, and the debugger window opens. You can now enhance the HTTP handler and return JSON in the response data stream. For the first example, you still hard-code the JSON in the ABAP code. You complete the `HANDLE_REQUEST` method in turn, as shown in Listing 5.32. This listing was shortened for clarity; you can download the complete listing from the book's web page.

JSON response

```
data: lv_json type string.

concatenate
'{ "week": ['
   '{ "we_day": "Monday",'
   '" we_comment": "Garfield says: I hate Mondays!",'
   '" we_rating": 0'
'},{'
   '" we_day": "Tuesday",'
   '" we_comment": "At least it's not Monday",'
   '" we_rating": 1'
" etc.
'}]}'

into lv_json.

server->response->set_status( code = 200 reason = 'OK' ).
server->response->set_cdata( data - lv_json ).
server->response->set_content_type(
                content_type - 'application/json' ).
```
Listing 5.32 JSON Return via the HTTP Handler

As a result, you obtain the same display as in the preceding example; the only difference is that the data now comes from an SAP system (see Figure 5.45).

Server roundtrip

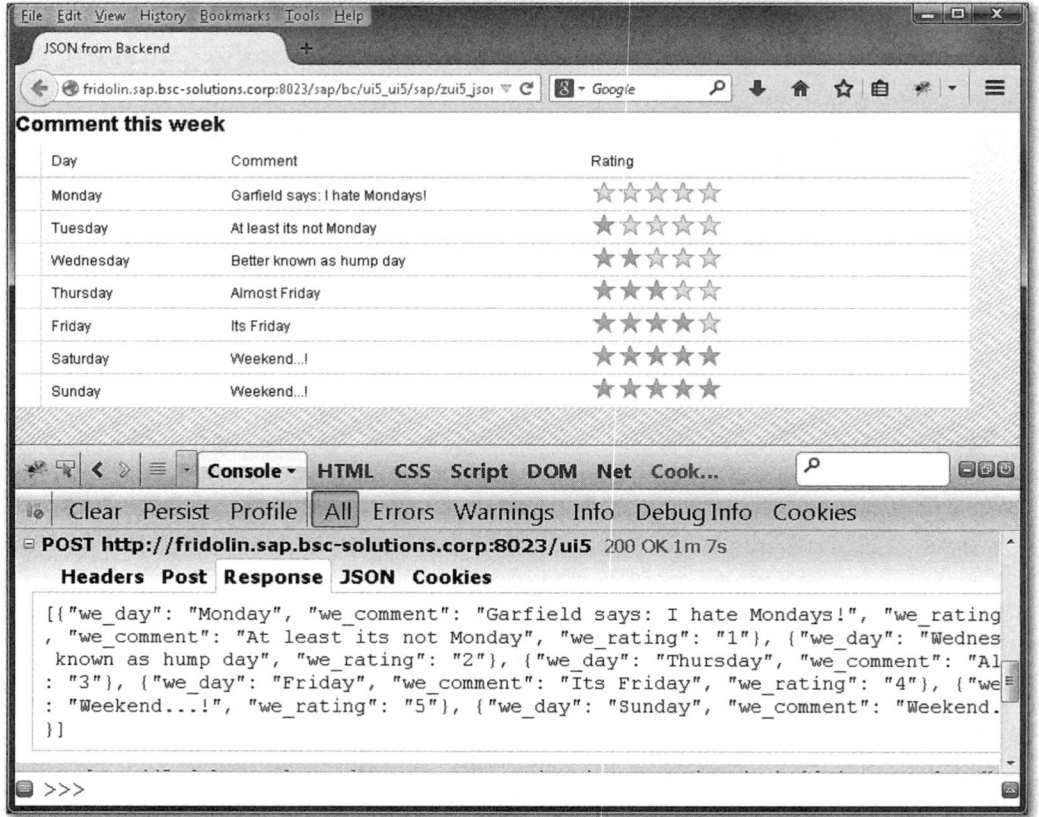

Figure 5.45 Server Roundtrip

Congratulations, you have just reached another milestone in SAPUI5 development: a complete "roundtrip" between the SAPUI5 frontend and the SAP backend. Even if this application is impressive, it has still two serious disadvantages:

1. The JSON is hardcoded in the source code.

2. Any request to this ICF node would get the JSON as a response.

There are several options for solving the first problem. There is the ZJSON project under *code.google.com/p/zjson/*, which provides two modules for creating and transforming JSON data. As an alternative, you can use the SAP-specific class CL_TREX_JSON_SERIALIZER; unfortunately, it has contained two known bugs for a long time. Both bugs can be easily removed;

for detailed instructions, see the SAP Community Network at *http://scn.sap. com/community/mobile/blog/2012/09/24/serialize-abap-data-into-json-format*. As of Basis Release 7.40, you have the option of calling the following transformation:

```
DATA(json_writer) = cl_sxml_string_writer=>create( type = if_
sxml=>co_xt_json ).
CALL TRANSFORMATION id SOURCE text = ls_
response RESULT XML json_writer.
```

The second problem is extremely easy to solve. In SAPUI5, you can also specify the AJAX request parameters, which are appended as a query string to the HTTP stream. This results, for example, in the complete syntax:

```
oModel.loadData("/ui5",
                { "application":"week", },
                false,
                "POST");
```

The POST method can be preferred because the transfer of the parameters in plain text via the URL can be critical in the SAP context.

You can read the transferred parameters via the method get_form_fields of the request object. In our example, this would result in the following listing of the HANDLE_REQUEST method (for the sake of clarity, the creation of *week.json* is stored in its own method; see Listing 5.33).

get_form_fields

```
data: lv_json              type string.
data: lt_query_string      type tihttpnvp.
field-symbols: <ls_query> type ihttpnvp.

server->request->get_form_fields(
                changing fields = lt_query_string ).

read table lt_query_string assigning <ls_query>
  with table key name = 'application'.

if sy-subrc <> 0 or <ls_query> is not assigned.
  server->response->set_status( code = '500'
        reason = 'Internal Server Error: No environment' ).
  exit.
endif.
```

```
      case <ls_query>-value.
        when 'week'.
          lv_json = get_week_comment( ).
        when others.
          server->response->set_status(
                      code    = 404
                      reason = 'not implemented' ).
          exit.
      endcase.

    server->response->set_status( code = 200 reason = 'OK' ).
    server->response->set_cdata( data   = lv_json ).
    server->response->set_content_type(
                      content_type = 'application/json' ).
```

Listing 5.33 HANDLE_REQUEST Method

AJAX parameter
transfer
Of course, you can freely extend the parameter transfer. If, for example, you have implemented not only a read method for the week but also a write method, you can transfer multiple parameters to differentiate the implementation in the SAP backend, as is the case in Listing 5.34.

```
oModel.loadData("/ui5",
                {"application":"week",
                 "action":"read" },
                false,
                "POST");
```

Listing 5.34 Transferring Multiple Parameters

For writing, the AJAX call corresponds to the content of Listing 5.35.

```
oModel.loadData("/ui5",
                {"application" : "week",
                 "action":"write" },
                false,
                "POST");
```

Listing 5.35 Transfer with the "write" Action

Stateful/stateless
For this example, you would work in a *stateless* manner. Stateless means that multiple requests are generally treated as independent transactions. A second request would again create the JSON that was shown previously,

and the requests would be treated without any reference to previous requests. SAPUI5 is designed in a manner that favors stateless applications; however, you can also work with SAPUI5 in a *stateful* manner. With a stateful application, you have a session in the backend in which each new request is handled. In our example, you could thus store JSON as an attribute in the class, read the attribute for the next request, and not determine JSON again.

In order to work in a stateful manner, two things are necessary:

► Set the session in the backend to stateful.

► Implement the processing class as a singleton.

You can use the statement `server->set_session_stateful( )` to easily set the session to stateful. The implementation of the processing class as a singleton is necessary so that you can also keep the data in the session and there can only be one instance of the class. With a normal ABAP class, you would create a new instance for each new request to the backend and would have gained nothing as a result. The following listing would thus result in stateful session handling.

```
"Singleton class
lo_stateful = zui5_stateful=>get_instance( ).
lv_json    = lo_stateful->get_week_comment( ).
" Set session stateful
server->set_session_stateful( ).
```

Listing 5.36 Stateful Session in the Backend

In this chapter, you learned about the basics of SAPUI5; you now know how to bind data to a UI element and how to change the display of the page by using your own CSS. What you're still missing is an overview of the individual UI elements that you already used to some extent in the examples in this chapter. In Chapter 6, these UI elements and controls will be discussed in more detail.

Summary

In this chapter, you will learn about the available UI elements: the controls. This will also introduce the layout options that are available.

6   SAPUI5 Controls

In the last chapter, you learned about the options for binding to UI controls, and this chapter will introduce the most common controls. Your "tool box" will then be complete, and you can begin to develop applications in SAPUI5.

The SAPUI5 framework is still a very young product and is being developed at full speed by SAP. Each new Service Pack entails new functions, new methods, and new controls. The goal of this book is not to indicate all controls with all parameters, but rather to refer to the existing API documentation. Once you know how to deal with the controls, you can develop the use of the individual controls based on the documentation.

API documentation

You can access the Demo Kit at *http://<HOST NAME>:<SERVICE>/sap/public/ bc/ui5_ui5/demokit* or, as of version 1.18, at *http://<HOST NAME>:<SERVICE>/ sap/bc/ui5_demokit*. In the Demo Kit, you will find the relevant documentation for each control in the API DOCUMENTATION section. If you have not yet installed the SAPUI5 library, you can also access the API documentation at *https://sapui5.netweaver.ondemand.com/sdk/*.

During the implementation, you should read the API documentation to determine whether the control is released, experimental, or deprecated (see Figure 6.1). You should consider this during the implementation and test it during each update to see whether anything has changed for these controls.

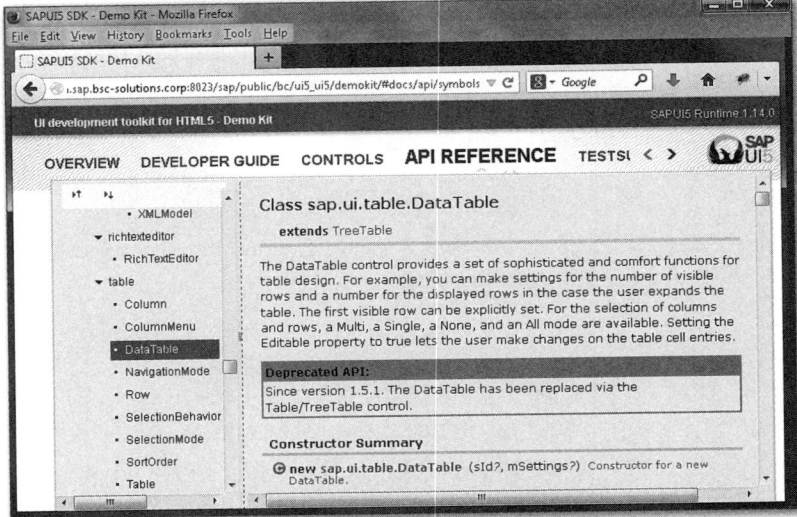

Figure 6.1 Example of a Deprecated Control

6.1 API Reference

The UI controls are divided into several thematically related namespaces. These include, among others:

Namespaces
▶ `sap.m` (for mobile devices)

▶ `sap.makit` (Mobile Analytics Kits)

▶ `sap.me` (enhancement of the `sap.m` class for mobile devices)

▶ `sap.ui` (UI controls)

▶ `sap.viz` (VIZ chart library)

Each of these namespaces is further subdivided in turn. If we now look at the example of the `sap.ui` class library, it is divided into the following classes, among others:

Classes

▶ sap.ui.app (base class for application classes)

▶ sap.ui.base (SAPUI5 base class)

▶ sap.ui.commons (most common UI controls)

▶ sap.ui.table (table controls)

▶ sap.ui.ux3 (SAP User Experience Controls)

For the controls, the *sap.ui.commons* library contains the most common ones, such as text or input fields, dropdown boxes, or the label control.

The *sap.ui.table* library is responsible for displaying table controls. The SAPUI5 library is *sap.ui.ux3*, with controls that implement the SAP User Experience Guidelines 3.0 (UX3; for example, Shell or Thing Inspector). The API Reference is also structured exactly according to this class schema (see Figure 6.2).

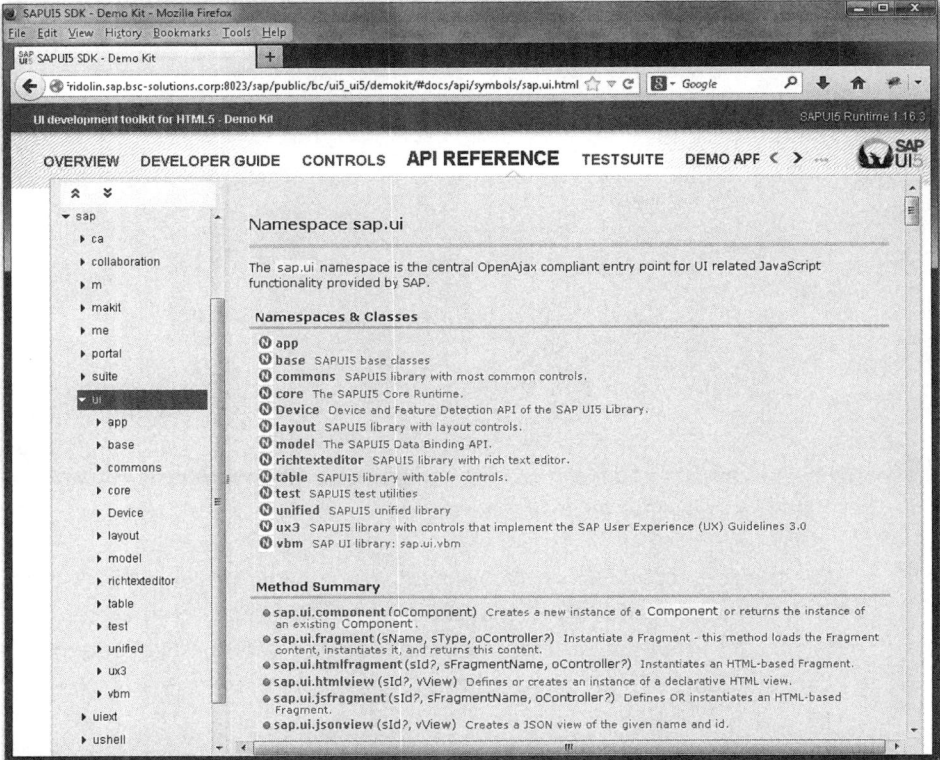

Figure 6.2 API Reference

sap.ui.commons.
Button The most important class for the development of desktop applications is the `sap.ui` class; for mobile application development, it's the `sap.m` class. For example, to use a button in your application, choose `sap.ui.commons.Button` in the API Reference (see Figure 6.3).

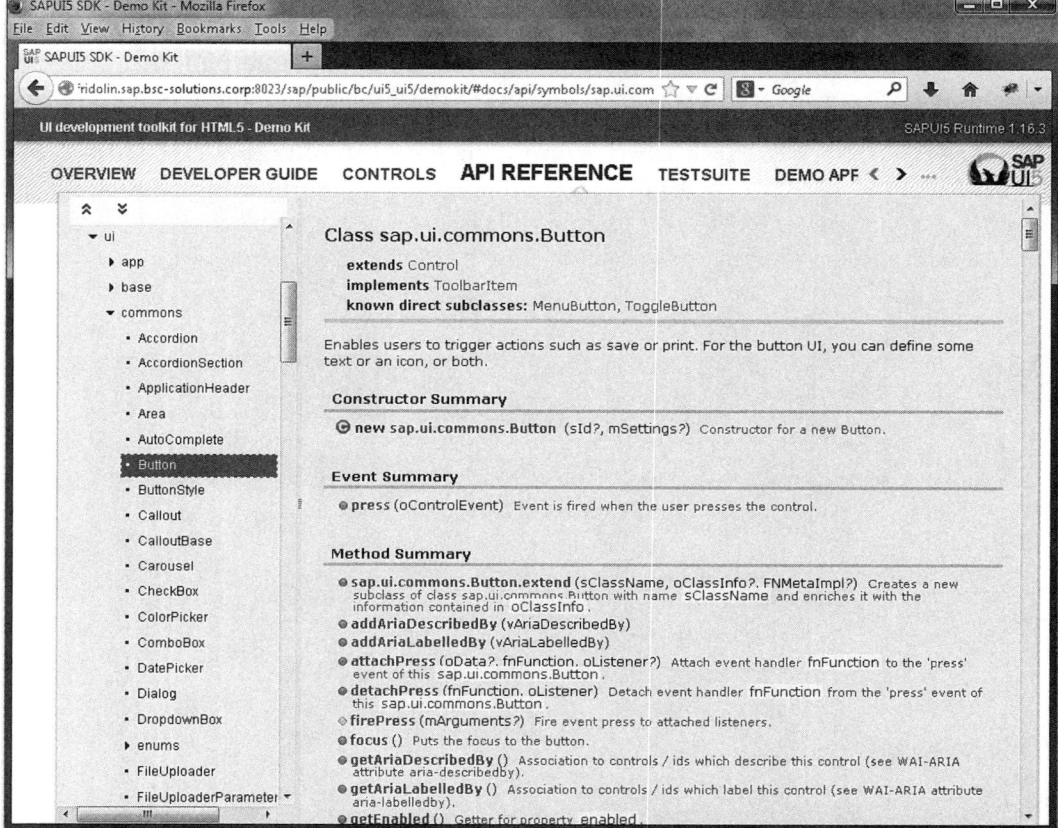

Figure 6.3 sap.ui.commons.Button

For the respective UI control, the constructor, the possible events, and the relevant methods are displayed in the API Reference. At this point, it's important to understand that you can also access methods of superordinate elements due to the inheritance. For example, the `sap.ui.commons.`

`Button` is derived from the control, and the control is derived in turn from the element, and so on, and therefore you can also access the methods of the superordinate element. These inherited methods are to be found below the specific methods of the respective element in the API Reference (see Figure 6.4).

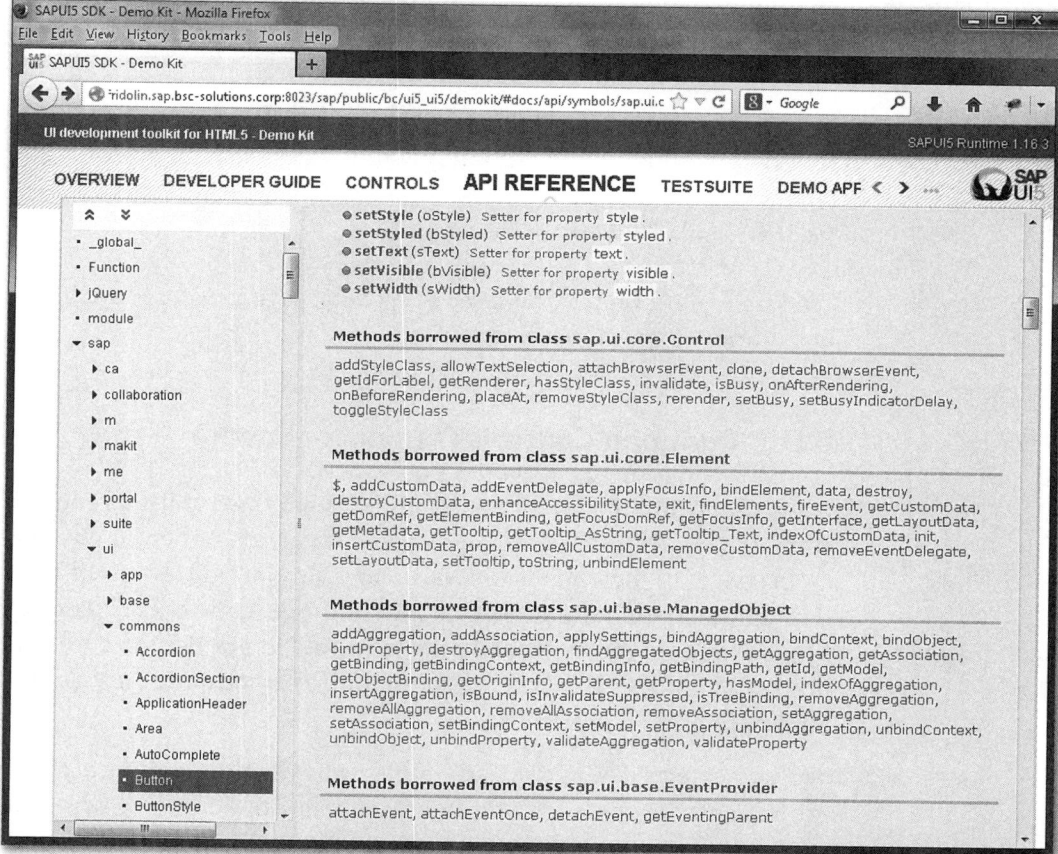

Figure 6.4 Inherited Methods

Thus, you can, for example, implement a tooltip for a button, because `sap.ui.commons.Button` inherits the method `setTooltip` from `sap.ui.core.Element` (see Figure 6.5).

```
 1  <!DOCTYPE HTML>
 2  <html>
 3  <head>
 4   <meta http-equiv="X-UA-Compatible" content="IE=edge">
 5   <meta http-equiv='Content-Type' content='text/html;charset=UTF-8' />
 6
 7  <script src="resources/sap-ui-core.js" id="sap-ui-bootstrap"
 8       data-sap-ui-libs="sap.ui.commons"
 9       data-sap-ui-theme="sap_bluecrystal">
10  </script>
11
12  <script>
13       var oButton = new sap.ui.commons.Button();
14       oButton.setText("Button");
15       oButton.setTooltip("This is a Tooltip");
16       oButton.placeAt("content");
17  </script>
18
19  </head>
20  <body class="sapUiBody">
21       <div id="content"></div>
22  </body>
23  </html>
```

Figure 6.5 setTooltip Inherited Method

Later on in this chapter, you'll see the general page structure and the use of controls by way of some examples.

6.2 Common Controls (sap.ui.commons)

As mentioned in the introduction, it makes no sense to list all controls with all methods and attributes. It would be better, rather, to give you an overview of the options in SAPUI5 and also introduce each of them through examples. You are encouraged at this point to try out as many as possible, to think about your own tasks, and to practice, practice, and practice. View the API documentation for each control, and try out the methods.

We will extensively practice using the individual controls in a practical example in Chapter 7, during the implementation of a complete application.

sap.ui.commons   The namespace sap.ui.commons contains the most common controls that you need in any application. These include input and output fields, checkboxes, buttons, menus, radio buttons, and so on. The various layout options are also implemented in this namespace. If you have already worked with the Web Dynpro development, you will be familiar with layouts such as the Matrix Layout. You use layouts such as these to arrange a page. In most cases, you not only implement a button in an

224

application, but you also arrange multiple elements. It is precisely for this arrangement that different layouts are available, which will be presented to you in detail now.

6.2.1 Layout

The individual layout options in SAPUI5 can be freely combined and nested. It's very easy to lose track of the layouts, especially at the start. If you are accustomed to the Graphical Screen Painter from ABAP, you will find designing a page via source code difficult at first. Figure 6.6 shows an example of a design.

Design on paper

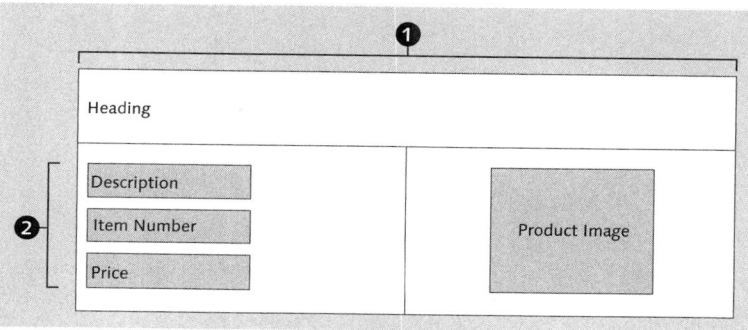

Figure 6.6 Establishing Layout

In order to implement a page in the design from Figure 6.6, two layouts are required: A two-column Matrix Layout ❶ as the outer framework and, within the second row of the Matrix Layout, a three-row vertical layout ❷ for the product description. Such a drawing will help you to find your way around the source code better. You'll soon see that you no longer need it for simple pages; however, a drawing is still a very good tool for complex page layouts.

Absolute Layout

The `AbsoluteLayout` control positions the controls with the CSS position statement `absolute` and is thus suitable only for areas with a fixed size. You create an instance of this control by using the constructor function `new sap.ui.commons.layout. AbsoluteLayout`.

USA map In the following example, you'll implement a page that displays a map of the USA with various cities. If you click on a city, the number of inhabitants of the relevant city is displayed. In Eclipse, create the project ZUI5_ABS_LAYOUT, and deselect the checkmark for CREATE AN INITIAL VIEW. For the sake of easier legibility, we will omit the MVC pattern for the moment. Below the *WebContent* folder, create an *img* subfolder, and copy the two images *usa.gif* and *dot.png* from the Appendix of this book to the *img* folder. The *index.html* file obtains the content of Listing 6.1. This listing was shortened for clarity; you can download the complete listing from the book's web page.

```
<script>
   //Absolute Layout
   var oMap = new sap.ui.commons.layout.AbsoluteLayout();
   USMap:
   oMap.setWidth("670px");
   oMap.setHeight("408px");

   //USA image
   oMap.addContent(new sap.ui.commons.Image({
           src : "img/usa.gif"
   }));

   // Position layout on the page
   oMap.placeAt("content");

//Function block ///////
   // Mark cities on the USA map.
   var addCity = function(oPosition, sName, sPopulation) {
      var oImage = new sap.ui.commons.Image({
              src : "img/dot.png",
              decorative : false
      });

      var showPopulation = function() {
         var oDialog1 = new sap.ui.commons.Dialog();
            oDialog1.setTitle(sName);
               var oText = new sap.ui.commons.TextView({
                       text : sPopulation
               });
         oDialog1.addContent(oText);
         oDialog1.addButton(new sap.ui.commons.Button({
              text : "OK",
```

```
                       press : function() {
                            oDialog1.close();
                       }
             }));
        oDialog1.open();
        };
        oImage.attachPress(showPopulation);
        oMap.addContent(oImage, oPosition);
    };

    // Cities
    addCity({
        left : "308px",
        top : "149px"
    }, "St. Louis", "3.502.000");
// ...
</script>
```

Listing 6.1 index.html with the AbsoluteLayout Control

Check in the project as a BSP page ZUI5_ABS_LAYOUT in the SAP back-end, and call the application via *http://<HOST NAME>:<SERVICE>/sap/bc/ui5_ui5/sap/zui5_abs_layout/* (see Figure 6.7).

Checking in

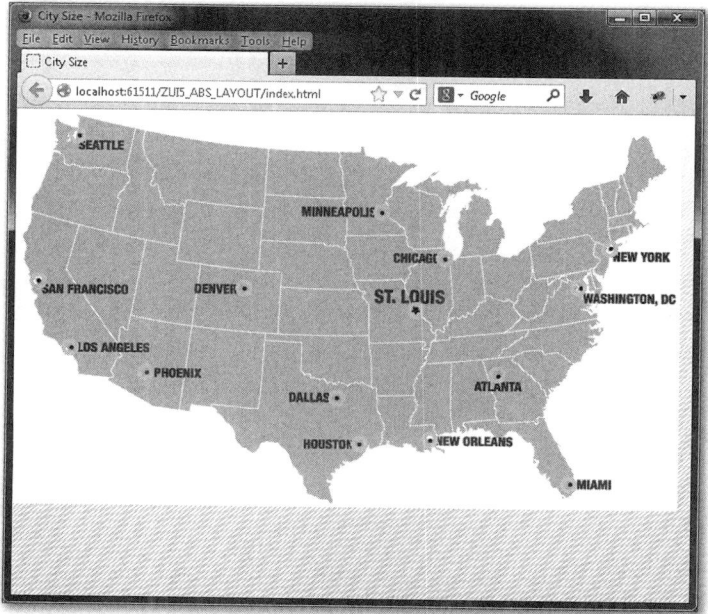

Figure 6.7 Absolute Layout in SAPUI5

Vertical Layout

You can use the `VerticalLayout` control to arrange UI elements vertically—that is, so that the individual UI elements are displayed one below the other. You create an instance of this control by using the constructor function `new sap.ui.commons.layout.VerticalLayout`.

Completing layout

In order to make the previous example of the USA map more user-friendly, add a heading with a small description in the following example. Then create a vertical layout and assign the layout to the heading and the USA map. Also replace the code above the function block from Listing 6.1 with Listing 6.2.

```
// Heading with description
var sHtmlText = "<h1>Guess size of the cities</h1>";
sHtmlText += "<p>Guess the number of inhabitants, ";
sHtmlText += "clicking on the appropriate city ";
sHtmlText += "will display the correct solution</p>";
var oHeader = new sap.ui.commons.FormattedTextView();
oHeader.setHtmlText(sHtmlText);

//Absolute Layout
var oMap = new sap.ui.commons.layout.AbsoluteLayout({
  width("670px");
  height("408px");
 });

//USA image
oMap.addContent(new sap.ui.commons.Image({
  src : "img/usa.gif"
}));

// Vertical layout with heading and map
var oLayout = new sap.ui.commons.layout.VerticalLayout({
  content: [oHeader, oMap]
});
// Attach the layout to the page
oLayout.placeAt("content");

//Function block ///////
...
```

Listing 6.2 Vertical Layout

Figure 6.8 shows how the map is now displayed in the browser.

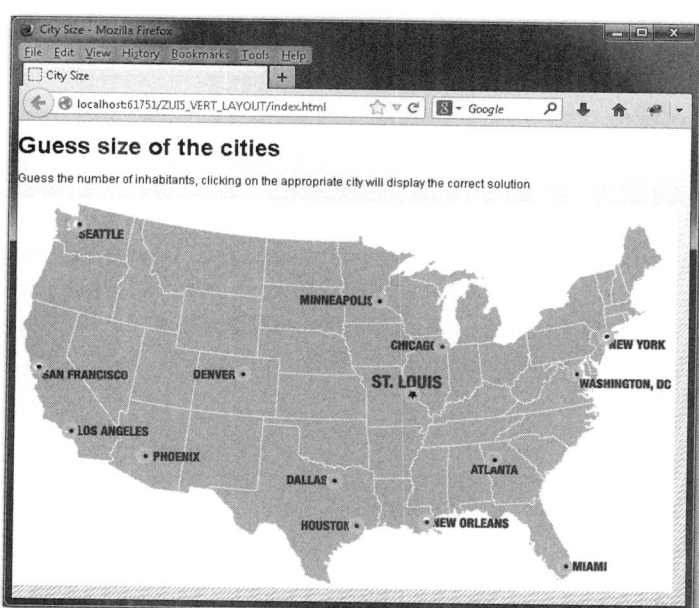

Figure 6.8   VerticalLayout Control

Horizontal Layout

You can use the HorizontalLayout control to arrange UI elements horizontally—that is, so that the individual UI elements are displayed next
to each other.

You create an instance of this control by using the constructor function
new sap.ui.commons.layout.HorizontalLayout. In order to display the
heading next to the image in the preceding example, you have to replace
only the constructor of the vertical layout with the horizontal layout (see
Listing 6.3).

```
// Horizontal layout with heading and map
var oLayout = new sap.ui.commons.layout.HorizontalLayout( {
                content: [oMap, oHeader]
            });
```

Listing 6.3   Horizontal Layout

When you execute this example in the browser, the heading is displayed to the right of the image.

Matrix Layout

You use the `MatrixLayout` control (`sap.ui.commons.layout.Matrix-Layout`) to assign a tabular form to the individual page elements; you can choose between a fixed number (attribute `layoutFixed = true`), or a variable number of columns (`layoutFixed = false`). In the latter case, the `MatrixLayout` control is calculated by the runtime based on the content. The `MatrixLayout` is comparable to the `<table>` statement in HTML; you can use the `rowSpan` property to link adjacent cells and use the `colSpan` property to link cells if one is below the other.

To illustrate the `MatrixLayout` control, create the project ZUI5_MATRIX in Eclipse and omit the Initial View. In order to make it easier to recognize the individual areas, create your own style definition as in Listing 6.4 after the bootstrap.

```
<style>
div {
    border: 1px solid blue;
    box-shadow: 5px 5px 5px gray;
    -moz-box-shadow: 5px 5px 5px gray;
    -webkit-box-shadow: 5px 5px 5px gray;
}
</style>
```

Listing 6.4 Style Definition

Button controls　In this simple example, first create seven button controls (see Listing 6.5).

```
<script>
// Buttons
var oButton_1 = new sap.ui.commons.Button();
oButton_1.setText("First Button");

var oButton_2 = new sap.ui.commons.Button();
oButton_2.setText("Second Button");

var oButton_3 = new sap.ui.commons.Button();
oButton_3.setText("Third Button");
```

```
var oButton_4 = new sap.ui.commons.Button();
oButton_4.setText("Fourth Button");

var oButton_5 = new sap.ui.commons.Button();
oButton_5.setText("Fifth Button");

var oButton_6 = new sap.ui.commons.Button();
oButton_6.setText("Sixth Button");

var oButton_7 = new sap.ui.commons.Button();
oButton_7.setText("Seventh Button");
```

Listing 6.5 Button Controls

Next, arrange the first two buttons with a fixed `MatrixLayout` control (see Listing 6.6).

Fixed MatrixLayout control

```
// fixed MatrixLayout
var oMatrixFix = new sap.ui.commons.layout.MatrixLayout({
            layoutFixed : true,
            width : '800px',
            columns : 2,
            widths : [ '400px', '400px' ]
        });
oMatrixFix.createRow(oButton_1, oButton_2);
oMatrixFix.placeAt("fix");
```

Listing 6.6 Fixed Matrix Layout

Arrange the next two buttons with a variable Matrix Layout (see Listing 6.7).

Variable MatrixLayout control

```
//variable MatrixLayout
var oMatrixVar = new sap.ui.commons.layout.MatrixLayout({
            layoutFixed : false
        });
oMatrixVar.createRow(oButton_3, oButton_4);
oMatrixVar.placeAt("var");
```

Listing 6.7 Variable Matrix Layout

Arrange the fifth button in a row by merging the two columns via the `colSpan` parameter. Write the last two buttons in a cell (see Listing 6.8).

Merging cells

```
//Merge cells
var oMatrixCell = new sap.ui.commons.layout.MatrixLayout({
                layoutFixed : true,
                width       : "100%",
                columns     : 2,
                widths      : [ '50%', '50%' ]
            });

var oRow = new sap.ui.commons.layout.MatrixLayoutRow();
oMatrixCell.addRow(oRow);

var oCell = new sap.ui.commons.layout.MatrixLayoutCell({
                colSpan : 2,
            });
// Center horizontally
oCell.setHAlign(sap.ui.commons.layout.HAlign.Center);

oCell.addContent(oButton_5);
oRow.addCell(oCell);

var oRow2 = new sap.ui.commons.layout.MatrixLayoutRow();
oMatrixCell.addRow(oRow2);

var oCell2 = new sap.ui.commons.layout.MatrixLayoutCell();

oCell2.addContent(oButton_6);
oRow2.addCell(oCell2);

oCell2.addContent(oButton_7);
oRow2.addCell(oCell2);

oMatrixCell.placeAt("cell");

</script>
</head>
<body class="sapUiBody" role="application">
   <div id="fix">
   <h1>Fixed MatrixLayout</h1>
   </div>
   <br>
   <div id="var">
   <h1>MatrixLayout with variable cell size</h1>
   </div>
```

```
    <br>
    <div id="cell">
    <h1>MatrixLayout, first row with merged cells</h1>
    </div>
</body>
</html>
```

Listing 6.8 MatrixLayout Control

In the browser, you can view the button arrangement with the selected Matrix Layout (see Figure 6.9).

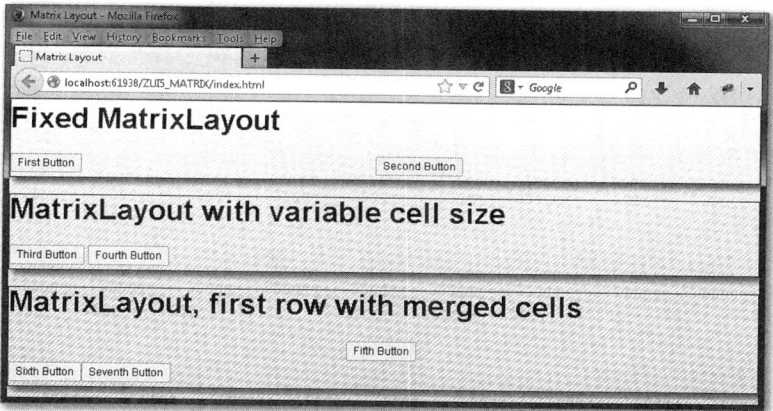

Figure 6.9 Matrix Layout

Border Layout

The BorderLayout control (sap.ui.commons.layout.BorderLayout) divides   **Subareas**
the screen area into five subareas:

▶ Top

▶ Begin

▶ Center

▶ End

▶ Bottom

Within the individual areas, you can freely embed any controls. This layout is very specific and is suitable only for pages that have this exact structure.

Constructor You create an instance of this control by using the constructor function `new sap.ui.commons.layout.BorderLayout`. In order to make it easier to recognize the individual areas, the areas are colored in the following example.

Example In Eclipse, create a project ZUI5_BORDER; omit the MVC pattern. In order to make it easier to recognize the individual areas, create your own style definition as in Listing 6.9 below the bootstrap.

```
<style type="text/css">
   .sapUiBorderLayoutTop { background-color: #F0AB00;}
   .sapUiBorderLayoutBegin {background-color: #e2001a;}
   .sapUiBorderLayoutCenter {background-color: #009ee0;}
   .sapUiBorderLayoutEnd {background-color: #00a02f;}
   .sapUiBorderLayoutBottom {background-color: #933588;}
</style>
```

Listing 6.9 Style Definition

BorderLayout control In the actual script block, create a `BorderLayout` control with the five areas TOP, BEGIN, CENTER, END, and BOTTOM. In this simple example, each area contains only a `TextView` control (see Listing 6.10).

```
<script>
// BorderLayout
var oBorderLayout = new sap.ui.commons.layout.BorderLayout
   ({
   width: "800px",
   height: "400px",
   top: new sap.ui.commons.layout.BorderLayoutArea({
        size: "20%",
        contentAlign: "center",
        content: [new sap.ui.commons.TextView(
               {text: '"Top"-Area' })]
        }),
   begin: new sap.ui.commons.layout.BorderLayoutArea({
        size: "20%",
        contentAlign: "left",
        content: [new sap.ui.commons.TextView(
               {text: '"Begin"-Area'})]
        }),
   center: new sap.ui.commons.layout.BorderLayoutArea({
        contentAlign: "center",
```

```
            content: [new sap.ui.commons.TextView(
                    {text: '"Center"-Area'})]
        }),
    end: new sap.ui.commons.layout.BorderLayoutArea({
        size: "20%",
        contentAlign: "right",
        content: [new sap.ui.commons.TextView(
                {text: '"End"-Area'})]
        }),
    bottom: new sap.ui.commons.layout.BorderLayoutArea({
        size: "10%",
        contentAlign: "center",
         content: [new sap.ui.commons.TextView(
                {text: '"Bottom"-Area'})]
        }),
    });

    oBorderLayout.placeAt("content");
</script>
```

Listing 6.10 BorderLayout Control

Figure 6.10 shows the five areas of the BorderLayout control.

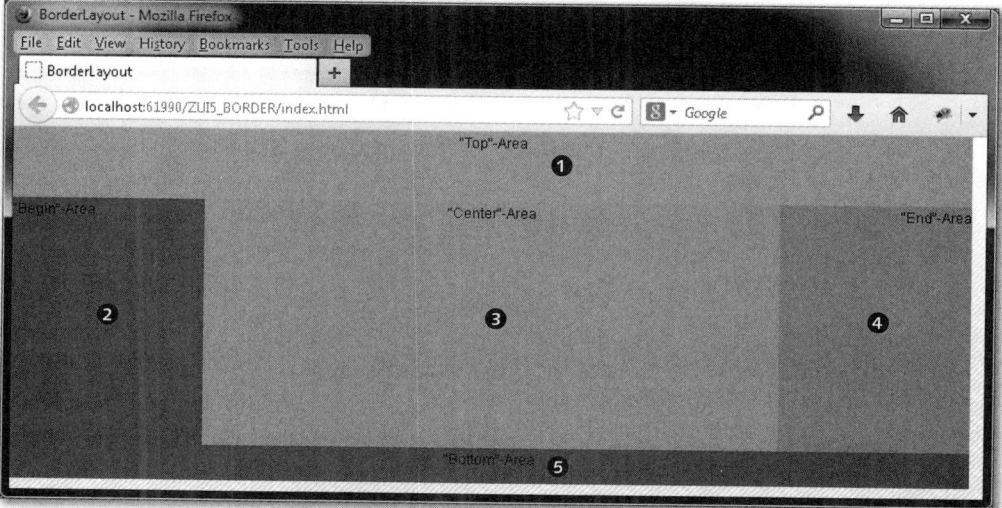

Figure 6.10 The Five Areas of the BorderLayout Control: ❶ "Top"-Area, ❷ "Begin"-Area, ❸ "Center"-Area, ❹ "End"-Area, ❺ "Bottom"-Area

Form Layout

There are four controls that you use when designing a form:

- ▶ Form
- ▶ FormContainer
- ▶ FormElement
- ▶ Layout

Form   The `FormControl` displays the actual form and wraps the `FormContainer`. The `FormContainer` controls are displayed in the form as a panel, and they wrap the `FormElement` controls; these include the actual form content such as input fields, checkboxes, and so on.

Example   The following example illustrates the relationship of the individual controls. In Eclipse, create a project ZUI5_FORM; omit the MVC pattern. In the application script area of the *index.html* file, insert the code from Listing 6.11.

```
<script>
// Layout for Form
var oLayout = new sap.ui.commons.form.GridLayout();

//FormElement
var oFormElement = new sap.ui.commons.form.FormElement();
// Title FormElement
oFormElement.setLabel("FormElement");
// Content FormElement
oFormElement.addField(new sap.ui.commons.TextField({
    value : "Content FormElement"
    }));

// FormElement2
var oFormElement2 = new sap.ui.commons.form.FormElement();
// Title FormElement
oFormElement2.setLabel("Another FormElement");
// Content FormElement
oFormElement2.addField(new sap.ui.commons.TextField({
    value : "Content FormElement 2"
    }));

// FormContainer
```

```
var oFormCont = newsap.ui.commons.form.FormContainer();
// Heading FormContainer
oFormCont.setTitle("FormContainer");
//Add FormElement
oFormCont.addFormElement(oFormElement);
oFormCont.addFormElement(oFormElement2);

// Form
var oForm = new sap.ui.commons.form.Form();
//Title
oForm.setTitle("Form");
// Set Layout
oForm.setLayout(oLayout);
//Add FormContainer to Form
oForm.addFormContainer(oFormCont);

oForm.placeAt("content");
</script>
```

Listing 6.11 Forms in SAPUI5

As a result, you obtain a simple form with one form container and two form elements (see Figure 6.11).

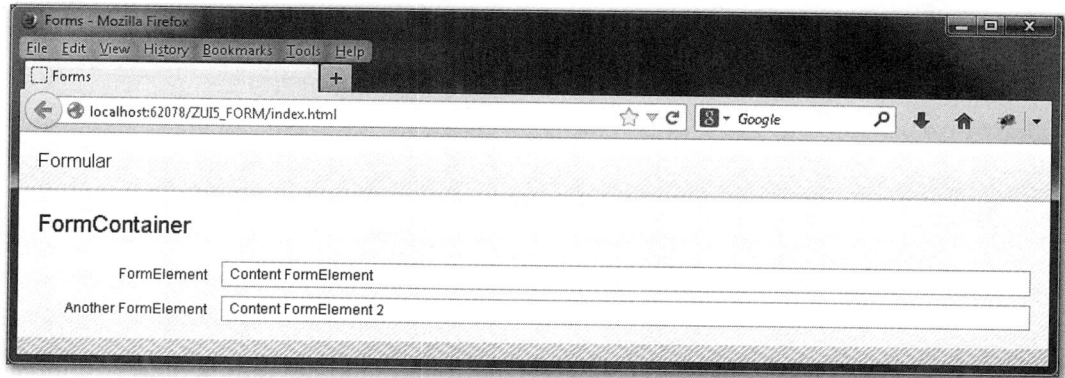

Figure 6.11 Simple Form

The form does not look particularly appealing due to its elongated fields. Two other layouts are available for arranging the form elements within the form: the Grid Layout and Responsive Layout.

Grid Layout

GridLayout grid   The Grid Layout is an extension of the Form Layout and is used to arrange the individual form fields in a grid within a form. The Grid Layout consists of a grid with 16 cells by default. If you set the property singleColumn to true, the grid is reduced to eight cells.

Constructor   You create an instance of this control by using the constructor function new sap.ui.commons.layout.GridLayout. You can use this grid to specify the number of occupied cells for a form element. Depending on whether or not you have set the parameter singleColumn, the available space is divided into 8 or 16 cells.

Example   In order to see the effect, create the project ZUI5_GRID in Eclipse. In this example, create two forms in the Grid Layout. Assign the property singleColumn = true to the first form. In the application script area of the *index.html* file, insert the code from Listing 6.12. The differences from the previous Listing 6.11 are in bold.

singleColumn true

```
<script>
// Layout for Form
var oLayout = new sap.ui.commons.form.GridLayout({
                                singleColumn:true
            });

//FormElement
var oFormElement = new sap.ui.commons.form.FormElement();
// Title FormElement
oFormElement.setLabel("FormElement");
// Content FormElement
oFormElement.addField(new sap.ui.commons.TextField({
    value : "Content FormElement",
    layoutData: new sap.ui.commons.form.GridElementData({
        hCells: "2"
        })
    }));

var oFormElement2 = new sap.ui.commons.form.FormElement();
// Title FormElement
oFormElement2.setLabel("Another FormElement");
// Content FormElement
oFormElement2.addField(new sap.ui.commons.TextField({
        value : "Content FormElement 2",
```

```
      layoutData: new sap.ui.commons.form.GridElementData({
         hCells: "4",
      })
   }));
// FormContainer
var oFormCont = new sap.ui.commons.form.FormContainer();
// Heading FormContainer
oFormCont.setTitle("FormContainer single Column - true");
//Add FormElement
oFormCont.addFormElement(oFormElement);
oFormCont.addFormElement(oFormElement2);

// Form
var oForm = new sap.ui.commons.form.Form();
//Title
oForm.setTitle("Form");
// Set Layout
oForm.setLayout(oLayout);
//Add FormContainer Form
oForm.addFormContainer(oFormCont);
oForm.placeAt("content");
```

Listing 6.12 GridLayout with singleColumn = true

Assign the property singleColumn = false to the second form. Copy the code from Listing 6.12, and insert it below the last statement (oForm. placeAt("content");). Adjust the constructor, and set the parameter singleColumn to false. To ensure that both forms can be displayed, you must declare your own <div> element in the UI area for the second form (see Listing 6.13).

singleColumn false

```
// Layout for Form
var oLayout = new sap.ui.commons.form.GridLayout({
                   singleColumn:false
            });
// Form as in Listing 6.12
...
oForm.placeAt("content2");
</script>
</head>
<body class="sapUiBody" role="application">
      <div id="content"></div>
      <div id="content2"></div>
```

```
</body>
</html>
```

Listing 6.13   GridLayout

Result As a result, you obtain one form in the eight-cell design and the second form in the 16-cell design (see Figure 6.12).

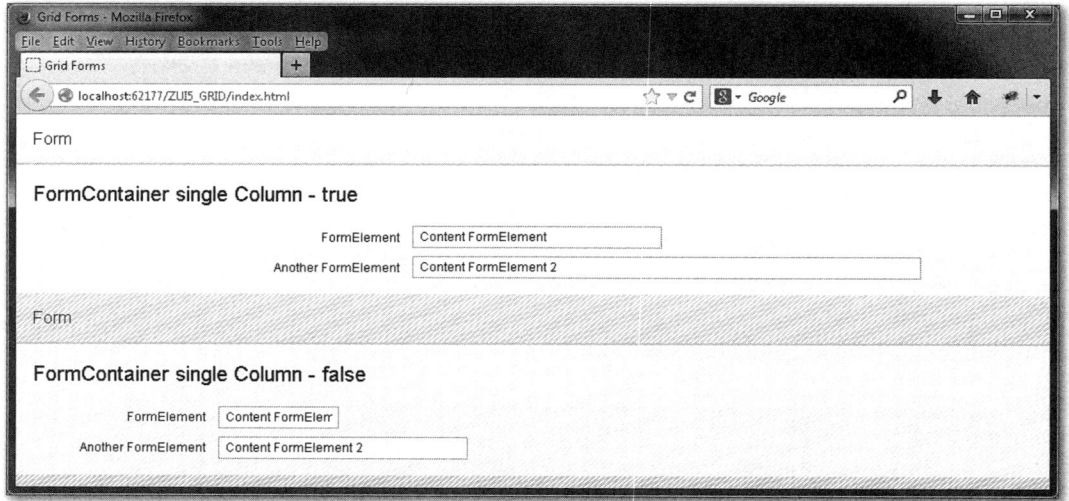

Figure 6.12   GridLayout

Responsive Layout

Weighting In the Responsive Layout, you set the individual form elements in relation to each other. You can assign a minimum width and a weighting to each element in this layout. The individual elements are displayed in one row as long as the width of elements is not less than their minimum width. The row is wrapped only if the width of an element is less than its minimum width.

You use the weighting to control their relative width to each other; that is, an element with a weighting of 2 takes twice as much space as an element with a weighting of 1. Listing 6.14 shows the same form as Listing 6.11; however, this time it is in the Responsive Layout.

```
<script>
// Layout for Form
var oLayout = new sap.ui.commons.form.ResponsiveLayout();

//FormElement
var oFormElement = new sap.ui.commons.form.FormElement();
// Title FormElement
oFormElement.setLabel("FormElement");
// Content FormElement
oFormElement.addField(new sap.ui.commons.TextField({
     value : "Content FormElement",
     layoutData: new
           sap.ui.commons.layout.ResponsiveFlowLayoutData({
                    weight: 1,
                    minWidth : 100
           })
 }));

var oFormElement2 = new sap.ui.commons.form.FormElement();
// Title FormElement
oFormElement2.setLabel("Another FormElement");
// Content FormElement
oFormElement2.addField(new sap.ui.commons.TextField({
     value : "Content FormElement 2",
     layoutData: new
           sap.ui.commons.layout.ResponsiveFlowLayoutData({
                    weight: 2,
                    minWidth : 250
           })
 }));

// FormContainer
var oFormCont = new sap.ui.commons.form.FormContainer();
// Heading FormContainer
oFormCont.setTitle("FormContainer");
//Add FormElement
oFormCont.addFormElement(oFormElement);
oFormCont.addFormElement(oFormElement2);

// Form
var oForm = new sap.ui.commons.form.Form();
//Title
```

```
oForm.setTitle("Form");
// Set Layout
oForm.setLayout(oLayout);
//Add FormContainer to Form
oForm.addFormContainer(oFormCont);

oForm.placeAt("content");
</script>
</head>
<body class="sapUiBody" role="application">
    <div id="content"></div>
</body>
</html>
```

Listing 6.14   Form with Responsive Layout

You see the effect of the weighting and minimum width best when you change the size of the window. As long as all elements fit in one row, they are displayed side by side, as shown in Figure 6.13.

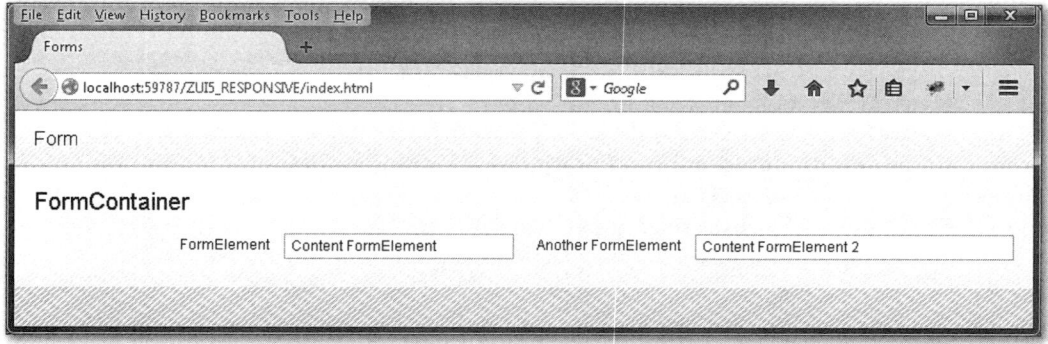

Figure 6.13   Responsive Layout in One Row

Wrapping row The row is wrapped once an element is less than its minimum size. In Figure 6.14, you can also see the effect of the weighting; the right element is twice as large as the left element.

As you can see, the form development in SAPUI5 is somewhat complex, but it is extremely flexible in its implementation in return. For simple forms, the library provides the Simple Form Layout.

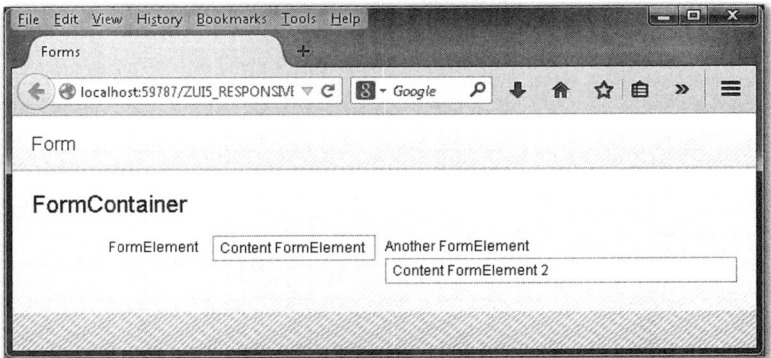

Figure 6.14 A Wrapping Row in Responsive Layout

Simple Form

In the `SimpleForm` container, insert only the content; the Simple Form generates the form, the form container, and the form element based on this transferred content. A control of type `Title` (`sap.ui.commons.Title`) creates a form container, a control of type `Label` (`sap.ui.core.Label`) creates a new form element, and all other controls are fields of the form element. In Listing 6.15, you'll create the same form as in Listing 6.11; however, use the `SimpleForm` control this time.

Simple Form control

```
<script>
// Constructor Simple Form
var oSimpleForm = new sap.ui.commons.form.SimpleForm();

// Create FormContainer
var oTitle = new
            sap.ui.commons.Title({text:"FormContainer"});
oSimpleForm.addContent(oTitle);
// FormElement
var oLabel = new sap.ui.commons.Label({text:"FormElement"});
oSimpleForm.addContent(oLabel);

// Content
var oText = new
    sap.ui.commons.TextField({value:"Content FormElement"});
oSimpleForm.addContent(oText);
// FormElement
var oLabel = new sap.ui.commons.Label({
```

```
                              text:"Another FormElement"
                    });
oSimpleForm.addContent(oLabel);
// Content
var oText = new sap.ui.commons.TextField({
                         value:"Content FormElement 2"
                    });
oSimpleForm.addContent(oText);

oSimpleForm.placeAt("content");
</script>
```

Listing 6.15 SimpleForm Control

As you can see from this simple example, the SimpleForm control really facilitates form development.

Before we leave the world of forms, an intriguing question remains to be answered: How can the data be transferred to the backend? The answer to this question is very simple: You learned about data binding models in Chapter 5, and this is the technique that you can use to transfer the form fields to the backend. You create a model and bind the input fields to it. When sending the data to the backend, you read the data from the model and attach the transfer to the data stream.

In the following example, take Listing 6.13 as the basis, bind the data to a JSON model, and transfer the data to the already familiar HTTP Handler (class ZUI5_HTTP_HANDLER). In Eclipse, create the project ZUI5_FORM_SEND without an Initial View, create an instance of the JSON Model, and bind it to the core element (see Listing 6.16).

```
<script>
// Create instance of the model
oModel = new sap.ui.model.json.JSONModel();
// Bind model to core
sap.ui.getCore().setModel(oModel);
```

Listing 6.16 Creating JSONModel

Form elements Next, create two form elements for the first and last names (see Listing 6.17).

```
// Layout for Form
var oLayout = new sap.ui.commons.form.GridLayout({singleColumn
:true});

//FormElement
var oFormElement = new sap.ui.commons.form.FormElement();
// Title FormElement
oFormElement.setLabel("First Name");
// Content FormElement
oFormElement.addField(new sap.ui.commons.TextField({
//Bind value to model
      layoutData: new sap.ui.commons.form.GridElementData({
                          hCells: "2"
                  })
}).bindValue({path: "/first_name"})); // Bind value

var oFormElement2 = new sap.ui.commons.form.FormElement();
// Title FormElement
oFormElement2.setLabel("last_name");
// Content FormElement
oFormElement2.addField(new sap.ui.commons.TextField({
layoutData: new sap.ui.commons.form.GridElementData({
                          hCells: "2",
              })
}).bindValue({path: "/Last Name"})); // Bind value
```

Listing 6.17 Form Elements

To ensure that the form can be sent, implement a Submit button. For the press event, send the form content to the backend; in our example, send it to the previously created ICF node ui5 (see Listing 6.18).

Send Form

```
//Submit button
var oFormElement3 = new sap.ui.commons.form.FormElement();
// Content FormElement
oFormElement3.addField(new sap.ui.commons.Button({
    "text": "Submit",
    "layoutData": new sap.ui.commons.form.GridElementData({
                          hCells: "1",
                  }),
    "press":function(){
```

```
var oResponse = jQuery.sap.sjax({
    "url":"/ui5",
    "type":"POST",
    "data":
sap.ui.getCore().getModel().getData()}); 
}}));
```

Listing 6.18 Send Form

Form

Finally, you have to transfer the form elements to a form and position them in the UI area (see Listing 6.19).

```
// FormContainer
var oFormCont = new sap.ui.commons.form.FormContainer();
// Heading FormContainer
oFormCont.setTitle("Enter Name");
//Add FormElement
oFormCont.addFormElement(oFormElement);
oFormCont.addFormElement(oFormElement2);
oFormCont.addFormElement(oFormElement3); //Submit button

// Form
var oForm = new sap.ui.commons.form.Form();
//Title
oForm.setTitle("Registration");
// Set Layout
oForm.setLayout(oLayout);
//Add FormContainer to Form
oForm.addFormContainer(oFormCont);
oForm.placeAt("content");
</script>
```

Listing 6.19 Form

Processing in the back end

In order to process the data in the SAP backend, you'll have to implement two things:

1. An AJAX call to the SAP backend

2. Reading and processing the form fields in the backend

In Figure 6.15, the server roundtrip for the example from Listing 6.19 is illustrated graphically.

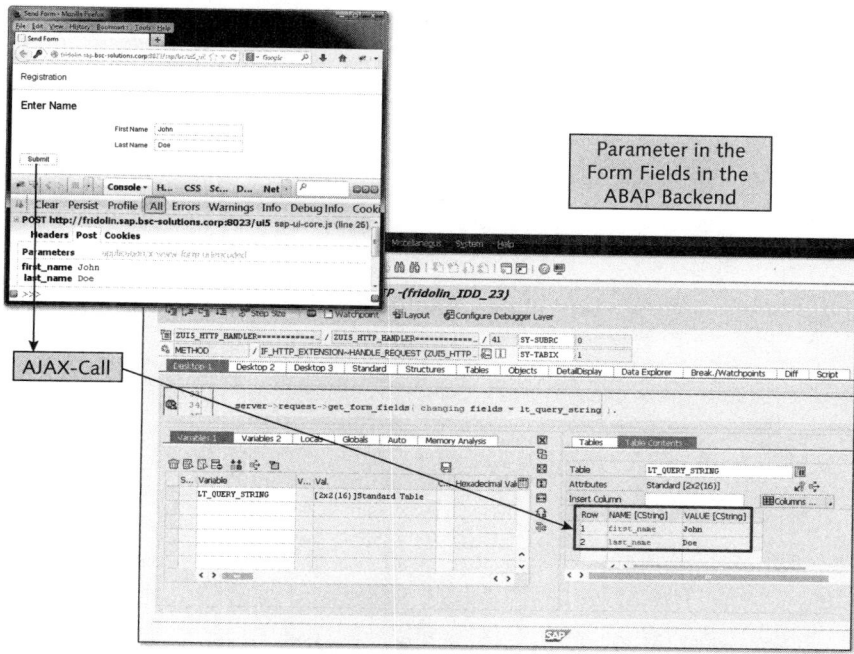

Figure 6.15 Form Processing in the SAP Backend

Panel Layout

You are probably already familiar with the Panel Layout (sap.ui.commons. Panel) from the Web Dynpro development. The Panel Layout consists of a header area and a body. You can display icons, text, and buttons in the header area, and it also contains the function for expanding and collapsing a Panel. In the Panel body, you can implement any UI controls and thus structure the page. As a small exercise, create the project ZUI5_PANEL in Eclipse, create a Panel Layout, and insert the Matrix Layout from Listing 6.20 into the Panel.

```
<script>
// Buttons
var oButton_1 = new sap.ui.commons.Button();
oButton_1.setText("First Button");
var oButton_2 = new sap.ui.commons.Button();
oButton_2.setText("Second Button");
```

```
// Fix MatrixLayout
var oMatrixFix = new sap.ui.commons.layout.MatrixLayout({
    layoutFixed : true,
    width : '800px',
    columns : 2,
    widths : [ '400px', '400px' ]
  });
oMatrixFix.createRow(oButton_1, oButton_2);

//Create instance of panel control
var oPanel = new sap.ui.commons.Panel();
//Title
oPanel.setTitle(new sap.ui.commons.Title({
   "text" : "Fix MatrixLayout"
}));
//Add matrix control to body of panel control
oPanel.addContent(oMatrixFix);
oPanel.placeAt("fix");
</script>
</head>
<body class="sapUiBody" role="application">
   <div id="fix"></div>
</body>
</html>
```

Listing 6.20   Panel Control

Figure 6.16 shows the Panel Layout in the browser.

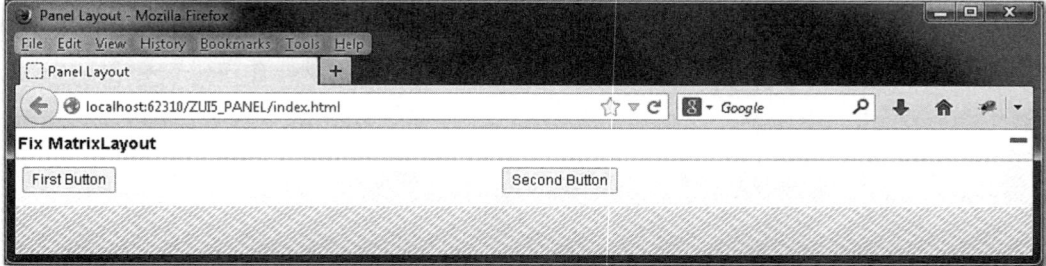

Figure 6.16   Panel Layout

Splitter Control

Panes

The Splitter Control (`sap.ui.commons.Splitter`) divides the relevant screen area into two areas, the *panes*. Within the panes, you can integrate any controls, and you can use the attribute `splitterOrientation` to specify whether the panes are to be arranged vertically or horizontally.

In the following example, create the project ZUI5_SPLITTER without an Initial View. In the *index.html* file, implement two splitter controls from Listing 6.21; the vertically-oriented splitter control includes the horizontally-oriented splitter control in the first pane. For illustration purposes, the splitter bar is given a dark color via CSS in this example.

```
<style>
.sapUiVerticalSplitterBar {
    background-color: #000066;
    }
.sapUiHorizontalSplitterBar {
    background-color: #000066;
    }
</style>

<script>
//Horizontal Splitter
var oSplitterH = new sap.ui.commons.Splitter("splitterH");
oSplitterH.setSplitterOrientation(
                    sap.ui.commons.Orientation.horizontal);
oSplitterH.setSplitterPosition("20%");
oSplitterH.setWidth("200px");
oSplitterH.setHeight("300px");
//Add text
var oTextView = new sap.ui.commons.TextView({
    text  : "First pane horizontal",
    design: sap.ui.commons.TextViewDesign.H1
    });
oSplitterH.addFirstPaneContent(oTextView);

// Text second pane
var oTextView2 = new sap.ui.commons.TextView({
    text  : "Second pane horizontal",
    design: sap.ui.commons.TextViewDesign.H1
    });
oSplitterH.addSecondPaneContent(oTextView2);
```

```
//Vertical Splitter
var oSplitterV = new sap.ui.commons.Splitter("splitterV");
oSplitterV.setSplitterOrientation(
                     sap.ui.commons.Orientation.vertical);
oSplitterV.setSplitterPosition("50%");
oSplitterV.setWidth("400px");
oSplitterH.setHeight("600px");

//Remove horizontal splitter in the first pane
oSplitterV.addFirstPaneContent(oSplitterH);

// Text second pane
var oTextView3 = new sap.ui.commons.TextView({
    text  : "Second pane vertical",
    design: sap.ui.commons.TextViewDesign.H1
   });
oSplitterV.addSecondPaneContent(oTextView3);

oSplitterV.placeAt("content");
</script>
```

Listing 6.21 Splitter Control

Figure 6.17 shows how the splitter controls are displayed in the browser.

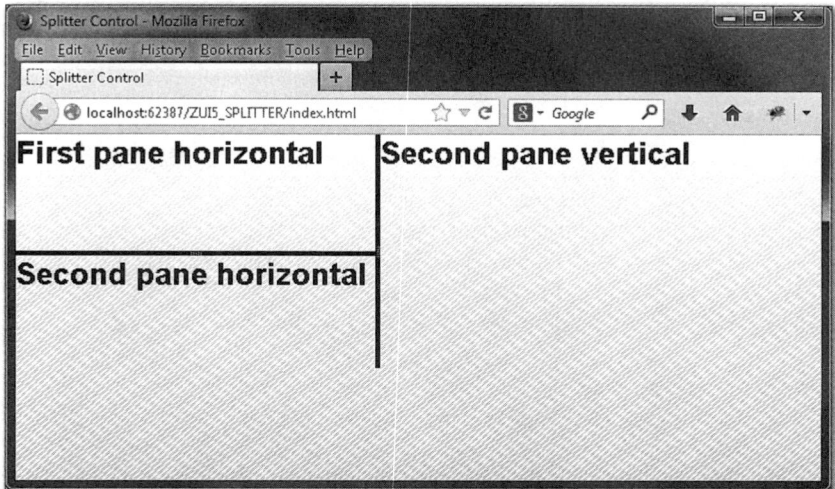

Figure 6.17 Splitter Control

Tabstrip Layout

You can use the Tabstrip Layout (sap.ui.commons.TabStrip) to display   Tabs
tabs on the assigned screen area. Each tab (sap.ui.commons.Tab) can in
turn include any UI elements.

In the following example, (see Listing 6.22), implement two simple tabs,   Example
each containing a text control (Eclipse project ZUI5_TABSTRIP).

```
<script>
//Tabstrip Layout
    var oTabStrip = new sap.ui.commons.TabStrip();
    oTabStrip.setWidth("300px");
    oTabStrip.setHeight("150px");

// First Tab
    var oTextView = new sap.ui.commons.TextView({
        text    : "First Tab",
        design : sap.ui.commons.TextViewDesign.H1
    });
    oTab = new sap.ui.commons.Tab();
    oTab.setTitle(new sap.ui.commons.Title({
        text : "First"
    }));
    oTab.addContent(oTextView);
// Add tab to the layout
    oTabStrip.addTab(oTab);
/// etc. //////

// Second Tab
    var oTextView2 = new sap.ui.commons.TextView({
        text : "Second Tab",
        design : sap.ui.commons.TextViewDesign.H1
    });
// Add tab to the layout
    oTab2 = new sap.ui.commons.Tab();
    oTab2.setTitle(new sap.ui.commons.Title({
        text : "Second"
    }));
    oTab2.addContent(oTextView2);

    oTabStrip.addTab(oTab2);
    oTabStrip.placeAt("content");
</script>
```

Listing 6.22 Tabstrip Layout

Figure 6.18 shows the Tabstrip Layout.

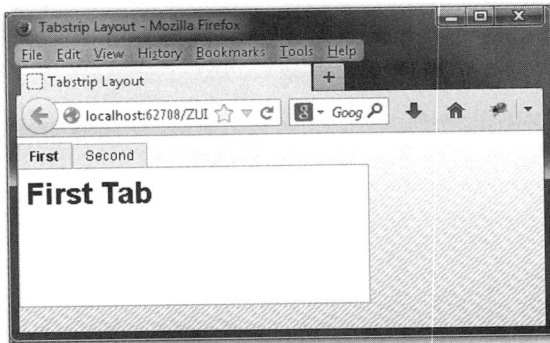

Figure 6.18 Tabstrip Layout

In Figure 6.19, you get a small glimpse of how very appealing pages can be even when designed through simple means. Figure 6.19 shows the home page of SAP Fiori and the new SAP HCM landing page.

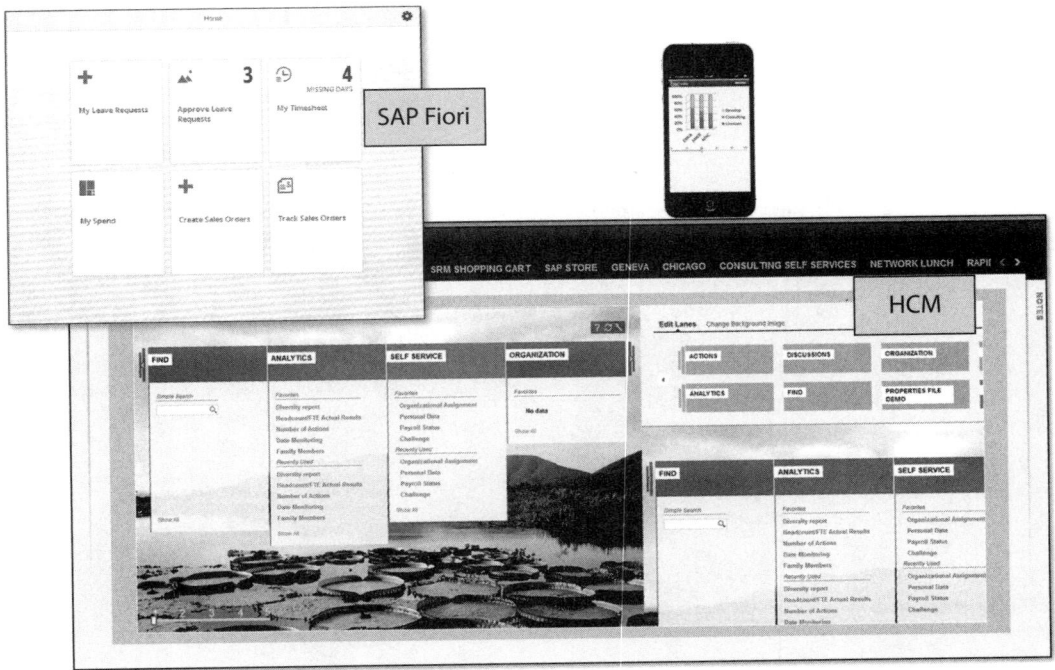

Figure 6.19 Examples of the Design Options

6.2.2 UI Controls

As mentioned in the introduction, the namespace `sap.ui.commons` contains the essential controls. These include texts, buttons, and images. In addition to these simple controls, there are also more complex controls, such as the `Accordion` control or the `ApplicationHeader` control. The controls are divided into three areas:

sap.ui.commons

▶ Simple controls with display functions

▶ Simple controls with input functions

▶ Complex controls

Simple Controls with Display Functions

The controls shown here can be used to display different content: text, images, and so on. Table 6.1 provides an overview of the simple controls with display functions.

Control	Description	Constructor
Button	Display of buttons	`sap.ui.commons.Button`
Formatted TextView	Formatted text	`sap.ui.commons.FormattedTextView`
HTML-Control	Wrapper for HTML	`sap.ui.core.HTML`
Image	Display of images	`sap.ui.commons.Image`
ImageMap	Image with superimposed map, for example, for hyperlinks	`sap.ui.commons.ImageMap`
Label	Text display	`sap.ui.commons.Label`
Hyperlink	Display of hyperlinks	`sap.ui.commons.Link`
TextView	Display of text	`sap.ui.commons.TextView`
Toggle-Button	Button active/inactive	`sap.ui.commons.ToggleButton`

Table 6.1 Simple Controls

Now it's your turn! In the following example, create a page that displays all the controls from Table 6.1. In Eclipse, create the project ZUI5_SIMPLE_CONTROL; below its *WebContent* folder, create an *img* folder. Copy the two images *HTML5_CSS3.jpg* and *HTML5_sticker.png* from the Appendix of this book to the *img* folder.

First, create a `MatrixLayout` control as the framework (see Listing 6.23).

```
<script>
// Fix MatrixLayout as outer layout
var oMatrixFix = new sap.ui.commons.layout.MatrixLayout({
        layoutFixed : true,
        width : '800px',
        columns : 2,
        widths : [ '200px', '600px' ]
});
```
Listing 6.23 Matrix Layout as Outer Layout

In this `MatrixLayout` control, implement the other controls, such as a `Button` (see Listing 6.24).

```
// Buttons ////////////////////////////////////////////////
var oTextView = new sap.ui.commons.TextView({
        text : "Button",
        design : sap.ui.commons.TextViewDesign.H1
});
var oButton = new sap.ui.commons.Button();
oButton.setText("Press me");
oMatrixFix.createRow(oTextView, oButton);
```
Listing 6.24 Text and Button Control

Formatted TextView and HTML-Control

Next, implement a `Formatted TextView` control and an HTML control to display formatted text (see Listing 6.25).

```
// Formatted TextView ///////////////////////////////////////
var oTextView = new sap.ui.commons.TextView({
        text : "Formatted TextView",
        design : sap.ui.commons.TextViewDesign.H1
});

var oFTV = new sap.ui.commons.FormattedTextView();
var sHtmlText = '<h1>Lorem ipsum</h1> dolor sit amet, ';
```

```
sHtmlText += 'consetetur sadipscing <h2>elitr</h2>,';
sHtmlText += 'sed diam nonumy <b>eirmod</b>';
oFTV.setHtmlText(sHtmlText);
oMatrixFix.createRow(oTextView, oFTV);

// HTML-Control /////////////////////////////////////////////
var oTextView = new sap.ui.commons.TextView({
     text : "HTML-Control",
     design : sap.ui.commons.TextViewDesign.H1
});
var oHtml = new sap.ui.core.HTML();
oHtml.setContent(sHtmlText);
oMatrixFix.createRow(oTextView, oHtml);
```
Listing 6.25 Formatted TextView and HTML-Control

Next, implement an `Image` control to display an image and an `ImageMap` control. With the `ImageMap` control, you can add a link to image areas by specifying their coordinates. In our example, you link the image areas to the Wikipedia entries for HTML5 and CSS3 (see Listing 6.26).

Image and ImageMap control

```
// Image ////////////////////////////////////////////////////
var oTextView = new sap.ui.commons.TextView({
     text : "Image",
     design : sap.ui.commons.TextViewDesign.H1
});
var oImage = new sap.ui.commons.Image();
oImage.setSrc("img/HTML5_sticker.png");
oMatrixFix.createRow(oTextView, oImage);

// ImageMap /////////////////////////////////////////////////
var oTextView = new sap.ui.commons.TextView({
     text : "Image Map",
     design : sap.ui.commons.TextViewDesign.H1
});

var oImage = new sap.ui.commons.Image();
oImage.setSrc("img/HTML5_CSS3.jpg");
oImage.setUseMap("Map");

var oMap = new sap.ui.commons.ImageMap();
oMap.setName("Map");
var aArea1 = new sap.ui.commons.Area({
```

```
        shape  : "rect",
        alt    : "HTML5",
        href   : "http://en.wikipedia.org/wiki/HTML5",
        coords : "35,60,215,240"
});
var aArea2 = new sap.ui.commons.Area({
        shape  : "rect",
        alt    : "CSS3",
        href   : "http://en.wikipedia.org/wiki/Cascading_Style_
Sheets",
        coords : "250,60,420,240"
});
oMap.addArea(aArea1);
oMap.addArea(aArea2);
oMap.placeAt("content");
oMatrixFix.createRow(oTextView, oImage);
```

Listing 6.26 Image and ImageMap Controls

Label, Hyperlink, TextView, and Toggle-Button controls

To conclude this example, implement a Label control, a Hyperlink control to display hyperlinks, a TextView control, and a Toggle-Button control, as shown in Listing 6.27.

```
// Label ////////////////////////////////////////////////////
var oTextView = new sap.ui.commons.TextView({
        text : "Label",
        design : sap.ui.commons.TextViewDesign.H1
});
var oLabel = new sap.ui.commons.Label();
oLabel.setText("Label Control");
oMatrixFix.createRow(oTextView, oLabel);


// Hyperlink ////////////////////////////////////////////////
var oTextView = new sap.ui.commons.TextView({
        text : "Hyperlink",
        design : sap.ui.commons.TextViewDesign.H1
});
var oLink = new sap.ui.commons.Link({
            text  : "A Link",
            href  : "www.w3.org",
            title : "W3 Consortium",
            target: "_blank"
        });
```

```
oMatrixFix.createRow(oTextView, oLink);

// Textview ///////////////////////////////////////////////
var oTextView = new sap.ui.commons.TextView({
      text : "TextView",
      design : sap.ui.commons.TextViewDesign.H1
});
var oTextView2 = new sap.ui.commons.TextView({
      text         : "TextView",
      semanticColor: sap.ui.commons.TextViewColor.Positive,
      design       : sap.ui.commons.TextViewDesign.H1
});
oMatrixFix.createRow(oTextView, oTextView2);

// Toggle Button ///////////////////////////////////////////
var oTextView = new sap.ui.commons.TextView({
      text : "Toggle-Button",
      design : sap.ui.commons.TextViewDesign.H1
   });

var oToggleButton1 = new sap.ui.commons.ToggleButton({
      text : "Active",
      pressed : true,
});

var oToggleButton2 = new sap.ui.commons.ToggleButton({
      text : "Inactive",
      pressed : false,
});

var oLayout = new sap.ui.commons.layout.HorizontalLayout({
         content: [oToggleButton1, oToggleButton2]
   });

oMatrixFix.createRow(oTextView, oLayout);
oMatrixFix.placeAt("content");
</script>
```

Listing 6.27 Simple Display Controls

You should now have a page with the control examples (see Figure 6.20). **Result** Pay special attention to the ImageMap control; in the image, both the 5 and the 3 have a hyperlink.

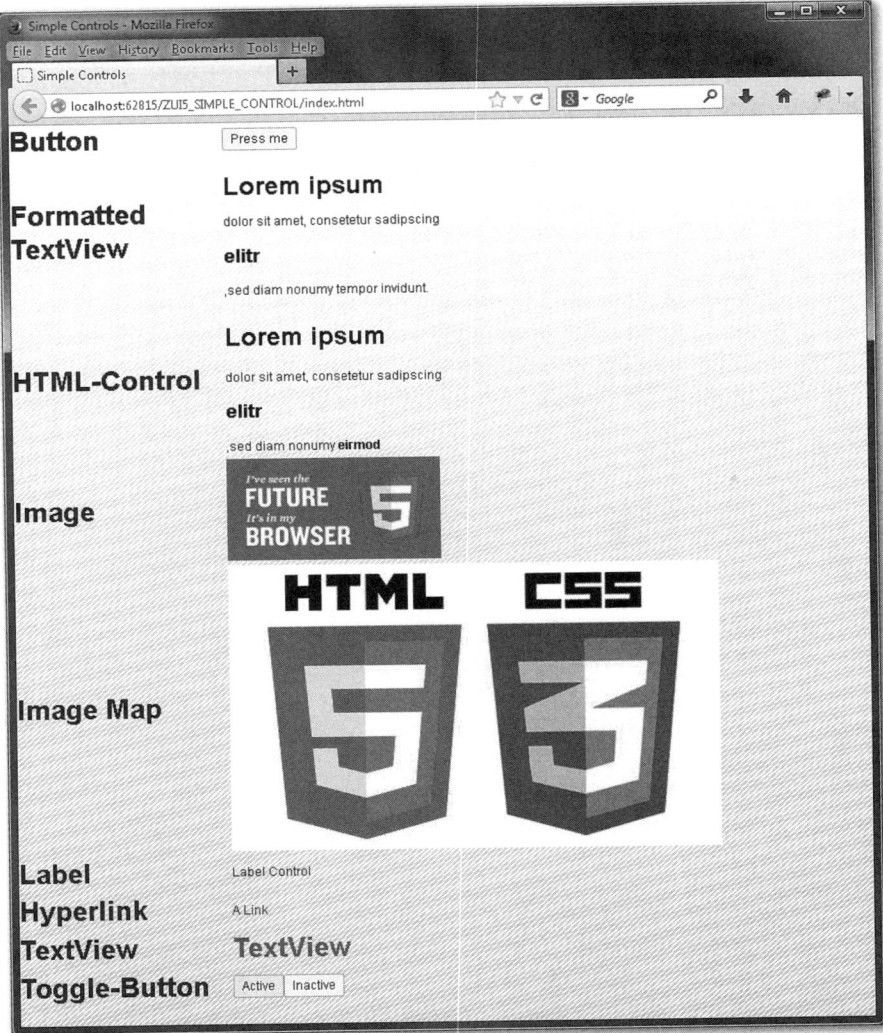

Figure 6.20 Example of an Application with Simple Controls

Simple Controls with Input

Controls involving user input include input fields, radio buttons, check-boxes, and so on. Table 6.2 provides an overview of the most important controls.

Control	Description	Constructor
AutoComplete	Input field with automatic completion	sap.ui.commons.AutoComplete
ComboBox	Values displayed as dropdown list	sap.ui.commons.ComboBox
DropdownBox	Same as ComboBox, with additional history and input help	sap.ui.commons.DropdownBox
DatePicker	Date selection	sap.ui.commons.DatePicker
FileUpload	File upload	sap.ui.commons.FileUploader
ListBox	Text as a selectable list	sap.ui.commons.ListBox
PasswordField	Field for password entry	sap.ui.commons.PasswordField
RadioButton	Display as radio button	sap.ui.commons.RadioButton and RadioButtonGroup
SearchField	Display as a search input field	sap.ui.commons.SearchField
TextArea	Multiline input field	sap.ui.commons.TextArea
TextField	Single-line input field	sap.ui.commons.TextField
CheckBox	Display as checkbox	sap.ui.commons.CheckBox
ValueHelpField	Display with F4 help	sap.ui.commons.ValueHelpField

Table 6.2 Controls with User Input

In the following example, create a page that displays all the controls from Table 6.2. The multiline UI controls are particularly suitable for data binding; we use the familiar *week.json* file in this example. In Eclipse, create the project ZUI5_VALUE_HOLD; below its *WebContent* folder, create a

Controls with input option

json folder. Copy the *week.json* file from the Appendix of this book to the *json* folder.

JSON Model

Create an instance of the JSON Model, and load the *week.json* file in the model. Use the `MatrixLayout` control as an external framework in this example (see Listing 6.28).

```
<script>
// Create instance of JSON Model
   var oModel = new sap.ui.model.json.JSONModel();

// Load JSON in model
   oModel.loadData("json/week.json");
   sap.ui.getCore().setModel(oModel);

// Fix MatrixLayout
var oMatrixFix = new sap.ui.commons.layout.MatrixLayout({
      layoutFixed : true,
      width : '800px',
      columns : 2,
      widths : [ '200px', '600px' ]
});
```

Listing 6.28 JSON Instance and External Framework

AutoComplete and ComboBox controls

The `AutoComplete` control automatically completes the user input based on the available values. If you enter a "T" in our example, the two values `Tuesday` and `Thursday` are proposed from the available values of JSON. The `ComboBox` control shows the available values as a dropdown list (see Listing 6.29).

```
// AutoComplete /////////////////////////////////////////////
var oTextView = new sap.ui.commons.TextView({
      text : "AutoComplete",
      design : sap.ui.commons.TextViewDesign.H1
});
var oAuto = new sap.ui.commons.AutoComplete({
      tooltip : "Enter weekday",
      items : {
         path : "/week",
            template : new sap.ui.core.ListItem({
            text     : "{we_day}"
         })
```

```
    }});
oAuto.setModel(oModel);
oMatrixFix.createRow(oTextView, oAuto);

// ComboBox ///////////////////////////////////////////////
var oTextView = new sap.ui.commons.TextView({
    text : "ComboBox",
    design : sap.ui.commons.TextViewDesign.H1
});

var oComboBox = new sap.ui.commons.ComboBox();
oComboBox.setModel(oModel);
var oItemTemplate = new sap.ui.core.ListItem();
oItemTemplate.bindProperty("text", "we_day");
oComboBox.bindItems("/week", oItemTemplate);

oMatrixFix.createRow(oTextView, oComboBox);
```

Listing 6.29 AutoComplete and ComboBox

The `DatePicker` control contains an input help for entering a date (see Listing 6.30).

DatePicker

```
// DatePicker ///////////////////////////////////////////////
var oTextView = new sap.ui.commons.TextView({
    text : "DatePicker",
    design : sap.ui.commons.TextViewDesign.H1
});

var date = new Date();
var properlyFormatted = date.getFullYear()
        + ("0" + (date.getMonth() + 1)).slice(-2)
        + ("0" + date.getDate()).slice(-2);

var oDatePicker = new sap.ui.commons.DatePicker();
oDatePicker.setYyyymmdd(properlyFormatted);
oDatePicker.setLocale("en-US");

oMatrixFix.createRow(oTextView, oDatePicker);
```

Listing 6.30 DatePicker Control

In contrast to the `ComboBox` control, you can implement an input help in the `DropdownBox` control. In addition, this control includes a history and

DropdownBox, FileUpload, and ListBox

displays the last selected entry. The FileUploader control enables you to upload files, and the ListBox control displays the available values as a list (see Listing 6.31).

```
// DropdownBox //////////////////////////////////////////
var oTextView = new sap.ui.commons.TextView({
    text : "DropdownBox",
    design : sap.ui.commons.TextViewDesign.H1
  });

var oDropdownBox = new sap.ui.commons.DropdownBox();
oDropdownBox.setModel(oModel);
var oItemTemplate = new sap.ui.core.ListItem();
oItemTemplate.bindProperty("text", "we_day");
oDropdownBox.bindItems("/week", oItemTemplate);

oMatrixFix.createRow(oTextView, oDropdownBox);

// FileUpload //////////////////////////////////////////
var oTextView = new sap.ui.commons.TextView({
    text : "FileUpload",
    design : sap.ui.commons.TextViewDesign.H1
});
var oSimpleFileUploader = new sap.ui.commons.FileUploader({
    uploadUrl : "ui5/",
    name : "simpleUploader",
    uploadOnChange : true
});

oMatrixFix.createRow(oTextView, oSimpleFileUploader);

// ListBox //////////////////////////////////////////
var oTextView = new sap.ui.commons.TextView({
    text : "ListBox",
    design : sap.ui.commons.TextViewDesign.H1
});

// Template for binding
var oItemTemplate = new sap.ui.core.ListItem();
oItemTemplate.setModel(oModel);
oItemTemplate.bindProperty("text", "we_day");

var oListBox = new sap.ui.commons.ListBox();
```

```
oListBox.bindAggregation("items", "/week", oItemTemplate);
oMatrixFix.createRow(oTextView, oListBox);
```
Listing 6.31 DropdownBox, FileUpload, and ListBox

With the `PasswordField` control, the entered text is masked, the `RadioBut-`
`ton` control displays the values as radio buttons, and the `SearchField`
control enables you to implement a search field (see Listing 6.32).

PasswordField, RadioButton, and SearchField

```
// PasswordField ///////////////////////////////////////////
var oTextView = new sap.ui.commons.TextView({
        text : "PasswordField",
        design : sap.ui.commons.TextViewDesign.H1
    });
oPassWord = new sap.ui.commons.PasswordField();
oMatrixFix.createRow(oTextView, oPassWord);


// RadioButton ///////////////////////////////////////////
var oTextView = new sap.ui.commons.TextView({
        text : "RadioButton",
        design : sap.ui.commons.TextViewDesign.H1
    });


//Template for binding
var oItemTemplate = new sap.ui.core.Item();
oItemTemplate.setModel(oModel);
oItemTemplate.bindProperty("text", "we_day");


// Radiobutton
var oRadioButton = new sap.ui.commons.RadioButtonGroup();
oRadioButton.bindAggregation(
                        "items", "/week", oItemTemplate);
oMatrixFix.createRow(oTextView, oRadioButton);


// SearchField ///////////////////////////////////////////
var oTextView = new sap.ui.commons.TextView({
        text    : "SearchField",
        design : sap.ui.commons.TextViewDesign.H1
    });


var oSearch = new sap.ui.commons.SearchField();
oMatrixFix.createRow(oTextView, oSearch);
```
Listing 6.32 PasswordField, RadioButton, and SearchField

To conclude this exercise, create a `TextArea` control, a `CheckBox` control, and a `ValueHelpField` control. For the `ValueHelpField` control, you can implement a function for displaying a value help in the `valueHelpRequest` parameter (see Listing 6.33).

```
// TextArea ////////////////////////////////////////////////////
var oTextView = new sap.ui.commons.TextView({
    text : "TextArea",
    design : sap.ui.commons.TextViewDesign.H1
  });
oTextArea = new sap.ui.commons.TextArea();
oTextArea.setRows(3);
oMatrixFix.createRow(oTextView, oTextArea);

//TextField //////////////////////////////////////////////////////
var oTextView = new sap.ui.commons.TextView({
    text   : "TextField",
    design : sap.ui.commons.TextViewDesign.H1
  });

  var oTextField = new sap.ui.commons.TextField();
  oMatrixFix.createRow(oTextView, oTextField);

//CheckBox //////////////////////////////////////////////////////
var oTextView = new sap.ui.commons.TextView({
    text : "CheckBox",
    design : sap.ui.commons.TextViewDesign.H1
  });
var oCheckBox = new sap.ui.commons.CheckBox();
oCheckBox.setText("CheckBox");

oMatrixFix.createRow(oTextView, oCheckBox);

//ValueHelpField //////////////////////////////////////////////////
var oTextView = new sap.ui.commons.TextView({
    text   : "ValueHelpField",
    design : sap.ui.commons.TextViewDesign.H1
  });
var oValueHelp = new sap.ui.commons.ValueHelpField();
oMatrixFix.createRow(oTextView, oValueHelp);

oMatrixFix.placeAt("content");
</script>
```

Listing 6.33 TextArea, CheckBox, and ValueHelpField

The resulting page shows the most common input-ready controls (see Figure 6.21).

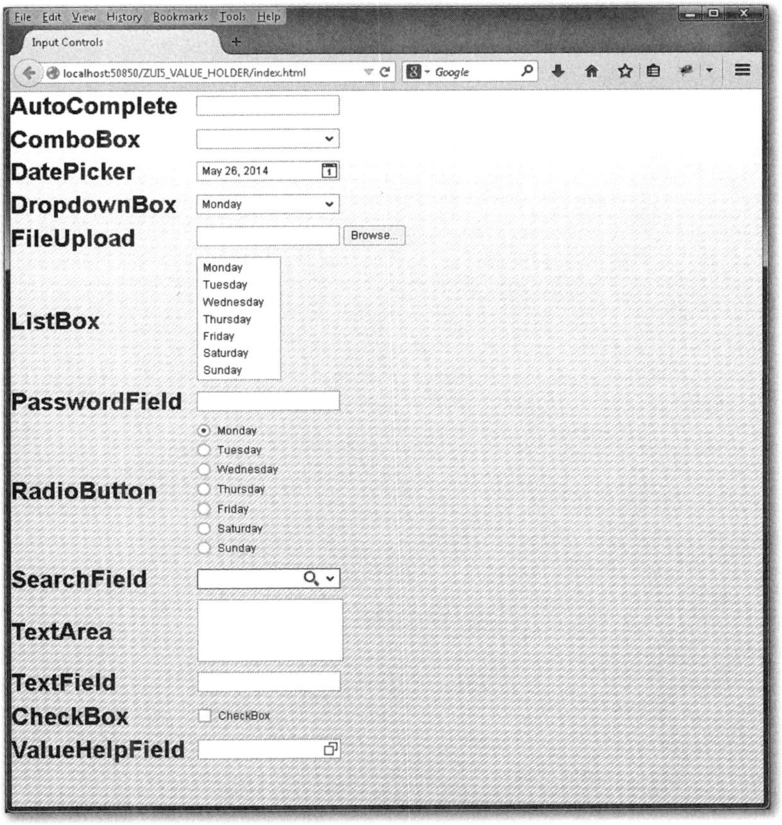

Figure 6.21 Input-Ready Controls

At this point, the question of how the file upload can be processed in the backend often arises. The content of the File Uploader is transferred as a byte string in the multipart segment of the HTTP request and can be read and processed there, similar to the header fields.

Processing File Uploader

In the following example, upload a file—for example, an image—to the SAP backend. First, add the upload function to the HANDLE-REQUEST method in the HTTP Handler ZUI5_HTTP_HANDLER. In the case statement case <ls_query>-value, insert the source code from Listing 6.34.

Back-end implementation

```
        types: begin of file,
                file_name     type  string,
                file_type     type  string,
                content_name  type  string,
                file_content  type  xstring,
             end of file.

        data: lv_content_type type string,
              lv_content_name type string,
              lv_filename     type string,
              ls_file         type file,
              lo_multipart    type ref to if_http_entity.

        data: lt_files          type table of file,
              lr_mime_rep        type ref to if_mr_api,
              lv_path            type string.
        field-symbols: <ls_query> type ihttpnvp,
                       <file>      type file.

  case <ls_query>-value.
  ...
  when 'upload'.
    "Multipart content for file uploads
    do server->request->num_multiparts( ) times.
      clear ls_file.
      lo_multipart = server->request->get_multipart(
                                         index = sy-index ).

      lv_content_type = lo_multipart->get_header_field(
         name = if_http_header_fields=>content_type ).
      lv_content_name = lo_multipart->get_header_field(
         name = if_http_header_fields_sap=>content_name ).
      lv_filename = lo_multipart->get_header_field(
         name = if_http_header_fields_sap=>content_filename ).

      if not lv_content_type is initial and
         not lv_content_name is initial and
         not lv_filename is initial.
        ls_file-file_content = lo_multipart->get_data( ).
        ls_file-content_name = lv_content_name.
        ls_file-file_type    = lv_content_type.
        ls_file-file_name    = lv_filename.
```

```
      append ls_file to lt_files.
    endif.
  enddo.
  "    "Save picture in MIME
  read table lt_files assigning <file> index 1.
  if sy-subrc = 0.
    concatenate 'SAP/PICTURES/' "MIME path
                <file>-file_name
                into lv_path.
    condense lv_path no-gaps.

lr_mime_rep = cl_mime_repository_api=>if_mr_api~get_api( ).

    lr_mime_rep->put(
      exporting
        i_url                       = lv_path
        i_content                   = <file>-file_content
        i_suppress_package_dialog   = 'X'
        i_dev_package               = '$TMP'
        i_suppress_dialogs          = 'X'
      exceptions
        parameter_missing           = 1
        error_occured               = 2
        cancelled                   = 3
        permission_failure          = 4
        data_inconsistency          = 5
        new_loio_already_exists     = 6
        is_folder                   = 7
        others                      = 8
           ).

    "Save path in appropriate manner.
    "....
endif.
```

Listing 6.34 File Upload in the SAP Backend

In Eclipse, create the project ZUI5_UPLOAD and, in the application area of the *index.html* file, add the source code from Listing 6.35.

```
<script>
   var layout = new sap.ui.commons.layout.MatrixLayout();
   layout.setLayoutFixed(false);
```

```
// FileUploader
var oFileUploader = new sap.ui.commons.FileUploader({
   name            : "upload",
   uploadOnChange : false,
   uploadUrl       : "/ui5?application=upload",
});
layout.createRow(oFileUploader);

// Upload Button
var oTriggerButton = new sap.ui.commons.Button({
   text  : 'Upload',
   press : function() {
      oFileUploader.upload();
   }
});
layout.createRow(oTriggerButton);
layout.placeAt("content");
</script>
```

Listing 6.35 File Upload with Connection to the SAP Backend

Breakpoint   Upload the SAPUI5 application to the SAP backend, and set an external breakpoint for the `case` statement `case <ls_query>-value`. After reading the multipart segment, you can see the file name and the file content as a byte string in the Debugger. After its transfer to the MIME Repository, you will find the file under the specified path—in our example, as shown in Figure 6.22, *SAP/PICTURES/*.

Now that you have an overview of the simple controls, you'll be introduced to the category of complex controls.

Complex Controls

Complex controls are predefined controls that consist mostly of a number of other controls. Complex controls include the following controls:

▶ `Accordion`: This control consists of several sections; in each section, you can include other controls in turn.

▶ `ApplicationHeader`: This control represents the header area of a page. You can include a menu, for example, in this control.

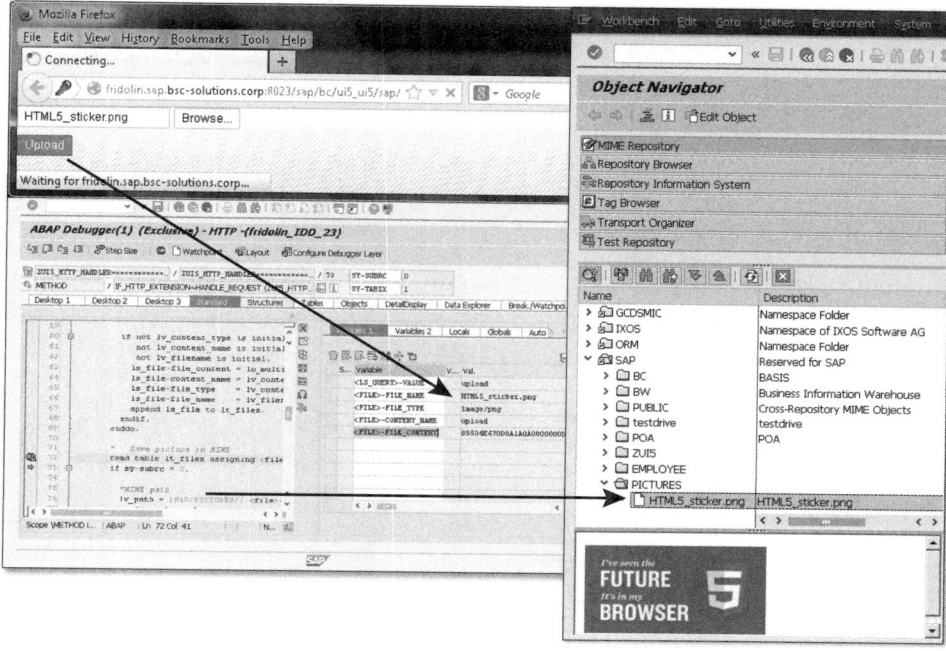

Figure 6.22 File Upload and Storage in the MIME Repository

▶ `Carousel`: This control can include several other controls, and you can navigate by button through the individual controls.

▶ `MenuBar`: This control represents several menu entries in a row.

▶ `RowRepeater`: This control repeats any UI control in a row-type display manner.

At this point, you are encouraged to view all controls using the API documentation and to implement them as examples; only practice makes perfect. In the following example, ZUI5_COMPLEX, from Listing 6.38, you will see examples of some controls. As you can see, the individual controls are always implemented according to the same schema:

▶ Call constructor

▶ Define properties, aggregations, and events

▶ Call control methods if required

ApplicationHeader
Set a `MatrixLayout` control as an external framework in this example. To begin, implement an `ApplicationHeader` control that displays the usual SAP header (see Listing 6.36).

```
<script>
   // Fix MatrixLayout as outer layout
   var oMatrix = new sap.ui.commons.layout.MatrixLayout({
      layoutFixed : true,
      width : '800px',
      columns : 2,
      widths : [ '200px', '600px' ]
   });

   // ApplicationHeader ///////////////////////////////
   var oTextView = new sap.ui.commons.TextView({
      text : "Application Header",
      design : sap.ui.commons.TextViewDesign.H2
   });

   //ApplicationHeader Control
   var oAppHeader = new sap.ui.commons.ApplicationHeader({
      logoText       : "Application Header",
      displayLogoff  : true,
      userName       : "John Doe",
      displayWelcome : true
   });
   oMatrix.createRow(oTextView, oAppHeader);
```

Listing 6.36 Application Header Control

MenuBar,
ToolBar, and
SegmentedButton
The controls `MenuBar`, `ToolBar`, and `SegmentedButton` are particularly suited to implementing toolbars (see Listing 6.37).

```
   // MenuBar ////////////////////////////////////////////
   var oTextView = new sap.ui.commons.TextView({
      text : "Menu Bar",
      design : sap.ui.commons.TextViewDesign.H2
   });

   var oMenuBar = new sap.ui.commons.MenuBar();

   var oMenuBarItem1 = new sap.ui.commons.MenuItem({
```

```
      text : "Menu 1"
});
oMenuBar.addItem(oMenuBarItem1);
var oMenuBarItem2 = new sap.ui.commons.MenuItem({
      text : "Menu 2"
});
oMenuBar.addItem(oMenuBarItem2);
var oMenu = new sap.ui.commons.Menu();
oMenuBarItem1.setSubmenu(oMenu);

// Submenu
var oMenuItem1 = new sap.ui.commons.MenuItem({
      text : "Submenu 1"
});
oMenu.addItem(oMenuItem1);
var oMenuItem2 = new sap.ui.commons.MenuItem({
      text : "Submenu 2"
});
oMenu.addItem(oMenuItem2);

oMatrix.createRow(oTextView, oMenuBar);

// ToolBar ///////////////////////////////////////////////
var oTextView = new sap.ui.commons.TextView({
      text : "Tool Bar",
      design : sap.ui.commons.TextViewDesign.H2
});

var oToolbar = new sap.ui.commons.Toolbar();

var oButton = new sap.ui.commons.Button({
      text : "Button 1",
});
oToolbar.addItem(oButton);

// Separator
oToolbar.addItem(new sap.ui.commons.ToolbarSeparator());

var oComboBox = new sap.ui.commons.ComboBox({
      items : [ new sap.ui.core.ListItem({
          text : "Combo 1"
```

```
      }), new sap.ui.core.ListItem({
         text : "Combo 2"
      }) ]
   });
   oToolbar.addItem(oComboBox);

   var oButton = new sap.ui.commons.Button({
      text : "Button 2",
   });
   oToolbar.addItem(oButton);
   oMatrix.createRow(oTextView, oToolbar);
   // SegmentedButton ////////////////////////////////////
   var oTextView = new sap.ui.commons.TextView({
      text : "Segmented Button",
      design : sap.ui.commons.TextViewDesign.H2
   });

var oSegmentedButton = new sap.ui.commons.SegmentedButton({
      buttons : [ new sap.ui.commons.Button({
         text : "Segment 1"
      }), new sap.ui.commons.Button({
         text : "Segment 2"
      }), new sap.ui.commons.Button({
         text : "Segment 3"
      }) ]
   });
   oMatrix.createRow(oTextView, oSegmentedButton);
```

Listing 6.37 MenuBar, ToolBar, and SegmentedButton

RoadMap   You are probably already familiar with the RoadMap control from Web Dynpro development. You can use it to define steps that, for example, will be executed in a wizard (see Listing 6.38).

```
   // RoadMap ////////////////////////////////////////////
   var oTextView = new sap.ui.commons.TextView({
      text : "Road Map",
      design : sap.ui.commons.TextViewDesign.H2
   });

   var oRoadMap = new sap.ui.commons.RoadMap({
      steps : [ new sap.ui.commons.RoadMapStep({
         label : "Step 1"
```

```
        }), new sap.ui.commons.RoadMapStep({
            label : "Step 2",
            subSteps : [ new sap.ui.commons.RoadMapStep({
                label : "Substep"
                }) ]
        }), new sap.ui.commons.RoadMapStep({
            label : "Step 3"
        }) ]
    });

    oMatrix.createRow(oTextView, oRoadMap);
    oMatrix.placeAt("content");
</script>
```

Listing 6.38 RoadMap Control

Figure 6.23 shows the complex controls in the browser.

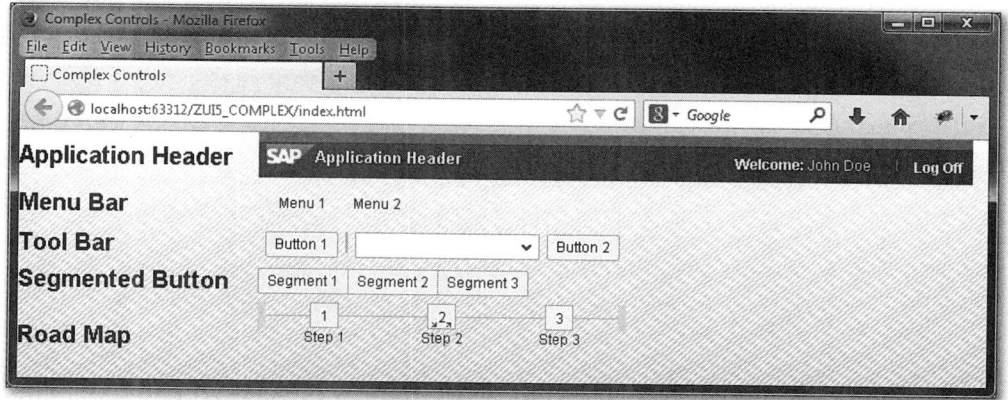

Figure 6.23 Complex Controls

6.3   UX3 Controls (sap.ui.ux3)

The SAP User Experience Guidelines 3.0 controls go one step further than the complex controls. The best-known example is the *Shell* (see Figure 6.24).

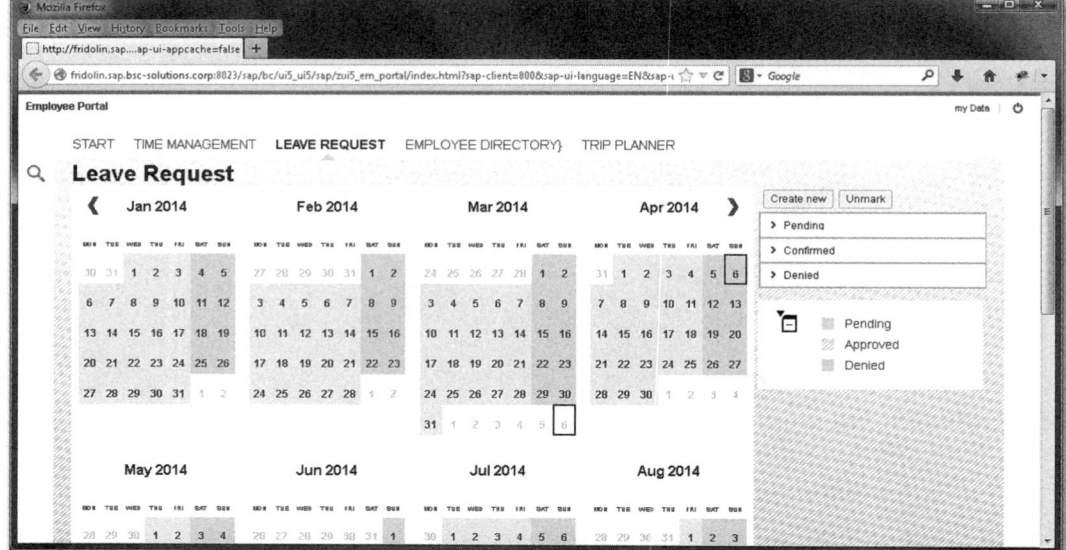

Figure 6.24 Shell UX3 Control

The Shell control provides different areas in which you can include navigation bars and more. The individual areas of the Shell are displayed in Figure 6.25:

❶ Application Title

❷ WorksetItem

❸ HeaderItem

❹ Pane Bar

❺ Content

❻ ToolPopUp

For many situations, the UX3 controls offer a complete framework—for example, as a navigation frame via the Shell control or also the notification bar for displaying messages. Because you will use most of the controls in the application example in Chapter 7, let's refrain from providing an example at this point.

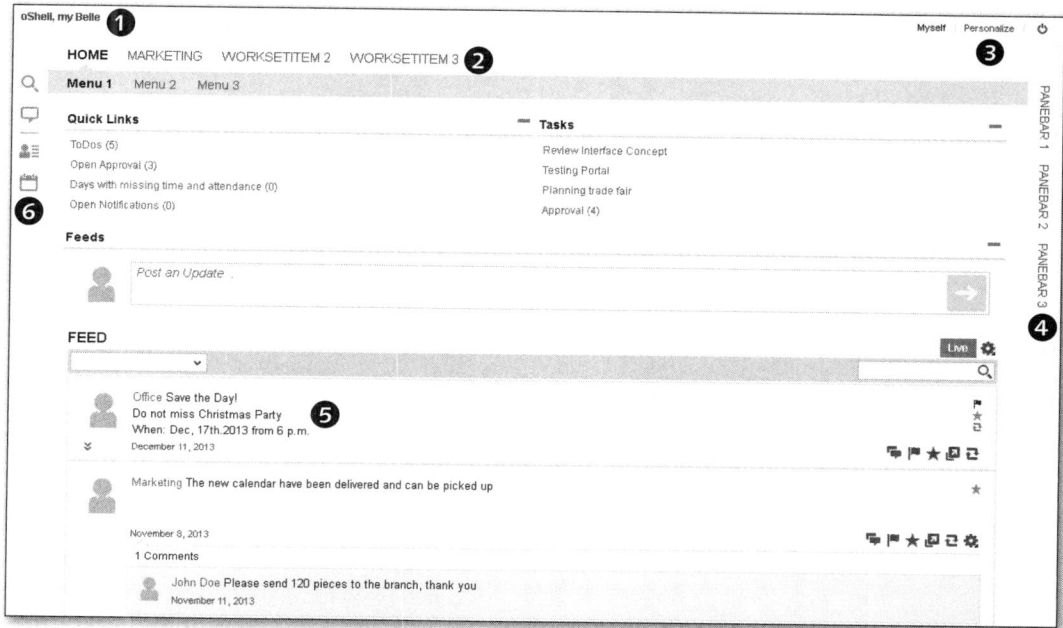

Figure 6.25 Areas of the Shell Control

6.4 Table Control (sap.ui.table)

As the name suggests, the class `sap.ui.table` implements the table control for displaying tabular information. You already used the control in Chapter 5, when you displayed the menu of the week during element binding.

sap.ui.table

6.5 Charts (sap.viz)

In the namespace `sap.viz`, the controls for the visualization of charts are summarized. Figure 6.26 shows a small selection of these options.

sap.viz

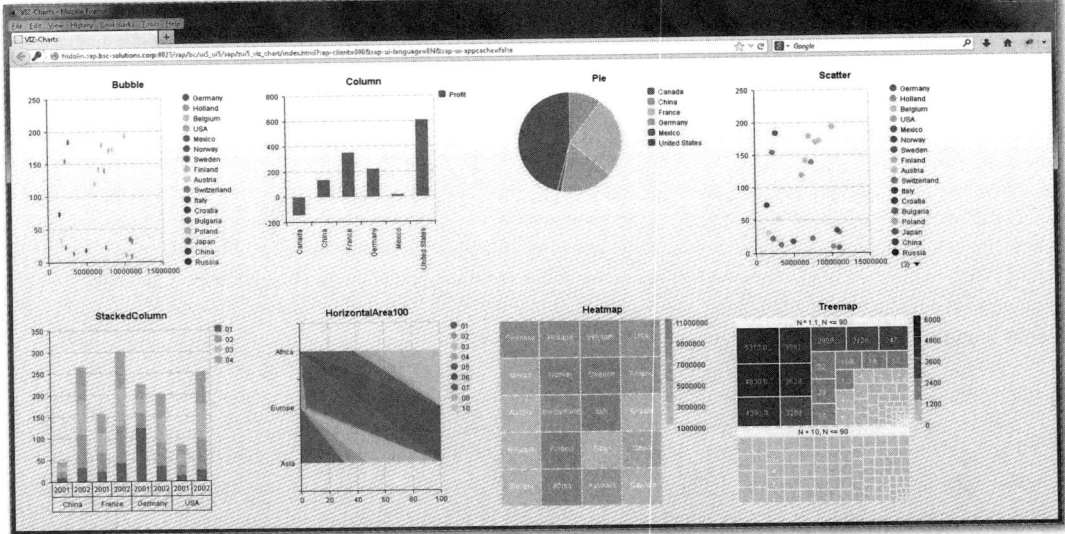

Figure 6.26 VIZ Controls

We will use these controls in Chapter 7 to display small statistics in the application.

6.6 Controls for Mobile Applications

The controls for applications developed specifically for mobile devices are summarized in the namespaces sap.m, sap.me, and sap.makit. The namespace sap.m is comparable with the sap.ui.commons namespace. The most common controls are summarized again in this namespace. The namespace sap.me is an extension of the sap.m namespace and currently includes mainly just the calendar control. We will also use this control in the application example. The namespace sap.makit is comparable with sap.viz; the chart controls for mobile devices are summarized here.

6.7 Suite Controls (sap.suite.)

sap.suite The naming convention suggests here that these controls were summarized specifically for areas of SAP Business Suite. These include, for example, a `BusinessCard` control, which bears a certain resemblance to a business card. As an example of this class, we've selected the `NoteTaker` control, with which you can record and manage notes.

Create the project ZUI5_NOTE with the source code from Listing 6.39. Remember to include the library *sap.suite.ui.commons* in the bootstrap.

Creating the project

```
<!DOCTYPE HTML>
<html>
  <head>
    <meta http-equiv="X-UA-Compatible" content="IE=edge">

    <script src="resources/sap-ui-core.js"
        id="sap-ui-bootstrap"
        data-sap-ui-libs="sap.ui.commons,
                          sap.suite.ui.commons"
    </script>

    <script>
    var oNoteTaker = new sap.suite.ui.commons.NoteTaker({
        visibleNotes : 2
    });

    oCard = new sap.suite.ui.commons.NoteTakerCard({
        uid : '4711',
        header: "Good News",
        body: "This is really good news",
        attachmentFilename : "Message.pdf"

    });
    oNoteTaker.addCard(oCard);
    //oCard.placeAt("content");
    oNoteTaker.placeAt("content");
    </script>

  </head>
  <body class="sapUiBody" role="application">
    <div id="content"></div>
  </body>
</html>
```

Listing 6.39 NoteTaker Control

Figure 6.27 shows an example of a `NoteTaker` control.

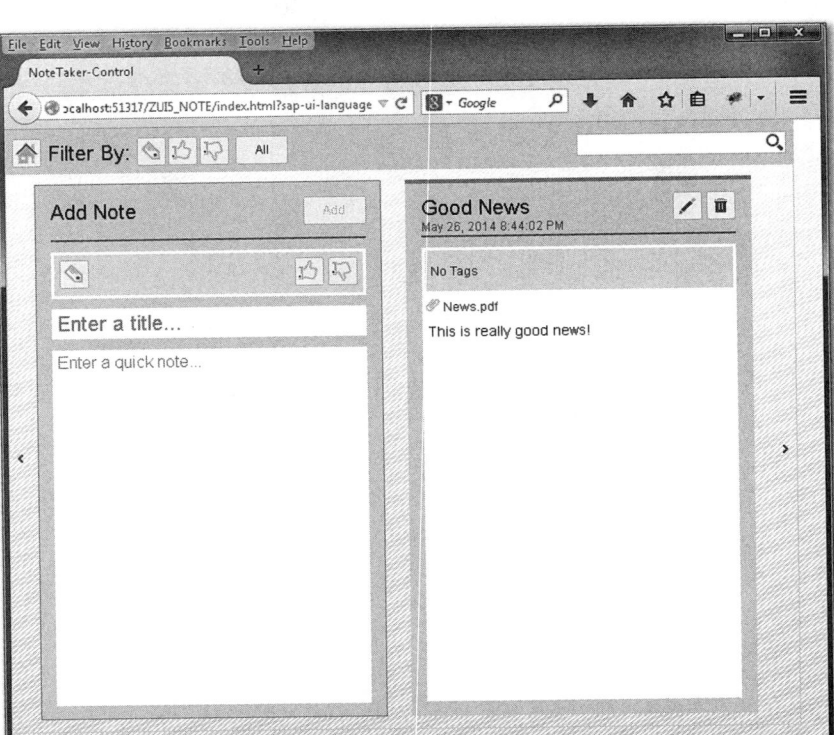

Figure 6.27 NoteTaker Control

To conclude this chapter, let's show how to develop your own controls.

6.8   Your Own Controls

If you've worked through the API documentation and the control library, you'll have noticed that the SAPUI5 library includes a large number of controls. It may nevertheless happen that you need a particular UI element in your business case that does not exist in the standard system. In SAPUI5, you can extend existing controls or implement completely new controls. For this purpose, an `extend` method is implemented in each UI control—for example, `sap.ui.commons.Button.extend` for extending the button control. If your own control is not based on an existing control, use the `extend` method of the core class: `sap.ui.core.Control.extend`.

You can now use this `extend` method to extend existing controls or to implement your own entirely new controls. Fortunately, certain methods, such as the `getter` and `setter` methods and the methods for registering events, are generated automatically by the SAPUI5 framework. As a result, it's very easy to implement your own controls.

extend

The constructor for a user-defined control contains metadata, public and private methods, an Event Handler, and the `renderer` method. This results in the content of Listing 6.40 as the basis for your own control.

```
sap.ui.core.Control.extend("MyControl", {
        metadata : { // Properties, Aggregations & Events
            properties : {},
            events: {},
            aggregations: {}
        },
    publicMethod: function() {},        // public Methods
    _privateMethod: function() {},      // private Methods
    init: function() {}                 //Initialization
    onclick: function (e) {},           //Event Handler
    renderer : function(oRm, oControl) {} //html statements
});
```

Listing 6.40 The Body of Your Own Control

In the `metadata` area, you define the properties, aggregations, and relevant events for the control. The SAPUI5 framework generates the relevant `getter` and `setter` methods for them. If, for example, you define the `Header` property:

```
properties : {"Header" : "string"}
```

you can use the `setter` method to set the value:

```
<Control>.setProperty("Header", "My Header");
```

The `renderer` method is responsible for the subsequent appearance of the controls. In this area, you define the HTML structure and thus the layout. At this point, you must pay attention: The method here is a static method, and so you cannot access the `this` method. An instance of the control and the `RenderManager` is transferred to you instead. The `RenderManager` is nothing more than a collector to which you transfer HTML fragments as a string. This is quite similar to the HTML control, in that the `RenderManager` takes care of the correct concatenation of HTML fragments and the corresponding positioning in the DOM.

Example As a simple example, implement your own control that displays the weather forecast for the next three days. This is a very simple service of the website *www.theweather.com*. Because we don't have to transfer any data to the service in this case, it's sufficient to implement only the `renderer` method. In Eclipse, create the project ZUI5_OWN_CONTROL, and extend the `index.html` file by adding the source code from Listing 6.41 to it. The result is shown in Figure 6.28.

```
<script>
// Weather Control
sap.ui.core.Control.extend("my.Weather",
{
    //metadata : {}, //is not required here
renderer : function(oRm, oControl) {
  oRm.write('<div ');
  oRm.write('id="cont_91dc83186187189b720bf75e94dabe06"> ');
  oRm.write('<span id="');
  oRm.write('h_91dc83186187189b720bf75e94dabe06">');
  oRm.write('Weather New York</span> ');
  oRm.write('<script type="text/javascript" ');
  oRm.write('src="http://www.theweather.com/wid_loader/');
  oRm.write('91dc83186187189b720bf75e94dabe06">');
  oRm.write("\<\/script>");
}
});
var oWeather = new my.Weather();
oWeather.placeAt('content');
</script>
```
Listing 6.41 Weather Control

As you can see, it's very easy to create a new control and to embed it in an SAPUI5 application. In Chapter 7, you'll implement a small application, and you will implement another control of your own in it.

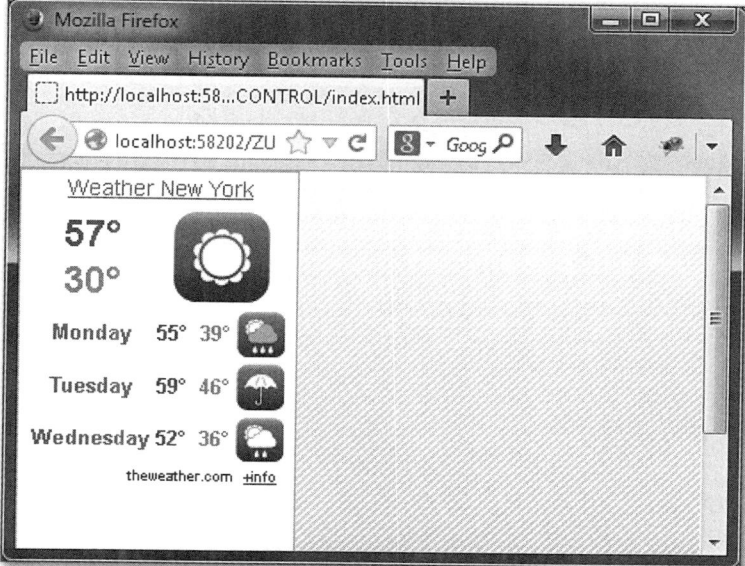

Figure 6.28 Weather Control

After the two preceding chapters, it's now time to merge the individual components of the SAPUI5 development—data binding, layout, controls, events, the connection to an SAP backend, and so on—into one application. You can thus deepen your existing knowledge and view a "real" application in the overall context.

A look ahead

In this chapter, everything you have learned so far will be combined, and you will develop a complete application in SAPUI5. In this application, you will use many controls from almost all of the libraries and thus consolidate the interaction of the individual components.

7   Development Example of an Application

The objective of this chapter is the implementation of an employee portal. This portal is intended to enable you to maintain your own data, create a leave request, and record your working times. An employee directory and a travel planning function will also be provided. In Chapter 10, we'll develop a suitable mobile app to approve leave requests.

Employee portal

The employee portal leaves potential for further development, so you can continue working on this portal and improving your skills in SAPUI5 after you have worked through this book.

Due to data privacy policies, the whole portal is based on your own database tables and does not read from the relevant master data tables of the SAP system. Of course, you can also access real data in your version.

7.1   The UI Design

SAPUI5 is, of course, the UI technology of choice; we will also use the ABAP stack of SAP Business Suite as the ERP system this time. Due to the fact that the development of UI (view) and database communication (model) in SAPUI5 are much more strictly separated than in the classic ABAP development, it's definitely advisable to think in advance about the necessary interfaces. Let's start with the UI design, because you can quickly derive the required services in the backend.

Tools   For internal purposes, you may prefer to use the whiteboard for UI design. Of course, you can also use any UI prototyping tools—for example, the open-source Pencil Project (*http://pencil.evolus.vn/*) or PowerPoint.

7.1.1   Start Page

Task List   On the Start page, a task list and a small statistic on tasks (open vs. done) will be displayed, and the option to create a new task will be available in the table display of the task list. The Start page should look something like Figure 7.1.

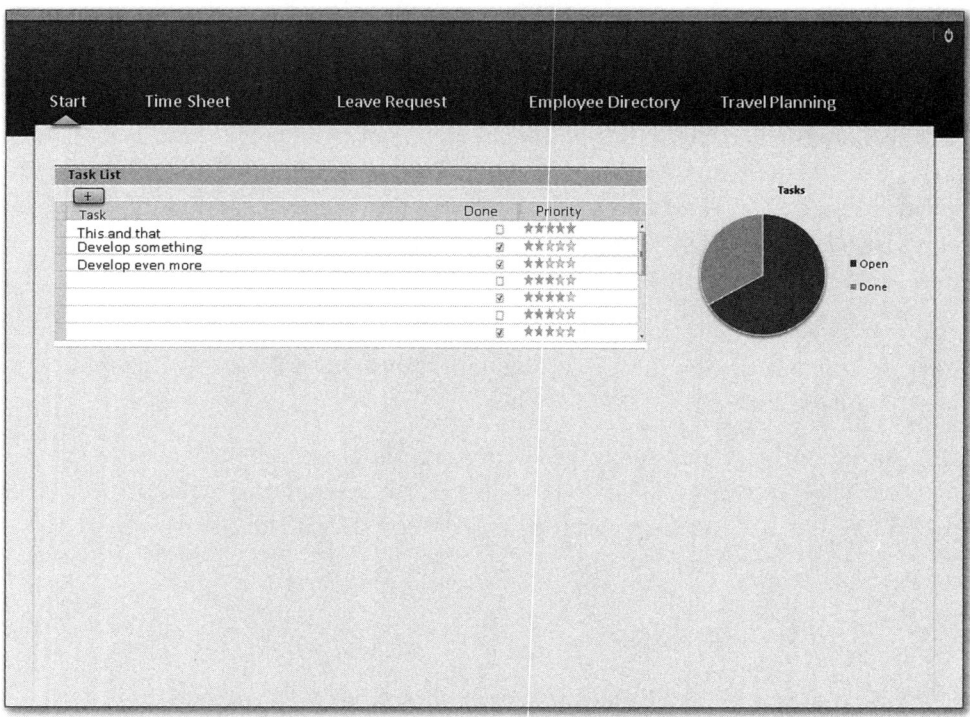

Figure 7.1   PowerPoint Mock-Up of the Start Page

Backend services   In order to meet these requirements, we need two services in the backend:

- ▶ Reading the task list
- ▶ Adding a task to the task list

7.1.2   Time Sheet

A table with the working times of the current month should be displayed on the Time Sheet page. It should be possible to enter times, and a small statistic on the last six months should be displayed. Figure 7.2 shows how a time sheet might look.

Entry of services performed

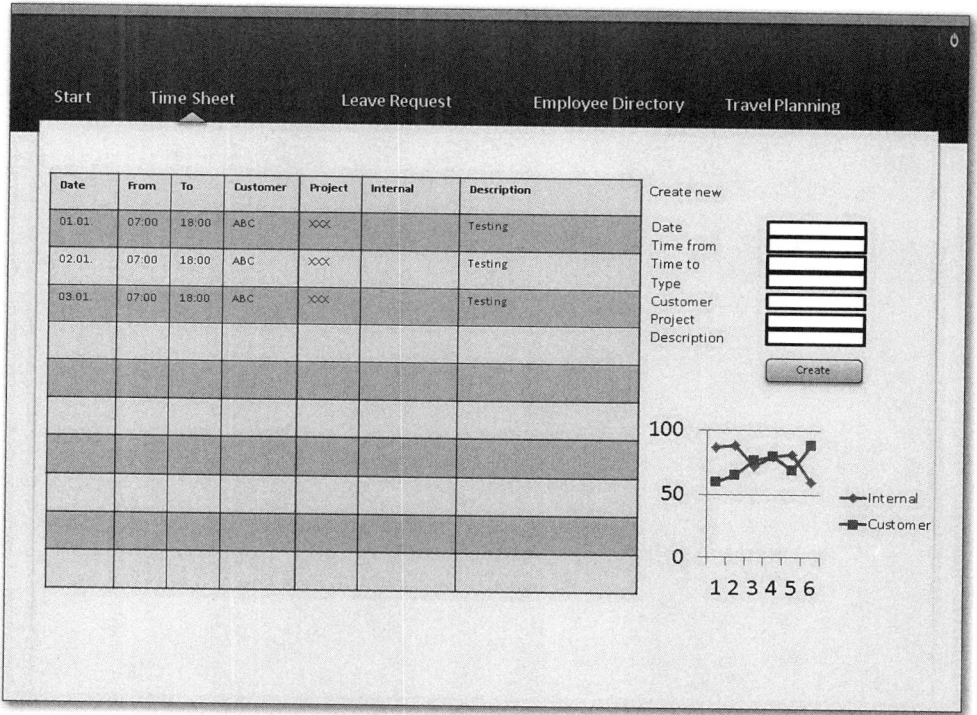

Figure 7.2   PowerPoint Mock-Up of the Time Sheet Page

In order to meet these requirements, we need three services in the backend:

Backend services

▶ Reading the current customers/projects for the input help

▶ Reading the working times of the last six months for the statistics and display of the current month

▶ Writing the recorded times

7.1.3 Leave Request

Maintaining leaves

On the Leave Request page, we need a calendar to be displayed in which the holiday that is entered is color coded. New leave days must be able to be marked in the calendar and the leave request sent to the SAP backend. Furthermore, the previous leave requests are to be displayed sorted, according to their status. Figure 7.3 shows how a Leave Request page might look.

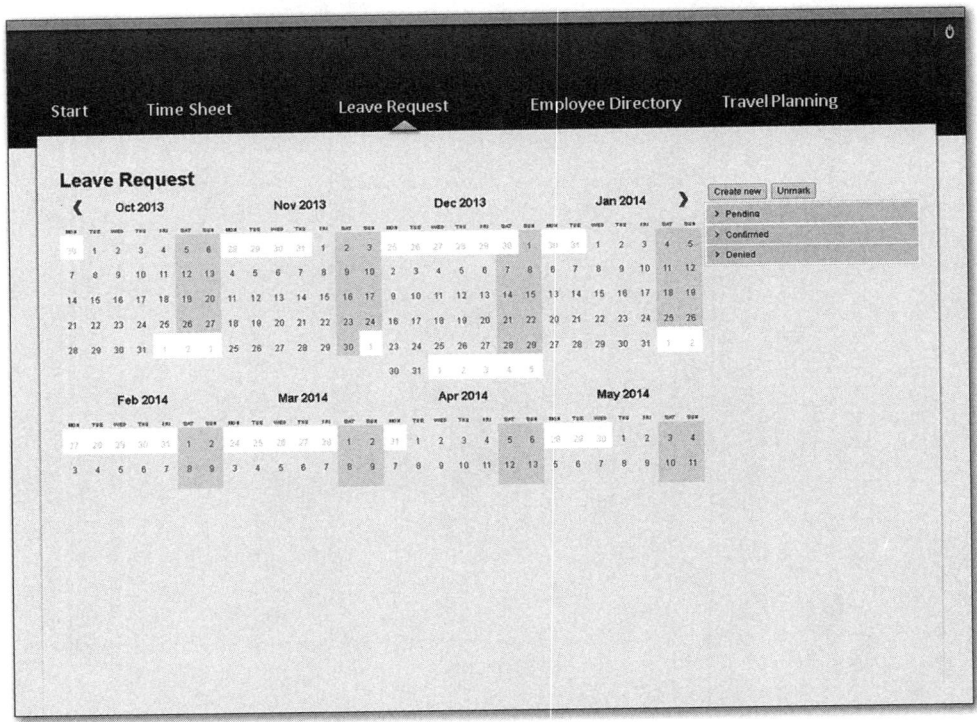

Figure 7.3 PowerPoint Mock-Up of the Leave Request Page

Backend services

In order to meet these requirements, we need two services in the backend:

▸ Reading the leave requests for the current year

▸ Saving new leave requests

7.1.4 Employee Directory

In the employee directory, employees are to be displayed with their email address and telephone number. A search function enables the targeted search for a specific person. In Figure 7.4, you can see how such an Employee Directory page might look.

Employee Directory

In order to meet these requirements, we need only one service in the backend: Reading the employee directory.

Backend services

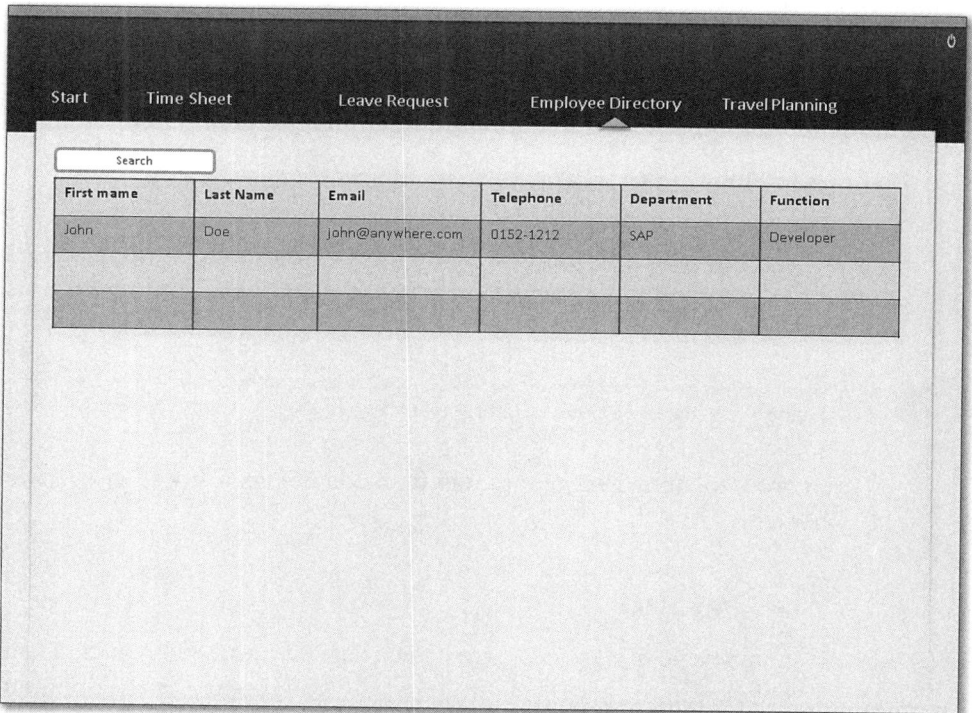

Figure 7.4 PowerPoint Mock-Up of the Employee Directory Page

7.1.5 Travel Planning

Travel planning is intended to embed Google Maps and offer the option of generating driving directions. Figure 7.5 shows a possible Travel Planning page.

Google Maps

287

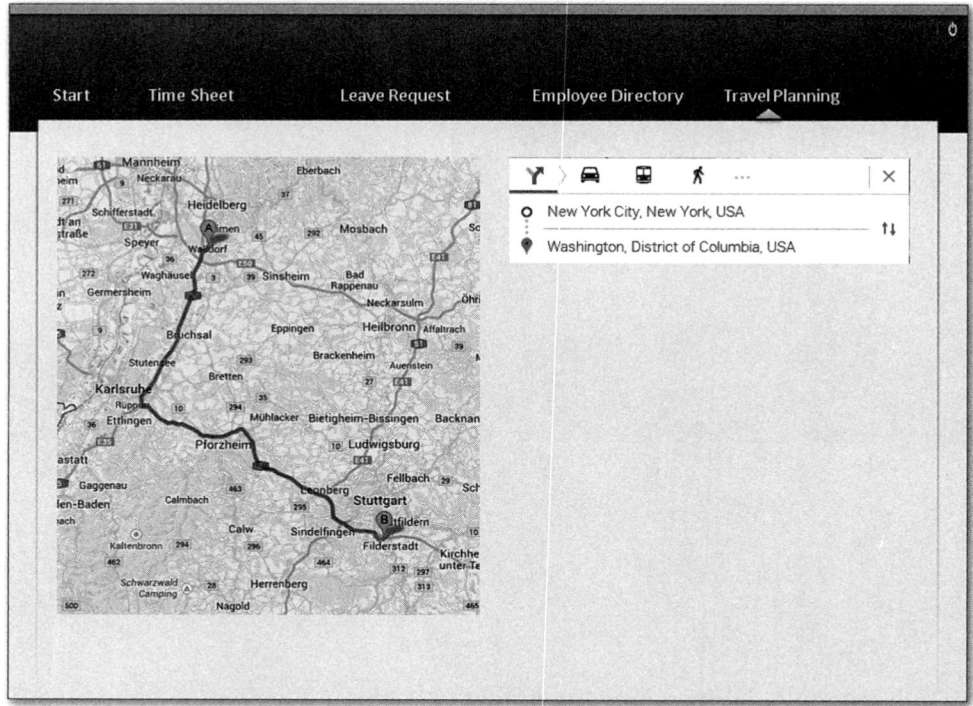

Figure 7.5 PowerPoint Mock-Up of Travel Planning Page

In order to meet these requirements, we do not need any services in the backend.

7.1.6 My Data

Personal data

It should be possible to change personal data (Department, Function, and Telephone) in the MY DATA area (Figure 7.6). There is also the option to upload a personal photo.

Backend services

In order to meet these requirements, we need three services in the backend:

▶ Reading personal data

▶ Saving the image

▶ Changing the selected personal data

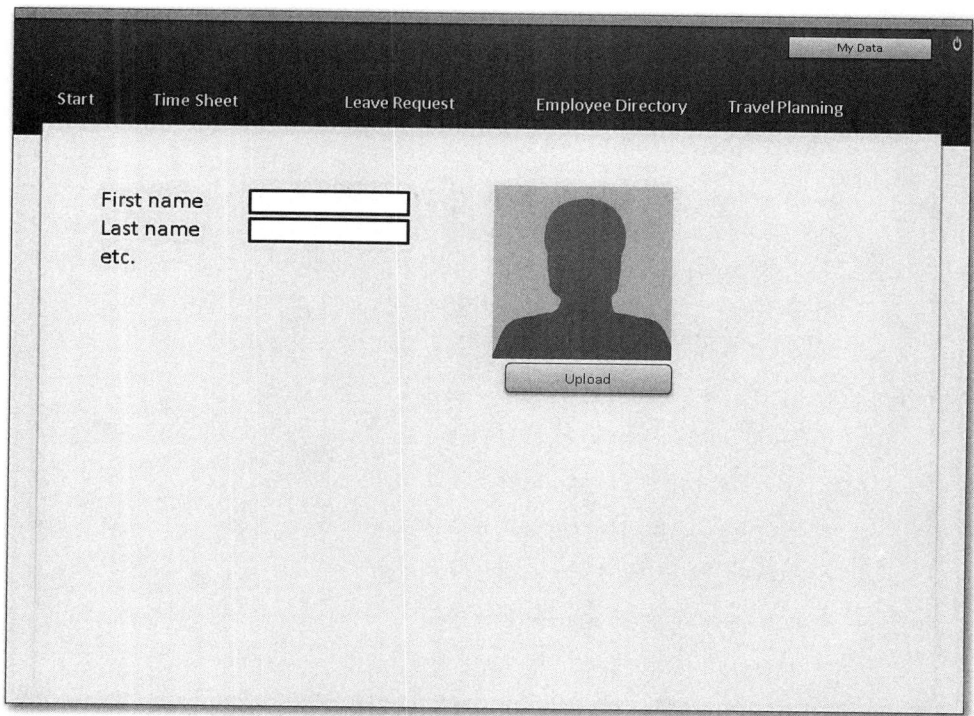

Figure 7.6 PowerPoint Mock-Up for My Data

Now that it's clear how the portal should look, we can think about the implementation in the backend.

7.2 Implementation

Because the main focus of this book is SAPUI5 and you are probably already very familiar with ABAP (and also to conserve space), let's omit the ABAP source code for backend integration, at this point. You can download a detailed description with code from the book's web page and integrate it in your example. If you do not want to implement the ABAP part yourself, you will also find the necessary ABAP objects as a transport request for download there.

Back-end implementation

Create the SAPUI5 application project ZUI5_PORTAL in Eclipse. For this application, we'll use the MVC architecture pattern again; when creating the project, select the checkmark CREATE AN INITIAL VIEW, and name the first view "main."

7.2.1 Basic Structure

We use the Shell control as the framework for the portal. We need the aforementioned pages as menu items. Next, create all required views. To do this, right-click the project and select NEW • VIEW from the context menu. Now, create the following views, and pay particular attention to uppercase and lowercase:

Creating views

- Start (view name `MyTask`)
- Time Sheet (view name `TimeSheet`)
- Leave Request (view name `LeaveRequest`)
- Employee Directory (view name `EmployeeSearch`)
- Travel Planning (view name `TripPlanner`)
- My Data (view name `MyData`)
- Messages and status display (view name `NotificationBar`)

The resultant project structure should look like Figure 7.7.

Implementing Shell control

Next, implement the Shell control in the `main` view. Create the MY DATA menu item in the header area (`headerItem`), and the other menu items are created in Shell's main menu (`WorksetItem`).

View

We have defined the display of tasks as the START page, which makes the `MyTask` view the initial content for the Shell. In addition, a `NotificationBar` control will always be displayed on each page; implement this in the `content` area of the Shell.

When you select MY DATA in the header area, the function `headerItemSelected` will also be called in the controller; this shows a `DialogBox` control. For the main menu, however, the function `worksetItemSelected` is called, and this function in turn calls the corresponding view. For the `main` view, this results in the code from Listing 7.1.

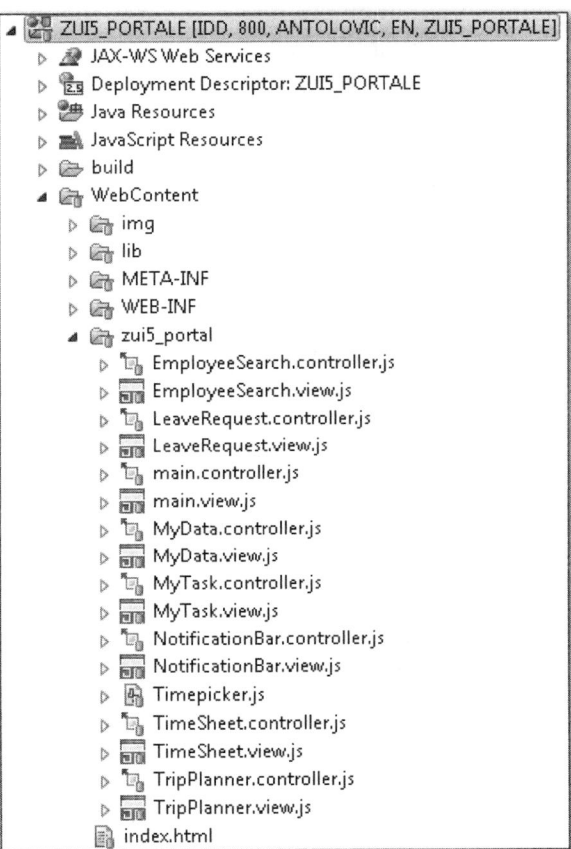

Figure 7.7 Project Structure of the Portal

```
createContent : function(oController) {
    var oMasterShell = new sap.ui.ux3.Shell("MainShell", {
        appTitle : "Employee Portal",
        showLogoutButton : false,
        showSearchTool : false,
        showInspectorTool : false,
        showFeederTool : false,
        designType : sap.ui.ux3.ShellDesignType.Crystal,
        headerItems : [ new sap.ui.commons.Button({
                text : "My Data",
                press : oController.headerItemSelected
            }) ],
        // Content
```

```
content : [ new sap.ui.view({
    id : "MyTask",
    viewName : "zui5_portal.MyTask",
        type : sap.ui.core.mvc.ViewType.JS
    }), sap.ui.view({
    id : "NotificationBar",
    viewName : "zui5_portal.NotificationBar",
    type : sap.ui.core.mvc.ViewType.JS
    }) ],
// Menu bar
worksetItems : [
    new sap.ui.ux3.NavigationItem("LP", {
        key : "MyTask",
        text : "Tasks"
    }), new sap.ui.ux3.NavigationItem("TM", {
        key : "TimeSheet",
        text : "Time Sheet"
    }), new sap.ui.ux3.NavigationItem("LR", {
        key : "LeaveRequest",
        text : "Leave Request"
    }), new sap.ui.ux3.NavigationItem("EL", {
        key : "EmployeeSearch",
        text : "Employee Directory"
    }), new sap.ui.ux3.NavigationItem("TP", {
        key : "TripPlanner",
        text : "Travel Planning"
    })
    ],
worksetItemSelected : oController.worksetItemSelected,
}); 
return oMasterShell;
}});
```

Listing 7.1 main View

Controller   Next, you can implement the View control in the main controller. In the controller, first read the selected menu entry from the event, then read the corresponding view name from the core, and then transfer the view name as content to the Shell. For the main controller, this results in the content of Listing 7.2.

```
worksetItemSelected: function(oEvent) {
   this.removeAllContent();
     // Read key from event
     var to = oEvent.getParameter("key");
     // Read view
     var oView = sap.ui.getCore().byId(to);
     if (oView == undefined)
       oView = new sap.ui.view({
           id: to,
           viewName:"zui5_portal." + to,
           type:sap.ui.core.mvc.ViewType.JS
         });
   // Set view
     this.addContent(oView);
   // Notification bar
    var oNoti = sap.ui.getCore().byId("NotificationBar");
    if (oNoti == undefined)
      oNoti= sap.ui.view({
        id:"NotificationBar",
        viewName:"zui5_portal.NotificationBar",
        type:sap.ui.core.mvc.ViewType.JS
          });
    this.addContent(oNoti);
  },

  headerItemSelected: function(oEvent) {
     var oView = sap.ui.getCore().byId("MyData");
     if (oView == undefined)
         var oView = new sap.ui.view({
             id: "MyData",
             viewName:"zui5_portal.MyData",
             type:sap.ui.core.mvc.ViewType.JS
         });
// Open My Data in the OverlayDialog control.
        var oOverlayDialog = new sap.ui.ux3.OverlayDialog({
                    width:"800px",
                    height:"500px"
                    close: function(){
                       oView.destroy();
                    }
                  });
```

```
                    oOverlayDialog.addContent(oView);
                    oOverlayDialog.open();

// Notification bar
    var oNoti = sap.ui.getCore().byId("NotificationBar");
    if (oNoti == undefined)
      oNoti= sap.ui.view({
        id:"NotificationBar",
        viewName:"zui5_portal.NotificationBar",
        type:sap.ui.core.mvc.ViewType.JS
      });
    this.oParent.addContent(oNoti);
  },
```

Listing 7.2   main Controller

Page content   To enable you to test the page, insert a short text in each view. Leave out the NotificationBar view for the moment; we will consider it separately in a little while. Insert the content of Listing 7.3 in each view, and adjust the text according to the page as you do; for example, use EMPLOYEE DIRECTORY for the EmployeeSearch view.

```
oText = new sap.ui.commons.TextView(
  {text :"Employee Directory"}); // Adjust for each page
var oLayout = new sap.ui.commons.layout.VerticalLayout({
  content: [oText]
});
return oLayout;
```

Listing 7.3   Dummy Content of Views

Bootstrap   Finally, you must add the UX3 library in the bootstrap so that the class for the Shell control is loaded (see Listing 7.4).

```
<script src="resources/sap-ui-core.js"
    id="sap-ui-bootstrap"
    data-sap-ui-libs="sap.ui.commons, sap.ui.ux3"
    data-sap-ui-theme="sap_bluecrystal">
</script>
```

Listing 7.4   Bootstrap

Result   Upload the project and test the page. As a result, you should see a Shell with the created menu entries and the corresponding texts, as in Figure 7.8.

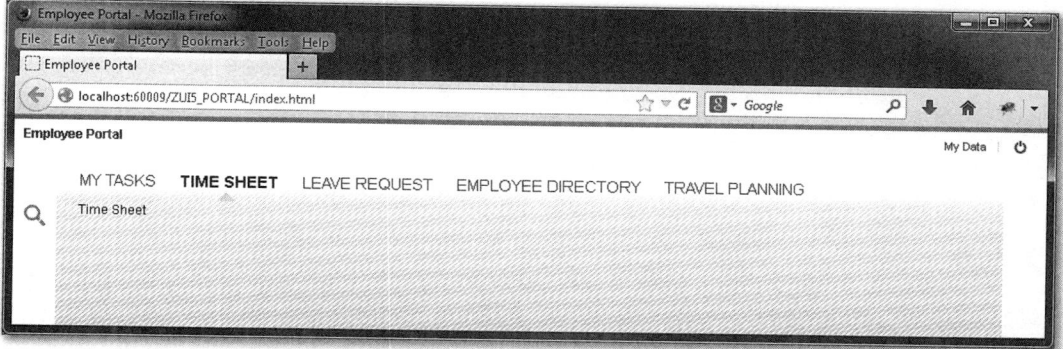

Figure 7.8 Finished Shell for the Portal

In this example, the design type, `sap.ui.ux3.ShellDesignType.Crystal`, was chosen because the Gold Reflection theme is a little too dark.

After each action, the individual methods of the ABAP class `ZUI5_ EMPLOYEE_PORTAL` return a message as JSON to the frontend. These messages are to be displayed in the portal. Here we use the `NotificationBar` control, but you can also introduce your own ideas, such as a `MessageBar` control. In the `NotificationBar` view, add the `NotificationBar` control, as displayed in Listing 7.5.

NotificationBar control

```
createContent : function(oController) {
    var oMessageNotifier =
        new sap.ui.ux3.Notifier("MessageNotifier",{
            title : "Messages"
        });
    var oNotiBar = new sap.ui.ux3.NotificationBar({
        visibleStatus : "Default"
    });
    oNotiBar.addStyleClass("slimNotificationBar");
    oNotiBar.setMessageNotifier(oMessageNotifier);
    return oNotiBar;
    }
});
```

Listing 7.5 NotificationBar View

As a result, a notification bar is displayed in the lower area (see Figure 7.9).

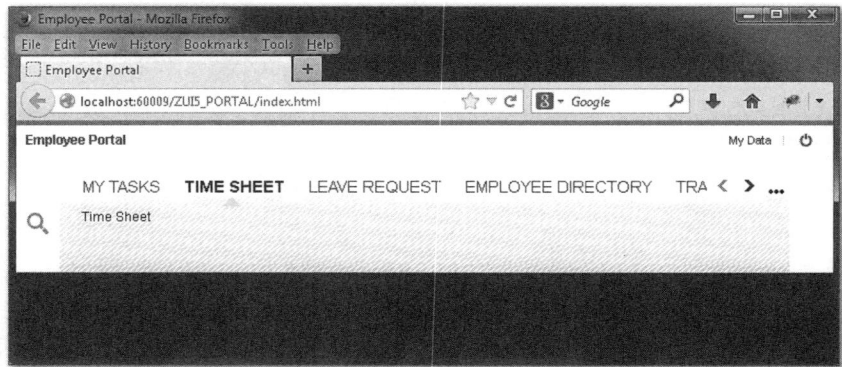

Figure 7.9 Portal with Notification Bar

We have the framework for our portal; now each page must be filled with the desired content. Let's begin with the employee directory, because this page has only a pure display function and is thus very easy to implement.

7.2.2 Employee Directory

For reading the employee directory, you implement the ABAP method GET_EMPLOYEES; this returns the employee data as JSON. Normally, it would be unlikely that you would implement both sides, frontend, and backend. For this reason, it's useful if you start by calling the HTTP request in the controller. That way, you can look at the returned JSON and use this information to implement the binding in the view.

Controller First, go to the EmployeeSearch controller, and in the onInit function, implement the service call for the employee directory, as shown in Listing 7.6.

```
onInit: function() {
    var oModel = new sap.ui.model.json.JSONModel();
    oModel.loadData(
            "/ui5/?application=portal&area=get_employees"
        );
    this.getView().setModel(oModel);
}
```

Listing 7.6 EmployeeSearch Controller

Now, upload the project, open the developer tools in the browser, and switch to the EMPLOYEE DIRECTORY in the menu. After calling the get_ employees service, you can view the JSON in the browser developer tools (see Figure 7.10).

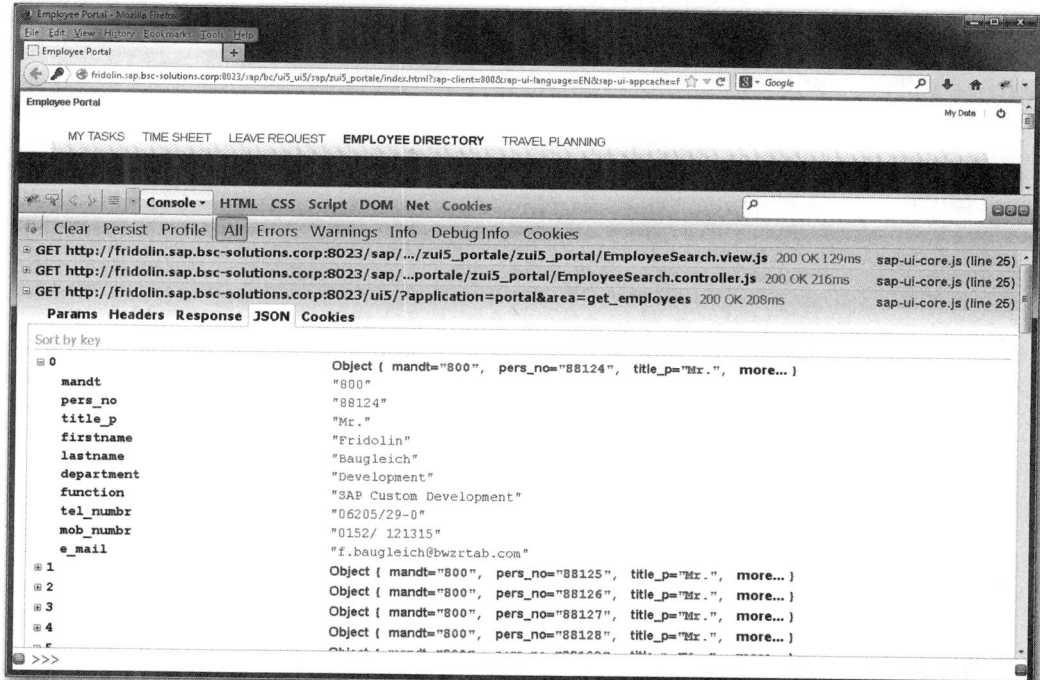

Figure 7.10 JSON of the get_employee Services

The return should not surprise you because, after all, you implemented the service yourself. For unknown sources, however, this approach can be very useful, because you can determine the necessary names and paths for the binding in this manner.

JSON return

You can use this information to implement the view now. Here, we've decided on a `RowRepeater` control with a small search function. You can also use a table control for this purpose; we've tried to use as many different controls as possible in this application example. First, create a `MatrixLayout` control as an external framework, a control for the header, and a control for the search field (see Listing 7.7).

View

```
createContent : function(oController) {
// Layout
var oLayout = new sap.ui.commons.layout.MatrixLayout({
        layoutFixed : true,
        columns : 1,
        width : "100%",
        widths : [ "100%" ]
    });
// Header
var oHeaderText = new sap.ui.commons.TextView({
        text:"Employee Directory",
        width:'500px',
        design : sap.ui.commons.TextViewDesign.H2
    });
oLayout.createRow(oHeaderText);
// Search field
var oTextFieldSearch = new
    sap.ui.commons.TextField("ES_TFS",{
      liveChange:  function(oEvent) {
// Filter by Last Name
        var para = oEvent.getParameters();
        if (para instanceof Object)
           para = para.liveValue;
        var oFilter = new sap.ui.model.Filter(
                   "lastname",
                    sap.ui.model.FilterOperator.Contains,
                    para);
        oRowRepeater.bindRows("/", oRowTemplate,"",oFilter);
      }
});
// Layout control for search field
var oHLayout = new sap.ui.commons.layout.HorizontalLayout({
            content:[
        new sap.ui.commons.Label({
        text:"Search",
           width:"100px"
           }),
           oTextFieldSearch]
});
oLayout.createRow(oHLayout);
```

Listing 7.7 Framework Layout

Next, create the `RowRepeater` control and bind the information from the JSON as individual columns to the control. This listing was shortened for clarity; you can download the complete listing from the book's web page.

RowRepeater
control

```
// RowRepeater
    var oRowRepeater = new sap.ui.commons.RowRepeater();
    oRowRepeater.setNoData(new sap.ui.commons.TextView({
        text: "No data found"
    }));
      oRowRepeater.setDesign("Standard");
      oRowRepeater.setNumberOfRows(10);
      oRowRepeater.setCurrentPage(1);

// Template
var oRowTemplate = new sap.ui.commons.layout.MatrixLayout();

var  matrixRow, matrixCell, control;
matrixRow = new sap.ui.commons.layout.MatrixLayoutRow();

// Last Name
  control = new sap.ui.commons.Label();
  control.bindProperty("text","lastname");
  matrixCell = new sap.ui.commons.layout.MatrixLayoutCell();
  matrixCell.addContent(control);
  matrixRow.addCell(matrixCell);

// Add the fields according to the same schema
// First Name (first name), Department (department),
// Function (function), Telephone (tel_numbr),
// Mobile Number (mob_numbr) and Email (email )
//

// Add row to RowRepeater
  oRowTemplate.addRow(matrixRow);

// Bind to RowRepeater
    oRowRepeater.bindRows("/", oRowTemplate);
    oLayout.createRow(oRowRepeater );
  return oLayout;
 }
});
```

Listing 7.8 EmployeeSearch View

The result of the implemented employee directory is displayed in Figure 7.11.

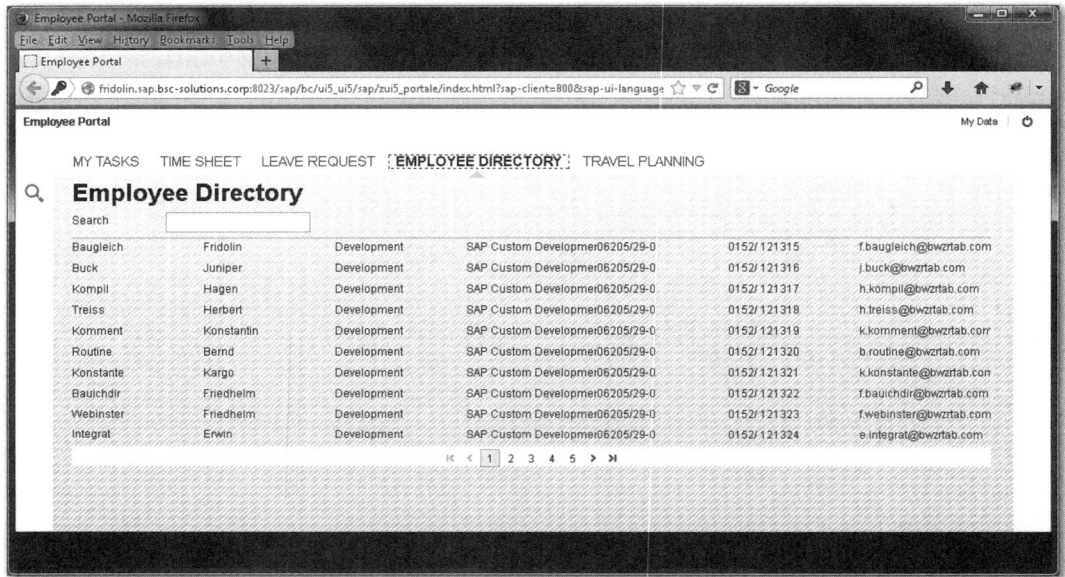

Figure 7.11 Employee Directory with Search Function

If you wish, you can use the built-in search function in the Shell so that the employee search is accessible from any other page. In the main view, set the Shell parameter ShowSearchTool to true for this purpose, and call the search function in the controller for the search. The content of Listing 7.9 is the result for the Shell (the relevant code portions are in bold; the unchanged parts are abbreviated).

```
var oMasterShell = new sap.ui.ux3.Shell("MainShell", {
... (abbreviated) ...
            showSearchTool : true,
    worksetItemSelected : oController.worksetItemSelected,
    search: [oController.search, oController]
});
... (abbreviated) ...
```

Listing 7.9 Shell with Search Function

Next, implement the `search` function in the `main` controller (see Listing 7.10). This function calls the view with the employee directory with the appropriate filter from the Shell search function.

```
search : function(oEvent, oContext) {
    var oSource = oEvent.getSource();
    oSource.setSelectedWorksetItem("ES");
    oSource.removeAllContent();
    var to = "EmployeeSearch";
    var oView = sap.ui.getCore().byId(to);
    if (oView == undefined)
        oView = new sap.ui.view({
                id : to,
                viewName : "zui5_portal." + to,
                type : sap.ui.core.mvc.ViewType.JS
            });
    oSource.addContent(oView);

    var oNoti = sap.ui.getCore().byId("NotificationBar");
    if (oNoti == undefined)
        oNoti = sap.ui.view({
                id : "NotificationBar",
                viewName : "zui5_portal.NotificationBar",
                type : sap.ui.core.mvc.ViewType.JS
            });
        oSource.addContent(oNoti);

// Determine search field in the employee directory
// based on the ID
    var sSearch =
            oEvent.getSource().getSearchField().getValue();
    sap.ui.getCore().getControl("ES_TFS").setValue(sSearch);
// Trigger event
sap.ui.getCore().getControl(
                    "ES_TFS").fireLiveChange(sSearch);
}
```

Listing 7.10 Shell Search Function in the main Controller

Figure 7.12 shows the newly implemented search function.

Figure 7.12 Shell Search Function

Next, we'll deal with travel planning.

7.2.3 Travel Planning

Google Maps

Integrate Google Maps for travel planning in the portal; this will allow your employees to better plan their travel times. You will find the relevant API documentation from Google at *https://developers.google. com/maps/*.

To be able to use this API, you must embed the relevant JavaScript as an external source below the bootstrap in the *index.html* file (see Listing 7.11).

```
<script src="https://maps.googleapis.com/maps/api/js?v=3.
exp&sensor=false">
</script>
```

Listing 7.11 Google API Script

In the view file, you will need two input fields for the start and destination of the route and a `<div>` area in accordance with the Google API documentation. This results in the content of Listing 7.12.

```
createContent : function(oController) {
// Layout Search fields
var oMatrix = new sap.ui.commons.layout.MatrixLayout({
    layoutFixed : true,
    columns : 5,
    width : "640px",
    widths : [ "50px", "150px", "50px", "150px", "120px" ]
});
```

```
// Input fields, which are transferred in the controller to the
// Google API.
    var oStartLabel = new sap.ui.commons.Label({
        text:"Start:", width:"50px"});
    var oFrom = new sap.ui.commons.TextField({
        width:"150px" });

    var oTargetLabel = new sap.ui.commons.Label({
        text:"Destination:", width:"50px"});
    var oTo = new sap.ui.commons.TextField({
        width:"150px",
        change:function(){
// Call controller function
                    oController.calcRoute(
                    oFrom.getValue(),oTo.getValue()
                     );
            }
    });

    var oSearchButton = new sap.ui.commons.Button({
            text : "Calculate route",
            press:function(){
            // Call controller function
                    oController.calcRoute(
                    oFrom.getValue(),oTo.getValue()
                    );
        }});

oMatrix.createRow(
      oStartLabel, oFrom, oTargetLabel , oTo, oSearchButton
);

// Here the required elements are set,
// which are used by the Google API in the controller.
  var oHtml = new sap.ui.core.HTML({
      id: "map_canvas",
      content:[
        '<div id="map_canvas" '+
        'style="float:left;min-width:500px;'+
        'width:70%;min-height:800px;height:100%;"></div>'+
        '<div style="float:right;width:30%;'+
        'height:100%;overflow:auto">'+
        '<div id="directions_panel" '+
```

```
                      'style="width:100%"></div></div>'
                           ]
         });
    // Page layout
    var oLayout= new sap.ui.commons.layout.VerticalLayout({
           width:"100%",
           height:"100%",
           content: [oMatrix, oHtml]}));

       return oLayout ;
     }
});
```

Listing 7.12   Travel Planning View

Controller   The two input fields START and DESTINATION must be transferred to the Google API in the controller, and the map in the included <div> area must be given the ID map_canvas. In the onAfterRendering method, set the starting point to *New York City* and create a Google Maps map (see Listing 7.13).

```
onAfterRendering: function() {
    var myOptions = {
    zoom: 13,
    center: new google.maps.LatLng(49.294449,8.636851),
                                       // New York City
       mapTypeId: google.maps.MapTypeId.ROADMAP
     }
   map = new
        google.maps.Map(document.getElementById("map_canvas"),
          myOptions);
},
```

Listing 7.13   onAfterRendering Method

Creating map   The method calcRoute is called if you click on CALCULATE ROUTE in the UI. This method consists of three functions; the first method, initialize, creates the Google Maps map (see Listing 7.14).

```
calcRoute : function(from, to) {
var directionsDisplay;
var directionsService = new google.maps.DirectionsService();
var map;
var oldDirections = [];
```

```
var currentDirections = null;

function initialize() { // creates the Google map
    var myOptions = {
      zoom : 13,
      center : new google.maps.LatLng(49.294449, 8.636851),
      mapTypeId : google.maps.MapTypeId.ROADMAP
  }
  map = new google.maps.Map(
            document.getElementById("map_canvas"),
            myOptions);
  directionsDisplay = new google.maps.DirectionsRenderer({
        'map' : map,
        'preserveViewport' : true,
        'draggable' : true
   });
  directionsDisplay.setPanel(
        document.getElementById("directions_panel"));

    google.maps.event.addListener(directionsDisplay,
        'directions_changed', function() {
          if (currentDirections) {
                  oldDirections.push(currentDirections);
              }
  currentDirections = directionsDisplay.getDirections();
        });
    calcRoute();
  }
```

Listing 7.14 initialize Method

The calcRoute function takes the values from the UI and sends them to   Calculating route
the Google API (see Listing 7.15).

```
function calcRoute() {
    var request = {
       origin : from,
       destination : to,
       travelMode : google.maps.DirectionsTravelMode.DRIVING
    };
  directionsService.route(
                request, function(response, status) {
      if (status == google.maps.DirectionsStatus.OK) {
```

```
document.getElementById("directions_panel").innerHTML = "";
directionsDisplay.setDirections(response);
var bounds = response.routes[0].bounds;
map.fitBounds(bounds);
addNotification("Route was calculated", "I");
} else {
addNotification("Error during the calculation", "E");
}
});
}
```

Listing 7.15 calcRoute Function

Google API messages The addNotification function transfers the Google API messages to the Notifier control (see Listing 7.16).

```
function addNotification(sText, sIcon) {
  var oMessageNotifier =
              sap.ui.getCore().byId("MessageNotifier");
  var oMessage = new sap.ui.core.Message({
            text : sText,
            timestamp : (new Date()).toUTCString()
  });
  switch (sIcon) {
  case "E":
    oMessage.setLevel(sap.ui.core.MessageType.Error);
    break;
  case "S":
    oMessage.setLevel(sap.ui.core.MessageType.Success);
    break;
  case "W":
    oMessage.setLevel(sap.ui.core.MessageType.Warning);
    break;
  case "I":
    oMessage.setLevel(sap.ui.core.MessageType.Information);
    break;
  default:
    oMessage.setLevel(sap.ui.core.MessageType.Information);
    break;
  }
    oMessageNotifier.addMessage(oMessage);
  }
```

```
  initialize();
},
});
```

Listing 7.16 AddNotification Function

As a result, you obtain a typical Google Maps view (see Figure 7.13), **Result**
from which you can calculate the route by entering the starting point
and destination.

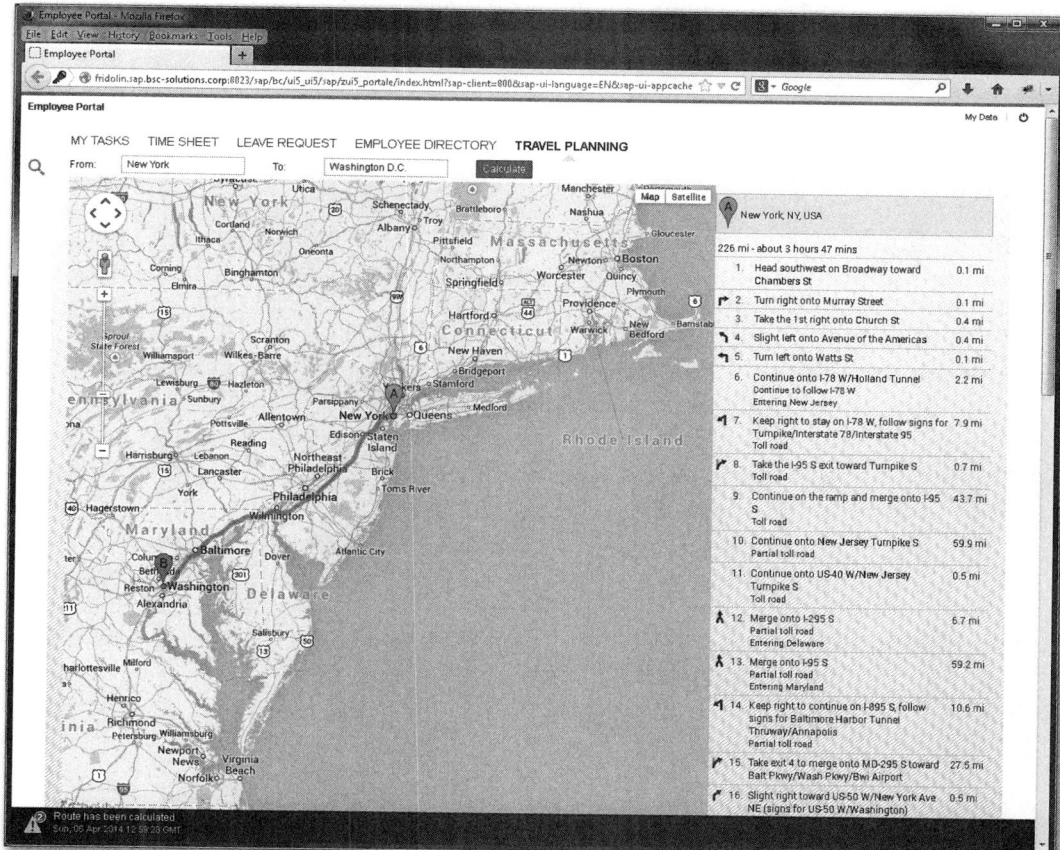

Figure 7.13 Google Maps in the Portal

Next, we'll implement the My Data area.

7.2.4 My Data

Binding
Here, as in the employee directory, you need to first implement the corresponding service call to determine the necessary information for the binding. Because you already know the service, however, you can start directly with the view and the binding. The service for reading the image is GET_PICTURE. Because Department, Function, Telephone, and Extension can be changed in this form, control IDs must be assigned to them. As a result, you can read the corresponding value in the controller and send it to the SAP backend. To ensure that the first column does not start directly at the edge of the page, we have created a CSS class margin and have assigned it to the elements in the left margin via the statement .addStyleClass("margin"). In the *index.html* file, insert the style definition from Listing 7.17 after the bootstrap.

```
<style>
  .margin { margin-left: 10px; }
</style>
```
Listing 7.17 Style Definition

Page layout
This page displays information such as first name on the left half of the screen. On the right side of the screen, an image is displayed, or the option of uploading an image is provided. In this example, we have chosen to use a MatrixLayout control as an external framework. The personal data is also wrapped in a MatrixLayout control, and the image is displayed using a VerticalLayout control. The distribution of layout controls is displayed in Figure 7.14.

Start with the external framework, and create a Matrix Layout with two columns (see Listing 7.18).

```
createContent : function(oController) {
// Basic layout
var oMatrix = new sap.ui.commons.layout.MatrixLayout({
    layoutFixed : true,
    width : '800px',
    columns : 2,
    widths : ['400px', '400px'] });
```
Listing 7.18 Matrix Layout as External Framework

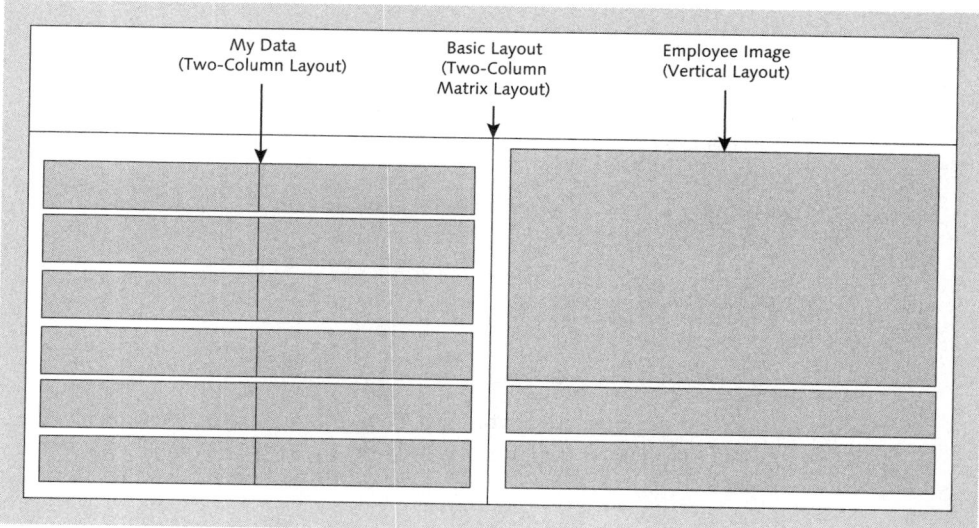

Figure 7.14 Page Layout

The heading covers the whole width of the layout. Create a Matrix Layout cell with colSpan 2, and assign this cell to the TextView control with the heading (see Listing 7.19).

Heading

```
var oCell = new sap.ui.commons.layout.MatrixLayoutCell({
    colSpan: 2 });
// Heading
var oTV = new sap.ui.commons.TextView({
    text : 'Personal Data',
    design : sap.ui.commons.TextViewDesign.H1
    }).addStyleClass("margin");
oCell.addContent(oTV);
oMatrix.createRow(oCell);
```

Listing 7.19 Heading

Also create a two-column Matrix Layout for the personal data, as displayed in Figure 7.14. The first column contains the name of the field, and the second column contains the actual field content. Listing 7.20 shows an example of how to implement the display of the last name. This listing was shortened for clarity; you can download the complete listing from the book's web page.

Personal data

```
// Personal Data form
var oMatrixPers = new sap.ui.commons.layout.MatrixLayout({
    layoutFixed : false,
    width : '300px',
    columns : 2 });
// Last Name
var oLabel = new sap.ui.commons.Label({
    text : 'Last Name' }).addStyleClass("margin");
var oTF = new sap.ui.commons.TextField({
    editable : false,
    value : '{lastname}',
    width : '200px' });
oLabel.setLabelFor(oTF);
oMatrixPers.createRow(oLabel, oTF);
// ... First Name, Company, Department, Function Address etc.

// Buttons
var oButton1 = new sap.ui.commons.Button({
    id : 'B-Change',
    text : 'Change',
    press : oController.toggle
}).addStyleClass("margin");

var oButton2 = new sap.ui.commons.Button({
    id : 'B-Save',
    text : 'Save',
    enabled: false,
    press : oController.save
});
oMatrixPers.createRow(oButton1, oButton2);
```
Listing 7.20 Personal Data

You can implement the fields FIRST NAME, COMPANY, DEPARTMENT, FUNC-TION, STREET AND CITY, TELEPHONE, FAX, and EMAIL according to the same schema as the LAST NAME field. Assign an ID to the fields DEPARTMENT, FUNCTION, and TELEPHONE; it's intended that employees will be able to change these values. When the user clicks the CHANGE button, these fields are ready for input.

Image   The image of the employee will be displayed on the right half of the screen, and the option of uploading an image will also be provided. As

shown in Figure 7.14, the information is displayed in a VerticalLayout
control (see Listing 7.21). Assign an ID in each case to the two controls
FileUploader and the Button; these controls only become active in change
mode. After uploading an image, cancel the rerender function of the
image control to display the uploaded image directly.

```
// Image
var oImg = new sap.ui.commons.Image("oImg",{
    height : '200px',
    src : '/ui5/?application=portal&area=get_picture' });
// FileUploader
var oFileUploader = new sap.ui.commons.FileUploader({
    id:"FileUploader",
    width:"350px",
    uploadOnChange: false,
    visible: false,
    uploadUrl: "/ui5?application=portal&area=set_picture",
    }).attachUploadComplete(
        function(){
            sap.ui.getCore().getControl("oImg").rerender();
        });

// The button starts the upload.
var oTriggerButton = new sap.ui.commons.Button({
    id:"UploadButton",
    text:'Upload',
    width:"100px",
    enabled: false,
    press:function() {
     oFileUploader.upload();
  }
  });
var oLayoutPic = new sap.ui.layout.VerticalLayout({
    content: [oImg, oFileUploader, oTriggerButton]
});
```

Listing 7.21 Employee Image

Finally, create a row of the external layout with the two layout controls
from Listing 7.20 and Listing 7.22, define the model binding, and return
the completed page definition.

```
oMatrix.createRow(oMatrixPers, oLayoutPic );
```

```
oMatrix.bindElement("/");
return oMatrix;
}});
```

Listing 7.22 Merging Left and Right Layout

Services and
functions

The service for reading your own data is GET_OWN_DATA, and the service for saving is SET_OWN_DATA. This means that you can call this service in the onInit function and write the data to a model. In addition to this function, the functions toggle and save from the view are required in the controller. In the save method, call the service for saving the data; the toogle method is used to switch between display and change mode. For the onInit method, this results in the content of Listing 7.23.

```
onInit : function() {
   var oModel = new sap.ui.model.json.JSONModel();
   oModel.loadData(
           "/ui5/?application=portal&area=get_own_data"
           );
   this.getView().setModel(oModel);
},
```

Listing 7.23 onInit Function in MyData Controller

Save function

In the view, you defined that clicking the SAVE button in the controller will call the save function (press : oController.save; see Listing 7.20). In this method, you read four changeable fields—DEPARTMENT, FUNCTION, TELEPHONE, and EXTENSION—and send this data to the SET_OWN_DATA service in the backend. For the save method, this results in the content of Listing 7.24.

```
save : function() {
var oCore = sap.ui.getCore();
var oParameters = {
  "Department" : oCore.getControl('department').getValue(),
  "Function" : oCore.getControl('function').getValue(),
  "Telephone" : oCore.getControl('telephone').getValue(),
  "telephone_ext" : oCore.getControl('telephone_ext').
getValue()
};
  $.ajax({
    url : "/ui5/?application=portal&area=set_own_data",
    contentType : "application/json",
```

```
    dataType : 'json',
    data : oParameters,
    success : function(data, textStatus, jqXHR) {
        sap.ui.getCore().byId("MyData").getController().
            addNotification(data.text,data.severity);
    sap.ui.getCore().getControl('B-Change').firePress();
    }});
},
```

Listing 7.24 save Function in MyData Controller

In the view (see Listing 7.20), you defined that clicking the CHANGE button will call the toggle function in the controller (press : oController.
toggle). This function switches to display or change mode depending on the previous status of the controls. This is easiest to achieve by using the logical NOT operator (!). For the toggle method, this results in the content of Listing 7.25.

Switching between display and change mode

```
toggle : function() {
    var oCore = sap.ui.getCore();
    var oControl = oCore.getControl('Department');
    oControl.setEditable(!oControl.getEditable());
    var oControl = oCore.getControl('Function');
    oControl.setEditable(!oControl.getEditable());
    var oControl = oCore.getControl('Telephone');
    oControl.setEditable(!oControl.getEditable());
    var oControl = oCore.getControl('Telephone_ext');
    oControl.setEditable(!oControl.getEditable());
    var oControl = oCore.getControl('FileUploader');
    oControl.setVisible(!oControl.getVisible());
    var oButton = oCore.getControl('UploadButton');
    oButton.setEnabled(!oButton.getEnabled());
    var oButton = oCore.getControl('B-Save');
    oButton.setEnabled(!oButton.getEnabled());
    oButton = oCore.getControl('B-Change');
    if (oButton.getText() == 'Change') {
        oButton.setText('Display');
    } else {
        oButton.setText('Change');
    } },
```

Listing 7.25 toggle Method in MyData Controller

Messages   In this controller, you use the function `addNotification` to transfer messages to the `Notifier` control. Copy the source code from Listing 7.16, and insert it below the `toggle` function in the controller file. Figure 7.15 shows the result in the browser.

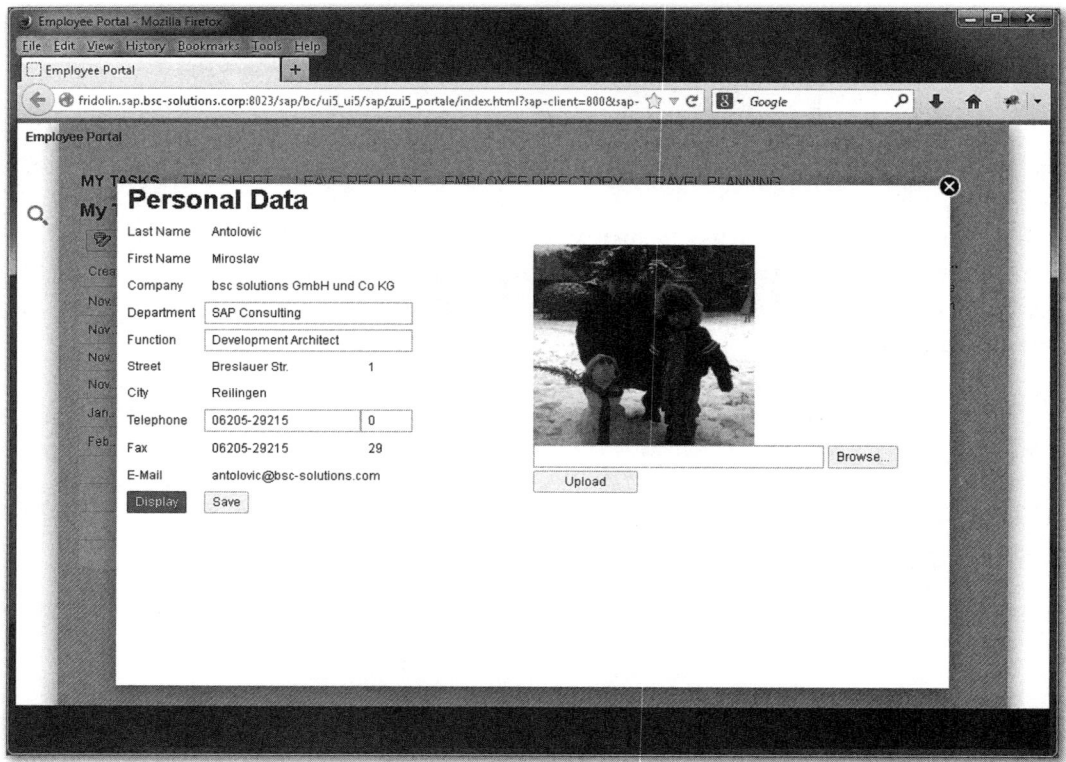

Figure 7.15   The My Data Area in the Portal

7.2.5   Tasks

On the START page, let's offer the option of maintaining a task list and of setting the tasks to DONE. In addition, a small statistic will be displayed that represents the ratio between open and done tasks as a chart. In the bootstrap, you have to include the *sap.viz* library to display charts and the *sap.ui.table* library to display tables. This changes the bootstrap as follows:

```
data-sap-ui-libs="sap.ui.commons, sap.ui.ux3,
                  sap.ui.table, sap.viz"
```

In the view, you receive the date fields from SAP as a special feature in the format YYYYMMDD. These fields must be formatted to make them easy to use. Here, you can use the DateTime type (see Listing 7.26), which you already learned about in Chapter 5.

```
oDateType = new sap.ui.model.type.DateTime({
    source : { pattern : "yyyyMMdd" },
    pattern : "MM.DD.YYYY"
});
```

Listing 7.26 DateTime Type

The field in the format YYYYMMDD is reformatted as MM.DD.YYYY by this typing. You specify this formatting in the relevant control as type; as a result, the fields are displayed correctly, as shown, for example, in Listing 7.27.

```
template : new sap.ui.commons.TextView({
    text : { path : "crea_date",
            type : oDateType
            }
    }),
```

Listing 7.27 Formatting Date

The other special feature of this view is the RatingIndicator control. This control also expects a value of type float here, so that you will also have to convert the value at this point using the function parseFloat (see Listing 7.28).

```
template : new sap.ui.commons.RatingIndicator({
    change : oController.markTaskDone,
    }).bindProperty("value", "priority", function(rating) {
        var fRate = parseFloat(rating);
            if (isNaN(fRate)) { fRate = 0; }
                return fRate;
        }),
```

Listing 7.28 Parsing Value in Float

When you create a new task, the add function will be triggered in the controller. For the ADD button, use a standard SAP symbol (*s_b_anno. gif*); you'll find this under the ICF node *sap/public/bc/icons/*. Because the

SAP icons and symbols

ICF node of your application is under *sap/bc/ui5_ui5/sap/zui5_portal*, you must first navigate four directories up in the ICF tree; from there, navigate down the other branch to the icons. This results in the path *../../../../ public/bc/icons/s_b_anno.gif*. This is displayed graphically in Figure 7.16.

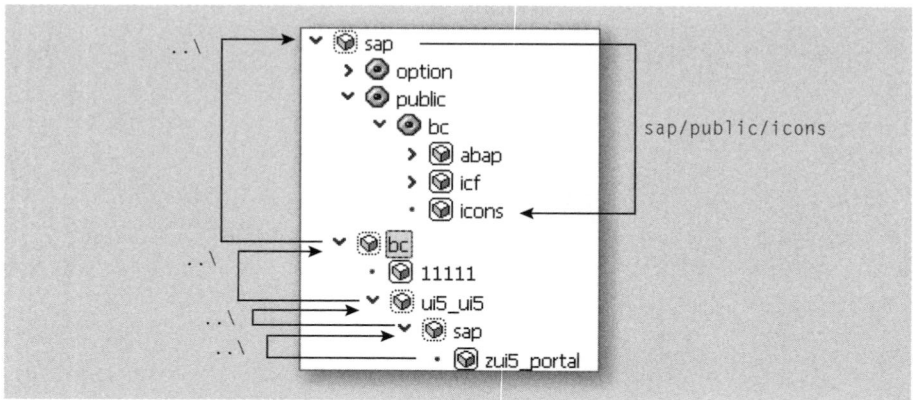

Figure 7.16 Path to the SAP Symbols

You will find the names of the individual icons in the MIME Repository, under *SAP/PUBLIC/BC/Icons*.

View   The chart will be displayed on the right, next to the task table. Create a MatrixLayout control with two columns as an external framework for this view (see Listing 7.29).

```
createContent : function(oController) {
// Basislayout
var oLayout = new sap.ui.commons.layout.MatrixLayout({
    layoutFixed : true,
    columns : 2,
    width : "100%",
    widths : [ "75%", "25%" ]
});
oText = new sap.ui.commons.TextView({
  text : "My Tasks"
});
```

Listing 7.29 Basic Layout for My Tasks

For the Task table, you need a function for formatting dates, as already **"My Tasks" table** shown in Listing 7.26, and you should also provide a button for creating a new task in the toolbar of the table. This results in the content of Listing 7.30.

```
// Header
var oHeaderText = new sap.ui.commons.TextView({
    text : "My Tasks",
    design : sap.ui.commons.TextViewDesign.H3
});
oLayout.createRow(oHeaderText);
// Format for date fields
oDateType = new sap.ui.model.type.DateTime({
    source : { pattern : "yyyyMMdd" },
    pattern : "MM.DD.YYYY"
});
// Table for "My Tasks"
var oTable = new sap.ui.table.Table({
  visibleRowCount : 10,
  firstVisibleRow : 1,
  editable : false,
  toolbar : sap.ui.commons.Toolbar({
    items : [ new sap.ui.commons.Button({
      text : "New Task",
      icon : "../../../../public/bc/icons/s_b_anno.gif",
      press : oController.add
    }) ]
  }),
  selectionMode : sap.ui.table.SelectionMode.Multi,
});
```

Listing 7.30 Table for My Tasks

The first two columns in the table are the date fields CREATED ON and DUE DATE. Listing 7.31 shows an example of the implementation of the column CREATED ON; implement the second column, DUE DATE, in a similar manner.

```
// Columns created on and due date
oTable.addColumn(new sap.ui.table.Column({
  label : new sap.ui.commons.Label({
    text : "Created on"
  }),
```

```
template : new sap.ui.commons.TextView({
  text : {
    path : "crea_date",
    type : oDateType
  }
}),
sortProperty : "crea_date",
filterProperty : "crea_date",
width : "8%"
}));
// "Due date" analogous, JSON path "due_date"
```

Listing 7.31 Date Fields

The column that contains the task texts does not offer any special features; the value must be parsed in float only for the PRIORITY column. For these columns, this results in the content of Listing 7.32.

```
oTable.addColumn( new sap.ui.table.Column({
    label : new sap.ui.commons.Label({
    text : "Task"
  }),
    template : new sap.ui.commons.TextView({
      text : { path : "task" }
  }),
    width : "40%"
}));

oTable.addColumn(new sap.ui.table.Column({
    label : new sap.ui.commons.Label({
      text : "Priority"
    }),
      template : new sap.ui.commons.RatingIndicator({
                editable : false
        }).bindProperty(
        "value", "priority", function(rating) {
          var fRate = parseFloat(rating);
                  if (isNaN(fRate)) { fRate = 0; }
                    return fRate;
          }),
        width : "16%"
}));
```

Listing 7.32 Task Texts and Priorities

In the last column of the table, implement a checkbox that you can use to set the individual tasks to DONE. When the status of the checkbox is changed, the function `markTaskDone` is to be called in the controller. For this column, this results in the content of Listing 7.33. Remember to bind the model to the table control with the `bindRows` function.

Doing tasks

```
oTable.addColumn(new sap.ui.table.Column({
  label : new sap.ui.commons.Label({ text : "Done" }),
  template : new sap.ui.commons.CheckBox({
    change : oController.markTaskDone,
    customData : [ new sap.ui.core.CustomData({
      key : "id",
      value : "{taskid}"
    }) ]
  }).bindChecked("done", function(checked) {
    var key = checked;
    switch (key) {
    case "X": return true;
    case "default": return false;
    }
  }),
  width : "10%"
}));
oTable.bindRows("/");
```

Listing 7.33 Setting Tasks to Done

On the right-hand side, a chart will be displayed that illustrates the distribution of open and done tasks. In this example, we've chosen the Donut chart type. The received data is processed in the controller, and the model is stored under the path PROJECTDATA (see Listing 7.36). For the chart, this results in the content of Listing 7.34.

Chart on task status

```
var oDataset = new sap.viz.ui5.data.FlattenedDataset({
  dimensions : [ {
    axis : 1,
    name : 'Done tasks',
    value : "{task}"
  }],
  measures : [ {
    name : 'Status',
    value : '{value}'
  }],
```

```
        data : {
          path : "/projectData"
        }});
// Create chart control
var oBarChart = new sap.viz.ui5.Donut("oTaskStatusBar", {
  width : "100%",
  height : "300px",
  title : {
    visible : true,
    text : 'Distribution of task status'
  },
  dataset : oDataset
});
```

Listing 7.34 Chart on Task Status

Finally, you have to add the table and chart control to the external `MatrixLayout` control (see Listing 7.35).

```
var oTableCell =
  new sap.ui.commons.layout.MatrixLayoutCell({
  content : oTable,
  vAlign : sap.ui.commons.layout.VAlign.Top
});
var oLayoutRightCell =
  new sap.ui.commons.layout.MatrixLayoutCell({
    content : oLayoutRight,
    vAlign : sap.ui.commons.layout.VAlign.Top
});
  oLayout.createRow(oTableCell, oLayoutRightCell);
  return oLayout;
}});
```

Listing 7.35 My Tasks View

onInit   In the controller, you need three functions for the task page. In the `onInit` function, you load the data via the `GET_TASK` method from the backend. The open and done tasks are counted for the small statistic and are bound as `projectData` to the model (see Listing 7.36).

```
onInit : function() {
    this.initLoad();
},
initLoad : function() {
```

```
var oModel = new sap.ui.model.json.JSONModel()
            .attachRequestCompleted(function(oData) {
var oTasks = oData.getSource().getProperty("/");
var iDone = 0; var iOpen = 0;
for ( var i = 0; i < oTasks.length; i++) {
  if (oTasks[i].done == "X")
    iDone++;
  else
    iOpen++;
 }


var oModel = new sap.ui.model.json.JSONModel({
    projectData : [ {
       Task : "Done", value : iDone
             }, {
       Task : "Open", value : iOpen
     } ]
  });
sap.ui.getCore().byId("oTaskStatusBar").setModel(oModel);
});


oModel.loadData("/ui5/?application=portal&area=get_task");
    this.getView().setModel(oModel);
},
```

Listing 7.36 onInit Function in MyTask Controller

If a task is marked as *done*, the function `markTaskDone` is called in the controller (see Listing 7.33). In this function, the `SET_TASK` method has to be called in the SAP backend (see Listing 7.37). After successfully calling the backend method, the `initLoad` method is called in the controller so that the chart is rerendered.

Setting task to "done"

```
markTaskDone : function(oEvent) {
var oRows = oEvent.getSource().oParent.getCells();
var bSelected = oRows[4].getChecked();

var sSelected = "X";
if (!bSelected)
  sSelected = " ";
var oParameters = {
  "taskid" : oRows[4].data("id"),
  "done" : sSelected,
```

```
};

$.ajax({
url : "/ui5/index.html?application=portal&area=set_task",
contentType : "application/json",
dataType : 'json',
data : oParameters,
success : function(data, textStatus, jqXHR) {
  sap.ui.getCore().byId("MyTask").getController()
      .addNotification(data.text, data.severity);
// Re-render view so that the statistics are updated.
sap.ui.getCore().byId("MyTask").getController().initLoad();
  }
});
},
```

Listing 7.37 Setting Tasks to Done

Creating new task
When you call the add function from the view, a dialog box is displayed in which you can create a new task. We've decided on a ToolPopup control; of course, you can also use a different control.

```
add : function(oEvent) {
var oDP = new sap.ui.commons.DatePicker();
var oTF = new sap.ui.commons.TextField();
var oRI = new sap.ui.commons.RatingIndicator();

var oSimpleForm = new sap.ui.commons.form.SimpleForm({
maxContainerCols : 1,
layout : sap.ui.commons.form.SimpleFormLayout.GridLayout,
content : [
new sap.ui.commons.Title({text : "Create task" }),
new sap.ui.commons.Label({text : "Due date"}),
oDP,
new sap.ui.commons.Label({text : "Task"}),
oTF,
new sap.ui.commons.Label({text : "Priority"}),
oRI,
new sap.ui.commons.Button({
      text : "Create",
      press : function() {
        var oParameters = {
            "due_date" : oDP.getYyyymmdd(),
```

```
                "done" : " ",
                "priority" : oRI.getValue(),
                "task" : oTF.getValue()
  };

  $.ajax({
  url : "/ui5/index.html?application=portal&area=set_task",
  contentType : "application/json",
  dataType : 'json',
  data : oParameters,
  success : function(data, textStatus, jqXHR){
  sap.ui.getCore().byId("MyTask").getController()
          .addNotification(data.text, data.severity);
  sap.ui.getCore().byId("MyTask").getController().initLoad();
      }});
    oTool.close();
    }}),
  new sap.ui.commons.Button({
    text : "Close",
    press : function() {
        oTool.close();
      }}) ]
  });

  var oTool = new sap.ui.ux3.ToolPopup({
    autoClose : true,
    content : new sap.ui.commons.layout.VerticalLayout(
      { width : "500px",
        content : [ oSimpleForm ]
        }),
    opener : oEvent.getSource()
  });
  oTool.open();
  },
```

Listing 7.38   Creating a Task

In this controller, you use the function addNotification to transfer messages to the Notifier control. Copy the source code from Listing 7.16, and insert it below the add function in the controller file. Figure 7.17 shows how the ratio between open and done tasks should look.

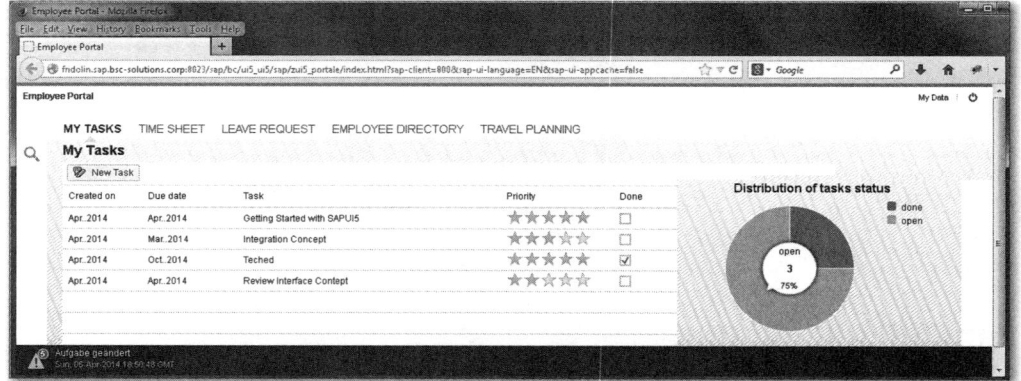

Figure 7.17 Distribution Statistic Based on Task Status

7.2.6 Time Sheet

Own control

For the TIME SHEET, we recommend that you create your own control for recording the hours. In this Custom control, two ComboBoxes are created: The first ComboBox displays the time in hours, and the second ComboBox displays the time in minutes. Below the ZUI5_PORTAL directory, create a new file called *Timepicker.js* for this purpose (see Figure 7.18).

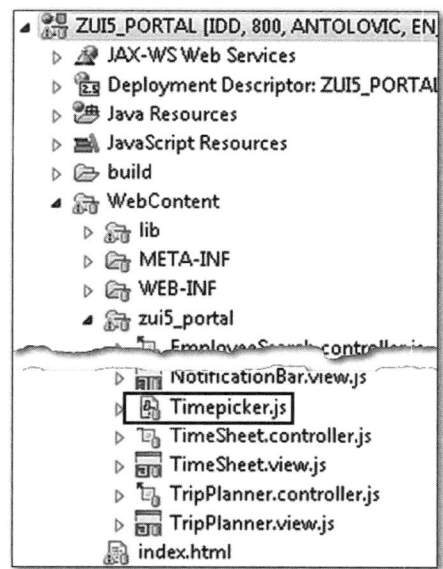

Figure 7.18 Timepicker.js

Because an external resource is involved, you have to use the function jQuery.sap.require to load the two required libraries *Control* and *Combo-Box*. In the TimePicker control, fill the first ComboBox with hourly values from 0 to 23 hours, and restrict to quarter-hourly values in the second ComboBox. In the *Datepicker.js* file, now enter the code from Listing 7.39.

Loading libraries

```
jQuery.sap.declare("zui5_portal.TimePicker");
jQuery.sap.require("sap.ui.core.Control");
jQuery.sap.require("sap.ui.commons.ComboBox");
// TimePicker control with HH MM
sap.ui.core.Control.extend("zui5_portal.TimePicker", {
    metadata : {
        properties : {
            "time" : "string"
        },
        aggregations : {
            "_hour" : {
                type : "sap.ui.commons.ComboBox",
                multiple : false,
                visibility : "hidden"
            },
            "_minutes" : {
                type : "sap.ui.commons.ComboBox",
                multiple : false,
                visibility : "hidden"
            }
        },
    events : {"submit" : {}}
    },
    init : function() {
        that = this;
        this.setProperty("time", "0000");
        // Hours
        this.setAggregation("_hour",
          new sap.ui.commons.ComboBox({
            width:"85px",
            items:[
                new sap.ui.core.ListItem({text:"00"}),
                new sap.ui.core.ListItem({text:"01"}),
//              etc. with value 02-21
                new sap.ui.core.ListItem({text:"22"}),
                new sap.ui.core.ListItem({text:"23"})
```

```
                        ],
                value:"00",
                  change: function(oEvent){
                    var sTime = this.oParent.getProperty("time");
                    var sMinutes = sTime.substr(2, 2);
                    var sHours = oEvent.getParameters().newValue;
                    this.oParent.setProperty(
                            "time",
                            sHours+sMinutes,
                            true
                    );
            }
      }));
        this.setAggregation("_minutes",
          new sap.ui.commons.ComboBox({
            width:"85px",
            items:[
                new sap.ui.core.ListItem({text:"00"}),
                new sap.ui.core.ListItem({text:"15"}),
                new sap.ui.core.ListItem({text:"30"}),
                new sap.ui.core.ListItem({text:"45"})
              ],
            value:"00",
            change: function(oEvent){
              var sTime = this.oParent.getProperty("time");
              var sHours = sTime.substr(0, 2);
              var sMinutes = oEvent.getParameters().newValue;
              this.oParent.setProperty(
                  "time",
                  sHours+sMinutes,
                  true);
          }
      }));
    },
    renderer : function(oRm, oControl) {
      oRm.write("<div");
      oRm.addClass("timePicker");
      oRm.writeClasses();
      oRm.writeControlData(oControl);
      oRm.write(">");
      oRm.write("<div>");
      oRm.renderControl(oControl.getAggregation("_hour"));
```

```
    oRm.write(":");
    oRm.renderControl(oControl.getAggregation("_minutes"));
    oRm.write("</div>");
    oRm.write("</div>");
    }
  });
```

Listing 7.39 TimePicker

The open-source library *Datejs* has proven itself useful for formatting date   Datejs
values. You can download this under *www.datejs.com* and integrate it into
your page. Below the *WebContent* directory, create a *lib* folder, and copy
the downloaded file to this directory (see Figure 7.19).

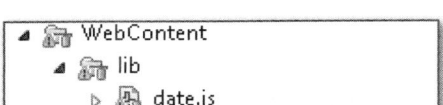

Figure 7.19 Datejs

Next, embed the two external resources below the bootstrap in the *index.
html* file (see Listing 7.40).

```
<!-- Date.js -->
  <script src="lib/date.js"></script>
<!-- Timepicker -->
  <script src="zui5_portal/Timepicker.js"></script>
```

Listing 7.40 Embedding the External Resources

In this view, first create a `MatrixLayout` control as an external layout.   View

```
createContent : function(oController) {
//Basic layout of the page
var oLayout = new sap.ui.commons.layout.MatrixLayout({
layoutFixed : true,
columns : 2,
width : "100%",
widths : [ "70%", "30%" ]
});

//Header with H1 formatting
var oHeaderText = new sap.ui.commons.TextView({
text:"Time Sheet",
```

```
design : sap.ui.commons.TextViewDesign.H1});
oLayout.createRow(oHeaderText);
```
Listing 7.41 External Framework of the Time Sheet Page

Date and Time
Date and time fields are displayed in the table. As in Listing 7.26, you also have to implement the formatting functions for these fields here. Listing 7.42 shows an example of the implementation of the first date field. This listing was shortened for clarity; you can download the complete listing from the book's web page. Implement the two fields FROM and TO in a similar manner; use the formatting function oTimeType for these fields.

```
oDateType = new sap.ui.model.type.DateTime({
source: {pattern: "yyyyMMdd"},
pattern: "MM.DD.YYYY"});  // DateType formatting

oTimeType = new sap.ui.model.type.Time({
source: {pattern: "hhmm"},
pattern: "hh:mm 'hours'"});     // DateType

//Structure of a table
var oTable = new sap.ui.table.Table({
    visibleRowCount:20,
    firstVisibleRow: 1,
    editable:false,
    selectionMode: sap.ui.table.SelectionMode.Multi,
});
var oColumn = new sap.ui.table.Column({
    label: new sap.ui.commons.Label({text: "Date"}),
    template: new sap.ui.commons.TextView().bindProperty(
            "text",
            "activity_date",
            oDateType),
    sortProperty: "date",
    filterProperty: "date",
    sorted:true ,
    sortOrder: sap.ui.table.SortOrder.Descending
});
oTable.addColumn(oColumn);
// time_from and time_to similar, each with oTimeType
```
Listing 7.42 Date and Time Fields

The next column implements a checkbox as an indicator for an internal project. In this column, you have to convert the ABAP values "X" and " " to the JavaScript-compliant values true and false. For this column, this results in the content of Listing 7.43.

```
oTable.addColumn(new sap.ui.table.Column({
   label: new sap.ui.commons.Label({text: "Internal"}),
   template: new sap.ui.commons.CheckBox({
       editable:false}).bindProperty(
                     "checked",
                     "internal",
       function(checked) {
         var key = checked;
         switch(key) {
         case "X": return true;
         case "default": return false;}
         }),
}));
```

Listing 7.43 Conversion to Boolean Values

The next two columns display the name of the customer and the project. Because you only have the ID, you have to determine the text of the ID for these two fields via a for loop (see Listing 7.44). With project names, note that the project ID can still occur twice and that you also have to compare the value with the customer ID as a result.

```
oTable.addColumn(new sap.ui.table.Column({
   label: new sap.ui.commons.Label({text: "Customer"}),
   template: new sap.ui.commons.TextView().bindProperty(
     "text", "customer_id", function(s){
     // Determine customer name for customer number
     if (s==zero)
     return;
       var oProperty =
          this.getModel().getProperty("/customer");
     for (var i=0; i < oProperty.length; i++){
       if (oProperty[i].customer_id == s)
         return oProperty[i].customer_text;
     }
     }),
}));
```

```
oTable.addColumn(new sap.ui.table.Column({
  label: new sap.ui.commons.Label({text: "Project"}),
  template: new sap.ui.commons.TextView().bindProperty(
        "text",
        "project_id",
    function(s){
     if (s==zero)
       return;
     var sPath = this.getBindingContext().getPath();
     var oCurrentRow = this.getModel().getProperty(sPath);
     var oProperty =
               this.getModel().getProperty("/projects");
     for (var i=0;i < oProperty.length;i++){
       // Project ID and customer ID match
       if ((oProperty[i].project_id == s)&&
         (oProperty[i].customer_id ==
                               oCurrentRow.customer_id))
         return oProperty[i].project_desc;
     }}),
}));
```

Listing 7.44 Determination of Customer and Project Names

Deleting entry and filter binding
The next column contains the description of the activity involved. It should be possible to delete a row. We've decided on the typical SAP DELETE icon in this column also. The special feature of this column is that the required data for deleting is transferred to the controller via the CustomData attribute. The binding table is rather unusual also. Because you obtain the last six months in the service from the backend, the TIME AND ATTENDANCE table would become very complex. For this reason, set a filter on the binding and thus avoid the complicated dividing up of the data. The external library *Datejs* is also used here (see Listing 7.45).

```
oTable.addColumn(new sap.ui.table.Column({
  label: new sap.ui.commons.Label({text: "Description"}),
  template:
    new sap.ui.commons.TextView().bindProperty(
        "text", "description"),
}));

oTable.addColumn(new sap.ui.table.Column({
  template: new sap.ui.commons.Button({
```

```
   lite: true,
   icon : "img/s_b_dele.gif",
   press: oController.removeTimeEntry,
   customData:[
      new sap.ui.core.CustomData({
      key:"DelKey",
      value:"{username}&{activity_date}&
                     {time_from}&{time_to}"})
   ]
 }),
}));
// Filter for the last two months
var oFilter = new sap.ui.model.Filter(
    "activity_date",
    sap.ui.model.FilterOperator.GE,
    Number(Date.today().addMonths(-1).toString(
      "yyyyMMdd"
      )));
oTable.bindRows("/time_report","","",oFilter);
```
Listing 7.45 Deleting Entry and Filter Binding

This completes the implementation of the table for displaying the recorded   Recording times
times. On the right-hand side, now implement a small form for recording
the working times. This form is also implemented as a framework in a
MatrixLayout control. First, create the MatrixLayout control, and implement a DatePicker control for selecting the date. The Custom control from
Listing 7.39 is used to record the times. For these fields, this results in
the content of Listing 7.46:

```
//Layout for the right-hand column of the matrix layout
var oLayoutRight = new sap.ui.commons.layout.MatrixLayout({
layoutFixed : true,
columns : 2,
width : "100%",
widths : ["35%", "65%"]
}).addStyleClass("margin");

//Create a DatePicker control
var oDatePicker = new sap.ui.commons.DatePicker({
width:"175px"});

//Create a TimePicker control
```

```
var oTimePickerFrom  = new zui5_portal.TimePicker();

//Create a TimePicker control
var oTimePickerTo  = new zui5_portal.TimePicker();
```
Listing 7.46 Time Recording

Customer and project

To select the customer and project names, implement two combo boxes. When a customer is selected in the customer name combo box, only the projects of the selected customer are to be displayed there. This is achieved because you determine the selected customer when binding the projects and then display only the projects that belong to the selected customer (see Listing 7.47).

```
//Template for combo boxes
var oItemTemplateCustomer = new sap.ui.core.ListItem({
text:"{customer_text}",
key:"{customer_id}"
});
var oItemTemplateProjects = new sap.ui.core.ListItem({
text:"{project_desc}",
key:"{project_id}"
});

//Create a ComboBox control
var oComboBoxCustomers = new sap.ui.commons.ComboBox({
width:"175px",
editable:false,
items: {path:"/customer",
  template:oItemTemplateCustomer},
change: function(oEvent){
//If this combo box is changed,
//the corresponding combo box of the projects must
//also be filtered and adjusted again.
var oFilter = new sap.ui.model.Filter(
        "customer_id",
        sap.ui.model.FilterOperator.EQ,
        this.getSelectedKey());
oComboBoxProjects.unbindItems();
oComboBoxProjects.bindItems(
        "/projects",
        oItemTemplateProjects,"" ,
        oFilter);
```

```
oComboBoxProjects.setValue("");
}});
//Create a ComboBox control
var oComboBoxProjects = new sap.ui.commons.ComboBox({
     width:"175px",
     editable: false
});
```

Listing 7.47 Selecting Customer and Project

Next, implement two radio buttons for selecting if an internal project or **Radio buttons**
a customer project is involved. The two ComboBoxes from Listing 7.47
should be visible only when the CUSTOMER radio button is selected.

```
var oLayoutRB = new sap.ui.commons.layout.MatrixLayout();
oLayoutRB.setLayoutFixed(false);
oLayoutRB.setWidth("175px");
oLayoutRB.setColumns(2);

//Create a RadioButton control
var oRB1 = new sap.ui.commons.RadioButton({
  text : 'Internal',
  groupName : 'Group1',
  selected : true,
  select : function() {
    oComboBoxCustomers.setEditable(false);
    oComboBoxProjects.setEditable(false);
    oComboBoxCustomers.setSelectedKey("");
    oComboBoxProjects.setSelectedKey("");
    }
});

//Create a RadioButton control
var oRB2 = new sap.ui.commons.RadioButton({
  text : 'Customer',
  groupName : 'Group1',
  select : function() {
    oComboBoxCustomers.setEditable(true);
    oComboBoxProjects.setEditable(true);
    }
});
//Place the created radio buttons in the layout
oLayoutRB.createRow(oRB1, oRB2);
```

333

Describing and saving

Next, create a control for the DESCRIPTION and a button for saving the data you entered. In the previous pages, you used the ID to read the necessary values of the UI controls for an action. In Listing 7.48, transfer the instances of the UI controls to the function and thus avoid having to read the values via the ID of controls in the controller.

```
//Create a TextArea control
var oTA = new sap.ui.commons.TextArea({
    width : '175px',
    height : '120px'
});

//Create a Button control
var oButtonCreate = new sap.ui.commons.Button({
width:"175px",
text:"Save",
press: function (oEvent){
  //Call function to create a time entry.
  oController.createNewEntry(
      oDatePicker,
      oTimePickerFrom,
      oTimePickerTo,
      oComboBoxCustomers,
      oComboBoxProjects,
      oTA,
      oRB1);
}
});
```

Listing 7.48 Saving Recorded Times

Row for form field

For each form field, create a row in the Layout control with a descriptive text and the actual control (see Listing 7.49).

```
//Fill the layout with the newly created controls
oLayoutRight.createRow(oTV);
oLayoutRight.createRow(
 new sap.ui.commons.Label({text:"Date"}),oDatePicker);
oLayoutRight.createRow(
 new sap.ui.commons.Label({text:"From"}),oTimePickerFrom);
oLayoutRight.createRow(
 new sap.ui.commons.Label({text:"To"}),oTimePickerTo);
oLayoutRight.createRow(
```

```
new sap.ui.commons.Label({text:"Type"}),oLayoutRB);
oLayoutRight.createRow(
 new sap.ui.commons.Label({text:"Customer"}),
                                oComboBoxCustomers);
oLayoutRight.createRow(
 new sap.ui.commons.Label({text:"Project"}),
                                oComboBoxProjects);
oLayoutRight.createRow(
 new sap.ui.commons.Label({text:"Description"}),oTA);
oLayoutRight.createRow("",oButtonCreate);
```
Listing 7.49   Form Layout

On this page, let's also implement a small `Chart` control that displays the   **Chart control**
ratio between internal and external costs (see Listing 7.50).

```
//Create a dataset for displaying a chart
   var oDataset = new sap.viz.ui5.data.FlattenedDataset({
       dimensions : [
                     {         axis : 1,
                               name : 'Month',
                               value : "{Month}"
                     }],
           measures : [
                     {         name : 'Internal',
                               value : '{internal}'
                     },{
                         name : 'Customer project',
                         value : '{external}'
                     }],
           data : {path : "/projectData"}
   });
   // Create chart control
   var oBarChart = new sap.viz.ui5.Line("oTimeChart",{
           width : "100%", height : "300px",
           title : { visible : true,
                     text : 'Project distribution'
           },
           dataset : oDataset
   });
```
Listing 7.50   Chart Control

Finally, you have to merge the individual screen areas in the external `MatrixLayout` control (see Listing 7.51).

```
oCell1 = new sap.ui.commons.layout.MatrixLayoutCell(
            {colSpan : 2 }
            );
oCell1.addContent(oBarChart);
oLayoutRight.createRow(oCell1);
var oTableCell = new sap.ui.commons.layout.MatrixLayoutCell(
    { content:oTable,
      vAlign : sap.ui.commons.layout.VAlign.Top
    });
var oLayoutRightCell =
    new sap.ui.commons.layout.MatrixLayoutCell(
        { content:oLayoutRight,
          vAlign : sap.ui.commons.layout.VAlign.Top
        });
//now place the whole page in the MatrixLayout
    oLayout.createRow(oTableCell , oLayoutRightCell);
    return oLayout;
    }
});
```

Listing 7.51 Time Sheet View

In the controller, call the `INIT_TS` service in the initialization phase. This returns the values for the customer and project combo boxes and also returns the recorded times of the last six months. The last two months are displayed in the SERVICE entry sheet (see view), and you need the full six months only for the statistics display.

In the `onInit` function, read the entered data from the backend and write the processed data to a model for the `Chart` control. For this function, this results in the content of Listing 7.52.

```
onInit: function() {
  // Init load of the data
  this.initLoad();
},
onBeforeRendering: function() {
  // Init load of the data
  this.initLoad();
```

```
  },
  initLoad: function(){
  var oModel =
    new sap.ui.model.json.JSONModel().attachRequestCompleted(
    function(oData){
      // Load all time entries
      var oTime=oData.getSource().getProperty("/time_report");
      // This loop calculates the duration.
      for (var i=0;i<oTime.length;i++){
        var oItem= oTime[i];
        var dStart = Date.parseExact(oItem.time_from,"HHmmss");
        var dEnd   = Date.parseExact(oItem.time_to,"HHmmss");
        var iDuration = (dEnd-dStart)/1000;
        // Month in text form
        oTime[i].duration = iDuration;
        var dDay =
              Date.parseExact(oItem.activity_date,"yyyyMMdd");
        oTime[i].month = dDay.toString("MMMM");
  }
  iInternal = 0;
  iExternal = 0;
  // JSON for Chart control
  sSummary = '{ "projectData" :[';
  for (var i=0;i<oTime.length;i++){
    if (i != 0){
      if(oTime[i].month != oTime[i-1].month){
        sSummary+= '{"Month" :"'
            +oTime[i-1].month
            +'","internal":"'
            +iInternal/3600
            +'","external":"'+
            iExternal/3600+'"},';
            iInternal=0;
            iExternal=0;
      }
    }
  // Internal then iInternal + Duration
    if(oTime[i].internal == "X"){
      iInternal+=oTime[i].duration;
    }
    else{
      // External, then iExternal + Duration
```

```
        iExternal+=oTime[i].duration;
    }
    if ((i+1)==oTime.length){
        sSummary+= '{"Month" :"'
        +oTime[i-1].month
        +'","internal":"'
        +iInternal/3600
        +'","external":"'
        +iExternal/3600+'"}]}';
    }
}
var oModel = new sap.ui.model.json.JSONModel( );
oModel.setJSON(sSummary);
sap.ui.getCore().byId("oTimeChart").setModel(oModel);
});
oModel.loadData("/ui5/?application=portal&area=init_ts");
    this.getView().setModel(oModel);
},
```

Listing 7.52 onInit Function

createNewEntry   When you create a new entry, the function `createNewEntry` is called in the controller (see Listing 7.48). Because the instances of the UI controls were transferred directly to the controller, you can read the corresponding values directly. For this function, this results in the content of Listing 7.53.

```
createNewEntry: function(
    oDatePicker, oTimePickerFrom, oTimePickerTo,
    oComboBoxCustomers, oComboBoxProjects,
    oTA, oCb){
  // Reading the parameter to be sent for the backend
var oParameters= {
        "date" :      oDatePicker.getYyyymmdd(),
        "timeFrom":  oTimePickerFrom.getTime(),
        "timeTo":    oTimePickerTo.getTime(),
        "customer": oComboBoxCustomers.getSelectedKey(),
        "project": oComboBoxProjects.getSelectedKey(),
        "internal" : oCb.getSelected(),
        "comment" : oTA.getValue()
};
// Validation, whether all values were entered
if(oParameters.date=="")
```

```
sap.ui.getCore().byId(
   "TimeSheet").getController().addNotification(
               "Select date","E");
if(oParameters.comment=="")
sap.ui.getCore().byId(
   "TimeSheet").getController().addNotification(
               "Enter description","E");
if ( ( Number ( oParameters.timeTo ) -
       Number (oParameters.timeFrom) ) < 1 )
sap.ui.getCore().byId(
   "TimeSheet").getController().addNotification(
               "Time incorrect","E");
if(((oParameters.customer =="") ||
   (oParameters.project=="")) &&
   (oParameters.internal != true))
sap.ui.getCore().byId(
   "TimeSheet").getController().addNotification(
           "Select Customer - Project","E");
 $.ajax({          //Ajax to backend
   url : "/ui5/index.html?application=portal&area=set_ts",
   contentType : "application/json",
   dataType : 'json',
   data: oParameters,
   // Call initLoad of this controller again
   success : function(data, textStatus, jqXHR) {
     sap.ui.getCore().byId("TimeSheet").getController().
                  addNotification(data.text,data.severity);
     sap.ui.getCore().byId(
               "TimeSheet").getController().initLoad();
       }
 });
},
```

Listing 7.53 createNewEntry Function

In this controller, you use the function addNotification to transfer mes-   Messages
sages to the Notifier control. Copy the source code from Listing 7.16,
and insert it below the createNewEntry function in the controller file.
Figure 7.20 shows the time sheet in the browser.

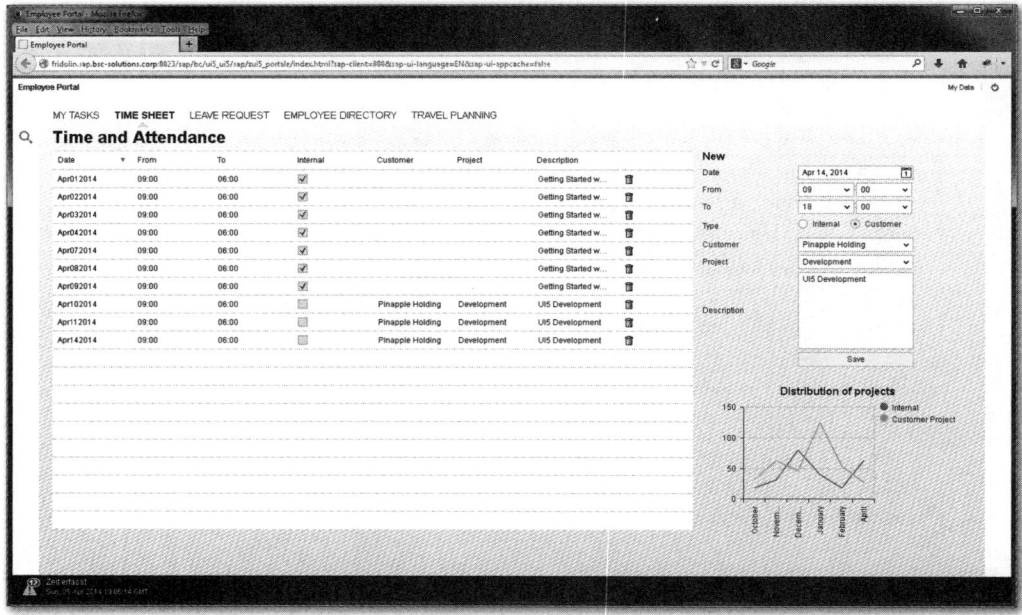

Figure 7.20 Time Sheet

7.2.7 Leave Request

Page layout   As the last component of the employee portal, the option of creating a
leave request is to be made available. At this point, let's choose the Calendar control from the *sap.me* library. This control displays a calendar
in which you can select the days and, together with the CalendarLegend
control, it offers all features that are necessary for a leave request. On the
right-hand side, the previous leave requests are displayed in an Accordion
control, sorted by status.

The style sheet for the Calendar control was available only for the Blue
Crystal theme in the current version of the library, version 1.16.5. For this
reason, two changes are needed in the bootstrap of the application: changing the theme to Blue Crystal and adding the *sap.me* and *sap.m* libraries.

```
<script src="resources/sap-ui-core.js"
        id="sap-ui-bootstrap"
        data-sap-ui-libs="sap.ui.commons, sap.ui.ux3,
                          sap.ui.table, sap.viz,
```

```
                              sap.m, sap.me"
                data-sap-ui-theme="sap_bluecrystal">
  </script>
```

Listing 7.54 Bootstrap

In this view, select a `MatrixLayout` control as the basic layout and cre- **Calendar control**
ate a `Calendar` control. This control displays a total of six months (see
Listing 7.55).

```
createContent : function(oController) {
// Basic Layout
var oLayout = new sap.ui.commons.layout.MatrixLayout({
  layoutFixed : true,
  columns : 2,
  width : "100%",
  widths : [ "75%", "25%" ]
});
//Header
var oHeaderText = new sap.ui.commons.TextView({
  text:"Leave request",
  design : sap.ui.commons.TextViewDesign.H1});
oLayout.createRow({height: "30px"}, oHeaderText );
//Calendar Control
var oCalendar = new sap.me.Calendar("LeaveRequestCalendar",
  {design: sap.me.CalendarDesign.Approval});
// Properties
  oCalendar.setEnableMultiselection(true);
  oCalendar.setSingleRow(false);
  oCalendar.setMonthsToDisplay(6);
  oCalendar.setWeeksPerRow(1);
  oCalendar.setFirstDayOffset(1);
  oCalendar.setMonthsPerRow(3);
  oCalendar.setDayHeight(35);
```

Listing 7.55 Calendar Control

On the right-hand side of the screen, an `Accordion` control displays **Accordion control**
the requests grouped according to the status CREATED, APPROVED, and
REJECTED. This is achieved by aggregation binding (see Listing 7.56).

```
oDateType = new sap.ui.model.type.DateTime({
  source: {pattern: "yyyyMMdd"},
  pattern: "MM.DD.YYYY'-'"});
```

```
//  Aggregation binding for Accordion
var oItemTemplate = new sap.ui.commons.TextView({
   text:{
     parts:[{
         path:"start_date",
         type: new sap.ui.model.type.DateTime({
                 source: {pattern: "yyyyMMdd"},
                 pattern: "MM.DD.YYYY'-'"})
     },{
         path:"end_date",
         type: new sap.ui.model.type.DateTime({
                 source: {pattern: "yyyyMMdd"},
                 pattern: "MM.DD.YYYY' /'"})
     },{
         path:"type",
         formatter:oController.Convert
     },{
         path:"descr",
     },
   ]
   },
   customData: new sap.ui.core.CustomData({
         key:"id",
         value:"{req_id}"
       }),
 });
```

Listing 7.56 Aggregation Binding to Accordion Item

Accordion section   You can now instantiate the Accordion control and create an accordion section for each status. Listing 7.57 shows an example of the implementation for the status CREATED (status value 01). In a similar manner, create an accordion section for the status APPROVED (status 02) and for the status REJECTED (status 03).

```
// Accordion control with status grouping
var oAccordion = new sap.ui.commons.Accordion();
oAccordion.setWidth("100%");
//Status Created
var oSection1 = new sap.ui.commons.AccordionSection({
  title: "Created",
  content:[ new sap.ui.commons.layout.VerticalLayout({
     content: {
```

```
            path: "/",
            filters: new sap.ui.model.Filter(
                "status", sap.ui.model.FilterOperator.EQ, "01"),
            template: oItemTemplate
            }})
    ]
});
oAccordion.addSection( oSection1 );
//...Status 02 and 03 similarly
// Legend
var oLegend = new sap.me.CalendarLegend();
oLegend.setExpanded(true);
oLegend.setLegendForType01("Pending Approval");
oLegend.setLegendForType04("Approved");
oLegend.setLegendForType06("Rejected");
```
Listing 7.57 Accordion Control

To create a leave request, implement a button that when clicked, calls the function openCreateDialog in the controller. A second button can be used to remove the marking of the days in the calendar. This button calls the function unmark in the controller (see Listing 7.58).

Creating leave request

```
// Toolbar
var oToolbar = new sap.ui.commons.Toolbar();
oToolbar.setStandalone(false);
oToolbar.setDesign(sap.ui.commons.ToolbarDesign.Flat);

var oButton1 = new sap.ui.commons.Button({
  text : "New",
  press : oController.openCreateDialog
});
oToolbar.addItem(oButton1);

var oButton2 = new sap.ui.commons.Button({
  text : "Remove",
  press : oController.unmark
});
oToolbar.addItem(oButton2);
```
Listing 7.58 Toolbar

Finally, you have to add the Calendar control and the Accordion control to the external MatrixLayout control again (see Listing 7.59).

```
var oCalendarCell = new
    sap.ui.commons.layout.MatrixLayoutCell({
       content:oCalendar,
       vAlign : sap.ui.commons.layout.VAlign.Top
});
var oAccordionCell = new
    sap.ui.commons.layout.MatrixLayoutCell({
       content:[oToolbar,oAccordion,oLegend],
       vAlign : sap.ui.commons.layout.VAlign.Top
});
oLayout.createRow(oCalendarCell, oAccordionCell );
return oLayout;
}});
```

Listing 7.59 Leave Request View

Controller   In the controller, the function INIT_ABS is used to provide the already created leave requests in the backend. In addition to the leave requests, the possible status for the leave types and processing status are also transferred (see Listing 7.60).

```
onInit: function() {
  this.initLoad();// Init Model
},
initLoad: function(){  // Init Model for Dropdowns
    var oModel = new sap.ui.model.json.JSONModel();
        oModel.loadData(
                "/ui5/?application=portal&area=init_abs");
    sap.ui.getCore().setModel(oModel,"init_abs");
},
onAfterRendering: function() {
  this.loadModel();
},
loadModel: function(){
  // Read leaves in the model
  var oModel = new sap.ui.model.json.JSONModel();
  oModel.attachRequestCompleted("",this.markLeaves);
  oModel.loadData(
              "/ui5/?application=portal&area=get_absence");
  this.getView().setModel(oModel);
},
```

Listing 7.60 Loading Data from the Backend

After the data is loaded, call the function `markLeaves` to mark the already created requests in the calendar (see Listing 7.61).

```
markLeaves: function(){
  // Connection to Calendar
  var oCalendar =
            sap.ui.getCore().byId("LeaveRequestCalendar");
// Read status
var aInitData =
        sap.ui.getCore().getModel(
        "init_abs").getProperty("/status");
// This is the model in this case
// Read all subitems via path
var aItems = this.getProperty("/");
for(var j=0; j < aInitData.length; j++){
  for ( var i=0 ; i < aItems.length ; i++ ){
  // Set selection from start to finish
  if (aInitData[j].status_key == aItems[i].status)
    oCalendar.toggleDatesRangeSelection(
      sap.ui.getCore().byId(
                "LeaveRequest").getController().toDate(
                    aItems[i].start_date),
      sap.ui.getCore().byId(
                "LeaveRequest").getController().toDate(
                    aItems[i].end_date),
          true);
    }
var aSelected = oCalendar.getSelectedDates();
var oType={};
switch(aInitData[j].status_key){
// Selection variant is selected here based on the status
  case "01":
      oType=sap.me.CalendarEventType.Type01;
      break;
  case "02":
      oType=sap.me.CalendarEventType.Type04;
       break;
  case "03":
      oType=sap.me.CalendarEventType.Type06;
      break;
  default:
      oType=sap.me.CalendarEventType.Type07;
      break;
```

```
// Change display type of all selected dates
oCalendar.toggleDatesType( aSelected, oType, true);
// Remove selection
oCalendar.unselectAllDates();
}},
```

Listing 7.61 Marking Entries in the Calendar

Converting date

The date is converted using the help function `toDate` (see Listing 7.62).

```
toDate : function(str){
    if (str==zero)
      return;
    String(str);
    var y = str.substr(0,4),
    m = str.substr(4,2) - 1,
    d = str.substr(6,2);
    var D = new Date(y,m,d);
    return D;
},
```

Listing 7.62 Date Conversion

Creating leave request

The CREATE button calls the function `openCreateDialog` in the controller. This function opens a dialog box for creating a new leave request (see Listing 7.63).

```
openCreateDialog: function(oEvent) {
  // Access to the calendar of the view
  var oCalendar =
        sap.ui.getCore().byId("LeaveRequestCalendar");
  // Read selected dates
  var oSelectedDates = oCalendar.getSelectedDates();
  // Error message if no dates were selected
  if (oSelectedDates.length==0)
    return sap.ui.getCore().byId(
      "LeaveRequest").getController().Error(
            "No dates selected");
  // Error message if start date is later than end date
  var sStartDate = sap.ui.getCore().byId(
              "LeaveRequest").getController().toYyyymmdd(
              oSelectedDates[0]);
  var sEndDate = sap.ui.getCore().byId(
              "LeaveRequest").getController().toYyyymmdd(
```

```
                    oSelectedDates[oSelectedDates.length - 1]);
if (sStartDate > sEndDate)
    return sap.ui.getCore().byId("LeaveRequest")
          .getController().Error(
        "Start date later than end date");

// Form to create the request
    var oComboBox1 = new sap.ui.commons.ComboBox();
    var oTextArea = new sap.ui.commons.TextArea({
        cols : 50,
        rows : 6,
        wrapping : sap.ui.core.Wrapping.Off,
  });
    var oItemTemplate = new sap.ui.core.ListItem({
      text:"{abs_text}",
      key:"{abs_key}"});
oComboBox1.setModel(sap.ui.getCore().getModel("init_abs"));
oComboBox1.bindItems("/absence",oItemTemplate);
  // Create dialog
  var oDialog1 = new sap.ui.commons.Dialog({
    title :     "New request",
    content:[
     new sap.ui.commons.layout.VerticalLayout({
      content:[new sap.ui.commons.layout.HorizontalLayout({
       content:[new sap.ui.commons.Label({
                  text:"Period : ",
                  width:"100px",
                  required: true }),
                  new sap.ui.commons.Label({
                  text:oSelectedDates[0]+ " - "+
                  oSelectedDates[oSelectedDates.length-1],}),
                  ] }),
          new sap.ui.commons.layout.HorizontalLayout({
            content:[ new sap.ui.commons.Label({
                  text:"Type : ",
                  width:"100px",
                  required: true}),
                  oComboBox1,
              ] }),
          new sap.ui.commons.layout.HorizontalLayout({
            content:[ new sap.ui.commons.Label({
                  text:"Reason : ",
                  width:"100px"}),
```

347

```
                          oTextArea
                    ] })
              ]
         })
      ],
 // Send request to backend
    buttons:[
        new sap.ui.commons.Button({
            text: "Send",
            press: function(oEvent){
 // Parameters for AJAX
            var oParameters= {
              "startDate" : sap.ui.getCore().byId(
                    "LeaveRequest").getController().toYyyymmdd(
                        oSelectedDates[0]),
               "endDate":    sap.ui.getCore().byId(
                    "LeaveRequest").getController().toYyyymmdd(
                        oSelectedDates[oSelectedDates.length-1]),
                "reason":  oComboBox1.getSelectedKey(),
                "comment":    oTextArea.getValue()
        };
         if (oComboBox1.getSelectedKey()=="")
         // Verify that entries are not empty
         return sap.ui.getCore().byId(
               "LeaveRequest").getController().Error(
               "Fill required fields");
         // Remove markings from calendar
         oCalendar.unselectAllDates();
        $.ajax({
        url :
          "/ui5/index.html?application=portal&area=set_absence",
        contentType : "application/json",
        dataType : 'json',
        data: oParameters,
        success : function(data, textStatus, jqXHR) {
          sap.ui.getCore().byId(
            "LeaveRequest").getController().addNotification(
                  data.text, data.severity);
                oDialog1.close();
          sap.ui.getCore().byId(
            "LeaveRequest").getController().loadModel();
                }});
        }}),
```

```
      new sap.ui.commons.Button({
        text: "Cancel",
        press:function(){
          oDialog1.close();
        } })
    ]
});
  oDialog1.open();//Open actual dialog
},
```

Listing 7.63 Creating a Leave Request

If no days have been marked in the calendar, an error message is output via the `Error` function (see Listing 7.64).

```
Error : function (string) {
// Error message
  jQuery.sap.require("sap.ui.commons.MessageBox");
    sap.ui.commons.MessageBox.show(string,
    sap.ui.commons.MessageBox.Icon.ERROR,
    "Error");
  },
```

Listing 7.64 Outputting an Error

The function `toYyyymmdd` converts the date fields to the backend-compatible format YYYYMMDD when creating a request (see Listing 7.63). For this function, this results in the content of Listing 7.65.

```
toYyyymmdd : function(date){
    date = String(date);
    date = date.substr(4);
    var theDate = Date.parseExact(date,"MMM dd yyyy");
    var yyyymmdd = theDate.toString("yyyyMMdd");
    return yyyymmdd;
  },
```

Listing 7.65 Converting Date

The UNMARK button calls the function `unmark` in the controller and removes the markings in the calendar (see Listing 7.66).

```
unmark: function() {
  // Deletes all markings from the calendar
  var oCalendar =
```

```
                    sap.ui.getCore().byId("LeaveRequestCalendar");
          oCalendar.unselectAllDates();
       },
```

Listing 7.66 Unmarking

Formatter function

The function `Convert` is called as a formatter for the entries in the `Accordion` control (see Listing 7.56) and inserts a slash between the request type and reason in each case.

```
Convert: function(sString){
  // Insert slash
  if (sString==zero)
    return;
  var oProperty = sap.ui.getCore().getModel(
               "init_abs").getProperty("/absence");
      for (var i=0;i<oProperty.length;i++){
        if (oProperty[i].abs_key == sString)
            return oProperty[i].abs_text +" / ";
      }
},
```

Listing 7.67 Formatter Function

In this controller, you use the function `addNotification` to transfer messages to the `Notifier` control. Copy the source code from Listing 7.16, and insert it below the `Convert` function in the controller file. Figure 7.21 shows the finished application for creating leave requests.

A look ahead

You can now create leave requests in your employee portal. What is missing is a function with which you can approve or reject a leave request. We will deal with this task in Chapter 10, in which you will develop an approval app specifically for smartphones and tablets.

As you may have noticed in this chapter, the implementation effort required on the backend side should not be underestimated. For this reason, the next chapter introduces an alternative to the Custom ICF handler: SAP Gateway.

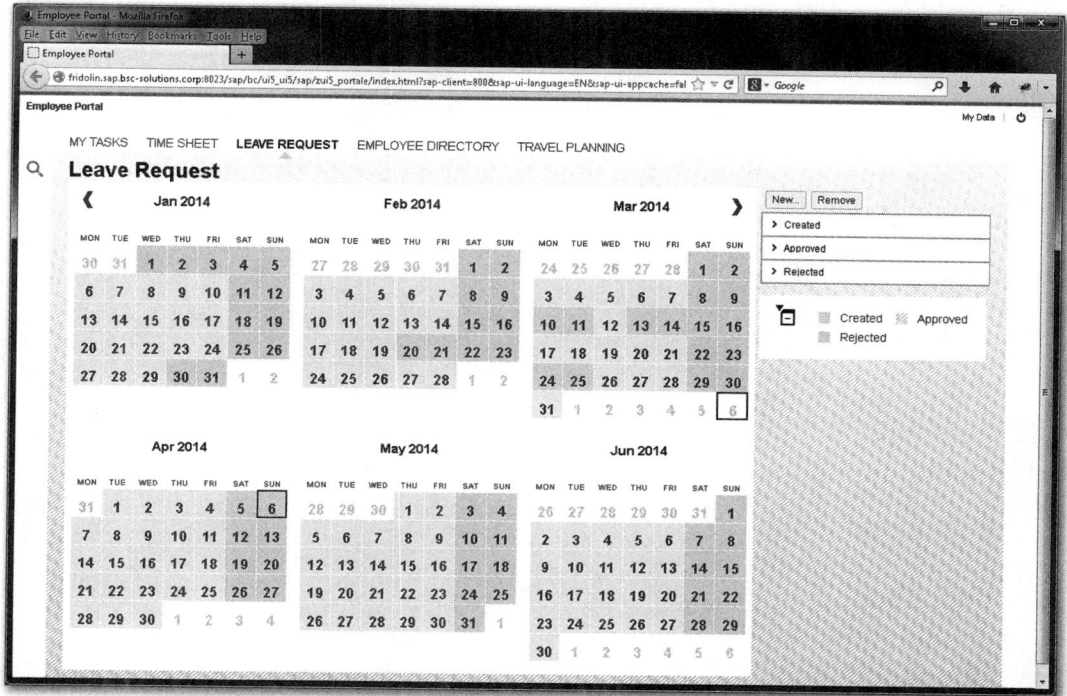

Figure 7.21 Leave Request

In this chapter, you'll create an OData service in SAP Gateway and use it in your SAPUI5 application.

8   SAP Gateway

SAP Gateway allows you easy and direct access to SAP backend services based on the standard OData Protocol (OData = Open Data). You first learned about these OData services in Chapter 5. In this chapter, you'll be shown how to create an OData service with SAP Gateway and consume it in your SAPUI5 application.

OData

8.1   Basic Principles of SAP Gateway

SAP Gateway and its services basically work in a stateless manner, and are thus particularly well-suited for use in mobile applications. SAP Gateway consists of several components, which are displayed in Figure 8.1.

The add-on component IW_BEP contains the ABAP classes for OData Channel Development and event handling; the two components IW_FND and GW_CORE form the actual core of OData Development and contain the runtime and the OData libraries.

As mentioned in Chapter 5, SAP Gateway supports the Open Data Protocol (also known as OData) and is based on the REST architecture. REST stands for Representational State Transfer and describes a programming paradigm for web applications. REST is characterized by the following five properties:

REST

- ▶ Addressability
- ▶ Statelessness
- ▶ Different representations
- ▶ Operations (GET, POST, PUT, and DELETE for HTTP)
- ▶ Use of hypermedia

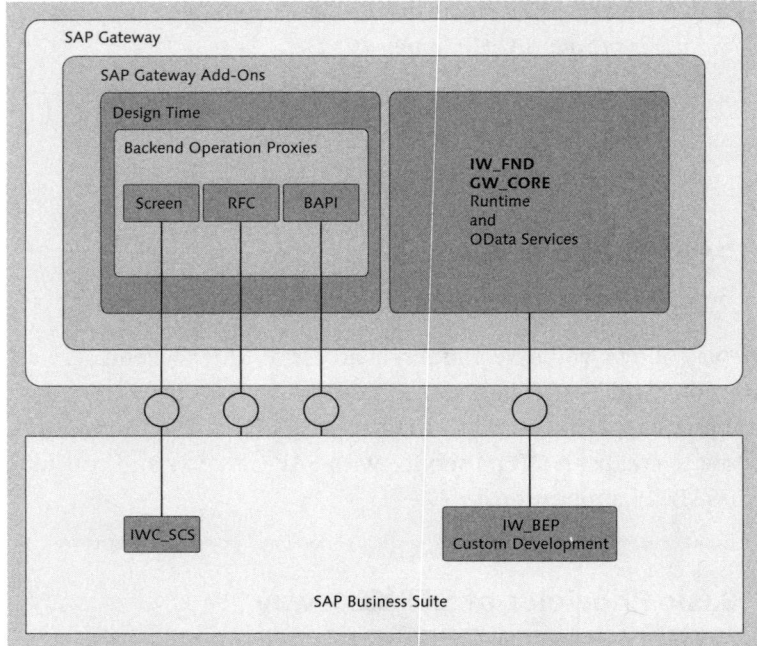

Figure 8.1 SAP Gateway Components

CRUD OData services support the basic database operations: writing, reading, updating, and deleting (the CRUD operations; CRUD = **C**reate, **R**ead, **U**pdate, and **D**elete).

For SAPUI5 development, it's only important to understand that the gateway is used as a *communication layer* between the web application (SAPUI5) and the SAP backend (ABAP). In the last chapter, you used your own ICF handler and had to implement the communication between SAPUI5 and the ABAP backend in that ICF handler.

SAP Gateway Service Builder For stateless applications, this part of the work will be assumed by SAP Gateway. In this chapter, you will model a service for your portal in SAP Gateway Service Builder and consume this service in your SAPUI5 application. Always bear in mind that you can implement only stateless applications with the gateway.

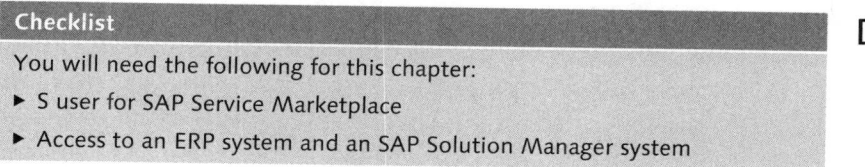

You will need the following for this chapter:

- S user for SAP Service Marketplace
- Access to an ERP system and an SAP Solution Manager system

8.2 Installation

SAP Gateway can be installed as an add-on in existing SAP systems (see Figure 8.2).

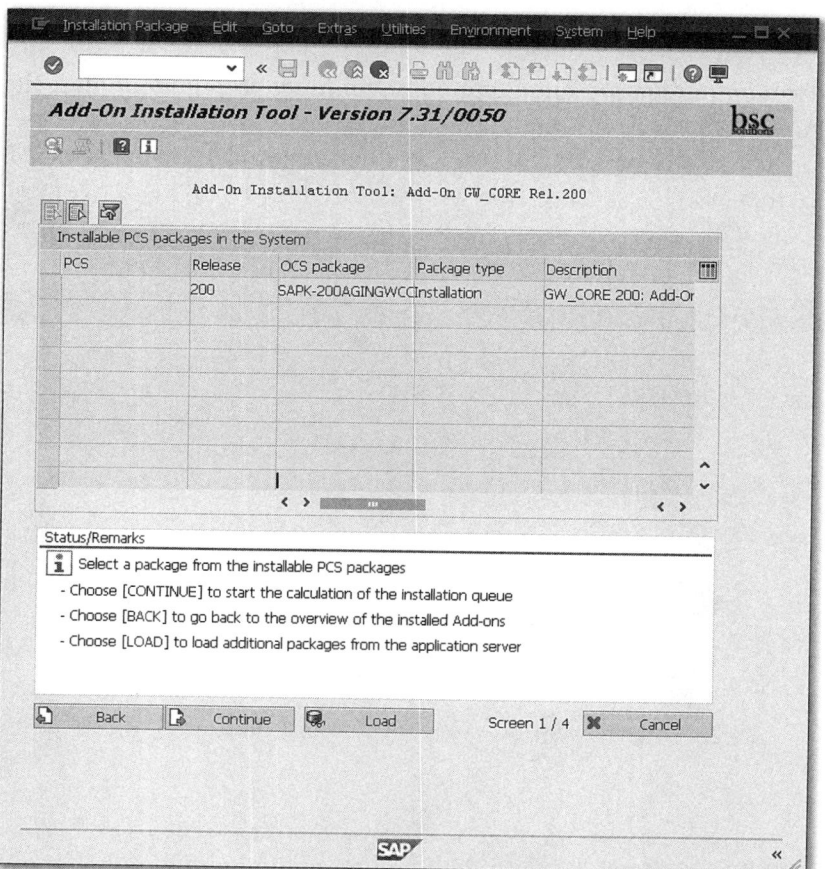

Figure 8.2 Installation of SAP Gateway

The installation packages are available in the SAP Software Download Center (*http://service.sap.com/swdc*) under INSTALLATIONS AND UPGRADES • A-Z INDEX • N • SAP GATEWAY • SAP GATEWAY 2.0 • INSTALLATION AND UPGRADE. Install the Gateway as described in SAP Note 1569624 (Installation/Delta Upgrade of SAP Gateway 2.0) in the relevant SAP system. For the OData services, you need the following components:

- GW_CORE 200 (Core)
- IW_FND 250 (Foundation)
- IW_BEP 200 (Business Enablement Provisioning)

8.3 Configuration

Configuration Guide

After successful installation, you must configure the Gateway with the SAP Customizing Implementation Guide (IMG). To do so, call Transaction SPRO; you will find the Gateway Configuration under the path SAP CUSTOMIZING IMPLEMENTATION GUIDE • SAP NETWEAVER • GATEWAY (see Figure 8.3).

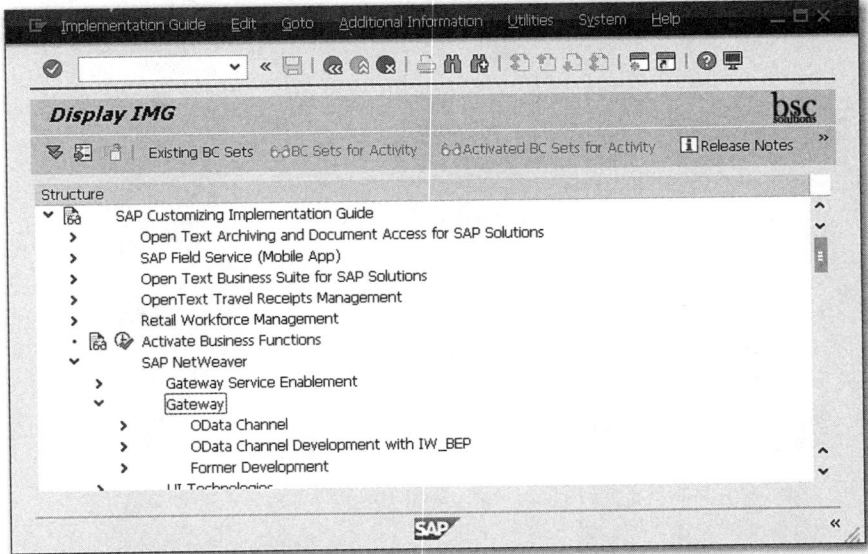

Figure 8.3 Implementation Guide

Configure the Gateway in accordance with the Configuration Guide; you will find the Guide at *http://help.sap.com* under SAP NETWEAVER • SAP GATEWAY • CONFIGURATION GUIDE. You will only be shown the absolute minimum configuration at this point; of course, this means that you're not yet using the full potential of SAP Gateway.

First, activate the gateway; you will find the relevant IMG activity by following the path SAP CUSTOMIZING IMPLEMENTATION GUIDE • SAP NETWEAVER • GATEWAY • ODATA CHANNEL • CONFIGURATION • ACTIVATE OR DEACTIVATE SAP GATEWAY. The required ICF nodes are activated as a result, and the Gateway services can thus be accessed from the Internet.

You now have to create a system alias and assign this alias to the local gateway. You will find the necessary activity under the path SAP CUSTOMIZING IMPLEMENTATION GUIDE • SAP NETWEAVER • GATEWAY • ODATA CHANNEL • CONFIGURATION • CONNECTION SETTINGS • SAP GATEWAY TO SAP SYSTEM • MANAGE SAP SYSTEM ALIASES. Maintain the entry for the system there, select the LOCAL GW and FOR LOCAL APP checkboxes, and specify NONE as the RFC Destination (see Figure 8.4).

Creating a system alias

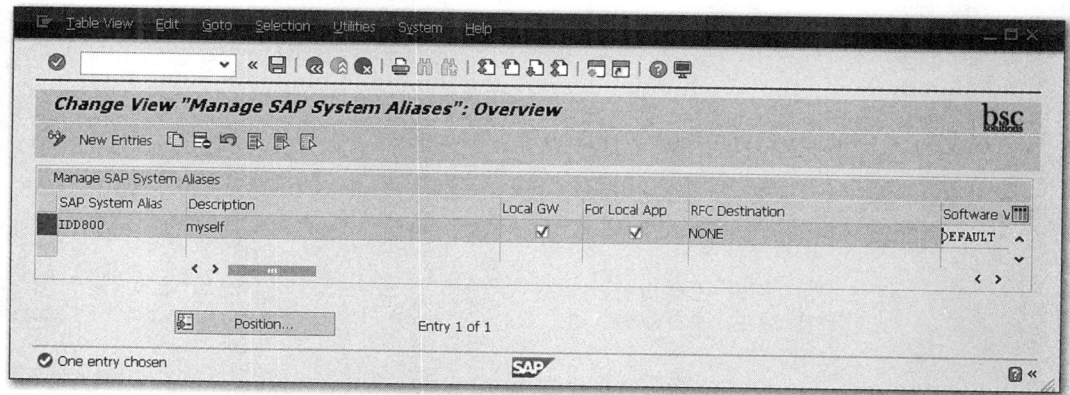

Figure 8.4 Creating a System Alias

After you've set these options, you'll be able to create a simple service and consume it in an SAPUI5 application.

8.4   Implementing OData Service

Transaction SEGW In the following scenario, we'll implement a service for the employee portal from Chapter 7. This will provide you with a good idea of how much the development effort is reduced by using the Gateway. SAP Gateway Service Builder (Transaction SEGW) is a Design Time tool that allows you to create a service with various tools. This transaction supports you throughout the entire lifecycle of a service. SAP Gateway Service Builder provides an OData-compliant modeling environment for creating and maintaining OData services. In the Service Builder, you can generate the necessary components of an OData service, including:

▶ SAP Gateway runtime artifacts such as the Model Provider Class (MPC), the Data Provider Class (DPC), the model, and the actual service

▶ OData artifacts such as the entity set, the entity type, and the properties

A detailed explanation of all SAP Gateway options would be beyond the scope of this book. Under *http://help.sap.com* • SAP NETWEAVER • SAP GATEWAY • SAP GATEWAY DEVELOPER GUIDE, you will find comprehensive documentation on this topic. Within the scope of this book, you'll now create a sample service so that you can see how easy it is to generate a service and provide it for your applications with the Gateway. Start SAP Gateway Service Builder via Transaction SEGW.

Defining sample service In the menu, choose PROJECT • CREATE, and create the project ZUI5_POR-TAL (see Figure 8.5).

As a result, the four directories DATA MODEL, SERVICE IMPLEMENTATION, RUNTIME ARTIFACTS, and SERVICE MAINTENANCE are created (see Figure 8.6).

Creating data model In the DATA MODEL directory, you define the data model of the corresponding services. Here, you can create a completely new data model, upload a data model (EDMX file), or create a data model based on a DDIC structure or based on an RFC or BOR definition. In this example, we'll create a service for MY TASKS from the employee portal; this is based on the DDIC structure ZUI5_TASK that you created in Chapter 7.

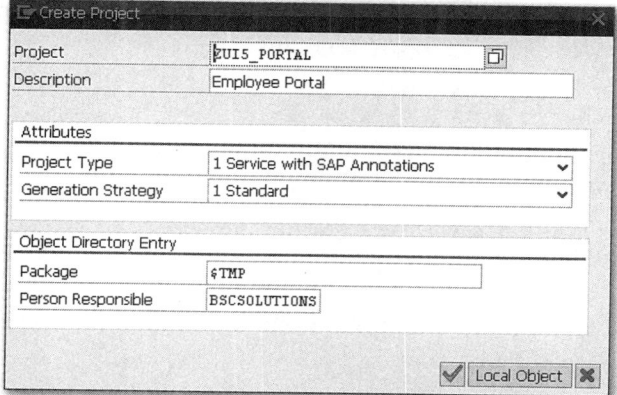

Figure 8.5 Create Project

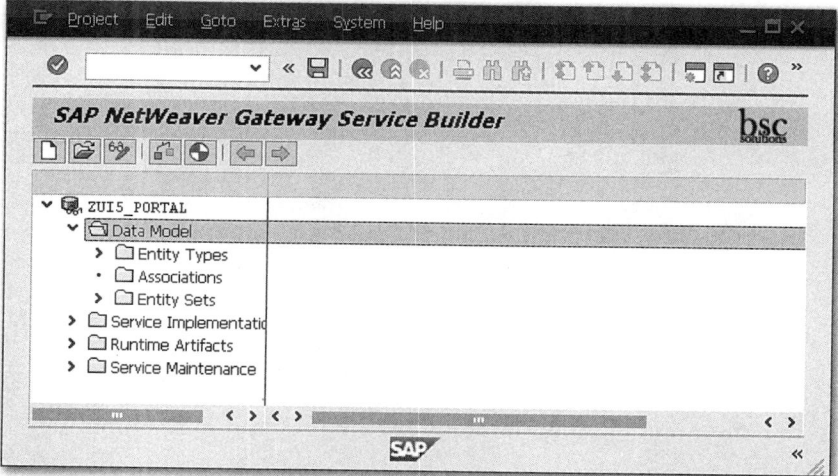

Figure 8.6 Directory Structure of a Project

Right-click the DATA MODEL node to open the context menu and choose IMPORT • DDIC STRUCTURE (see Figure 8.7).

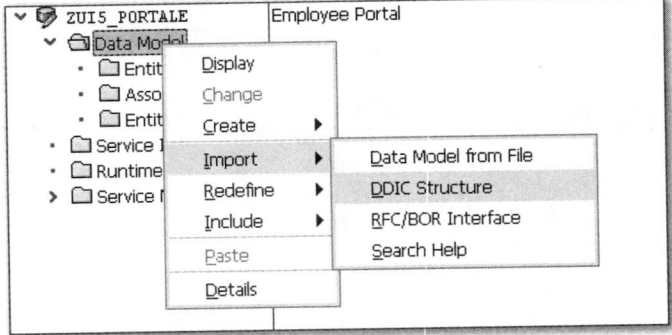

Figure 8.7 Import DDIC Structure

In the next dialog box, specify ZUI5_TASK as the ABAP structure, and press ⌈Finish⌋ (see Figure 8.8).

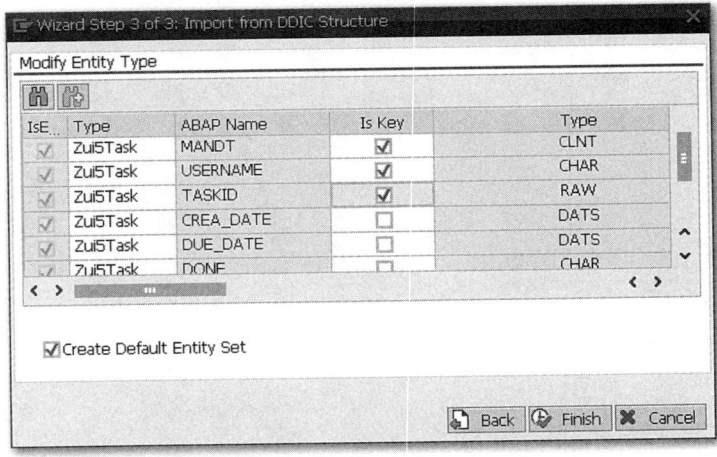

Figure 8.8 DDIC Import

Field definition   Theoretically, you can now change the names of all fields or exclude fields from consideration; however, we don't want to make any changes in this simple example. Leave everything set to the default values, and confirm the field selection by clicking NEXT. The imported structure is now included as an entity type in the data model, and all selected fields are displayed as a property (see Figure 8.9).

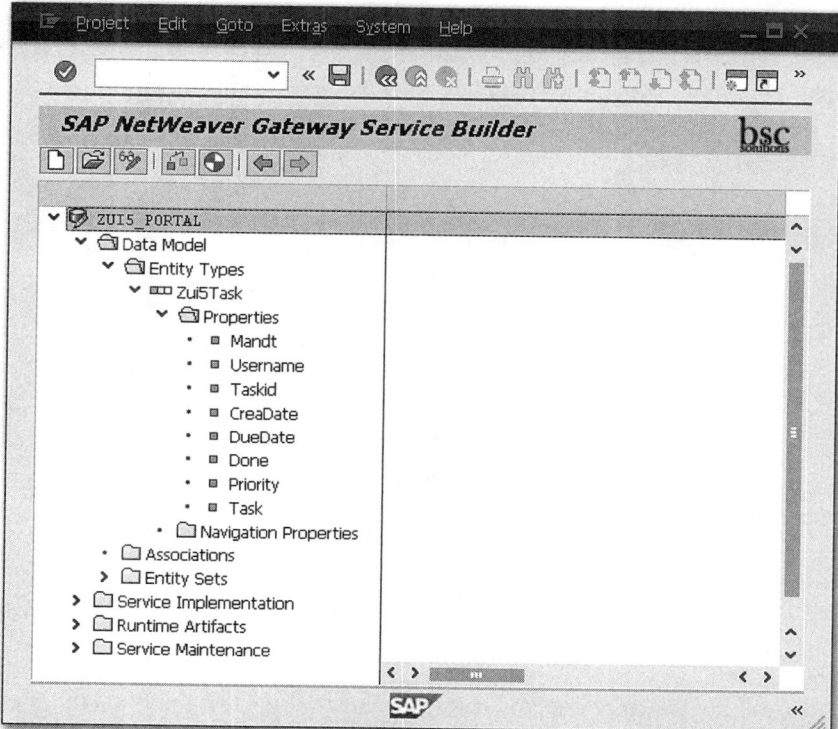

Figure 8.9 DDIC Structure as Entity Type

Entity types are used in a Service Builder project to describe the structure **Entity types** of the data in the Entity Data Model (EDM). An entity type stands for a specific data type, such as a purchase order item or, as in our example, a task list. Entity types include the following:

▶ A unique name

▶ A key that can be defined by one or more properties

▶ Properties (optional)

▶ Navigation properties (optional); needed, for example, for navigating between different associations

Double-click the PROPERTIES folder below the entity you created. In this view, you can specify the properties of each field in this service. In addition to their names, you can specify here, per field, whether the field is to be CREATABLE, UPDATABLE, SORTABLE, or filterable (FILT.) or whether null values will be possible for this field (NULLABLE; see Figure 8.10). The INVERT button is particularly useful here. For a selected column, this button changes the property of all fields; this is especially useful for larger structures.

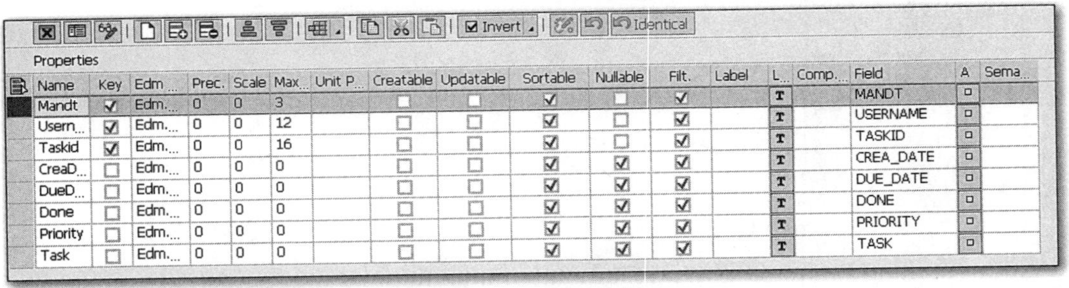

Figure 8.10 Changing Properties Per Field

In this simple example, we would like to define the fields CREATABLE, UPDATABLE, SORTABLE, and FILT. Select the relevant columns, and choose INVERT.

Entity set Next, you have to define an entity set. Entity sets group the instances of an entity type with instances of any type that is derived from this entity type. To put it simply, you define a data structure with the entity type and the instances of the given structure with the data set.

This may seem slightly overcomplicated at this point, but bear in mind that the provision of a simple table as a service, although suitable for our example, is not particularly realistic. You usually have header information, items, and possibly additional customer data, vendor master data, prices and conditions, the purchase order corresponding to an invoice, and so on. You can imagine that the modeling then becomes much more complex, and this strict separation makes even more sense.

Defining entity set If you double-click ENTITY SETS in the navigation tree on the left, all entity sets for this project are displayed in the right-hand area of the screen. In the right-area area, now click APPEND ROW to define a new entity set (see Figure 8.11).

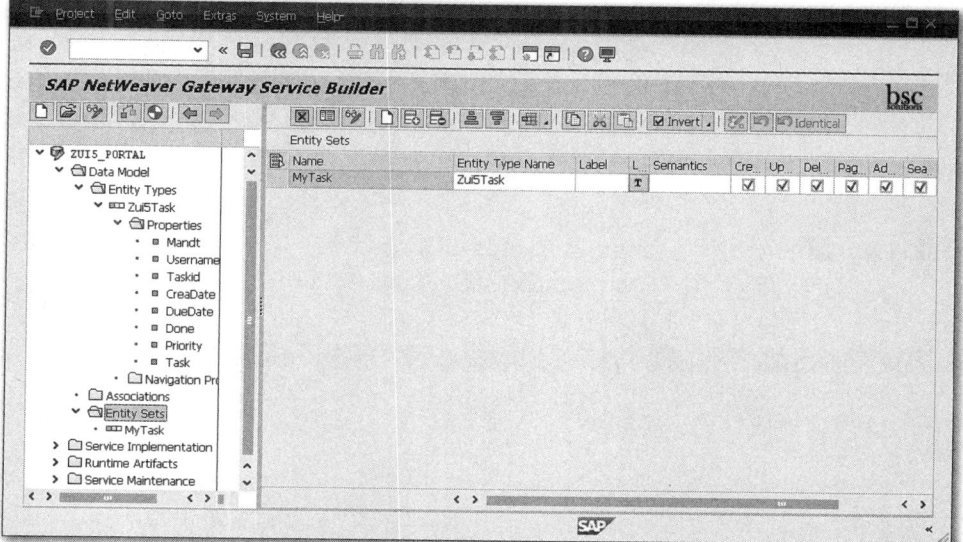

Figure 8.11 Creating an Entity Set

Assign MYTASK as the name, and select ZUI5TASK as the entity type. In this view, you can also use checkbox selection to define whether the entity set (instance) is to be creatable, updatable, and so on. In this example, select the checkmarks for CREATABLE, UPDATABLE, and DELETEABLE. After you have defined the entity set, you can now generate the service (see Figure 8.12). To do so, follow the menu path GENERATE • PROJECT.

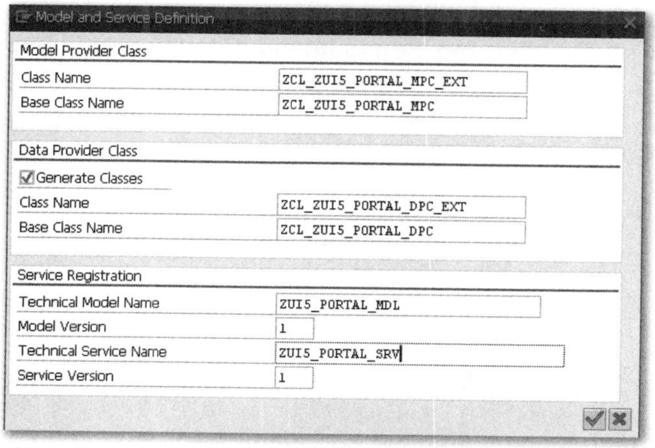

Entity type

Figure 8.12 Generating the Model and Service

Generated classes   The Service Builder already proposes names for the classes and the service to be generated. Here, you have the option of renaming the objects according to the naming conventions in your company. For our simple example, let's use the name "proposals" and confirm this by clicking NEXT. In the next dialog box, choose LOCAL OBJECT as the object catalog entry.

Generation log   After the generation of the runtime objects, a corresponding log is displayed in the Service Builder (see Figure 8.13).

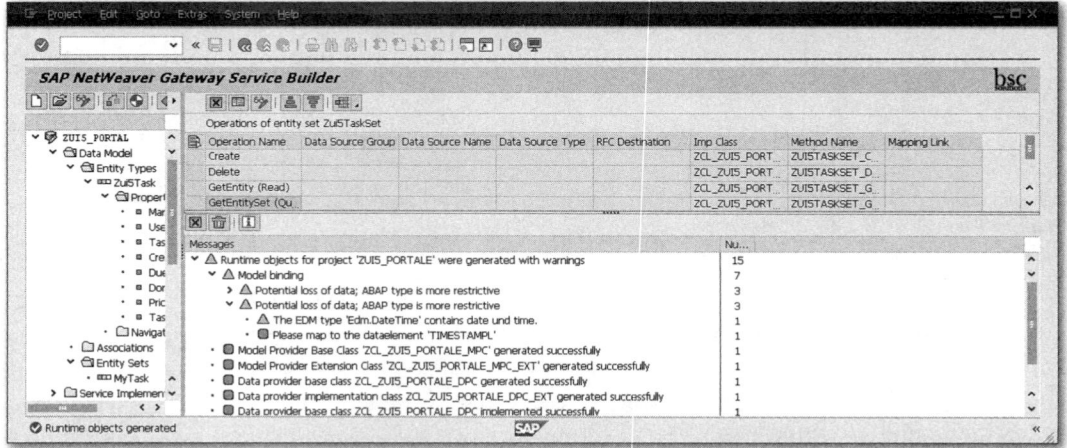

Figure 8.13   Generated Runtime Objects

After the successful generation of the runtime objects, you can activate and test the service. To do so, call Transaction /IWFND/MAINT_SER-VICE. In this transaction, you will see the services that were already created. Add the service you just created by choosing ADD SERVICE (see Figure 8.14).

System alias   Now select the system alias according to Customizing and the service ZUI5_PORTAL_SRV you just created, and press Enter; see Figure 8.15.

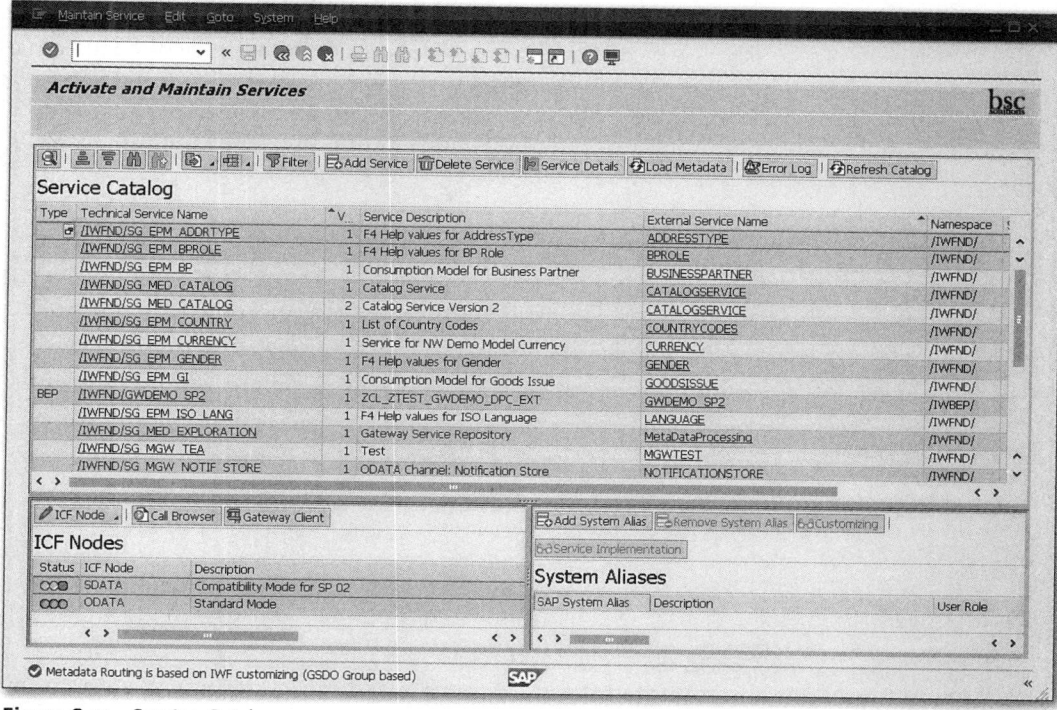

Figure 8.14 Service Catalog

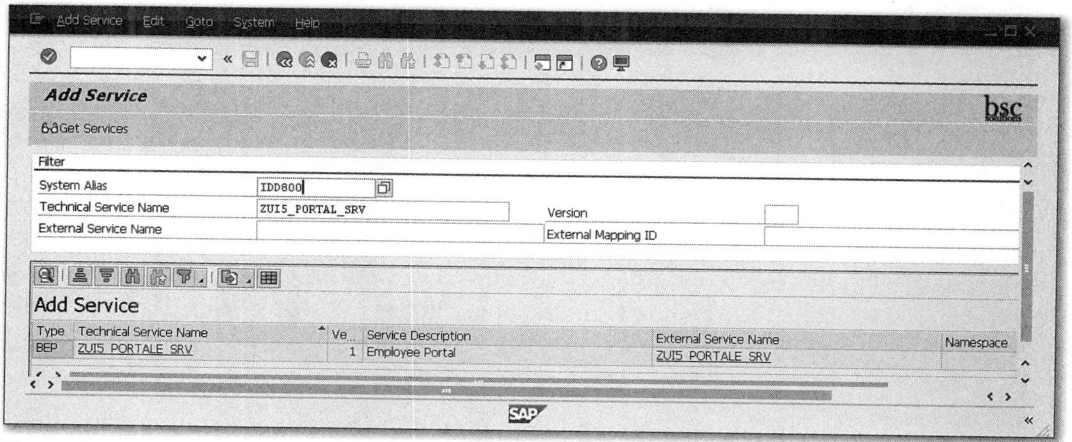

Figure 8.15 Add Service

Detailed information In the lower part of the screen, the service is displayed; click on the Technical Service Name, and a dialog box opens with detailed information about this service (see Figure 8.16).

Set all options as in Figure 8.16, and confirm your selections by pressing Enter.

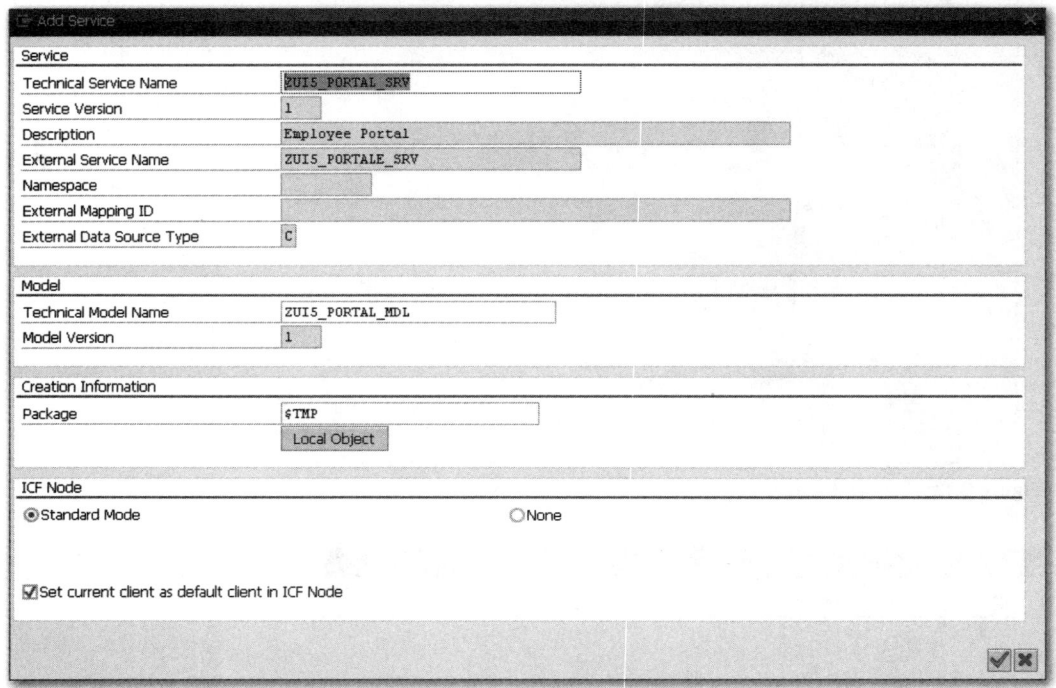

Figure 8.16 Detailed Information about the Service

Activating service You can now see your service in the Service Catalog. Click on the Technical Service Name so that the service is displayed with the system alias in the lower area of the catalog. Choose ICF Node • Activate to activate the ICF node for your service (see Figure 8.17).

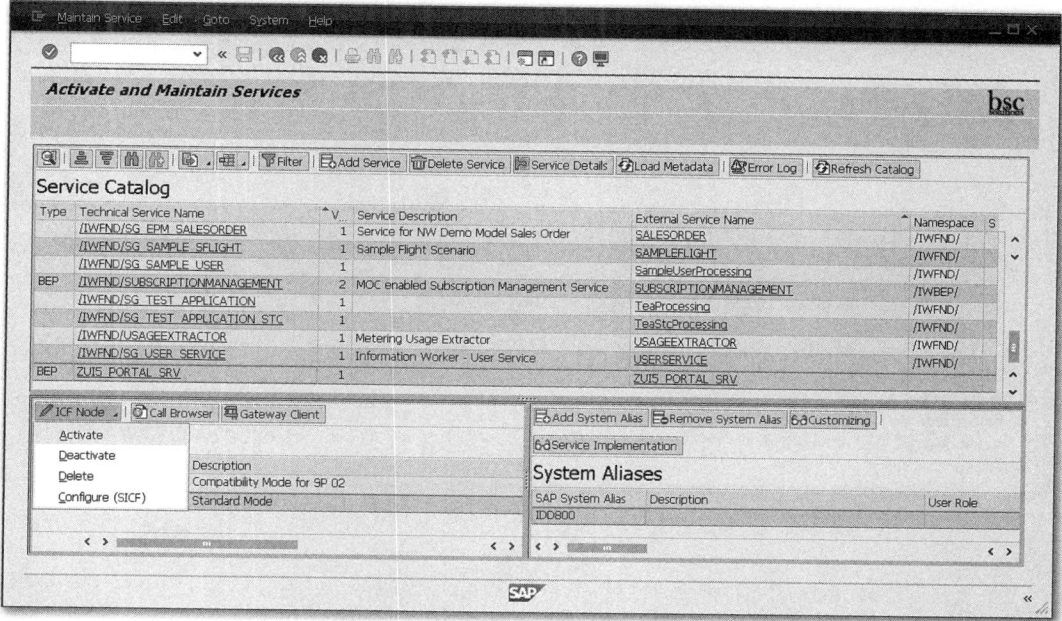

Figure 8.17 Activating the ICF Node

In Transaction SICF, under the path SAP • OPU • ODATA • SAP, you'll now find the active service ZUI5_PORTAL_SRV, as shown in Figure 8.18.

Virtuelle Hosts / Services	Documentation	Referenz Service
∨ 🔲 default_host	VIRTUAL DEFAULT HOST	
▸ 🌐 bsc	bsc solutions	
∨ 🌐 sap	SAP NAMESPACE; SAP IS OBLIGED NOT T...	
▸ ◉ option	RESERVED SERVICES AVAILABLE GLOBALLY	
▸ ◉ public	PUBLIC SERVICES	
∨ 🌐 opu	OData for SAP Products	
∨ 🌐 odata	Standard Mode	
▸ 🌐 iwfnd	Namespace	
∨ 🌐 sap	Namespace	
· 🌐 zui5_portal_srv		
▸ 🌐 sdata	Compatibility Mode for SP 02	
▸ 🌐 utils	Utility services	

Figure 8.18 ICF Service

After you have activated the service, you can test the service by clicking CALL BROWSER (see Figure 8.17). As a result, the service definition should be displayed in XML (see Figure 8.19).

Testing service

Figure 8.19 Service Definition in XML

At this point, we should take a closer look at the URL. In this example, the URL is

http://<HOST>:<PORT>/sap/opu/odata/sap/ZUI5_PORTAL_SRV/?$format=xml

The question mark is followed by the query options. You use these parameters to specify the return of entities. Table 8.1 provides an overview of the parameter values.

Parameter	Description
$orderby	Sorting of the entity entries
$top	Selects only n elements
$skip	Selects the entries from n + 1
$filter	Filter criteria
$expand	Specifies which nodes are to be loaded in expanded form
$format	Definition of the return format
$select	Returns the subset of the specified properties

Table 8.1 Query Parameters

SAPUI5 supports the use of these parameters; you can specify this directly   **Example in SAPUI5**
when binding, as Listing 8.1 shows:

```
oControl.bindElement(
  "/<ENTITY_TYPE> {
    expand: "NAVIGATION_PROPERTY",
    select: "Property_1, Property_2..."
});
oTable.bindRows({
  path: "/<NAVIGATION_PROPERTY>",
  parameters:
    { select: " Property_1, Property_2...""  }
});
```

Listing 8.1 OData Binding in SAPUI5

You can also test the individual query parameters from the Service Catalog.
To do so, click GATEWAY CLIENT. A new window now opens in which the
relevant service is displayed. By clicking ADD URI OPTION ❶, you can
append the respective query options to the URL ❷ and test them directly
by clicking EXECUTE ❸ (see Figure 8.20).

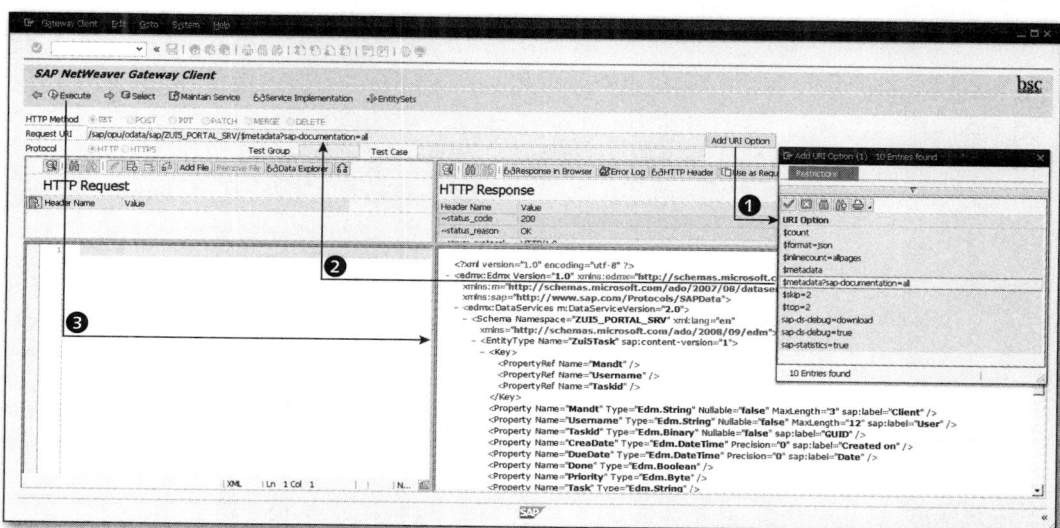

Figure 8.20 Testing Query Parameters

369

Finally, we have to implement the relevant query method `GetEntitySet` for our example. We would like to read all tasks of the logged-on user from the Gateway Service, similar to our own implementation in the class `ZUI5_EMPLOYEE_PORTAL=>GET_TASK`.

In the Service Builder, go to the SERVICE IMPLEMENTATION section for this purpose. There you will find information on the relevant class and method names (see Figure 8.21).

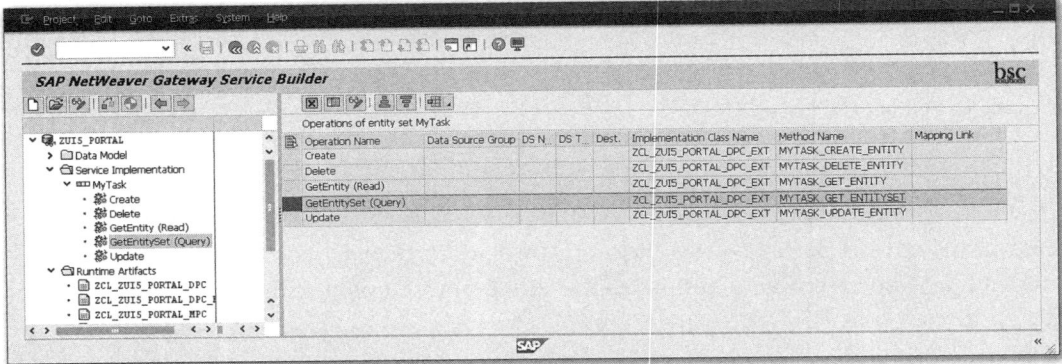

Figure 8.21 Service Implementation

Redefining method Use the context menu to call the ABAP Workbench directly for operation `GetEntitySet`. Now, redefine the method `MYTASK_GET_ENTITYSET` in the ABAP Workbench (see Figure 8.22). As you can see from the interface definition, you have to return the data in the export parameter `ET_ENTITYSET`.

Data record selection Now, add the selection of data records from the table ZUI5_TASK to the method (see Listing 8.2). In this table, you have saved the tasks from the portal.

```
select * from zui5_task into
            corresponding fields of table et_entityset
            where username = sy-uname.
```

Listing 8.2 MYTASK_GET_ENTITYSET Method

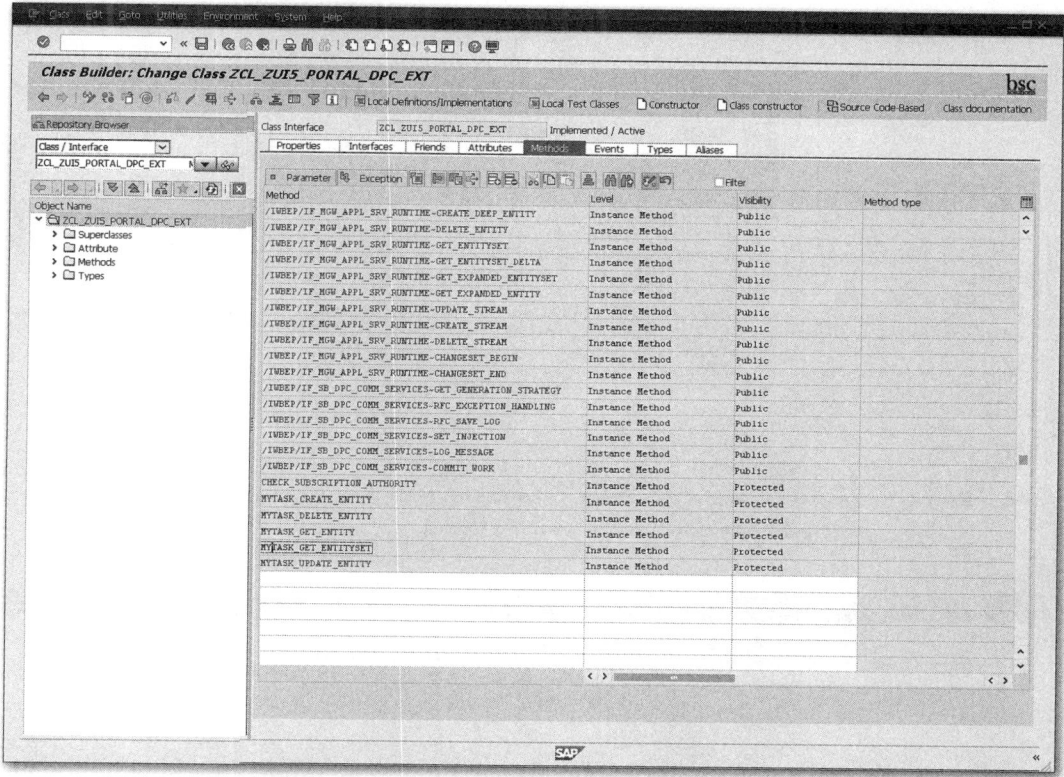

Figure 8.22 Redefining Method

The service is now consumable, at least in read mode. In the browser, call the URL *http://<HOST>:<PORT>/sap/opu/odata/sap/ZUI5_PORTAL_SRV/ MyTask/?$format=json*, and the system displays a JSON file with the results of the service (see Figure 8.23).

At this point, of course, the expected result may not be displayed on the first attempt. In the event of an error, the initial focal point is the Service Catalog, which Figure 8.24 shows. There, you can display the error log for each service by clicking ERROR LOG.

Troubleshooting

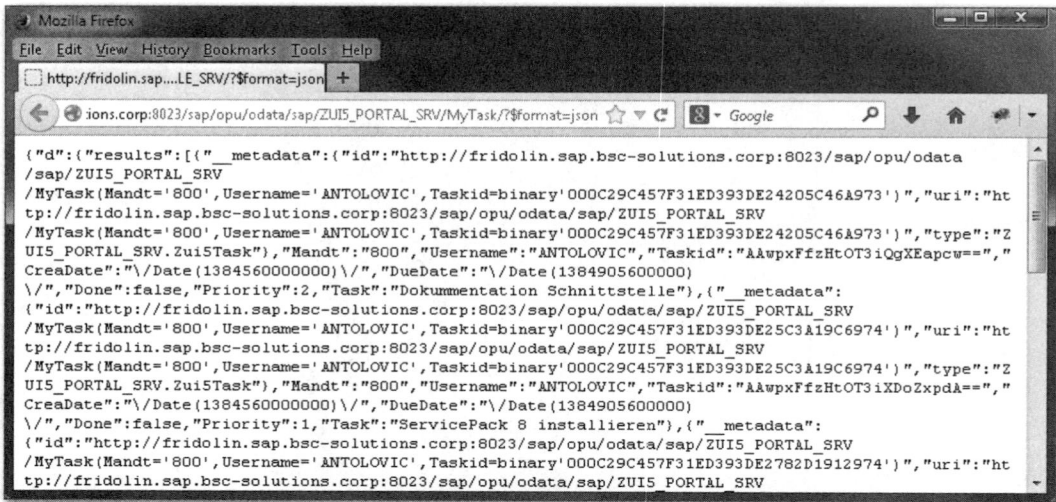

Figure 8.23 JSON Result from the Service

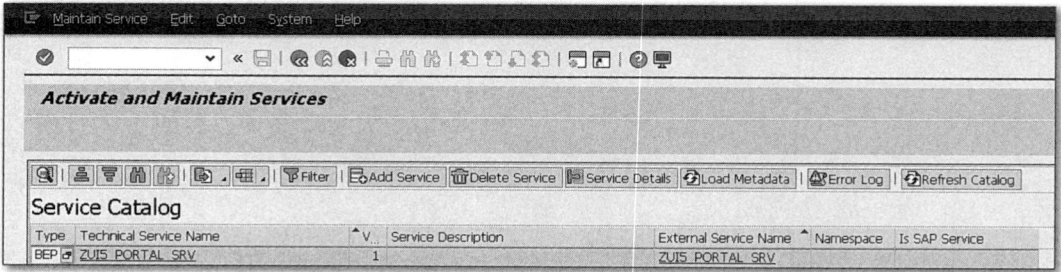

Figure 8.24 Error Log

In the current version, the errors unfortunately are not directly displayed; you first have to choose RE-SELECT to set the error log entries to DEFAULT SETTING: ONLY TODAY, ALL USERS. In the example in Figure 8.25, previously, the checkmark was removed for NULLABLE in the property definition of the service and manipulated a data record in the database in such a way that it deleted the date from the DUE_DATE field.

You can very easily identify and remedy this error using the error log. The error log even shows that the error occurred in the data record of row 6.

Service definition   Let's now take a look back at the service definition in Figure 8.10. There, you specified that all fields are to be sortable and filterable. It's a good idea not to filter the data in a fixed manner in the code, but to make the filtering, sorting, and paging of the data dependent on the request.

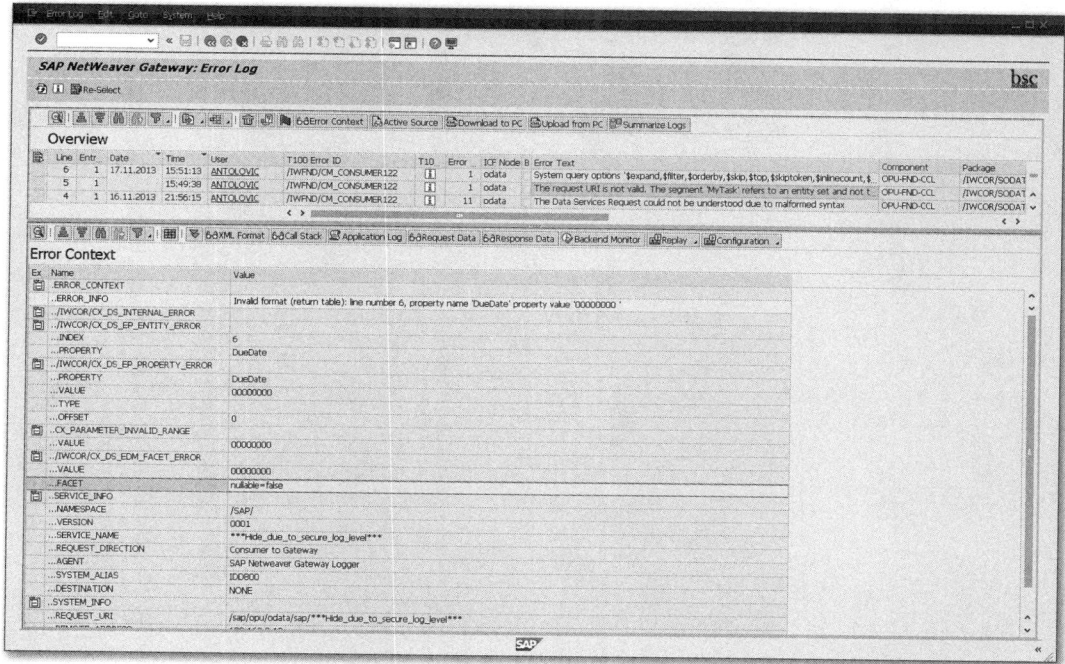

Figure 8.25 Error Log

Paging in this context means that you can request only a certain subset—for example, ten data records—from the service. This is especially relevant if you read very large volumes of data; but, for example, only ten data records are displayed on the page in the application. In this case, you can request the data records 1 to 10 from the service, and if you click, for example, NEXT or PAGE 2, you request the next ten data records from the service.

If you now look at the interface of the method MYTASK_GET_ENTITYSET, you see that the necessary information was transferred to you via the interface.

Interface

▶ IT_FILTER_SELECT_OPTIONS: Filter criteria

▶ IT_ORDER: Sort order

▶ IS_PAGING: Paging structure

The specification of the individual URL parameters can be found at *www. odata.org/documentation/odata-v2-documentation/uri-conventions/*. For our example, this would result in an implementation as in Listing 8.3.

```
method mytask_get_entityset.
  data: lt_task        type table of zui5_task,
        ls_filter_user type /iwbep/s_mgw_select_option,
        lt_tech_order  type /iwbep/t_mgw_tech_order,
        lt_sorting     type abap_sortorder_tab,
        lv_min type i,
        lv_max type i.


  field-symbols:
        <order>      type /iwbep/s_mgw_tech_order,
        <sorting>    type abap_sortorder,
        <task>       type zui5_task,
        <entityset>  type zcl_zui5_portal_mpc=>ts_zui5task,
        <so_user>    type /iwbep/s_mgw_select_option.

  "Filter --------------------------------------------------
  read table it_filter_select_options
            assigning <so_user>
            with key property = 'Username'.

  if sy-subrc <> 0.
    assign ls_filter_user to <so_user>.
  endif.

  select * from zui5_task into
            corresponding fields of table et_entityset
            where username in <so_user>-select_options.

  "Sorting --------------------------------------------------
  if io_tech_request_context is bound.
    lt_tech_order = io_tech_request_context->get_orderby( ).

    loop at lt_tech_order assigning <order>.
      append initial line to lt_sorting assigning <sorting>.
      " Convert to ABAP type
      <sorting>-name = <order>-property.
      if <order>-order = 'desc'.
        <sorting>-descending = abap_true.
      elseif <order>-order = 'asc'.
```

```
        <sorting>-descending = abap_false.
      endif.
      <sorting>-astext = abap_true.
    endloop.

    sort lt_task by (lt_sorting).
  endif.


  "Paging -----------------------------------------------
  if is_paging-skip is not initial.
    lv_min = is_paging-skip + 1.
  else.
    lv_min = 1.
  endif.
  if is_paging-top is not initial.
    lv_max = is_paging-skip + is_paging-top.
  else.
    lv_max = lines( lt_task ).
  endif.

  loop at lt_task from lv_min to lv_max
                              assigning <task>.
    append initial line to et_entityset
                              assigning <entityset>.
    move-corresponding <task> to <entityset>.
  endloop.

endmethod.
```

Listing 8.3 MYTASK_GET_ENTITYSET Method with Filter, Sorting, and Paging

After you have set up the Gateway Service, you can consume it in your SAPUI5 application.

8.5   Consuming OData Service

The processing of an OData service in SAPUI5 is very easy: First, create an instance of the `sap.ui.model.odata.ODataModel` class, and transfer this as a parameter of the URL to your service. The data binding works in a similar manner as the familiar JSON Model (see also Chapter 5).

Creating project In Eclipse, create the project ZUI5_ODATA, and omit creating the Initial View. Because you have already implemented the filter on the user name in the service (see Listing 8.3), you can transfer this filter directly to the service in SAPUI5. To do so, define an OData filter (class `sap.ui.model.odata.Filter`) with the desired filter criteria and transfer it to the binding method. First, create an instance of the `sap.ui.model.odata.ODataModel` class (see Listing 8.4).

```
<!DOCTYPE HTML>
<html>
<head>
<TITLE>OData Service</TITLE>
<meta charset="UTF-8">
<meta http-equiv="X-UA-Compatible" content="IE=edge">

<script src="resources/sap-ui-core.js" id="sap-ui-bootstrap"
  data-sap-ui-libs="sap.ui.commons, sap.ui.table"
  data-sap-ui-theme="sap_goldreflection">
</script>

<script>
    // OData Model
    var oModel = new sap.ui.model.odata.ODataModel(
                    "/sap/opu/odata/sap/ZUI5_PORTAL_SRV/");
    sap.ui.getCore().setModel(oModel);
```

Listing 8.4 Creating ODataModel Instance

Table For this simple example, now create a table with the two columns USER-NAME and TASK (see Listing 8.5).

```
    // Table as output
    var oTable = new sap.ui.table.Table({
        width : "100  %",
        rowHeight : 30,
        visibleRowCount : 5,
        title : "Task list as OData service",
        navigationMode : sap.ui.table.NavigationMode.Paginator,
        selectionMode : sap.ui.table.SelectionMode.None
    });
// Username
    oTable.addColumn(new sap.ui.table.Column({
        id : "Username",
```

```
            label : new sap.ui.commons.Label({
                text : "User"
            }),
        template : new sap.ui.commons.TextView({
                text : "{Username}"
        }),
    }));
    oTable.addColumn(new sap.ui.table.Column({
        label : new sap.ui.commons.Label({
                text : "Task"
        }),
        template : new sap.ui.commons.TextView({
                text : "{Task}"
        }),
    }));

    // Bind model
    oTable.setModel(oModel);
```

Listing 8.5 Table with Username and Tasks

Finally, create a filter for the last name. To avoid making the example unnecessarily complicated, the username is hard-coded in this example (see Listing 8.6). In the portal application from Chapter 7, you would determine the username via the GET_OWN_DATA service and thus make the filter call variable.

Filter for last name

```
    // Define filter
    var oFilter = new sap.ui.model.odata.Filter('Username',
        [{
            operator : "EQ",
            value1 : "ANTOLOVIC" //Adjust to own user
        }]);

    // Bind rows from model
    oTable.bindRows({
            path : "/MyTask",
            filters : [ oFilter ]
        });
    oTable.placeAt("content");
</script>
</head>
<body class="sapUiBody" role="application">
```

```
        <div id="content"></div>
    </body>
</html>
```

Listing 8.6 OData Filter

As a result, you obtain a page with the tasks for the user as you have defined them in the filter criteria (see Figure 8.26).

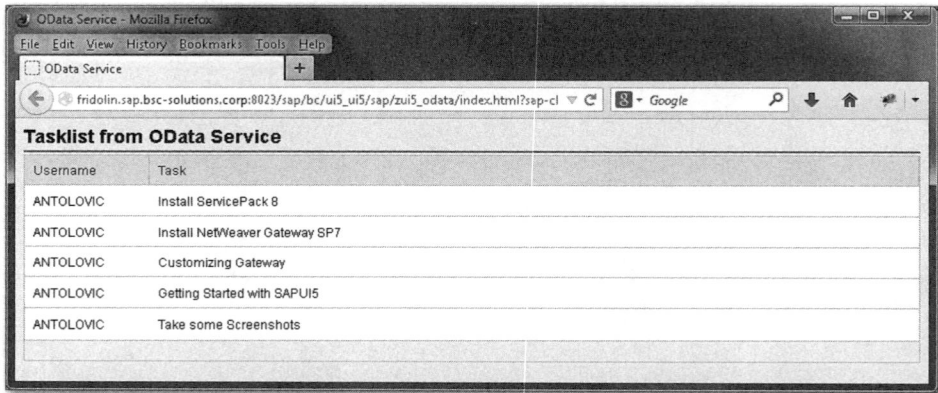

Figure 8.26 OData Service in SAPUI5

Breakpoint   If you set a session breakpoint in the method MYTASK_GET_ENTITYSET and call the page again, you can see very nicely how the filter parameters are transferred to the service (see Figure 8.27).

A look ahead   As you have seen, you can use SAP Gateway to very quickly and very effectively define OData services and provide them for your SAPUI5 applications. Its true strength is mainly demonstrated with more comprehensive services, in which you include multiple database tables in one context and link them via associations. In the Service Catalog, you'll find many sample services that you can view and also execute directly.

We'll now leave the ABAP world and turn our attention to SAP HANA. In the next chapter, you'll be shown how to implement SAPUI5 applications in SAP HANA.

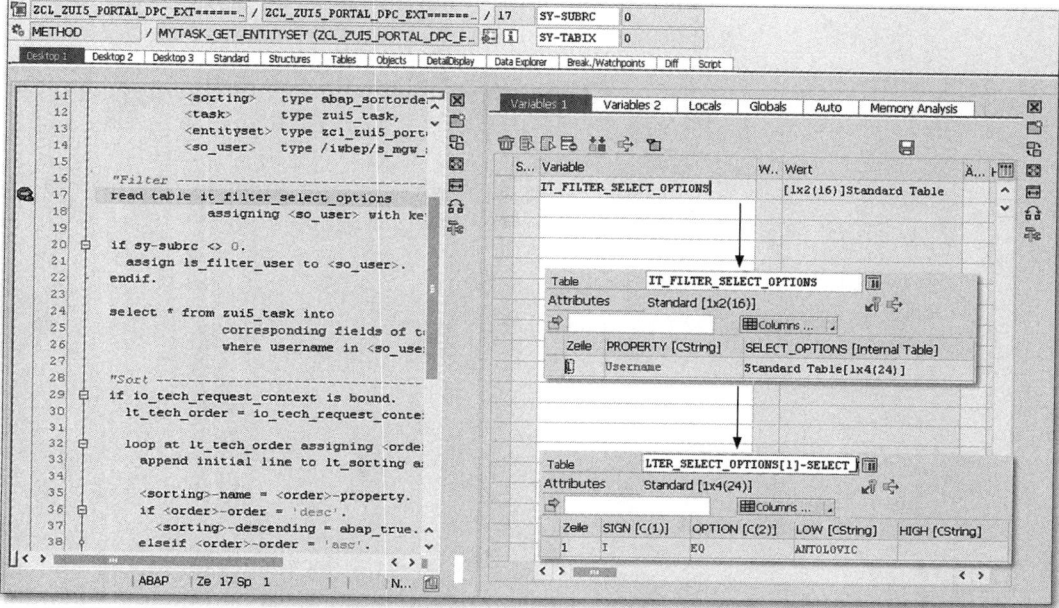

Figure 8.27 Filter Parameters in the OData Service

In this chapter, you will learn the basics of SAP HANA. You will develop a calculation view and use it as an OData service in your SAPUI5 application.

9   SAP HANA

SAP for HANA is based on an in-memory database technology, and thus allows for much faster data accesses. The data lies in the memory there and is no longer read by the much slower hard drive. In addition to the speed benefit of the memory access with SAP HANA, the data is no longer stored only in a row-based manner, as in traditional database systems, but also in a column-based manner. Due to this data store form, the entire row is no longer read; instead, targeted access to just one column of a table is allowed. Thus, arithmetic operations are performed much faster, and this system also allows parallel processing with multiple processors, as shown in Figure 9.1.

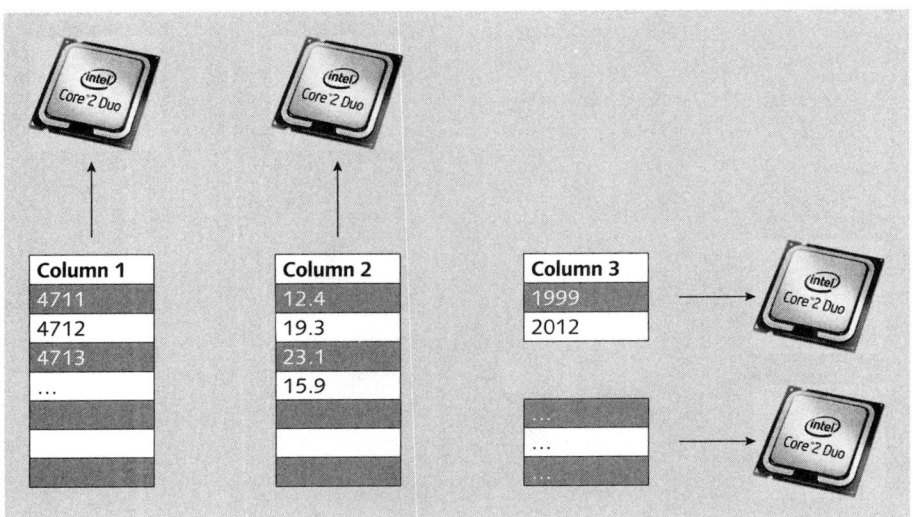

Figure 9.1   Parallel Processing

HANA views Data modeling takes place in SAP HANA by using views. There are currently three types of views:

► *Attribute views* are used to establish a context (for example, a text name for the material) for master data.

► *Analytic views* are an OLAP (Online Analytical Processing) cube: an n-dimensional array of data.

► *Calculation views* aggregate multiple tables or analytic views and are mostly used for the output in reporting tools.

Each view type is managed by its own engine. Figure 9.2 shows the various engines.

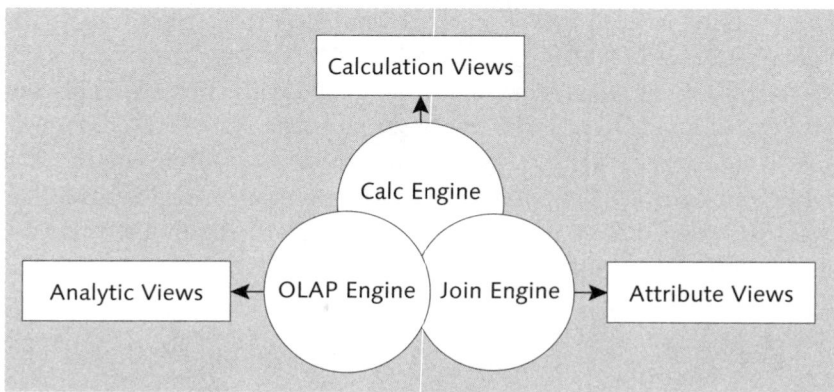

Figure 9.2 SAP HANA Engines

9.1 XS Engine

Extended
Application
Services
SAP HANA is not just a database; it's also a platform. The Extended Application Services (XS for short) are an important aspect of this platform. XS is both an application server and a web server, and thus forms the basis for the development of an application in SAPUI5 with SAP HANA. XS is not a standalone technology; it's firmly integrated in the SAP HANA database. As a result, the speed benefits of SAP HANA also apply to XS. With XS, you have the option of executing applications with a HTTP-based user interface directly in SAP HANA.

How can SAPUI5 applications now be developed in SAP HANA? We'll answer this question in the chapter ahead. This book will be limited to only the most essential terms of HANA development. More detailed instructions can be found in the SAP HANA Developer Guide at *http:// help.sap.com/hana/SAP_HANA_Developer_Guide_en.pdf*.

Checklist
You will need the following for this chapter: ▶ Access to a HANA instance   ▶ SAP HANA Studio

[⬆]

You will now be shown the necessary steps for the development by using the free SAP HANA Cloud. If you already have access to SAP HANA, you can skip Section 9.2 and proceed immediately to Section 9.3.

9.2   HANA Access

If you do not have SAP HANA, you can apply for free access at *https:// account.hanatrial.ondemand.com*.

Click REGISTER on the aforementioned page, and complete the registration form. After a few minutes, you will receive an email with an activation link. After successful activation, you can register with your user name and password in the SAP HANA Cloud Platform Cockpit under *https:// account.hanatrial.ondemand.com/cockpit*. First, you have to create a package for your XS applications. In the Cockpit, go to HANA XS APPLICATIONS, and click NEW PACKAGE. Assign, for example, "sapui5" as the name, and save your changes (see Figure 9.3).

By creating the package, a database schema of the same name is created— *sapui5*, in our example. In the Cockpit, you will find all previously created schemas in the DATABASE SCHEMAS menu item. After you have created the package, click TOOLS, and you will be redirected to the web page *https:// tools.hana.ondemand.com*. There, you will find the HANA Cloud Platform SDK for Java EE 6 Web Profile in the SAP HANA CLOUD PLATFORM TOOLS area. Download the SDK, and unpack the zip directory into any folder.

Database schema

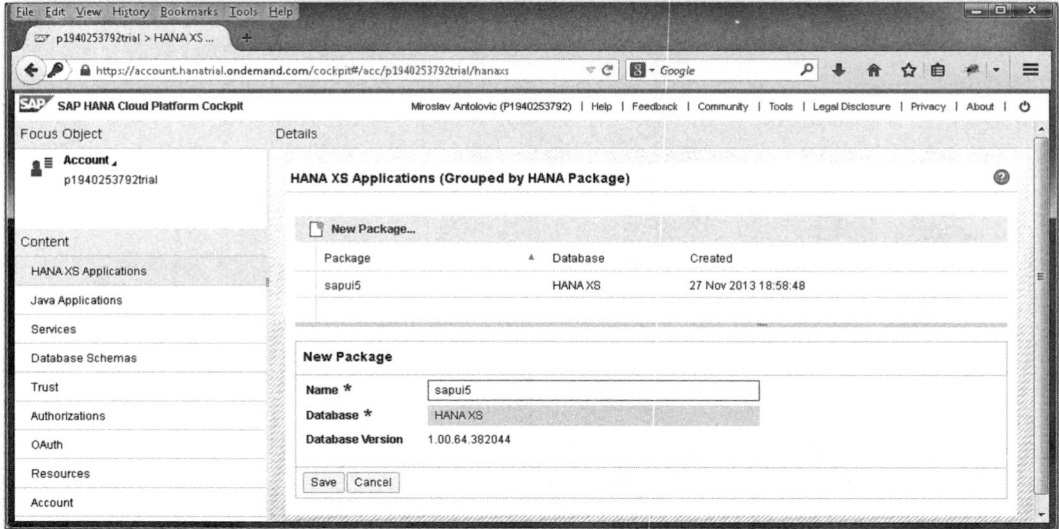

Figure 9.3 Creating an XS Package

After unpacking into the *tools* directory, create a new file with the extension *.properties*, as shown in Figure 9.4.

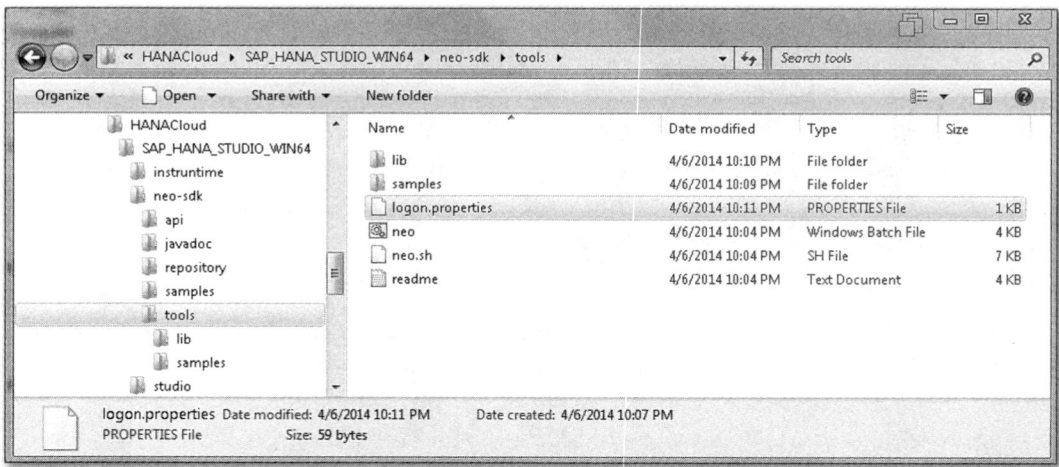

Figure 9.4 logon.properties

In the *logon.properties* file, enter the account information according to the following schema, and save the changes (see Figure 9.5):

▶ Account = <ACCOUNT>

▶ Host = *hanatrial.ondemand.com*

▶ USER = <USER NAME>

We will need the *.properties* file later to create a DB tunnel.

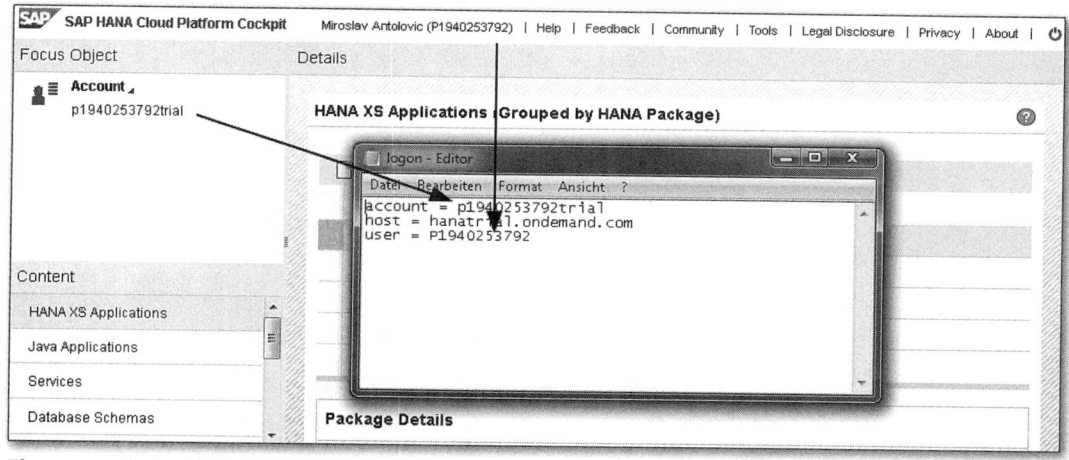

Figure 9.5 logon.properties

From the web page *https://hanadeveditionsapicl.hana.ondemand.com/hanade-vedition/*, download SAP HANA Studio and the SAP HANA Client. After unpacking, you can start the installation by double-clicking the HDBSETUP file. This will open the Installation Manager; select an installation directory, and confirm your selection by clicking NEXT. SAP HANA Studio will now be installed. After installing Studio, install Client in the same manner.

SAP HANA Studio

Next, depending on the version of SAP HANA Studio you have installed, you have to install the necessary plug-ins:

Plug-ins

▶ Eclipse Faceted Project Framework

▶ Eclipse Faceted Project Framework JDT Enablement

- ▶ Eclipse Java EE Developer Tools
- ▶ Eclipse Java Web Developer Tools
- ▶ WST Common Core
- ▶ Jetty Core: Servlets and webapps

Proceed as usual via the menu path HELP • INSTALL NEW SOFTWARE, and in the WORK WITH field specify the page *http://download.eclipse.org/releases/juno*. Select the relevant plug-ins, and install them. SAP Note 1747308 contains the current installation guide with the current list of necessary plug-ins.

From the update page *https://tools.hana.ondemand.com/juno*, install the SAP HANA Cloud Platform Tools, the SAP HANA Cloud Integration Tools, and the UI Development Toolkit for HTML5.

DB tunnel · After their successful installation, you can create the database tunnel to the HANA database. The DB tunnel is necessary for you to log on to the HANA database with the locally installed SAP HANA Studio. For this purpose, open the program command prompt (*cmd.exe*).

Navigate within command prompt to the *tools* directory in which you created the *logon.properties* file (see Figure 9.4). Now, enter the command `neo.bat open-db-tunnel -i <SCHEMA NAME> logon.properties`, where you replace `<SCHEMA NAME>` with the name of the created schema (`sapui5` in our example), and press ⌷Enter⌷; see Figure 9.6.

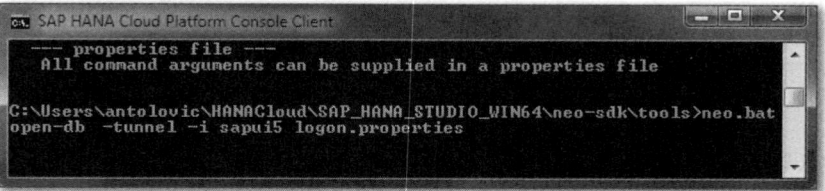

Figure 9.6 Creating DB Tunnel

After you have entered your password, the temporary access data will be displayed (see Figure 9.7). Do not close this window under any circumstances; if you do, the DB tunnel will also be closed.

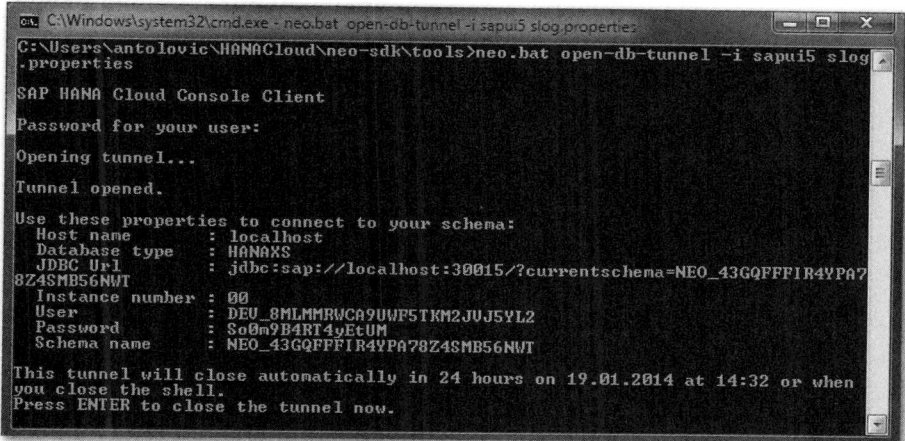

Figure 9.7 Access Data

You can now establish a connection in SAP HANA Studio with this access data. To do so, open SAP HANA Studio, right-click the HANA Systems area, and then click Add System (see Figure 9.8).

Adding system

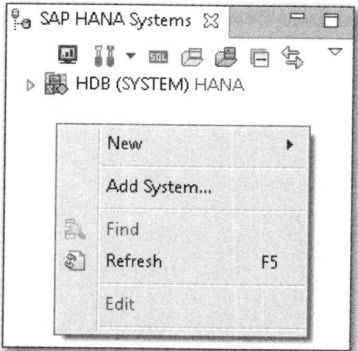

Figure 9.8 Adding a New System

A wizard now opens in which you can enter the information of the DB tunnel connection. In the first window, enter "localhost" under Host Name and "00" in the Instance Number field and click Next.

In the second window, enter the user name and the password of the DB tunnel (see Figure 9.7) and click NEXT. The DB tunnel assigns a new password for each connection. Because the password is saved in SAP HANA Studio and because the Studio connects directly with the HANA database when it opens, your user is locked due to the failed logons. To prevent this, switch off the autoreconnect function in the third window. To do this, deselect the AUTO-RECONNECT checkbox, and save your entries by clicking FINISH.

New logon   If you would like to log on again, open a new DB tunnel; a new password is assigned by the system as a result. Then right-click to open the context menu of the system, and select the PROPERTIES entry in the context menu. In the DATABASE USER LOGON area, you can enter the new password and connect Studio with the HANA instance (see Figure 9.9).

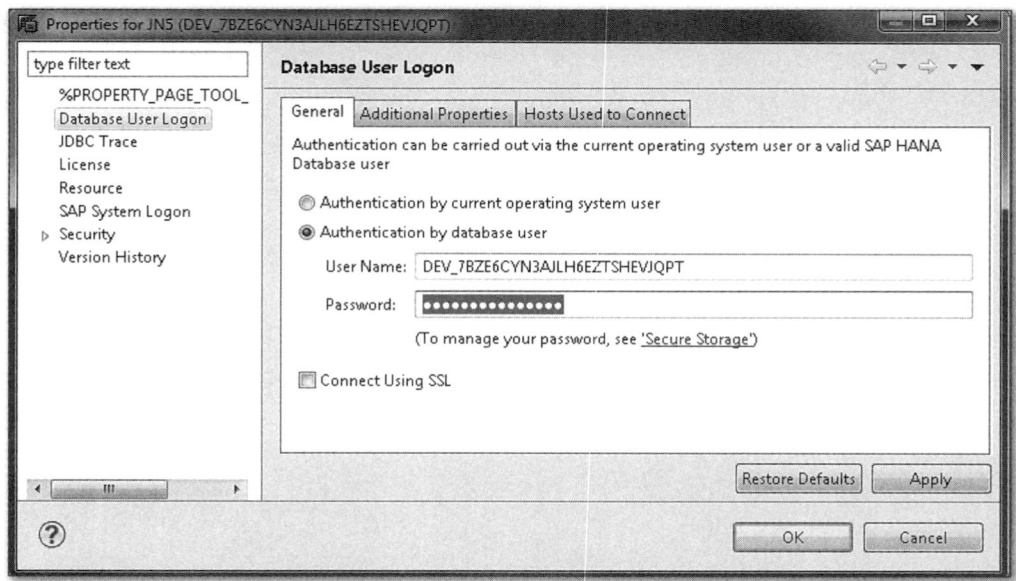

Figure 9.9 New Connection

After you have added the HANA system, you can configure access to the SAP HANA Repository. To do so, follow the menu path WINDOWS • PREFERENCES, navigate in this window to SAP HANA DEVELOPMENT •

REPOSITORY ACCESS, and, under LOCATION, enter the path to the *regi.exe* file of the SAP HANA Client (see Figure 9.10).

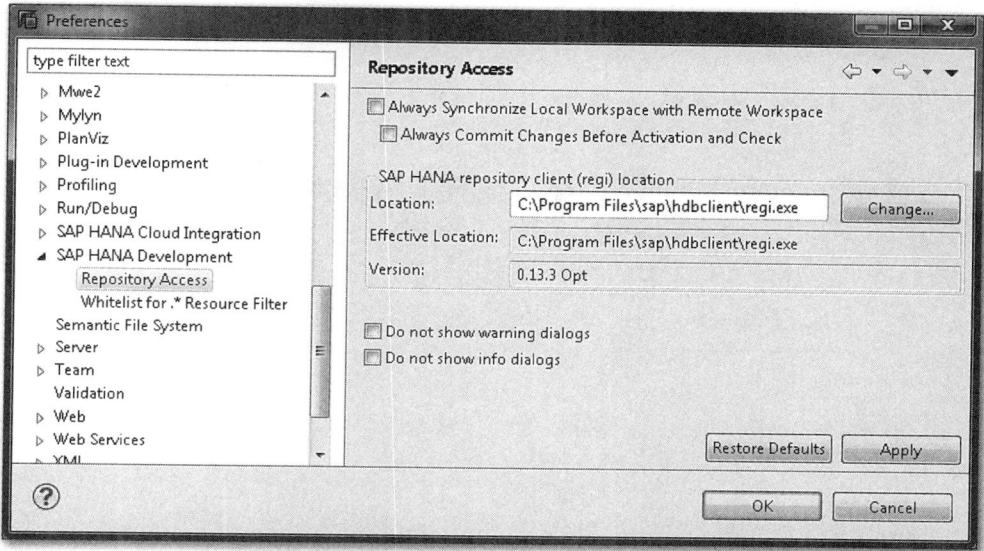

Figure 9.10 Access to the SAP HANA Repository

9.3   Implementation of the Sample Application

As noted in the introduction, the Extended Application Services provide the runtime environment for SAPUI5 applications. For this reason, first create an XS project. In SAP HANA Studio, follow the menu path FILE • NEW PROJECT, select SAP HANA DEVELOPMENT • XS PROJECT in the wizard, and click NEXT.

Enter, for example, "myFirstUI5" as the project name, and click FINISH.   .xsaccess
To enable you to call your application later, you have to configure access to the SAP HANA Cloud in your XS project. Make sure that you are in the SAP HANA DEVELOPMENT view in SAP HANA Studio. Now switch to the Project Explorer, and call the context menu of the XS project. In the context menu, select NEW • FILE, and, in each case, create a file with the file extension *.xsapp* and a file with the file extension *.xsaccess*; do not assign any names to these files (see Figure 9.11).

The *.xsapp* file remains empty; in the *.xsaccess* file, insert the statement from Listing 9.1.

```
{
"exposed" : true
}
```

Listing 9.1   .xsaccess File

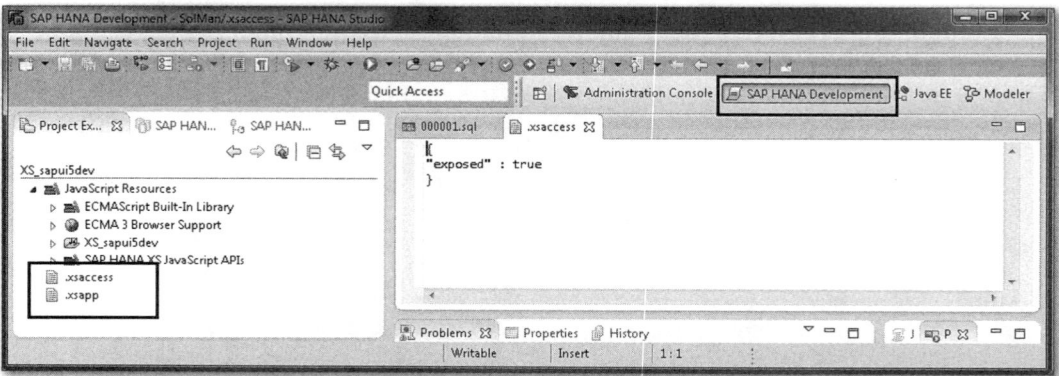

Figure 9.11   Creating .xsaccess File

The OData service that you will create later will be accessible due to this statement.

Repository workspace

Next, you have to create a *repository workspace*. The repository workspace is a local directory in which you can work with the project-related objects. When you check out a package from the repository, SAP HANA copies the content of the package to your workspace.

To do this, switch to the SAP HANA REPOSITORIES tab, and use the context menu to create a new repository. Assign a name—for example, "sapui5"— to the workspace, and click FINISH (see Figure 9.12).

Uploading project

After you have created the repository workspace, you can upload the project in Project Explorer to the SAP HANA Cloud. Similar to the Team Provider function, you can link the project via the context menu of the project (TEAM • SHARE PROJECT) with the SAP HANA Repository. In the dialog box that is now displayed, select SAP HANA REPOSITORY (see Figure 9.13), and click NEXT.

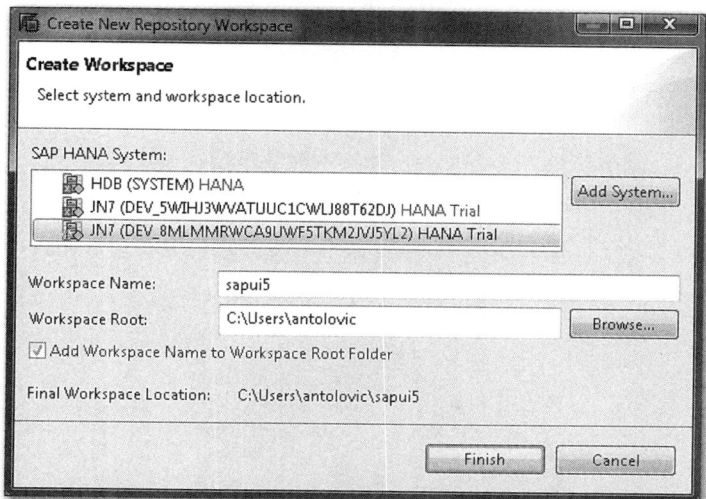

Figure 9.12 Creating the Repository

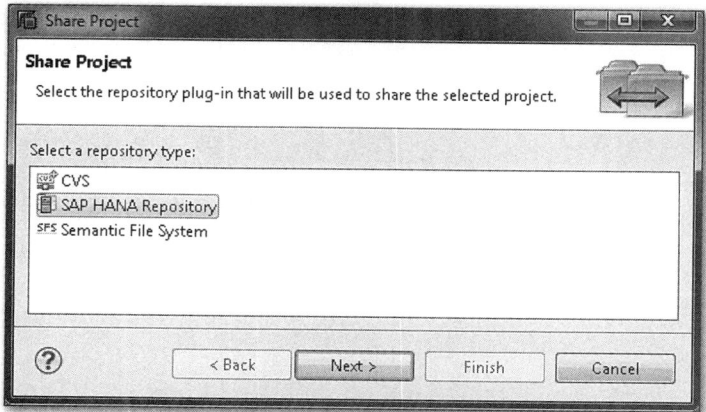

Figure 9.13 Loading a Project in the SAP HANA Repository

On the next screen, select the previously created repository workspace and repository package. At this point, it's important that you select the repository package via the BROWSE button; do not enter it directly in the field (see Figure 9.14). With SPS 06, which was current at the time of writing this book, an error occurred in which the project could not be activated if the package had previously been entered directly in the input field. Click FINISH.

Repository

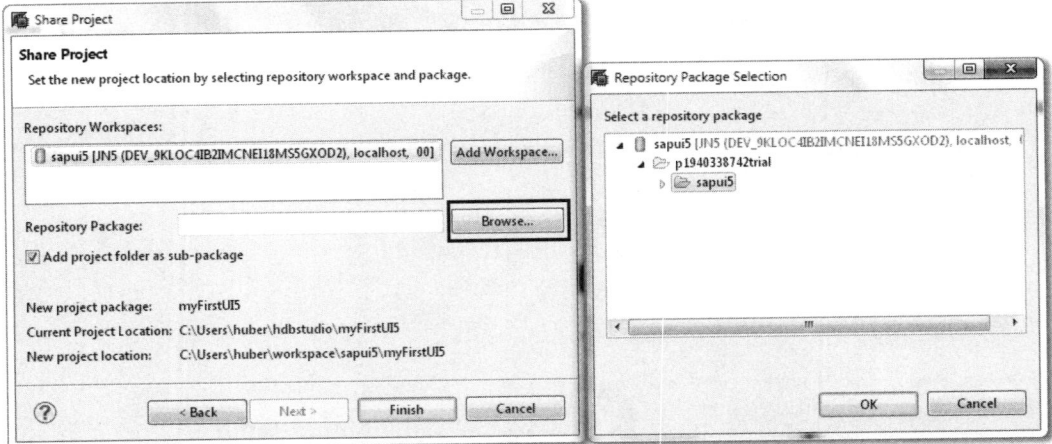

Figure 9.14 Selecting the Workspace

You can then activate the project via the context menu of the project (TEAM • ACTIVATE). As a result, your XS project is now visible in the Cockpit (see Figure 9.15).

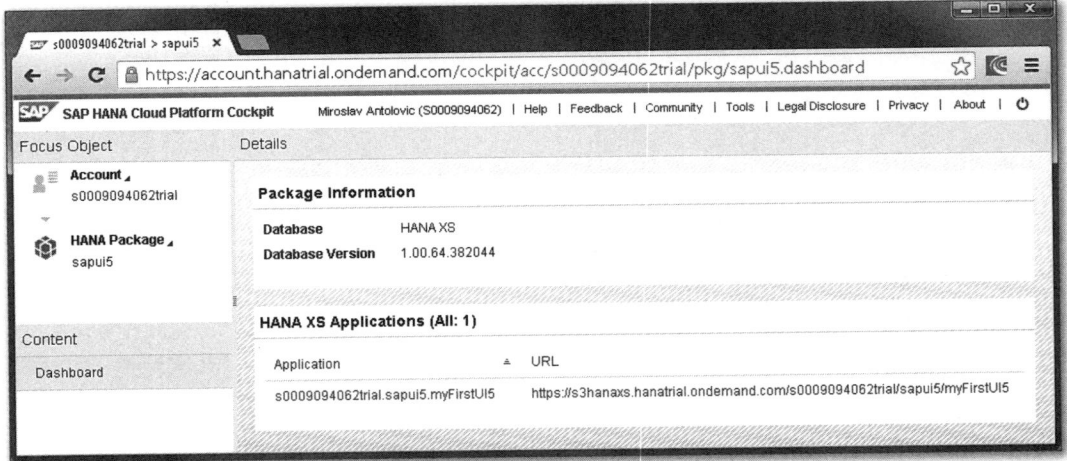

Figure 9.15 SAP HANA Cloud Platform Cockpit

Next, you'll model a calculation view, which you'll then consume in your SAPUI5 application as an OData service. The example used here is based on the EPM demo scenario, which you will find under the database schema EPMSAMPLEDATA in the HANA test version. If you would like to implement this example on another HANA instance, you can download the demo content from SAP Service Marketplace (see *http://help.sap.com/hana/SAP_HANA_Interactive_Education_SHINE_en.pdf*).

Calculation view

In this example, you'll implement a display of orders broken down according to *buyer* (see Figure 9.16). The orders are in the table SNWD_SO, and the buyer information is in the table SNWD_BPA.

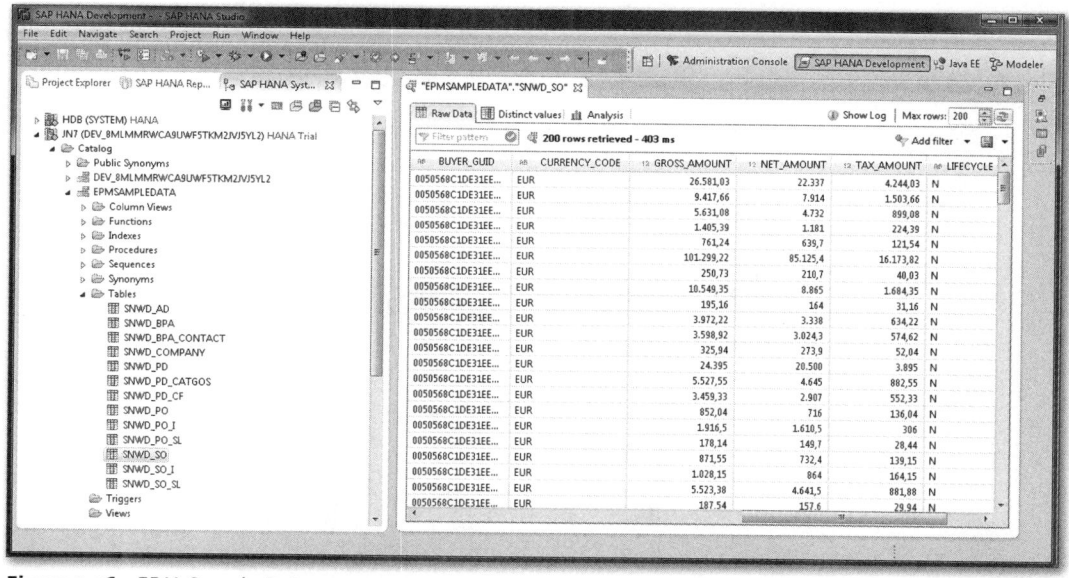

Figure 9.16 EPM Sample Data

Using the context menu of your project, now select New • Calculation View (see Figure 9.17) to create a calculation view with the name CV_SALESORDER.

Creating a calculation view

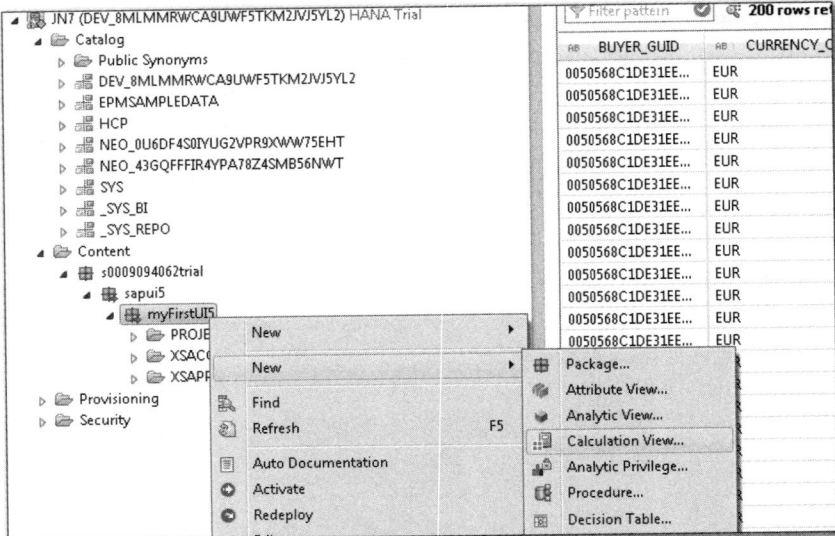

Figure 9.17 Creating a Calculation View

Leave all other settings unchanged (see Figure 9.18), and click FINISH.

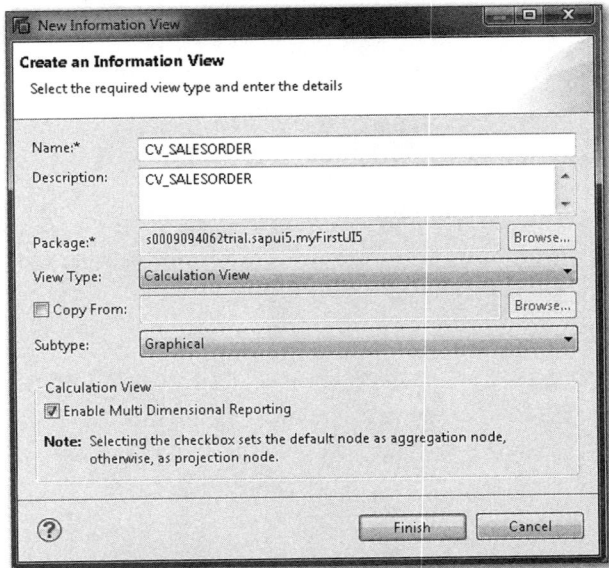

Figure 9.18 Calculation View Wizard

On the right-hand side in the Scenario Editor, add a Join node. To do this, first click JOIN NODE ❶ in the toolbar, and then click below the aggregation node in the free area ❷ (see Figure 9.19).

Join node

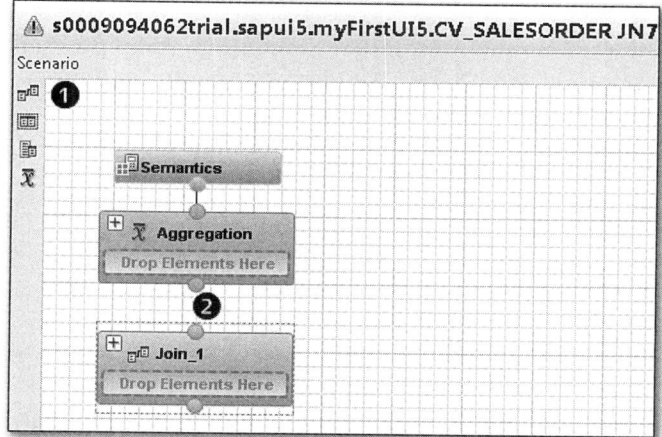

Figure 9.19 Creating a Join Node

Link the join node to the aggregation node by clicking on the circle on the join node, holding down the mouse button, and linking this circle with the circle on the aggregation node. Next, include the two tables SNWD_BPA and SNWD_SO from the EPSSAMPLEDATA schema in the join node by drag and drop, and link the two tables in the DETAILS view via BUYER_GUID in the table SNWD_BPA and NODE_KEY in the table SNWD_SO (see Figure 9.20).

Table join

Now, add the fields EMAIL_ADDRESS, PHONE_NUMBER, COMPANY_NAME, GROSS_AMOUNT, NET_AMOUNT, and TAX_AMOUNT to the output by using the context menu to select the entry ADD TO OUTPUT.

Adding fields to the output

Now, switch to the join view by double-clicking the AGGREGATION NODE in the Scenario Editor. Again, add the fields EMAIL_ADDRESS, PHONE_NUMBER, COMPANY_NAME, GROSS_AMOUNT, NET_AMOUNT, and TAX_AMOUNT to the output via the context menu. Because you can display the data in SAP HANA in an authorization-based manner, you can assign *analytical authorizations*. Analytical authorizations are used to provide different users access to various parts of the data in the same view, depending on their user role. Because we want to omit this in our

Analytical authorizations

simple example, deselect the checkbox for ENABLE ANALYTIC PRIVILEGE in the SEMANTICS view. To do this, double-click SEMANTICS in the Scenario Editor, and remove the checkmark for ENABLE ANALYTIC PRIVILEGE in the Properties section (see Figure 9.21).

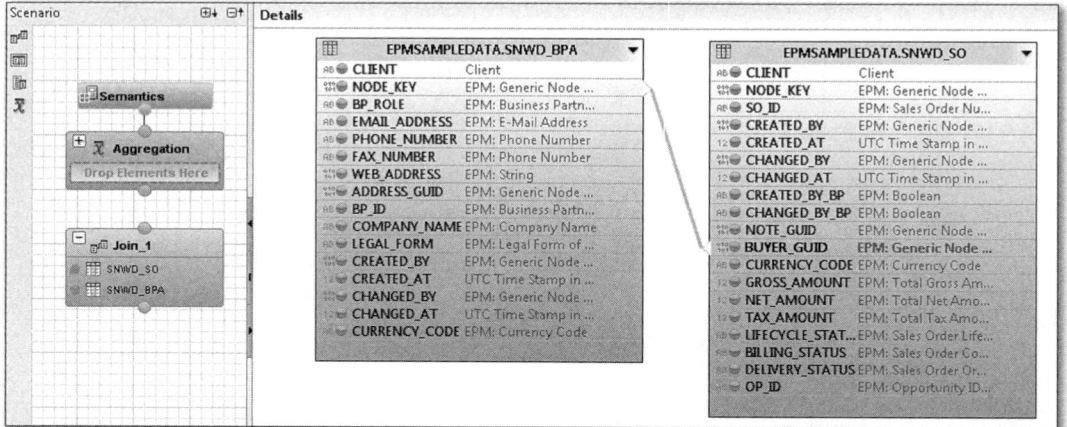

Figure 9.20 Join of Both Tables

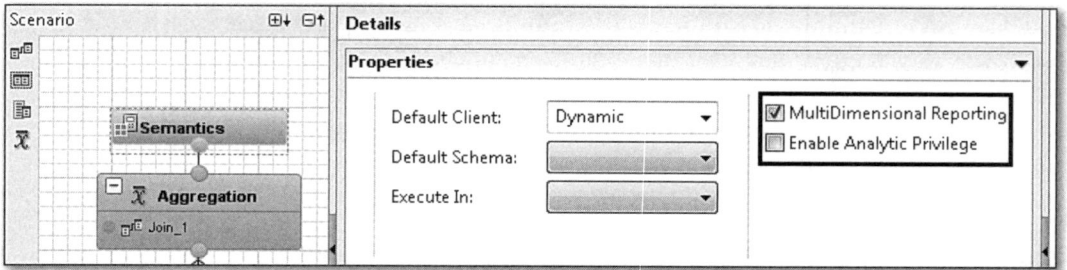

Figure 9.21 Removing Analytical Authorization

Field type   Also ensure that the three fields GROSS_AMOUNT, NET_AMOUNT, and TAX_AMOUNT are of type MEASURE. Define quantifiable data such as sales or amount as type MEASURE and all other fields as type ATTRIBUTE (see Figure 9.22).

Save and activate your view, and check in the JOB LOG that the activation was successful (see Figure 9.23).

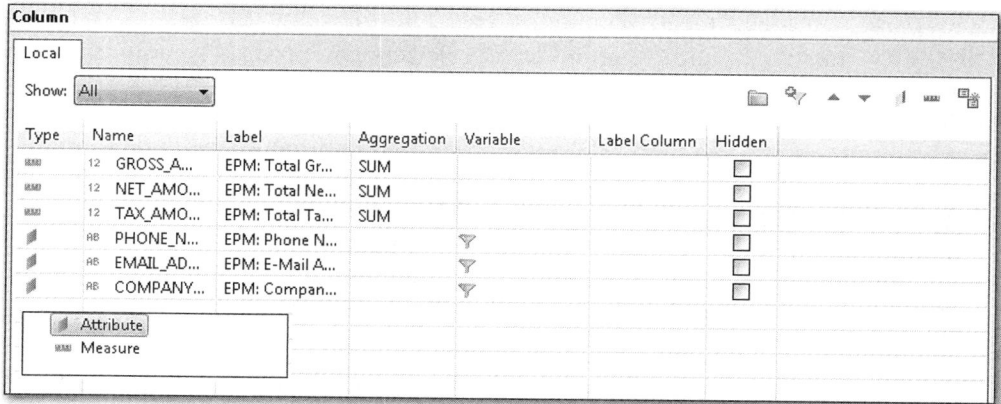

Figure 9.22 Field Types Measure and Attribute

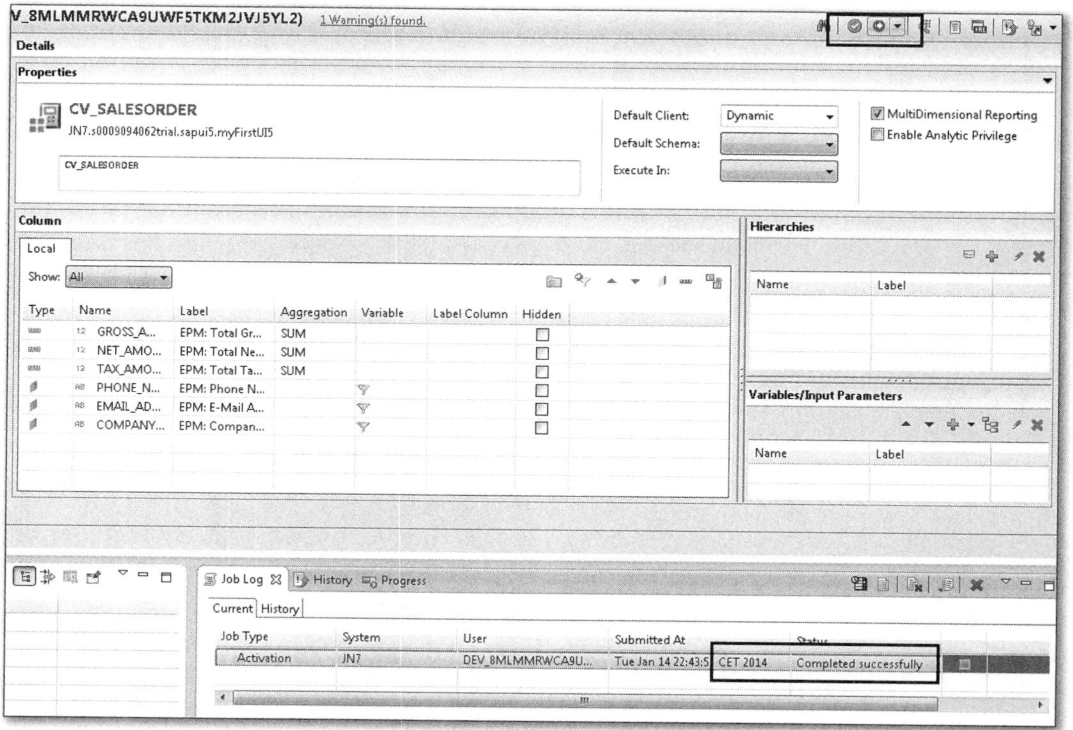

Figure 9.23 Activating the View

Assigning
authorization

To enable the system user to access the view you just created, you must assign the authorization for the relevant view. You assign authorizations in SAP HANA with a script. To do this, switch to the Quick Launch of the MODELER view on the SQL CONSOLE (see Figure 9.24).

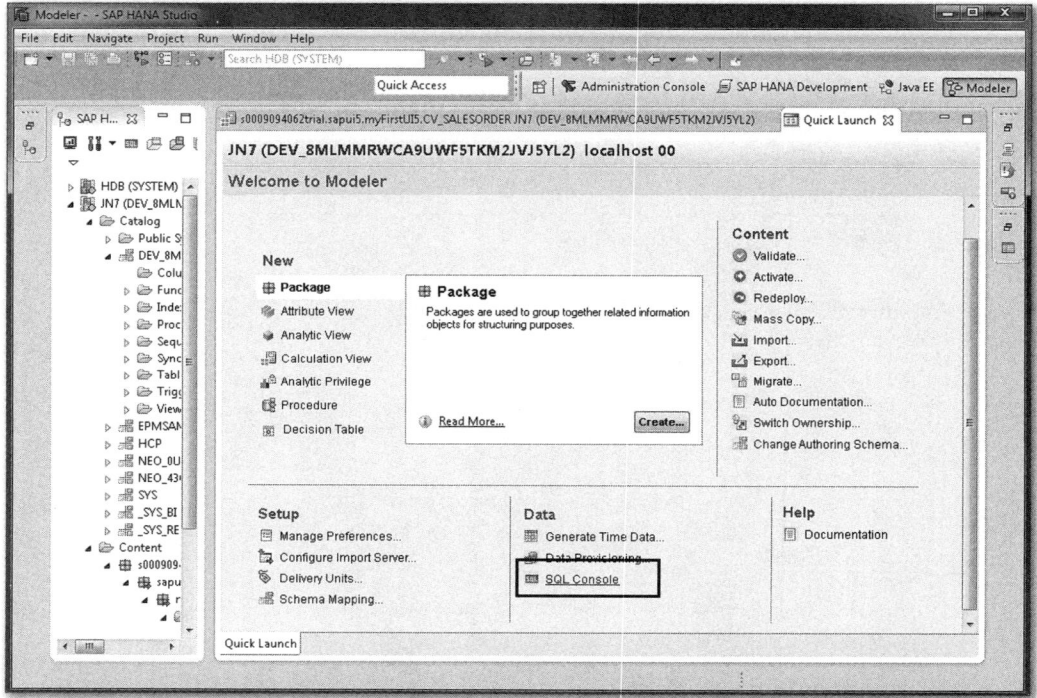

Figure 9.24 SQL Console

In the SQL CONSOLE, enter the command CALL "HCP" . "HCP_GRANT_SELECT_ON_ACTIVATED_OBJECTS", and execute it. You assign the system user the authorizations for the activated object via this procedure. You execute this step each time after you have created a view.

After successfully executing the procedure, you can display the data in the preview of the calculation view you created. To do this, go into the context menu of the catalog node, and click REFRESH. Under the schema _SYS_BIC • COLUMN VIEWS, after updating, you will find the calculation view CV_SALESORDER that you created. You can execute the data preview via the context menu of the view (see Figure 9.25).

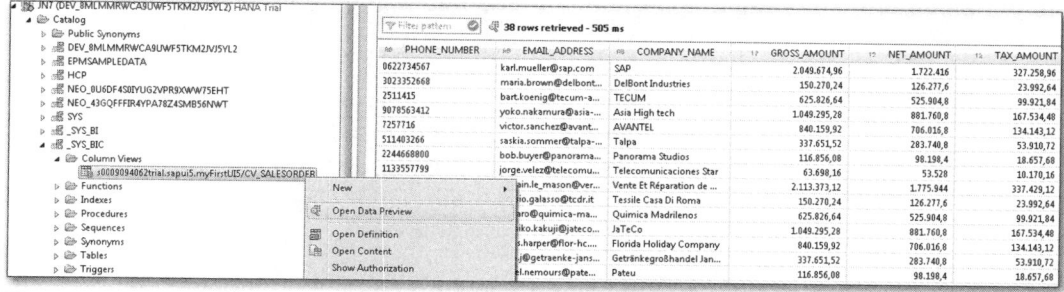

Figure 9.25 Data Preview

To enable you to access the data of the view, you now have to implement an OData service that provides the data from the created calculation view as an OData service. Below your XS project, create a SERVICES directory with an ORDER.XSODATA file for this purpose. For the syntax for the service, see Listing 9.2.

OData Service

```
service namespace "myFirstUI5.services" {
"_SYS_BIC"."s0009094062trial.sapui5.myFirstUI5/CV_SALESORDER"
as "order" keys generate local "ID";
}
```

Listing 9.2 OData Service

The syntax for the service is "<SCHEMA NAME>"."<PATH_TO_THE_VIEW>"; adjust the values accordingly (see Figure 9.26).

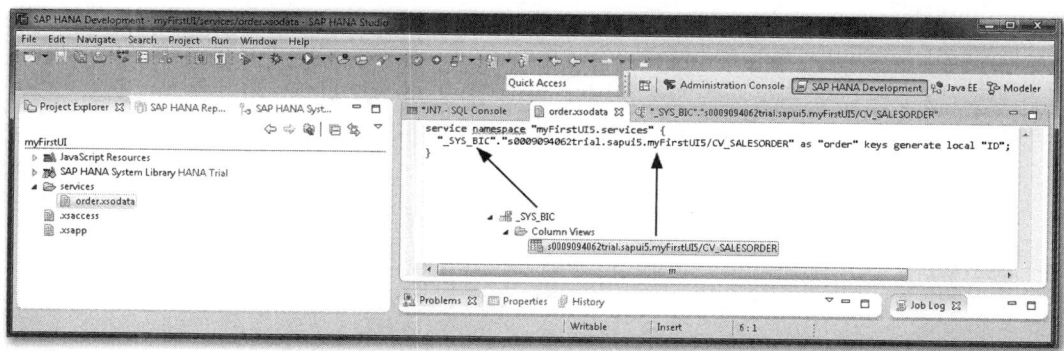

Figure 9.26 OData Service

If your OData service was now to refer to an analytic view, the syntax would change as shown in Listing 9.3.

```
service namespace "myFirstUI5.services" {
"<PATH>/AN_SALESORDER.analyticview" as "orders"
keys generate local "ID" aggregates always;
}
```

Listing 9.3   OData Service with an Analytic View

Authorization   You now need to create a role for the read authorization to this view. In your project, create a ROLES directory and create a file with the name *access.hdbrole* in this directory. Then insert the content from Listing 9.4.

```
role s0009094062trial.sapui5.myFirstUI5.roles::access {
sql object s0009094062trial.sapui5.myFirstUI5:CV_SALESORDER.
calculationview : SELECT;
}
```

Listing 9.4   Authorization Role

Also replace the values again here according to your user name, the database schema, and the project name (see Listing 9.5).

```
role <USER>.<SCHEMA>.<PROJECT>::<ROLE NAME> {
sql object <USER>.<SCHEMA>.<PROJECT>:<VIEW>.
calculationview : SELECT ;
}
```

Listing 9.5   General Syntax of an Authorization Role

Activate the service and the role via the context menu (TEAM • ACTIVATE). You now have to assign the new authorization role again to your user. Execute the following script in the SQL Editor:

```
call "HCP"."HCP_GRANT_ROLE_TO_USER"('s0009094062trial.
sapui5.myFirstUI5.roles::access','S0009094062');
```

Again, replace the script here with your values. You've now assigned the created role access to your user name.

Implementation   This concludes the preparatory work, and you can now implement an
in SAPUI5   SAPUI5 application that uses the OData service and displays the data from the calculation view. To do this, create a new application project, assign "ui5_hana" as its project name, and omit creating the Initial View.

You can consume the OData service in the same way you learned about in Chapter 8. You create an instance of the OData Model and specify the relative path to your *xsodata* file in the constructor—for example:

```
var oModel = new sap.ui.model.odata.ODataModel(
"../../../myFirstUI5/services/order.xsodata");
```

For the *index.html* file, this results in the content of Listing 9.6. This listing was shortened for clarity; you can download the complete listing from the book's web page.

```
<!DOCTYPE HTML>
<html>
<head>
<meta charset="UTF-8">
<meta http-equiv="X-UA-Compatible" content="IE=edge">
<script src="/sap/ui5/1/resources/sap-ui-core.js"
id="sap-ui-bootstrap"
data-sap-ui-libs="sap.ui.commons, sap.ui.table"
data-sap-ui-theme="sap_bluecrystal">
</script>

<script>
// SAP-HANA-OData-Service
var oModel = new sap.ui.model.odata.ODataModel(
"../../../myFirstUI5/services/order.xsodata");

// Table display
var oTable = new sap.ui.table.Table({
title: "Buyer orders",
visibleRowCount : 5,
navigationMode:
sap.ui.table.NavigationMode.Paginator
});

oTable.addColumn(new sap.ui.table.Column({
label: new sap.ui.commons.Label({
text: "Buyer"}),
template: new
sap.ui.commons.TextView().bindProperty(
"text", "COMPANY_NAME"),
}));
```

```
// Shortened; insert the other columns here according to
// the same schema

// Bind model and rows
oTable.setModel(oModel);
oTable.bindRows("/order");

oTable.placeAt("content");
</script>
</head>
<body class="sapUiBody" role="application">
<div id="content"></div>
</body>
</html>
```

Listing 9.6 SAPUI5 Application in SAP HANA

Upload the application to the repository, and click BROWSE to select your
XS project as the repository package (see Figure 9.27). Make sure this
time that you select the XS project as the repository package; this is one
level lower than shown in Figure 9.14.

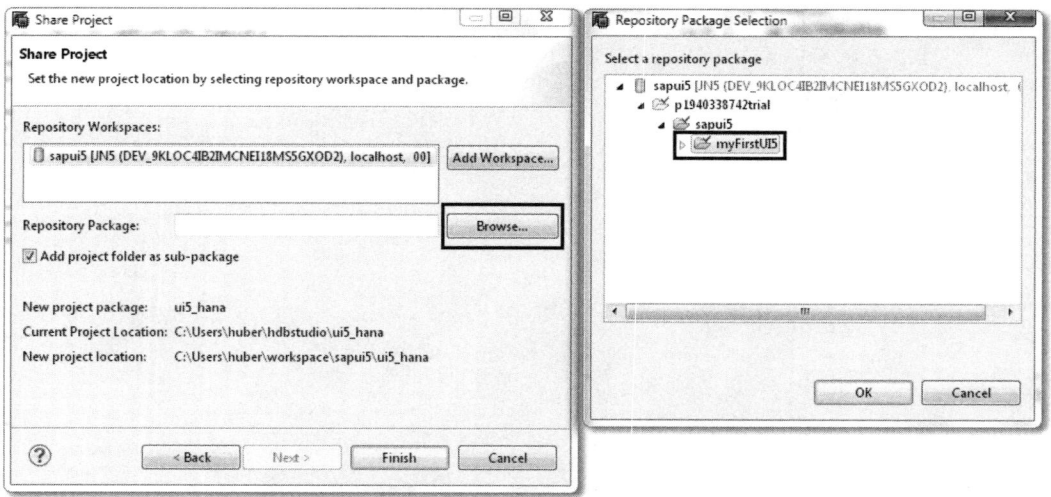

Figure 9.27 Uploading the Project

You can activate the project via the context menu of the project (TEAM • **Activating project**
COMMIT and TEAM • ACTIVATE). After the successful activation, you can
call your application via the URL *https://s3hanaxs.hanatrial.ondemand.
com/s0009094062trial/sapui5/myFirstUI5/ui5_hana/WebContent/index.html*.
Again, replace the path here with your values (see Figure 9.28).

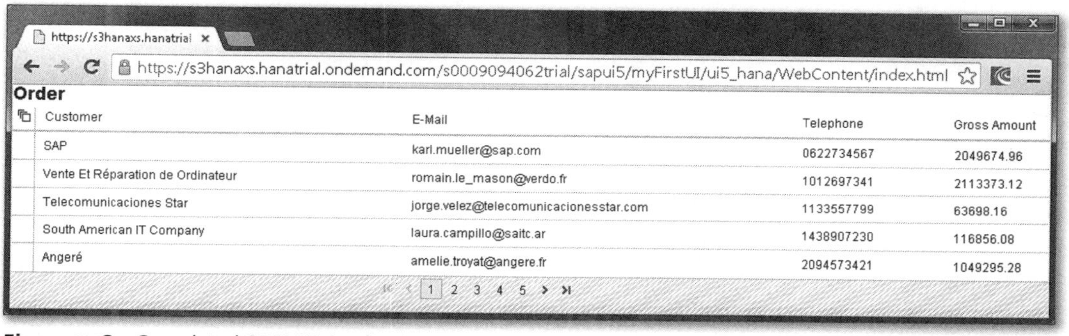

Figure 9.28 Completed SAPUI5 Application

Congratulations! You have just successfully implemented your first SAPUI5
application in SAP HANA! As you can see from this small example, the
SAPUI5 development in SAP HANA works in exactly the same manner as
in an ABAP backend system. You can implement the various views of SAP
HANA as OData services, and, as you already learned in previous chapters,
you can embed them in the SAPUI5 application via the OData model.

In this chapter, you will learn about the library for mobile applications. By implementing an application example, you will be lead through the world of development for mobile devices.

10   Mobile Applications

The development of mobile applications presents a whole new set of challenges. On the one hand, as a company you have to consider the issue of security. A smartphone or tablet PC is lost more easily than an installed PC in the office—and a dishonest finder would have very easy access to sensitive corporate data in the event of a lack of safety precautions.

On the other hand, there are many different manufacturers of mobile devices and thus also different operating systems, such as iOS, Android, BlackBerry OS, or Windows Phone. You usually use many different devices in your company and hence many different platforms. The bring-your-own-device approach, which takes into account the desire of employees to be able to use their private devices for business purposes, represents a major challenge for a company. How can you ensure that the employee will assume personal responsibility for eliminating every security vulnerability via software updates or that the latest virus scanner is always installed on these personal devices?

Bring your own device

The large number of operating systems in use poses a challenge at the technical level for developers. If you are now developing, for example, a native application for Android, you must develop it again for iOS and perhaps even for Windows Phone. This fact means, of course, that a huge implementation and maintenance effort is involved. Fortunately, every mobile device "understands" HTML5, CSS3, and JavaScript—and thus SAPUI5 also! With SAPUI5, you can develop cross-platform Hybrid Web Container applications and make them available for most devices.

Multiple platforms

Last but not least, with SAP Fiori, SAP has introduced a product on the market that was specifically designed for mobile devices and implemented in SAPUI5 (see Figure 10.1).

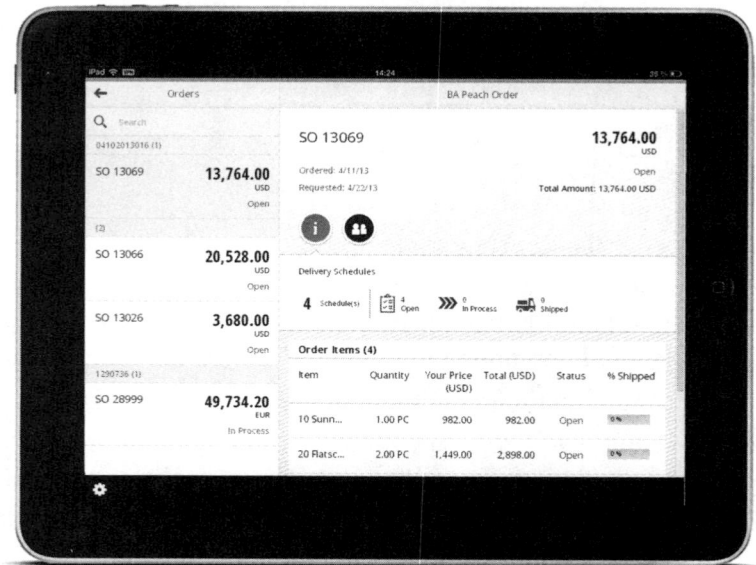

Figure 10.1 SAP Fiori

SAP Fiori

With SAP Fiori, users can currently access the 25 most important functions of SAP Business Suite via mobile devices. You can use SAP Fiori, for example, to approve travel or purchasing requests, update customer information, or create leave requests.

In this chapter, you'll be introduced to the development options for mobile devices with SAPUI5. You'll also implement a mobile application for the approval of leave requests entered from the portal from Chapter 7.

[☞]

Checklist
You will need the following for this chapter:
▶ An installed and configured Eclipse development environment
▶ Access to an SAP ERP system with an installed SAPUI5 library
▶ An emulator for mobile devices, such as Ripple
▶ Google Chrome as a browser

10.1 Installation

The simulation of mobile devices is currently best supported by Google Chrome, so first download Google Chrome (via *https://chrome.google.com/*), and install it on your PC.

You can simulate mobile devices in the browser with Ripple Emulator. The emulator is available at *http://emulate.phonegap.com*. At the start, you are asked what platform you would like to use. Select, for example, MOBILE WEB (DEFAULT); the page is displayed in a frame, which simulates the corresponding device. You can now enter the URL to your application in the middle pane (see Figure 10.2).

Emulator

Figure 10.2 Ripple Emulator

On the left-hand side, you can select various devices and view your application in different resolutions (see Figure 10.3).

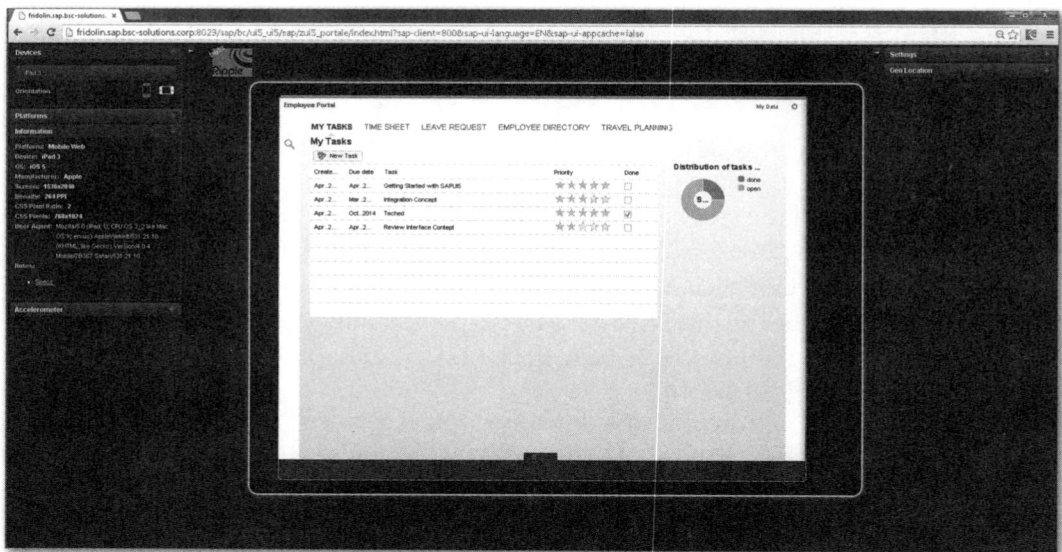

Figure 10.3 Preview of the Page in a Mobile Device

10.2 Introduction to SAPUI5 for Mobile

With *sap.m*, SAPUI5 introduces a special control library for mobile devices, such as tablets and smartphones. *sap.m* is based on the same runtime as the controls for the desktop area and uses the same infrastructure for data binding, the Model View Controller concept, and so on. Due to this common ground, it's much easier for the application developer to port a desktop application to an application for mobile devices and vice versa.

Themes   The themes Blue Crystal ❶ and Mobile Visual Identity ❷ are available for the development of applications for mobile devices; the MVI theme is not being further developed (see Figure 10.4). The Blue Crystal theme has the advantage that it's also available for desktop applications, and it thus allows for a uniform appearance for desktop and mobile applications.

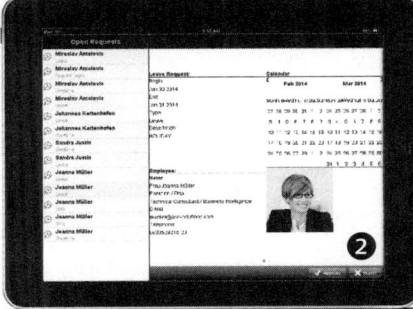

Figure 10.4 Themes for Mobile Applications

10.3 Developing Mobile Solutions with SAPUI5

The development of an application for mobile devices is very similar in SAPUI5 to the development of desktop applications. Therefore, let's discuss only the differences in the remainder of this chapter.

10.3.1 Page Layout of Mobile Applications

The first difference involves the bootstrap of the page; this difference is due more to browsers than to mobile development. Before you integrate your application in an app format with PhoneGap or a similar tool, test the application in the browser. Because mobile devices are mostly controlled

Bootstrap

with your finger, you can inform the browser via a parameter that mobile events (touching, swiping, and so on) are to be simulated using the mouse. To enable you to simulate these events in the browser, you have to add `data-sap-ui-xx-fakeOS` to the bootstrap and thus inform the browser as to which operating system is to be simulated (see Listing 10.1).

- `sap-ui-xx-fakeOS="android"`: Android simulation
- `sap-ui-xx-fakeOS="ios"`: Apple iOS
- `sap-ui-xx-fakeOS="blackberry"`: BlackBerry OS
- `sap-ui-xx-fakeOS="winphone"`: Windows Phone

```
<script src="resources/sap-ui-core.js"
    id="sap-ui-bootstrap"
    data-sap-ui-libs="sap.m"
    data-sap-ui-theme="sap_bluecrystal"
    data-sap-ui-xx-fakeOS="blackberry">
</script>
```

Listing 10.1 Bootstrap of a Mobile Application

As an alternative to the bootstrap, you can also specify this parameter in the URL.

Root control The second difference is that you have to define a root control. This control is responsible for controlling individual pages.

The *sap.m* library provides an app control (`sap.m.App`), which you define as the root control in the simplest case. You have to specify this control only for the first page to be displayed. You can imagine the root control as a container that assumes the control and management of individual pages.

The third difference is that you should use controls from the `sap.m.` class if possible; therefore, instead of `sap.ui.commons.Label()`, use `sap.m.Label()`. Of course, you can also use all other UI controls; the `sap.m.` controls are optimized only for viewing on mobile devices.

As a small exercise, create the project ZUI5_MOBILE in Eclipse now, and make sure that you choose the MOBILE option as the target device (see Figure 10.5).

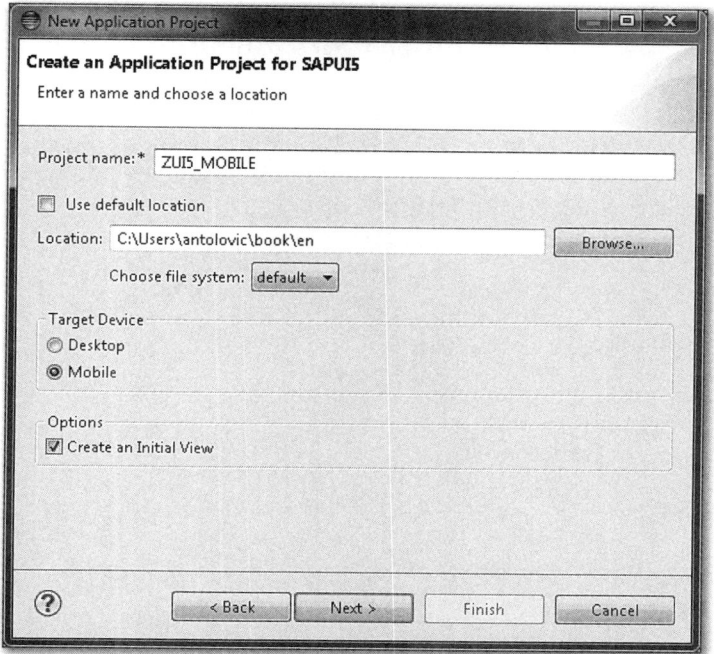

Figure 10.5 Mobile Target Device

This page should display only a selection field for a date; this results in Listing 10.2.

Selection field for date

```
<!DOCTYPE HTML>
<html>
  <head>
   <title>Date</title>
    <meta http-equiv="Content-Type"
                    content="text/html;charset=UTF-8"/>
    <meta http-equiv="X-UA-Compatible" content="IE=edge">

    <script src="resources/sap-ui-core.js"
        id="sap-ui-bootstrap"
        data-sap-ui-libs="sap.m"
        data-sap-ui-theme="sap_mvi"
        data-sap-ui-xx-fakeOS="blackberry" >
   </script>
   <script>
```

```
// App-Control
  var oApp = new sap.m.App ({initialPage:"date"});

// A page with date field
    var oPage = new sap.m.Page ("date", {
        title: "Date",
        content : new sap.m.DateTimeInput({
        type : sap.m.DateTimeInputType.Date,
        })
    });
// Add page to app control
    oApp.addPage(oPage);

//Place app control in HTML page
    oApp.placeAt("content");

    </script>
  </head>
  <body class="sapUiBody" role="application">
    <div id="content"></div>
  </body>
</html>
```

Listing 10.2 First Application for Mobile Devices

Themes

As you can see in Figure 10.6, the sap_mvi theme adapts to the native appearance of the respective device—for example:

❶ sap_mvi on the BlackBerry operating system

❷ sap_mvi on the Android operating system

❸ sap_blue_crystal on Android or Blackberry

If you use the Blue Crystal theme, the page is always displayed the same way regardless of the platform.

Within the app control, you can use other full-screen controls, such as the sap.m.Page control or the sap.m.Carousel control. For SAP Fiori, for example, the Fiori shell is used as the home page (see Figure 10.7).

Figure 10.6   Result: Date Display

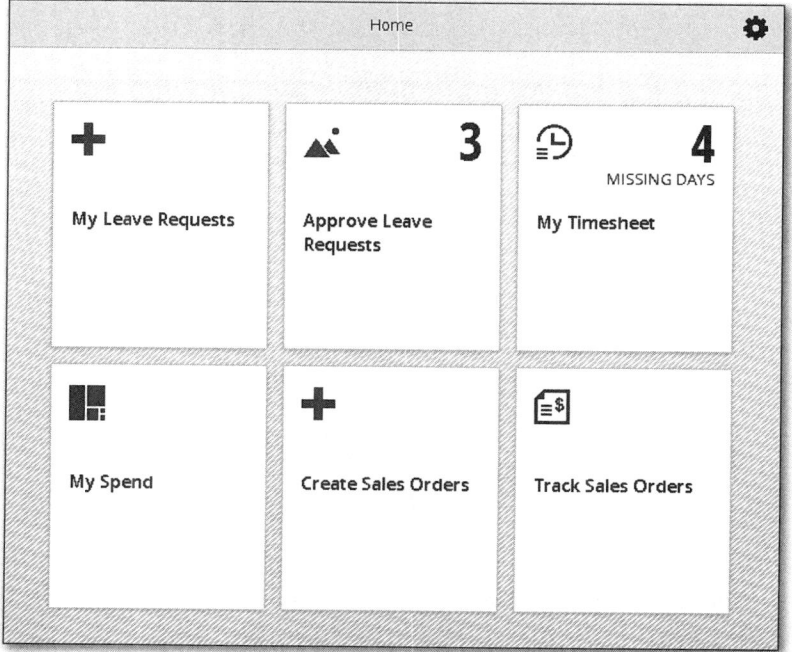

Figure 10.7   SAP Fiori Home Page

10.3.2 Page Navigation

navigate event

As you saw in the example in Listing 10.2, it is very easy to develop an application for mobile devices with SAPUI5. Usually, an application consists of more than one page, and you want to navigate between different views and pages within the application. The class `sap.m.Class` provides the two events `navigate` and `afterNavigate` for navigation purposes. These two events were inherited from the central element `NavContainer`. In the `navigate` event, you can use the event parameters to identify from which page the user has come (`from` parameter) or where he would like to go (`to` parameter). An exact description of all parameters is available in the API reference. In addition to this central event control in the app control, the `NavContainer` control also fires events within the displayed page. These include the following:

▶ `beforeHide` (before leaving the source page)

▶ `beforeFirstShow` (event on the target page, before it is shown for the first time)

▶ `beforeShow` (event on the target page, before it is shown)

▶ `afterShow` (after the target page has been shown)

▶ `afterHide` (after leaving the source page)

ZUI5_MO_NAV

As a small exercise, now create the project ZUI5_MO_NAV with the source code from Listing 10.3. This small application consists of two pages, but the second page is only accessible if you have pushed the slider on the front page as far to the right as possible.

```
<!DOCTYPE HTML>
<html>
  <head>
  <meta http-equiv="X-UA-Compatible" content="IE=edge" />
  <meta http-equiv="Content-Type"
                    content="text/html;charset=UTF-8" />
  <title>Navigation</title>

  <script src="resources/sap-ui-core.js"
     id="sap-ui-bootstrap"
     data-sap-ui-libs="sap.ui.commons, sap.m"
     data-sap-ui-theme="sap_bluecrystal"
     data-sap-ui-xx-fakeOS="blackberry" >
```

```
     </script>

<script>
 // App-Control
 var oApp = new sap.m.App ({initialPage:"page1"});

 // Initial page
 var oPage1 = new sap.m.Page ("page1", {
   title: "Entry",
   content : [
          // Text
     new sap.m.Text ({
                text : "Swipe to Unlock"
                }),
         // Slider
     new sap.m.Slider ({
       max: 100,
       change: function(oControlEvent){
        if (oControlEvent.getParameter("value") == "100"){
           var oButton = sap.ui.getCore().byId("GoOn");
           oButton.setEnabled(true);
          }},
       liveChange: function(oControlEvent){
         if (oControlEvent.getParameter("value") == "100"){
            var oButton = sap.ui.getCore().byId("GoOn");
            oButton.setEnabled(true);
           }},
        }),
         // Navigation
     new sap.m.Button ("GoOn", {
          text : "Go On",
          enabled : false,
          press: function() {
               oApp.to("page2");
           }
       }),
    ]
 });


// Second page
var oPage2 = new sap.m.Page("page2", {
    title: "Welcome",
```

```
        // Back button
        showNavButton: true,
        // Navigation to home page
        navButtonPress: function(){
            oApp.back();
        },
        content : new sap.m.Text({
        text:"Welcome to the world of mobile applications"})
  });

oApp.addPage(oPage1);
oApp.addPage(oPage2);

oApp.placeAt("content"); //
  </script>
</head>
<body class="sapUiBody">
  <div id="content"></div>
</body>
</html>
```

Listing 10.3   Page Navigation

Upload the page to the SAP system, and view the result in the Ripple
emulator (see Figure 10.8).

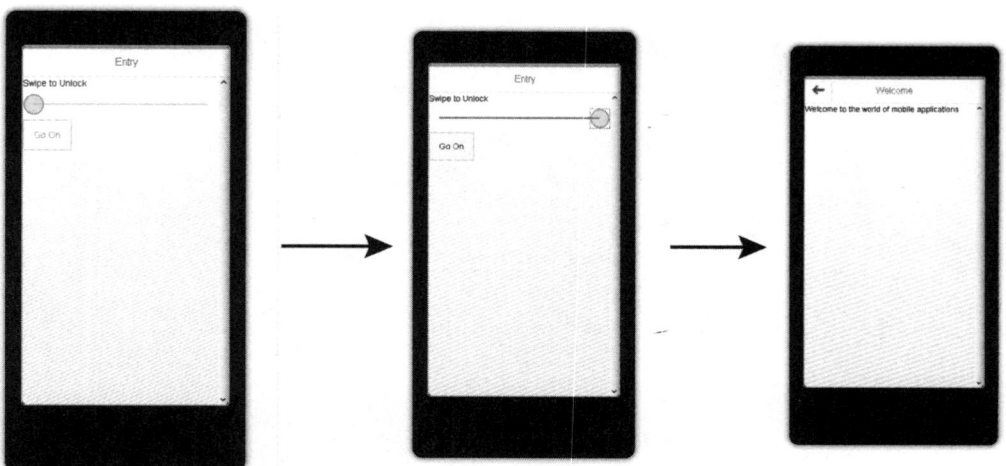

Figure 10.8   First Application with Page Navigation

10.3.3   Where Am I?

When developing for mobile devices, the question of on which device the application is running and whether a smartphone or tablet is involved is sometimes of interest. Depending on the device in question, you may, for example, want to change the behavior or the layout of the pages. Unfortunately, this question is not so easy to answer nowadays. There are now desktop monitors and notebooks with touchscreen functions, there are netbooks that are somewhere between a laptop and a tablet in terms of size, and some smartphones are larger than tablets; all of these devices may be in use, so ultimately you can never really be sure as to the exact device on which your application is running.

Regardless of this fact, you can find out via the jQuery library whether the device, for example, has a touchscreen and whether it's a tablet or a smartphone (you can also check the screen resolution in case of doubt). The most important functions include the following:

▶ `jQuery.support.touch`
   Does the device have a touchscreen?

▶ `jQuery.device.is.desktop`
   Is the device a desktop PC?

▶ `jQuery.device.is.tablet`
   Is the device a tablet?

▶ `jQuery.device.is.phone`
   Is the device a smartphone?

The complete list is available in the API documentation under JQUERY • DEVICE • IS. You can also use the `jQuery.device.is` function to determine whether the device is held upright or horizontally:

▶ `jQuery.device.is.landscape`: horizontal

▶ `jQuery.device.is.portrait`: upright

If the device is rotated during use, the event `orientationChange` is triggered (see Listing 10.4).

```
oApp.attachOrientationChange(function(evt) {
    if (evt.getParameters().landscape) {
        // Changes
```

```
    }
});
```

Listing 10.4 Event when Orientation Changes

10.3.4 SplitApp Control

If you look at Figure 10.1 and Figure 10.4, you'll notice that the layout of the pages corresponds to the typical layout of tablets. On the left-hand side, you have a list view, and when you select an entry the details of the entry are displayed on the right-hand side. This layout is achieved by the `SplitApp` control The `SplitApp` control divides the screen area into a master section ❶ and a detail section ❷ (see Figure 10.9).

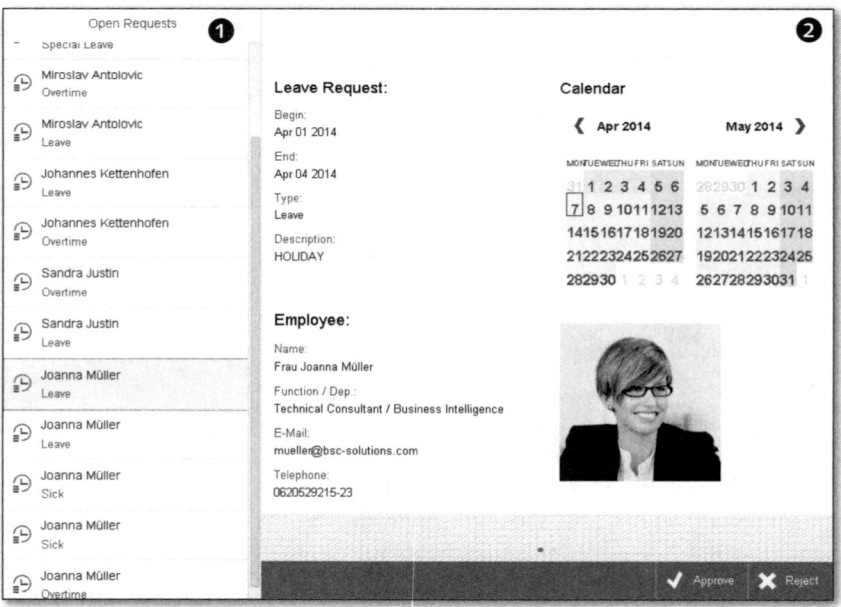

Figure 10.9 SplitApp Control

On smartphones, only the master pane is displayed initially with the `SplitApp` control. If an entry is selected, the corresponding detail page is displayed (see Figure 10.10).

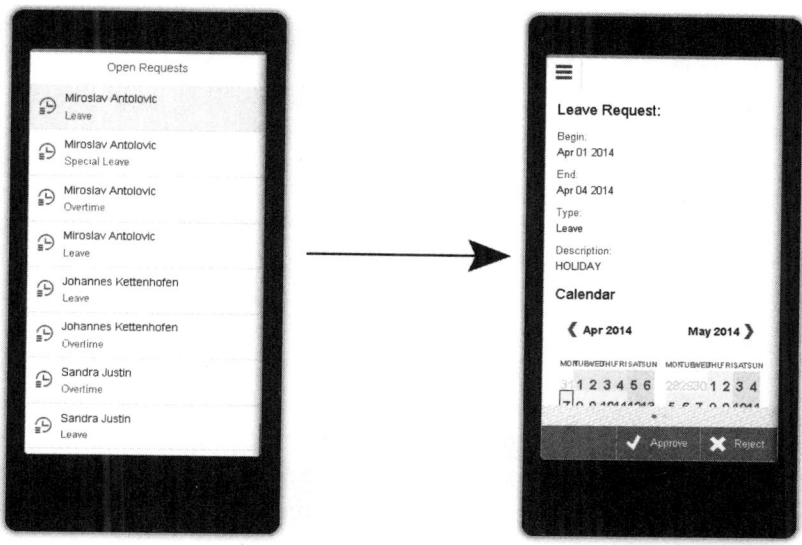

Figure 10.10 SplitApp Control on Smartphones

The application example in Section 10.4 illustrates the use of the SplitApp control.

10.3.5 Events on Mobile Devices

You also have slightly different events on mobile devices than on a desktop PC that use your fingers:

Events

- ▶ Touch events
- ▶ Swipe events
- ▶ Scroll events

These events enable you, for example, to handle typical *swiping* and call a function. In our application example, we'll use this event to navigate from the detail list to an overview of the open leave requests of a person.

The complete list of events can be found at *http://api.jquerymobile.com/category/events/*.

10.4   Application Example

To deepen your knowledge, let's now develop an application that will display the leave requests from the portal. If an entry is selected, the corresponding request is displayed, and the two editing options APPROVE and REJECT are offered.

10.4.1   Backend Implementation

Approval app   We stored the leave requests in the database table ZUI5_ABSENCE of the portal from Chapter 7. Similar to the class implementation in Chapter 7, we thus require a service that will read the open requests as well as a service that will set the status of the requests accordingly to *approved* or *rejected*. Because we would also like to display the image of the employee in the approval app, we need another service that will read the image. For this purpose, create the class ZUI5_MOBILE with the following methods:

▶ HANDLE_REQUEST: Dispatcher function

▶ GET_APPROVAL: Read requests

▶ SET_APPROVAL: Approve/reject requests

▶ GET_PICTURE: Read image

The interface of all methods is the same as the interface definition from Chapter 7 (see Figure 10.11).

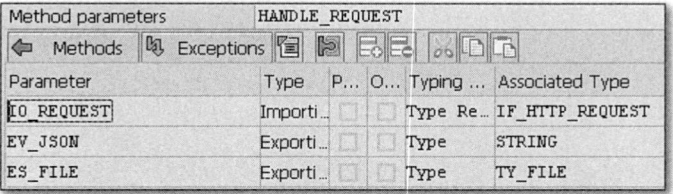

Figure 10.11   Interface Definition

Method HANDLE_REQUEST

HANDLE_   The method HANDLE_REQUEST acts again as a dispatcher and calls the cor-
REQUEST   responding function depending on the parameter AREA (see Listing 10.5).

```
    data: lv_form             type string,
          exception           type ref to cx_root,
          ref                 type ref to data,
          lo_json             type ref to zui5_json_serializer,
          ls_message          type s_message,
          lv_error(1).

  lv_form = to_upper( io_request->get_form_field( 'area' ) ).

  if sy-subrc <> 0 or lv_form is initial.
      ls_message-severity = 'E'.
      ls_message-text     = 'Form field AREA is missing'.
      lv_error            = abap_true.
    else.
      try.
          call method (lv_form)
            exporting
              io_request = io_request
            importing
              es_file    = es_file
              ev_json    = ev_json.
        catch cx_sy_dyn_call_error into exception.
          ls_message-severity = 'E'.
          ls_message-text     = exception->get_text( ).
          lv_error            = abap_true.
      endtry.
    endif.

  if lv_error = abap_true.
    create object lo_json
      exporting
        data = ls_message.
    lo_json->serialize( ).
    ev_json = lo_json->get_data( ).
  endif.
```

Listing 10.5 Method HANDLE_REQUEST

Method GET_APPROVAL

The method GET_APPROVAL reads all open requests (status 01), their pos-   **GET_APPROVAL**
sible statuses, and the addresses of the applicants (see Listing 10.6).

```
data: ls_approval        type zui5_approval,
      ls_message         type s_message,
      lt_dd07v           type standard table of dd07v,
      alias              type bapialias,
      address            type bapiaddr3,
      return             type standard table of bapiret2,
      lo_json            type ref to zui5_json_serializer.

field-symbols: <abs_type>    type zui5_abs,
               <abs>         type zui5_absence_t,
               <ab>          type zui5_absence,
               <addresses>   type zui5_address_t,
               <address>     type zui5_address,
               <abs_types>   type zui5_abs_t,
               <stat>        type zui5_stat,
               <stats>       type zui5_stat_t,
               <dd07v>       type dd07v.

"Absence types
assign component 'ABS_TYPE'    of structure ls_approval
                                       to <abs_types>.
"Status
assign component 'STATUS_TYPE' of structure ls_approval
                                       to <stats>.
"Requests
assign component 'ABSENCE' of structure ls_approval
                                       to <abs>.
"Addresses
assign component 'ADDRESS' of structure ls_approval
                                       to <addresses>.

select * from zui5_absence into table <abs>
                          where status = '01'
                          order by username.

if sy-subrc <> 0.
  ls_message-severity = 'E'.
  ls_message-text     = 'No open requests found'.
endif.

loop at <abs> assigning <ab>.
  at new username.
```

```
    call function 'BAPI_USER_GET_DETAIL'
      exporting
        username = <ab>-username
      importing
        address  = address
        alias    = alias
      tables
        return   = return.

  if not address is initial.
    append initial line to <addresses> assigning <address>.
      move-corresponding address to <address>.
      <address>-username    = <ab>-username.
      <address>-usr_function = address-function.
      <address>-img_path     = alias-useralias.
  endif.
 endat.
endloop.

 call function 'DDIF_DOMA_GET'
   exporting
     name         = 'ZUI5_ABS_TYPE'
     langu        = sy-langu
   tables
     dd07v_tab    = lt_dd07v
   exceptions
     illegal_input = 1
     others       = 2.

 if sy-subrc <> 0.
   ls_message-severity = 'E'.
   ls_message-text     = 'Read ZUI5_ABS_TYPE failed'.
 else.
   loop at lt_dd07v assigning <dd07v>.
     append initial line to <abs_types>
                        assigning <abs_type>.
     <abs_type>-abs_key  = <dd07v>-domvalue_l.
     <abs_type>-abs_text = <dd07v>-ddtext.
   endloop.
 endif.

 clear: lt_dd07v.
```

```
call function 'DDIF_DOMA_GET'
  exporting
    name          = 'ZUI5_STATUS'
    langu         = sy-langu
  tables
    dd07v_tab     = lt_dd07v
  exceptions
    illegal_input = 1
    others        = 2.

if sy-subrc <> 0.
  ls_message-severity = 'E'.
  ls_message-text     = 'Read ZUI5_ABS_TYPE failed'.
else.
  loop at lt_dd07v assigning <dd07v>.
    append initial line to <stats>
                          assigning <stat>.
    <stat>-status_key = <dd07v>-domvalue_l.
    <stat>-status_text = <dd07v>-ddtext.
  endloop.
endif.

if not ls_message is initial.
  create object lo_json
    exporting
      data = ls_message.
else.
  create object lo_json
    exporting
      data = ls_approval.
endif.
lo_json->serialize( ).
ev_json = lo_json->get_data( ).
```

Listing 10.6 Method GET_APPROVAL

Method SET_APPROVAL

SET_APPROVAL   The method SET_APPROVAL sets the status of the request according to the decision in the approval app to status 02 (approved) or 03 (rejected); see Listing 10.7.

```abap
data: lt_query_string    type tihttpnvp,
      ls_abs             type zui5_absence,
      lv_update          type abap_bool,
      lo_json            type ref to zui5_json_serializer,
      ls_message         type s_message.
field-symbols: <ls_query> type ihttpnvp.

io_request->get_form_fields(
          changing fields = lt_query_string ).

loop at lt_query_string assigning <ls_query>.
  <ls_query>-name = to_upper( val = <ls_query>-name ).
  case <ls_query>-name.
    when 'REQ_ID'.
      if not <ls_query>-value is initial.
        ls_abs-req_id  = <ls_query>-value.
        lv_update = abap_true.
      endif.
    when 'STATUS'.
      ls_abs-status = <ls_query>-value.
  endcase.
endloop.

if lv_update = abap_true.
  update zui5_absence set status = ls_abs-status
                    where req_id = ls_abs-req_id.
endif.

if sy-subrc = 0.
  ls_message-severity = 'S'.
  ls_message-text     = 'Request successfully changed'.
else.
  ls_message-severity = 'E'.
  ls_message-text     = 'Data was not changed'.
endif.

create object lo_json
  exporting
    data = ls_message.
lo_json->serialize( ).
ev_json = lo_json->get_data( ).
```

Listing 10.7 Method SET_APPROVAL

Method GET_PICTURE

GET_PICTURE   The method GET_PICTURE loads the image of the relevant employee (see Listing 10.8).

```
data: lt_query_string    type tihttpnvp,
      lv_pic             type string,
      path               type string,
      lr_mime_rep        type ref to if_mr_api,
      content            type xstring,
      lo_json            type ref to zui5_json_serializer,
      ls_message         type s_message.
field-symbols: <ls_query> type ihttpnvp.

io_request->get_form_fields(
        changing fields = lt_query_string ).

loop at lt_query_string assigning <ls_query>.
  <ls_query>-name = to_upper( val = <ls_query>-name ).
  case <ls_query>-name.
    when 'IMG_PATH'.
      lv_pic  = <ls_query>-value.
  endcase.
endloop.

if not lv_pic is initial.
 es_file-file_name = lv_pic.
 path = |SAP/EMPLOYEE/{ lv_pic }|.

lr_mime_rep = cl_mime_repository_api=>if_mr_api~get_api( ).
   lr_mime_rep->get(
      exporting
        i_url                = path
        i_check_authority    = abap_false
      importing
        e_content            = es_file-file_content
        e_mime_type          = es_file-file_type
      exceptions
        parameter_missing    = 1
        error_occured        = 2
        not_found            = 3
        permission_failure   = 4
        others               = 5
```

```
          ).

    if sy-subrc <> 0.
      ls_message-severity = 'W'.
      ls_message-text      = 'Read from MIME failed'.
    else.
      ls_message-severity = 'S'.
      ls_message-text      = 'Image loaded'.
    endif.
  else.
    ls_message-severity = 'S'.
    ls_message-text      = 'Image not found'.
  endif.

  create object lo_json
    exporting
      data = ls_message.
  lo_json->serialize( ).
  ev_json = lo_json->get_data( ).
```

Listing 10.8 Method GET_PICTURE

HTTP Handler

Finally, you have to add the new application mobile to the HTTP handler. To do so, go to the class ZUI5_HTTP_HANDLER, and add the application to the case statement, as shown in Listing 10.9.

Extending HTTP handler

```
    case <ls_query>-value.
"  ...
      when 'mobile'.
        zui5_mobile=>handle_request(
          exporting
            io_request = server->request
          importing
            es_file    = ls_file
            ev_json    = lv_json
              ).
"  ...
```

Listing 10.9 HTTP Handler

You've now provided all services for the approval app in the backend, and we can start the SAPUI5 implementation.

10.4.2 Frontend Implementation

MVC pattern   Let's implement this example according to the MVC pattern. In Eclipse, create the project ZUI5_APPROVAL with MOBILE as the target device, and select the CREATE AN INITIAL VIEW checkbox (see Figure 10.12).

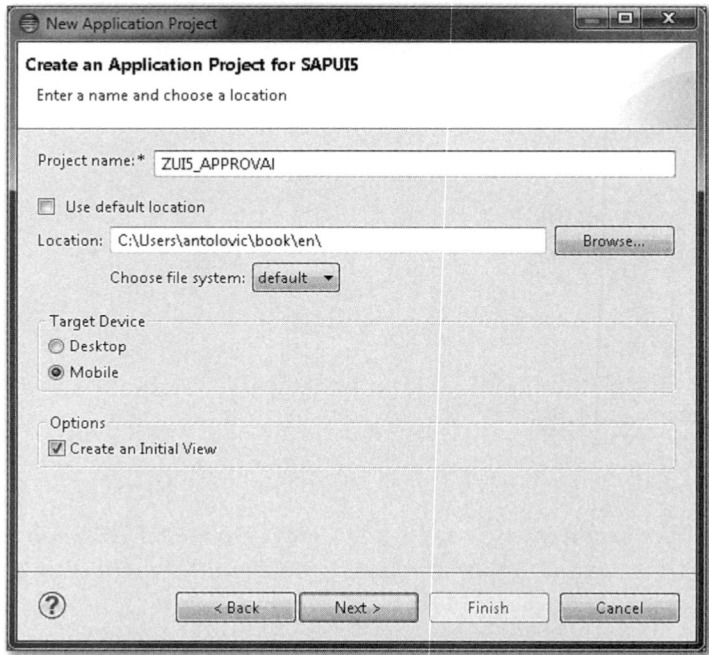

Figure 10.12 Approval App

Name the first view "App," and confirm your selection by clicking FINISH.

Basic Structure

App view   The App view assumes control of the application. Because this application is primarily designed for tablets, use the SplitApp control with the master view INBOX and the detail view APPROVE. Before selecting an entry from the list of open requests, an empty view is displayed on the right-hand side in the detail view; name this view "Empty."

Use the context menu of the project to create the views named "Inbox," "Approve," and "Empty," so that you have a directory structure as in Figure 10.13.

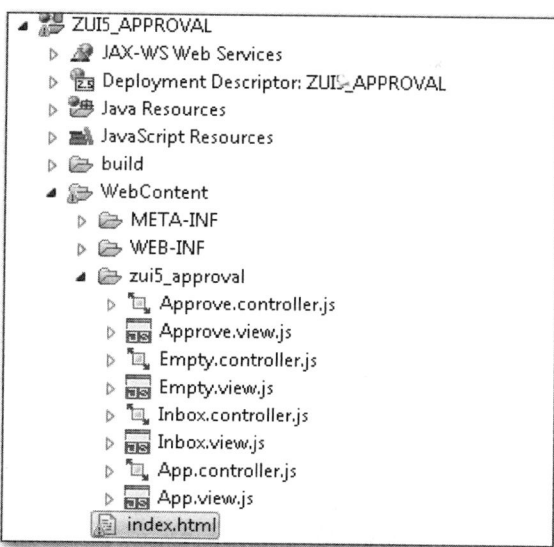

Figure 10.13 Directory Structure

As shown in Section 10.3.4, the SplitApp control consists of a master view and a detail view. In the App view, create the SplitApp control, and assign the Inbox view to the master pane and the Empty view to the details pane. For *app.view.js*, this results in the content of Listing 10.10.

app.view.js

```
createContent : function(oController) {
  // SplitApp-Control
  this.app = new sap.m.SplitApp({
  // Close master view if
  // branching to detail view
  afterDetailNavigate: function(){
    this.hideMaster();
  }
});

  // Empty view as detail
  this.app.addDetailPage(sap.ui.jsview(
      "zui5_approval.Approve",
```

```
        "zui5_approval.Empty")));

    // Inbox view as master
    this.app.addMasterPage(sap.ui.jsview(
        "zui5_approval.Inbox",
        "zui5_approval.Inbox")));

    // Important: address the master pane last
    // because only one of the two sides
    // is displayed on smartphones
    this.app.toDetail("zui5_approval.Empty");
    this.app.toMaster("zui5_approval.Inbox");

    // Return control
    return this.app;
  }
});
```
Listing 10.10 App View

Master view   When developing applications for mobile devices, you must always remember that a different resolution, and thus a different display, results for smartphones or tablets. For this reason, you must assign the master pane last when assigning the panes. This ensures that the master view is displayed first on a smartphone.

To enable you to test the application, add the code from Listing 10.11 to the Empty view and the Approve view. For now, assign only one title, "Master view" to the Inbox view and "Detail view" to the Empty view.

```
  return new sap.m.Page({
    title: "Detail view", // and "Master view"
    content: []
  });
```
Listing 10.11 Detail View and Master View

Upload the page to the SAP system, and view the result in the browser. As a result, the two screen areas should be displayed with their respective headings (see Figure 10.14).

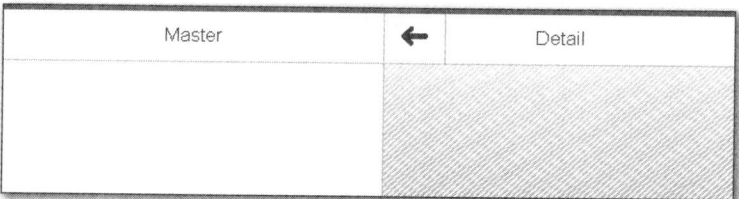

Figure 10.14 Split App

Inbox

Next, fill the Master view with the open requests from the SAP system; you obtain them via the method GET_APPROVAL. Use a list control from the *sap.m.* library to display the requests.

The GET_APPROVAL service is called in the Inbox controller. If the device is a tablet, the first entry in the list is selected automatically. For the onBeforeRendering function, this results in the content of Listing 10.12.

Controller

```
onBeforeRendering: function(){
  var oInbox = sap.ui.getCore().byId("inboxList");
  // Reset selection
  oInbox.removeSelections();
  // Load data from back end
  var oJSONDataModel =
    new sap.ui.model.json.JSONModel(
      "/ui5/?application=mobile&area=get_approval"
      ).attachRequestCompleted("", function(){
        // Select first entry immediately for
        // tablet
        if (!jQuery.device.is.phone){
          var aNavItems = oInbox.getItems();
            if (aNavItems.length > 0){
              oInbox.setSelectedItem(aNavItems[0]);
              aNavItems[0].fireTap();
            }
      }});
  // Bind model to core
  sap.ui.getCore().setModel(oJSONDataModel);
},
```

Listing 10.12 onBeforeRendering Function

In the view, the event object is transferred via the function `onBeforeFirst-`
`Show` (see Listing 10.15). You can therefore access the binding context of
the view directly in the controller. In the `onBeforeFirstShow` function,
the `bindListData` function is called (see Listing 10.13).

```
onBeforeFirstShow: function(oEvent){
  this.bindListData();
    if(oEvent.data.title){
      this.getView().page.setTitle(oEvent.data.title);
    }
},
```

Listing 10.13   onBeforeFirstShow Function

bindListData In the `bindListData` function, the binding to the list control is done via
a factory function. This function is executed once for each element in
the path /absence. As a result, each list item is mapped with the return
value of this function (see Listing 10.14).

```
bindListData: function(aFilters){
  // Remember "this" context
  var that = this;
  // Binding
  this.getView().oList.bindAggregation("items", {
    path: "/absence",
    factory: function(sId){
      return new sap.m.StandardListItem(sId, {
        icon: "img/Date.png",
        title: {
          path:"username",
          // Combine first name last name
            formatter: function(name){
            var oProperty =
                    this.getModel().getProperty("/address");
            for (var i=0; i<oProperty.length; i++){
              if (oProperty[i].username == name)
              return oProperty[i].firstname + " " +
              oProperty[i].lastname;
              }}},
        description: {
          path:"type",
          // Read the description for the type key
          formatter: function(type){
```

```
                var oProperty =
                        this.getModel().getProperty("/abs_type");
                for (var i=0; i<oProperty.length; i++){
                  if (oProperty[i].abs_key == type)
                    return oProperty[i].abs_text;
                  }
                }
            },
            // Set the type of the items
            // Telephone ->  Type Navigation
            // Tablet -> Type None
              type: jQuery.device.is.phone?
                sap.m.ListType.Navigation : sap.m.ListType.None,
            customData: [
              //Save REQ-ID as custom data
              new sap.ui.core.CustomData({
                key: "req_id",
                value: "{req_id}"
            }),
            ],
            // "Tap" event for mobile devices
              tap: [that.onListItemTap, that]
            });
          },
        filters: aFilters
    });
  },
});
```

Listing 10.14 bindListData Function

Now, add the list display to the Inbox view by transferring the list control View
to the page control as content. Make sure that you use the same ID as in
the controller (inboxList; see Listing 10.12). For the event navButtonTap
of the page control, you also transfer the controller object. As a result,
you change the context from the event object to the controller object and
can thus access the controller object directly with this in the controller
function. For the view, this results in the content of Listing 10.15.

```
onBeforeFirstShow: function(oEvent){
   this.getController().onBeforeFirstShow(oEvent);
},
createContent : function(oController) {
```

```
// New list control
this.oList = new sap.m.List("inboxList",{
  mode: jQuery.device.is.phone ?
  sap.m.ListMode.None : sap.m.ListMode.SingleSelectMaster,
});

// Add list control to page
this.page = new sap.m.Page({
  title: "Open requests",
  navButtonTap: [oController.onNavButtonTap, oController],
  content: [this.oList]
});

// Return page
return this.page;
}

});
```

Listing 10.15 Inbox View

Upload the page to the SAP system, and view the result in the browser. As a result, a list of open requests should be displayed in the Master pane (see Figure 10.15).

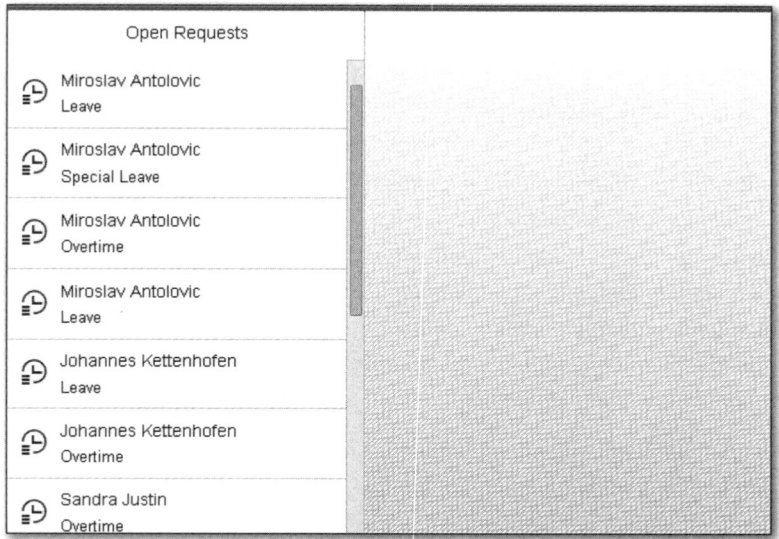

Figure 10.15 List of Open Requests

If you view the page using the Ripple plug-in, you will notice that only the list (Master view) is displayed in a smartphone.

Navigation

Next, we have to deal with navigation. If an entry is selected from the list of requests, information about this request should be displayed in the Detail pane. The easiest way to implement the navigation is with EventBus (`sap.ui.core.EventBus`). This class provides versatile options for the registration and management of events. In order to navigate between the pages, we have to register two events with EventBus, one for forward navigation and one for backward navigation. Furthermore, we have to implement the two functions for forward navigation (`NavTo`) and backward navigation (`NavBack`). In the `onInit` function of the app controller, the `EventBus` is first initialized and the relevant events are registered (see Listing 10.16).

EventBus

```
onInit : function() {
// Initialize EventBus
var that = this;
this.oEventBus = sap.ui.getCore().getEventBus();
this.oEventBus.subscribe("nav", "to", this.navTo, this);
this.oEventBus.subscribe("nav", "back", this.navBack, this);
this.oEventBus.subscribe(
  "app",
  "mode",
  function(sChannelId, sEventId, oData){
    this.getView().app.setMode(oData.mode);
}, this);

jQuery.sap.require("jquery.sap.history");
jQuery.sap.history({
  routes: [{
  path: "page",
  handler: function(params, navType) {
  if (!params || !params.id) {
  jQuery.sap.log.error("Invalid parameter: " + params);
   } else {
  that.oEventBus.publish("nav", "to", {
    viewId: params.id,
    navType: navType
  });
```

435

```
}}}],
  defaultHandler: function(navType) {
    that.oEventBus.publish("nav", "to", {
    viewId: "zui5_approval.Inbox",
    navType: navType
  });
 }});
},
```

Listing 10.16 onInit Function

Because we store the navigation in *jQuery.sap.history*, we can use the
function jQuery.sap.history.back(); for the back navigation. For the
navBack function, this results in the content of Listing 10.17.

```
navBack : function(sChannelId, sEventId, oData) {
  jQuery.sap.history.back();
},
```

Listing 10.17 navBack Function

navTo function In the navTo function, the two methods toMaster and toDetail of the
SplitApp control are used to navigate to the relevant page (see Listing
10.18).

```
navTo : function(sChannelId, sEventId, oData) {
var app = this.getView().app,
  sViewName = oData.viewName,
  sViewId = oData.viewId,
  oDataObject = oData.data,
  sNavType = oData.navType,
  oView;

if(!sViewId){ sViewId = sViewName;}

var bMaster = (sViewId.indexOf("zui5_approval.") !== -1);

if (sNavType === jQuery.sap.history.NavType.Back) {
  if(bMaster){ app.backMaster(); }
} else {
  if (!sap.ui.getCore().byId(sViewId)) {
    oView = sap.ui.jsview(sViewId, sViewName);
    (bMaster) ?
      app.addMasterPage(oView) : app.addDetailPage(oView);
```

```
    }
    (bMaster) ?
    app.toMaster(
      sViewId, oDataObject
        ) : app.toDetail(sViewId, oDataObject);
  }
// Write history entry
if (!sNavType && (bMaster || jQuery.device.is.phone)) {
  jQuery.sap.history.addHistory("page", {id: sViewId}, false);
}}});
```

Listing 10.18 navTo Function

Next, you can register the event when selecting an item in the Inbox view and process the event in the Inbox controller. Depending on the device, either the event onListSelect or onListItemTap is triggered. For this reason, you have to consider both events in your controller. Now, add the functions from Listing 10.19 to the Inbox controller.

Processing events

```
onListSelect: function(oEvent){
  var oBindingContext =
    oEvent.getParameter("listItem").getBindingContext(),

    sViewId = "detailApprove_" +
              oEvent.getParameter(
              "listItem").data("req_id");
  // Transfer event to EventBus
  sap.ui.getCore().getEventBus().publish("nav", "to", {
      viewName: "zui5_approval.Approve",
      viewId: sViewId,
      data: {
          bindingContext: oBindingContext
      }
  });
},


onListItemTap: function(oEvent){
  var oBindingContext =
    oEvent.oSource.getBindingContext(),

  sViewId = "detailApprove_" +
            oEvent.oSource.data("req_id");
  sap.ui.getCore().getEventBus().publish("nav", "to", {
```

```
        viewName: "zui5_approval.Approve",
        viewId: sViewId,
        data: {
            bindingContext: oBindingContext
        }
    });
},

//Navigation back
onNavButtonTap: function(){
    sap.ui.getCore().getEventBus().publish("nav", "back");
    },
```

Listing 10.19 Inbox Controller

onListSelect   In the Inbox view, you only have to extend the list control and call the function onListSelect from the controller when selecting an entry (see Listing 10.20).

```
// New list control
this.oList = new sap.m.List("inboxList",{
    mode: jQuery.device.is.phone ?
    sap.m.ListMode.None : sap.m.ListMode.SingleSelectMaster,
    select: [oController.onListSelect, oController]
});
```

Listing 10.20 Inbox View

Approval Page

Approve view   When designing the actual approval page, the details of the leave request, a selected calendar, details about the applicant, and the applicant's image are displayed. A Carousel control can also be used to navigate to a second page on which all open requests of the relevant person are displayed. In the approve view, first create the Calendar control in which the days to be approved are color coded (see Listing 10.21).

```
onBeforeFirstShow: function(oEvent){
    this.getController().onBeforeFirstShow(oEvent);
},
createContent : function(oController) {
// Format date
oDateType = new sap.ui.model.type.DateTime(
    {source: {pattern: "yyyyMMdd"},
```

```
        pattern: "MM.DD.YYYY"
    });

//Calendar control
this.oCalendar = new sap.me.Calendar();
this.oCalendar.setEnableMultiselection(false);
this.oCalendar.setSingleRow(false);
this.oCalendar.setMonthsToDisplay(2);
this.oCalendar.setWeeksPerRow(1);
this.oCalendar.setFirstDayOffset(1);
this.oCalendar.setMonthsPerRow(2);
this.oCalendar.setDayHeight(30);
```

Listing 10.21 Calendar Control

A small form with information about the duration of the request and the applicant is then displayed (see Listing 10.22). This example was shortened; you can download the complete listing from the book's web page.

Request duration and applicant

```
this.oLayoutLeaveRequest =
new sap.ui.layout.form.SimpleForm({
  maxContainerCols : 2,
  content : [
   new sap.ui.commons.Title({text: "Leave Request: "}),
   new sap.m.Label({ text: "Begin" }),
   new sap.m.Text({ text: {path:"start_date",
                   type: oDateType} }),
   new sap.m.Label({ text: "End" }),
   new sap.m.Text({ text: {path:"end_date",
                     type:oDateType} }),
   new sap.ui.commons.Title({ text: "Calendar"}),
   this.oCalendar,
   new sap.ui.commons.Title({text: "Applicant:" }),
   new sap.m.Label({ text: 'Name' }),
   new sap.m.Text({ text: { path:"username",
                   formatter: function (username){
        try{
    var oProperty = this.getModel().getProperty("/address");
        for (var i=0; i<oProperty.length; i++){
        if (oProperty[i].username == username)
          return oProperty[i].title_p + " "+
          oProperty[i].firstname + " "+
          oProperty[i].lastname;
        }}
      catch(e){} }}
```

```
                   }),
               new sap.ui.commons.Image({
                 src : {
                   path:"username",
                   formatter: function (username){
                     try{
          var oProperty = this.getModel().getProperty("/address");
                     for (var i=0;i<oProperty.length;i++){
                       if (oProperty[i].username == username)
                         return "/ui5/?application=mobile&area=get_
picture&img_path="  +
 oProperty[i].img_path;
                       }}
                   catch(e){}
                 }},
             height : '200px'
           }),
]
});
this.oBox =   new sap.m.VBox({
  items:[ this.oLayoutLeaveRequest ]
});
```

Listing 10.22   Form with Additional Information on the Request

Carousel control

In addition, all open requests of the relevant person are summarized in a list control and are displayed together with the form from Listing 10.22 in a Carousel control (see Listing 10.23).

```
this.oList = new sap.m.List(this.createId("DetailList"),
  { headerText : "Open requests of person",
    mode: jQuery.device.is.phone ?
    sap.m.ListMode.None : sap.m.ListMode.SingleSelectMaster,
    select: [oController.onListSelect, oController]
});


// Carousel control
this.oCarousel = new sap.m.Carousel({
  pages: [
    this.oBox, // Request
    this.oList // List of requests
  ]
});
```

Listing 10.23   Carousel Control

Finally, the footer with the two buttons REJECT and APPROVE is implemented and returned along with the Carousel control as a page. However, the Carousel control prevents the scrollbar from functioning, and you thus have to adjust the page design for smartphones. Use the Carousel control only if the device is not a smartphone. In the two functions, approve and decline, you use the customData attribute to transfer the ID of the approval request (see Listing 10.24).

Approve and decline

```
// Navigation
this.oFooter = new sap.m.Bar({
    contentRight: [
      new sap.m.Button({
        text : "Approve",
        icon : "sap-icon://accept",
        press : oController.approve,
        customData : [
              new sap.ui.core.CustomData({
                key:"id",
                value:"{req_id}"})
          ]
      }),
      new sap.m.Button({
        text : "Reject",
        icon : "sap-icon://decline",
        press : oController.decline,
        customData : [
              new sap.ui.core.CustomData({
                key:"id",
                value:"{req_id}"})
          ]
    }) ]
  });
// Carousel does not allow scrolling on smartphone
if (jQuery.device.is.phone){
  return this.page = new sap.m.Page({
    content: [ this.oLayoutLeaveRequest ],
    footer:  this.oFooter
  });
} else {
  return this.page = new sap.m.Page({
    content: [ this.oCarousel ],
    footer: this.oFooter
  });
```

```
    }
  }
});
```
Listing 10.24 Buttons and Page Layout

Approve controller
On the one hand, the binding of data must be carried out in the approve controller; on the other hand, the functions `approve` and `reject` require the `SET_APPROVAL` function to be called in the backend. Because you have also transferred the event object via the `onBeforeFirstShow` function in the Approve view (see Listing 10.21), you can access the binding context directly in the controller. In this function, the `markLeave` function for selecting the days in the calendar is called and a filter is applied to the user names for the Detail list. For the `onBeforeFirstShow` function, this results in the content of Listing 10.25.

```
onBeforeFirstShow: function(oEvent){
if(oEvent.data.bindingContext){
  // Set binding context
this.getView().page.setBindingContext(
                    oEvent.data.bindingContext);
  // Select entry in the calendar
  this.markLeave(oEvent.data.bindingContext);
  var oLeave = this.getView().getModel().getProperty(
      oEvent.data.bindingContext.getPath());
  // Filter on user name
  var oFilter1 = new sap.ui.model.Filter (
      "username",
      sap.ui.model.FilterOperator.EQ,
      oLeave.username);
  // Fill Detail list
  this.bindListData(oFilter1);
}
},
```
Listing 10.25 onBeforeFirstShow Function

bindListData function
The `bindListData` function fills the Detail list with the open requests of the person based on the filter on the user name (see Listing 10.26).

```
bindListData: function(aFilters){
  var that = this;
  this.getView().oList.bindAggregation("items", {
    path: "/absence",
```

```
  factory: function(sId){
    return new sap.m.StandardListItem(sId, {
      title: { parts : [{
          path : "start_date",
          type : new sap.ui.model.type.DateTime({
            source: {pattern: "yyyyMMdd"},
            pattern: "MM.DD.YYYY' - '"})
          },{
          path : "end_date",
          type: new sap.ui.model.type.DateTime({
            source: {pattern: "yyyyMMdd"},
            pattern: "MM.DD.YYYY"})
          } ] },
      description: {
        path:"type",
        formatter: function(type){
          var oProperty =
          this.getModel().getProperty("/abs_type");
          for (var i=0; i<oProperty.length; i++){
            if (oProperty[i].abs_key == type)
                return oProperty[i].abs_text;
          }}},
      type: jQuery.device.is.phone?
          sap.m.ListType.Navigation : sap.m.ListType.None,
      customData: [ new sap.ui.core.CustomData({
                    key: "req_id",
                    value: "{req_id}"
                    }),
                ],
      tap: [that.onListItemTap, that]
    });
  },
  filters: aFilters
  });
},
```

Listing 10.26 bindListData Function

The markLeave function selects the days in the calendar on the page, and the calendar display is centered around the date (see Listing 10.27).

markLeave function

```
markLeave: function(context){
    try{
    var oCalendar = this.getView().oCalendar;
```

443

```
        // Read context
        var oData =
                    sap.ui.getCore().getModel().getProperty(
                                    context.getPath()
                    );
        // Create date object
        var dFrom = new Date(oData.start_date.slice(0, 4),
                Number(oData.start_date.slice(4, 6))-1,
                oData.start_date.slice(6, 8));
        var dTo = new Date(oData.end_date.slice(0, 4),
                Number(oData.end_date.slice(4, 6))-1,
                oData.end_date.slice(6, 8));
        var dInit = new Date();

        // Init sets the calendar to +30 days.
        // Thus the calendar is centered around the request date
        dInit.setTime(dFrom.getTime()+ 30 * 24 * 60 * 60 * 1000);

        // Selected calendar for specified period
        oCalendar.toggleDatesRangeSelection(dFrom,dTo,true);
        //Set selection on selected fields
        oCalendar.toggleDatesType(oCalendar.getSelectedDates(),
            sap.me.CalendarEventType.Type01, true);
        //Deselect the selection
        oCalendar.unselectAllDates();
        oCalendar.setCurrentDate(dInit);
        }catch(E){}
    },
```

Listing 10.27   markLeave Function

Status change   The two functions approve and decline set the status of the request to *approved* (status 02) or to *rejected* (status 03). Because the status change in the backend is handled via the same method, SET_APPROVAL, you can combine these two calls in one function (see Listing 10.28).

```
approve: function(oEvent){
  this.process(oEvent, "02");
},

decline: function(oEvent){
  this.process(oEvent, "03");
},
```

```
process: function(oEvent, status){
// ID is transferred as Custom data.
  var sId = oEvent.getSource().data("id");
// Parameter for AJAX
  var oParameters= { "req_id" :    sId,
                     "status":     status,
                   };
//Ajax to back end
$.ajax({
  url :
  "/ui5/index.html?application=mobile&area=set_approval",
  contentType : "application/json",
  dataType : 'json',
  data: oParameters,
  success : function(data, textStatus, jqXHR) {
   // Display dialog box for success
     var oDialog = new sap.m.Dialog({
      rightButton: new sap.m.Button({
         text: "OK",
         press: function(){this.oParent.close();}
        }),
       content: [ new sap.m.Label({ text: data.text }) ]
       });

// When closing the dialog, the inbox is recreated
   oDialog.attachAfterClose( "",
    function(oEvent){
     var oInbox = sap.ui.getCore().byId("inboxList");
     oInbox.removeSelections();
     var oJSONDataModel =
     new sap.ui.model.json.JSONModel(
        "/ui5/?application=mobile&area=get_approval"
        ).attachRequestCompleted(
        "",
         function(){
          var aNavItems = oInbox.getItems();
          if (aNavItems.length > 0){
          sap.ui.getCore().byId(
                "inboxList"
                ).setSelectedItem(aNavItems[0]);
              aNavItems[0].fireTap();
           }
         });
```

445

```
                        sap.ui.getCore().setModel(oJSONDataModel);
                          });
                        oDialog.open();
                      }
                  });
             },
```

Listing 10.28 Approving or Rejecting Leave Request

Navigation The three functions onListSelect, onListItemTap, and onNavButtonTap for navigation on the page are still missing (see Listing 10.29).

```
onListSelect: function(oEvent){
  if (!jQuery.device.is.phone){
    // Reset Carousel
    var aPages = this.getView().oCarousel.getPages();
    this.getView().oCarousel.setActivePage(aPages[0].sId);
  }
  var oBindingContext = oEvent.getParameter(
      "listItem").getBindingContext();

  var sViewId = "detailApprove_" +
               oEvent.getParameter(
               "listItem").data("req_id");

  sap.ui.getCore().getEventBus().publish(
    "nav", "to", {viewName: "zui5_approval.Approve",
               viewId: sViewId,
               data: { bindingContext: oBindingContext }
  });
},
onListItemTap: function(oEvent){
 if (!jQuery.device.is.phone){
 // Reset Carousel
 var aPages = this.getView().oCarousel.getPages();
 this.getView().oCarousel.setActivePage(aPages[0].sId);
 }
 var oBindingContext = oEvent.oSource.getBindingContext();

  var sViewId = "detailApprove_" +
               oEvent.oSource.data("req_id");

  sap.ui.getCore().getEventBus().publish(
```

```
    "nav", "to", {viewName: "zui5_approval.Approve",
            viewId: sViewId,
            data: { bindingContext: oBindingContext }
  });
},

onNavButtonTap: function(){
  // is executed if the Hardware button
  // or the Back button is pressed
  sap.ui.getCore().getEventBus().publish( "nav", "back");
}
```

Listing 10.29 Page Navigation

The Completed Application

Start the application in the Chrome browser, and view the result in the Ripple emulator (see Figure 10.16).

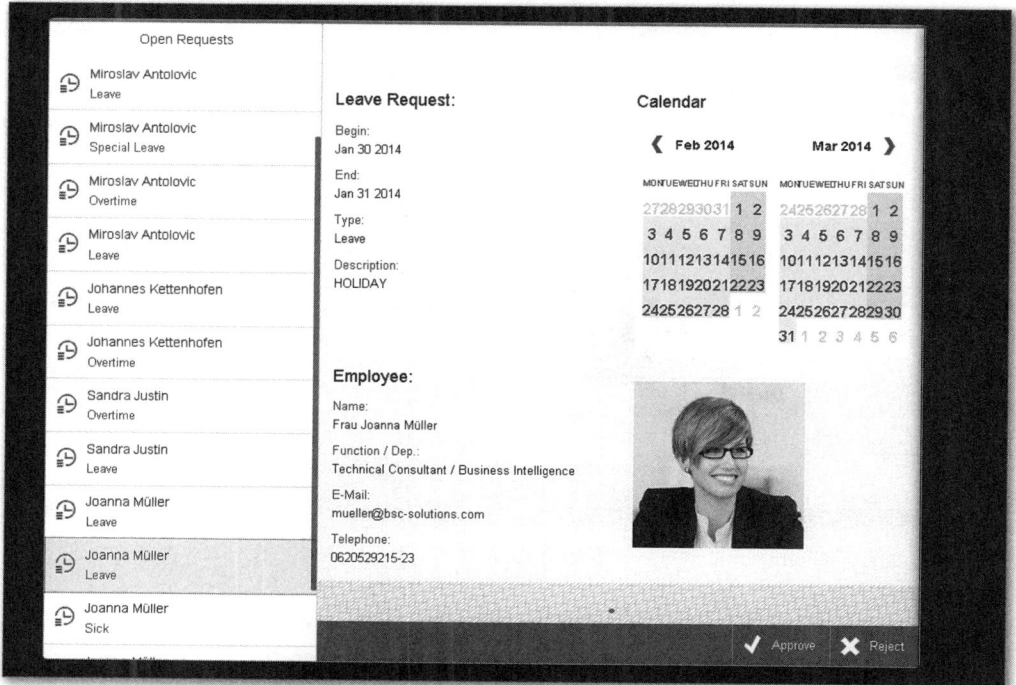

Figure 10.16 Approval App on Tablet

Implementation
in the various
systems

When you call the app, the Inbox with the open approvals is displayed on the left-hand side as expected. You can see the details of the selected request in the middle section. The Carousel control displays the typical points in the Detail list. From these points, the user recognizes that he has to swipe to navigate to the next page. In the toolbar, you will see the two buttons for approving or rejecting the request. In the implementation, we have specified that the Back button is not to be displayed on tablets. If you now simulate swiping with the mouse in the browser (click, hold the mouse button, and slide to the left), you will reach the next page with the open requests of the relevant person (see Figure 10.17).

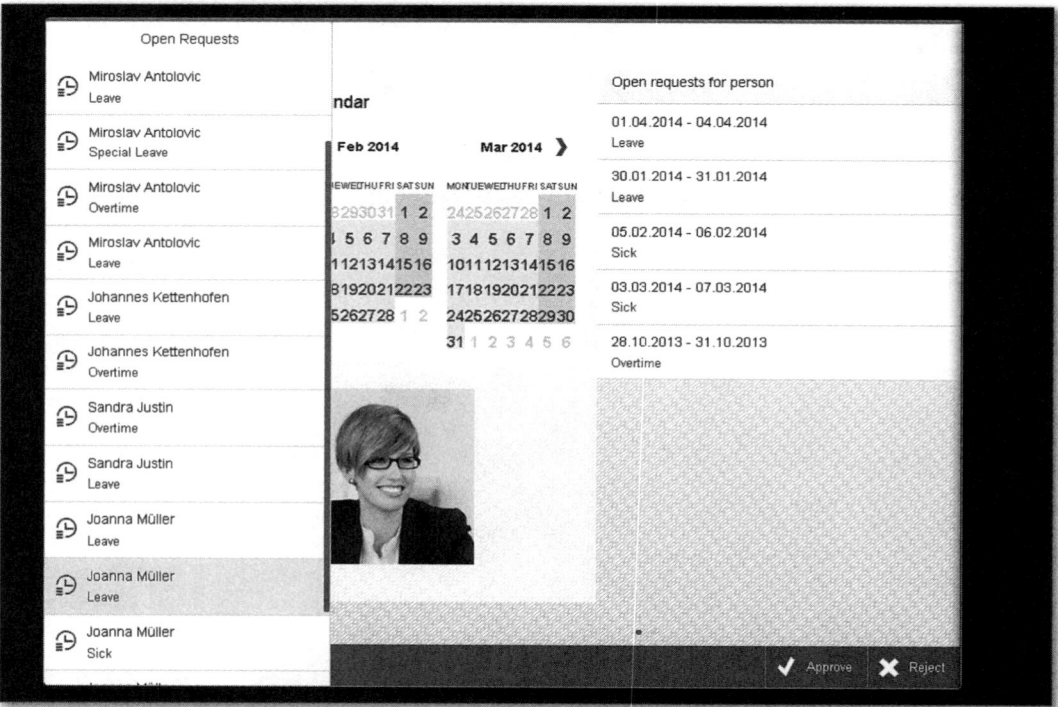

Figure 10.17 Swiping to Next Page

If you look at the app in a smartphone view, however (see Figure 10.18), you'll notice the following:

▶ Only the Inbox is displayed when loading the list.

▶ There is a Back button on the actual approval page.

▶ The Carousel control is not displayed.

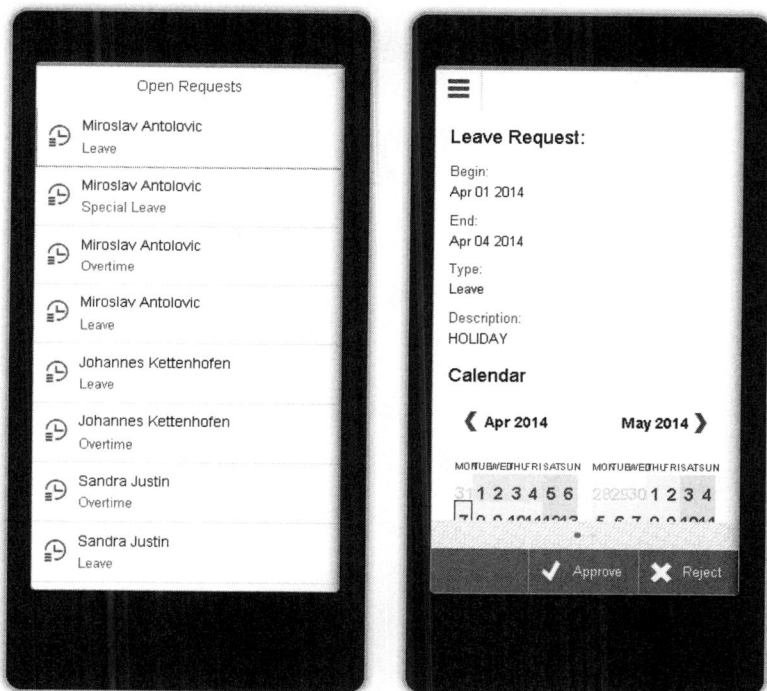

Figure 10.18 Smartphone View

In this chapter, you learned about the world of SAPUI5 development for mobile devices. You were shown that although the development of mobile applications involves some pitfalls, it's still possible to develop an appealing app with relatively little effort.

You should always pay particular attention to the variety of different devices for implementation. Here, the Ripple plug-in is ideal because you can simulate many devices with it. Fortunately, it's possible to determine devices using the jQuery.device.is functions, and navigation can also be very easily controlled by the EventBus class.

A look ahead   Returning to the quote from Galileo Galilei in the introduction, the hope
is that this book has helped you to discover the possibilities of SAPUI5
for yourself.

You have developed two excellent applications—the employee portal
and the approval app—but they are far from finished. Consider our joint
implementation Version 1.0. It's now your turn to develop Version 2.0,
and to enjoy doing so!

A   Further Sources of Information

A.1   Links

- *www.w3schools.com*

  Tutorials on HTML, CSS, and JavaScript

- *www.w3.org*

  Home page of the W3C

- *http://de.selfhtml.org/*

  Language reference for HTML, CSS, and JavaScript

- *http://scn.sap.com/community/developer-center/front-end*

  SAPUI5 in SAP Community Network

- *http://sap.github.io/openui5/*

  OpenUI5 initiative of SAP

- *http://help.sap.com/hana/SAP_HANA_Developer_Guide_en.pdf*

  SAP HANA Developer Guide

- *https://sapui5.netweaver.ondemand.com/sdk/*

  SAPUI5 Demo Kit

A.2   SAP Notes

- SAPUI5 Installation Guide

  Note 1747308 (Installation Guide: UI Development Toolkit for HTML5 [SAPUI5])

- SAP Gateway Installation Guide

  1569624 (Installation/Delta Upgrade of SAP Gateway 2.0)

A.3 Books

A.3.1 HTML

▶ Peter Müller, *Einstieg in CSS—Webseiten gestalten mit HTML und CSS*
(Bonn, Germany: Galileo Press GmbH, 2013). Available in German language only.

▶ Clemens Gull and Stefan Münz, *HTML5 Handbuch*
(Bonn, Germany: Franzis Verlag GmbH, 2011). Available in German language only.

A.3.2 JavaScript

▶ Thomas Theis, *Einstieg in JavaScript*
(Bonn, Germany: Galileo Press GmbH, 2013). Available in German language only.

▶ Christian Wenz, *JavaScript—Das umfassende Handbuch*
(Bonn, Germany: Galileo Press GmbH, 2014). Available in German language only.

▶ Christian Wenz, *JavaScript and AJAX*
(Bonn, Germany: Galileo Press GmbH, 2007).

A.3.3 jQuery

▶ Frank Bongers and Maximilian Vollendorf, *jQuery—Das Praxisbuch*
(Bonn, Germany: Galileo Press GmbH, 2013). Available in German language only.

▶ Carsten Bönnen, Volker Drees, André Fischer, Ludwig Heinz, and Karsten Strothmann, *OData and SAP NetWeaver Gateway*
(Boston, MA: SAP PRESS, 2014).

A.3.4 SAP HANA

▶ Thorsten Schneider, Eric Westenberger, and Hermann Gahm, *ABAP Development for SAP HANA*
(Boston, MA: SAP PRESS, 2014).

B   The Author

Miroslav Antolovic works as an SAP developer and trainer at bsc solutions GmbH & Co. KG. He studied Pharmacy at the University of Heidelberg and worked as a Java and web developer. In 1999, he started as an application developer in Product Lifecycle Management at SAP AG, and in 2004 he moved to REALTECH AG, where he developed SAP add-on products. From 2007 onwards, he worked as Head of SAP Development at SEEBURGER AG, until he finally moved to bsc solutions in 2010. You can contact Miroslav Antolovic at the following email address: *antolovic@bsc-solutions.com*.

Index

$expand, 368
$filter, 368
$format, 368
$orderby, 368
$select, 368
$skip, 368
$top, 368
<div> tag, 28
.properties file, 171
.xsaccess, 389
.xsapp, 389

A

ABAP in Eclipse, 112, 113
AbsoluteLayout control, 225
Accordion, 268
  control, 340, 342
  section, 342
Adapting CSS, 199
addStyleClass, 199
Aggregation binding, 175, 176, 341
AJAX, 97, 212, 244
  asynchronous processing, 99
  call, 246
  parameter transfer, 216
  readyState, 99
  SAP backend, 246
  synchronous processing, 99
AJAX() object, 101
A Link, 253, 256
Analytical authorization, 395
Analytic view, 400
AND operator, 62
API
  documentation, 132
  reference, 221
ApplicationHeader, 268
Application Header control, 270
Application, mobile, 276
Architecture pattern, 126

Assigning authorization, 398
Assignment operator, 61
Asynchronous JavaScript and XML ->
  see AJAX, 97
AutoComplete, 259, 260

B

Binding, 170
bindListData, 432, 442
Blue Crystal, 408
Boolean values, 59
Bootstrap, 150
BorderLayout control, 233
Browser, 19
  developer tools, 48, 199, 297
BSP application, 146
BusinessCard control, 277
Button, 253, 254

C

Calculation view, 393, 399
Calendar control, 276, 340
CalendarLegend control, 340
Carousel, 269
Chart, 275
  controls, 276
Checkbox, 259, 264, 319, 329
Class selector, 41
CL_HTTP_SERVER, 118
ComboBox, 259, 260, 261
Complex binding, 184
Constructor, 138, 222
  function, 134
Control
  your own, 278
Controller, 125, 127
Corporate design, 116
createContent, 140

CRUD operation, 173
CSS, 199
   hierarchy, 41
   parameters, 199
   selector, 42
   Sequence, 202
   specificity rule, 42
Custom control, 324, 331
CustomData attribute, 330

D

Database tunnel, 386
Data Binding
   JSON Model, 160
   OData Model, 160
   Resource Model, 160
   XML Model, 160
Data model, 358
Data Provider Class, 358
Data type, 191
Data typing, 191
Datejs, 327
DatePicker, 259, 261
   control, 331
DB tunnel, 385, 386
Demo kit, 107
Descendant selector, 41
Desktop target device, 132
Detail section, 418
DialogBox control, 290
Document body, 24
Document compatibility mode, 24
Document Object Model, 59
DOM, 59
   ContentLoaded, 87
   manipulation, 93
Dot notation, 90
DropdownBox, 259
   control, 261
Dropdown list, 260

E

Eclipse, 109
   code pattern, 134
   creating project, 127
   download, 109
   preview function, 137
   project Explorer, 146
ECMAScript, 47
EDMX file, 358
Element binding, 175, 179
Entity
   Data Model, 361
   set, 358, 362
   type, 358, 360, 361, 362
EPM demo scenario, 393
Event, 81, 91
   DOMContentLoaded, 87
   handler, 82
   listener, 83, 87, 135
   object, 82
   onAfterRendering, 131
   onBeforeRendering, 131
   onExit, 131
   onInit, 131
EventBus, 435
Events, 222
Extended Data Binding, 183
External resource, 327

F

Factory function, 87
fakeOS, 410
FileUpload, 259
FileUploader, 311
   control, 262
for loop, 329
Form, 236, 331
Formatted TextView, 253, 254
Formatter Class, 196
Formatting option, 192
FormContainer, 236
FormControl, 236
FormElement, 236

G

Gateway Service
  activate, 364
  error log, 371
  generate, 363
  query option, 368
  test, 364
GetEntitySet, 370
get_form_fields, 215
Google Maps, 302
GridLayout, 238
  singleColumn, 238
GUID, 185

H

HANDLE_REQUEST, 213, 118
HorizontalLayout control, 229
HTML
  control, 253, 254
  header area of document, 23
  headings tag, 25
  text markup, 29
  text paragraph, 26
  View, 129
HTTP
  communication, 212
  handler, 213
  request, 117
  status code, 100
HTTP_DISPATCH_REQUEST, 118

I

i18n, 171
ICF
  controller, 118
  node, 212, 245, 316
  service, 107
ICM, 118
  Monitor, 125
Icon, 316
ID selector, 41
if query, 62

Image control, 253, 255
Image Map, 253
  control, 255
Input help, 264
Installation SAPUI5, 106
Integer data type, 192
Internationalization, 171
Internet Communication Manager -> see
  ICM, 118

J

Java Runtime version
  JRE, 109
JavaScript
  event, 82, 83
  typeof, 62
  View, 129
JDBC, 173
Join node, 395
jQuery, 85
  AJAX() object, 101
  DOM manipulation, 93
  Dot notation, 90
  Event, 91
  Factory function, 87
  function, 95
  hasAttribute selector, 88
  Object, 87
  ready function, 87
  Selector, 87, 88
jQuery.device.is.desktop, 417
jQuery.device.is.phone, 417, 441
jQuery.device.is.tablet, 417
jQuery DOM manipulation -> see DOM
  manipulation, 93
jQuery event
  .bind, 93
  .blur, 93
  .change, 93
  .click, 93
  .dbclick, 93
  .hover, 93
  .keypress, 93
  .keyup, 93

jQuery event (Cont.)
  .mousemove, 93
  .on, 93
  library, 85
jQuery.support.touch, 417
JScript, 47
JSON, 162, 299
  Model, 162, 244, 260
  notation, 138
  relative path, 163
  response ABAP, 213
  View, 129

L

Label control, 253, 256
Language file, 171
Layout, 199, 225
LDML, 195
ListBox, 259
  control, 262
Local development, 145
Logon language, 173
Loose typing, 57

M

Master section, 418
MatrixLayout control, 230, 254
MenuBar, 269, 270
Method, 222
MIME Repository, 268, 316
Mobile application, 276
Mobile Visual Identity, 408
Model, 125, 126
Model Provider Class, 358
Model View Control architecture
  pattern -> see MVC architecture, 116
Model View Control -> see MVC, 116
Multipart segment, 265, 268
MVC, 116
  architecture pattern, 116, 126, 131, 289
  Controller, 127

MVC (Cont.)
  Model, 126
  Pattern, 127
  View, 126

N

Named binding, 183
NaN, 59
NavContainer, 414
Navigate event, 414
Negation operator, 62
NoteTaker control, 277
Notification bar, 274
Notifier control, 314
NOT operator, 313

O

OData, 173
  filter, 376
  Service, 174, 399
ODBC, 173
onAfterRendering, 304
onBeforeFirstShow, 432
Open Data Protocol, 173
OR operator, 62

P

Pane, 249
Panel control, 247
Parent-Child Binding, 179
parseFloat, 315, 318
PasswordField, 259
  control, 263
PhoneGap, 409
placeAt, 135
Point system, CSS weighting, 42
POST
  http, 215
Preview function, 206
Property binding, 175

R

RadioButton, 259, 263
Relational operator, 61
Renderer method, 279
Request, 117
Request object, 215
Rerender function, 311
Resource
    external, 327
    Model, 170
Response, 117
Responsive Layout, 240
    weighting, 240
Ripple Emulator, 407
RoadMap control, 272
RowRepeater, 269
    control, 297, 299
Runtime version, 154

S

SAP Fiori, 252
SAP Gateway, 174
    Data Model, 358
    Service Builder, 358
SAP HANA
    Aggregation node, 395
    Client, 385
    Developer Studio, 385
    hdbrole, 400
    OData service, 400
    Repository Package, 391
    Repository Workspace, 390
    SQL Console, 398
    Studio, 385
sap.m, 276, 408
sap.makit, 276
sap.m.App, 410, 412, 415
sap.m.Bar, 441
sap.m.Button, 415
sap.m.Carousel, 440
sap.me, 276
sap.me.Calendar, 341, 439
sap.me.CalendarEventType, 345
sap.me.CalendarLegend, 343

sap.m.List, 434, 440
sap.m.Page, 412, 415, 434, 441
sap.m.Slider, 415
sap.m.SplitApp, 429
sap.m.Text, 415
SAP NetWeaver Application Server
    ABAP, 117
sap.suite, 276
SAPUI5
    aggregation binding, 176
    API documentation, 132
    Application object, 131
    Application project, 127
    bindAggregation, 177
    bindProperty, 175
    Boolean variable (data type), 194
    bootstrap, 150
    Checking in, 146
    class, 154
    complex binding, 184
    component Tools IDE Plug-in, 113
    createContent, 140
    Custom control, 324
    data binding, 160
    data type, 191
    date (data type), 195
    debug mode, 154
    Demo Kit, 133
    determining language, 173
    element binding, 179
    embedding library, 154
    Event listener, 135
    extended data binding, 183
    floating-point number (data type),
        193
    HTML View, 129
    Installation, 106
    installation instructions, 107
    installation package, 106
    integer (data type), 192
    JavaScript View, 129
    JSON View, 129
    language-dependent file, 170
    library, 109
    loadData, 212
    MVC, 138

SAPUI5 (Cont.)
 named binding, 183
 namespace, 154
 Namespace, 220
 Notation, 138
 Page body, 131
 placeAt, 135
 platform, 116
 Predefined event, 131
 property binding, 175
 renderer, 326
 resource, 152
 runtime version, 154
 setModel, 175
 strings (data type), 193
 support packages, 106
 Team Provider, 109, 113, 141
 themes, 155
 time (data type), 196
 XML View, 129
 your own type, 196
sap.ui class, 222
sap.ui.commons, 224, 253
sap.ui.commons.Accordion, 342
sap.ui.commons.AccordionSection, 342
sap.ui.commons.Button, 303, 310, 311,
 334, 343, 348
sap.ui.commons.ComboBox, 325, 332,
 333, 347
sap.ui.commons.DatePicker, 322, 331
sap.ui.commons.Dialog, 347
sap.ui.commons.FileUploader, 311
sap.ui.commons.form.SimpleForm, 322
sap.ui.commons.form.
 SimpleFormLayout.GridLayout, 322
sap.ui.commons.Image, 311
sap.ui.commons.Label, 298, 299, 303,
 310, 347
sap.ui.commons.layout.Horizontal-
 hLayout, 298, 347
sap.ui.commons.layout.Matrix-hLayout,
 298, 299, 308, 316, 341
sap.ui.commons.layout.
 MatrixLayoutCell, 299, 309
sap.ui.commons.layout.
 MatrixLayoutRow, 299

sap.ui.commons.layout.Vertical-
 hLayout, 294, 304, 342, 347
sap.ui.commons.MessageBox, 349
sap.ui.commons.RadioButton, 333
sap.ui.commons.RatingIndicator, 318
sap.ui.commons.RowRepeater, 299
sap.ui.commons.TextArea, 334, 347
sap.ui.commons.TextField, 298, 303,
 310
sap.ui.commons.TextView, 298, 309,
 316, 318, 341, 342
sap.ui.commons.Toolbar, 317, 343
sap.ui.core.Control.extend, 325
sap.ui.core.CustomData, 441
sap.ui.core.EventBus, 435
sap.ui.core.HTML, 303
sap.ui.core.ListItem, 332, 347
sap.ui.layout.VerticalLayout, 311
sap.ui.model.Filter, 298, 331, 332, 343,
 442
sap.ui.model.FilterOperator, 331, 332
sap.ui.model.json.JSONModel, 296,
 321, 337
sap.ui.model.odata.Filter, 376
sap.ui.model.odata.ODataModel, 375
sap.ui.model.type.DateTime, 317, 328,
 341
sap.ui.model.type.Time, 328
sap.ui.table, 275, 314
sap.ui.table.Column, 317, 318, 328
sap.ui.table.Table, 317, 328
sap.ui.ux3, 273
sap.ui.ux3.NotificationBar, 295
sap.ui.ux3.Notifier, 295
sap.ui.ux3.OverlayDialog, 293
sap.ui.ux3.Shell, 291
sap.ui.ux3.ToolPopup, 323
sap.viz, 275, 314
sap.viz.ui5.data.FlattenedDataset, 319,
 335
sap.viz.ui5.Line, 335
sap.viz.ui5.Pie, 320
SE63, 189
SearchField, 259
 control, 263
SegmentedButton, 270

SEGW, 358
Selector, 41
Semantic separation, 24
Service Marketplace, 113
Shell
   content, 290
   control, 290
   designType, 295
   headerItem, 290
   search function, 300
   WorksetItem, 290
SimpleForm container, 243
singleColumn, 239
SMTP, 118
SplitApp-Control, 418, 429
Splitter Control -> see
   splitterOrientation, 249
splitterOrientation, 249
Standard plug-ins, 112
   SAP symbol, 315
Stateful, 217
Stateless, 216
String concatenation, 60
Style guide, 117
System alias, 357

T

Tab, 251
Table control, 275
Tabstrip Layout, 251
Tag
   <footer> , 24
   <header>, 24
   <section>, 24
Task handler, 118
TCP/IP, 118
Team Provider, 113, 141
   functions, 109
Template, 176
TextArea, 259, 264
Text
   element, 188
   type, 185

TextField, 259
   liveChange, 298
TextView, 253, 256
Theme, 155, 204
   blue crystal, 155
   gold reflection, 155
   high contrast black, 155
   mobile visual identity, 156
   platinum, 155
Theme Designer, 203
   basis Theme, 204
   preview function, 206
Theming, 199
Toggle-Button, 253, 256
ToolBar, 270
ToolPopup control, 322
Transaction SICF, 107
   SMICM, 125
Translation
   object types, 185
   tool, 173
Transportable object, 145
Type conversion, 61
Type selector, 41

U

UI controls, 154
UI Development Toolkit for HTML5,
   107
Universal selector, 41
User Experience Guideline, 273
UX3 controls, 273

V

ValueHelpField, 259, 264
Variable value
   undefined, 59
   zero, 59
VerticalLayout control, 228
View, 125, 126
   Initial, 128

W

W3C standard, 81
Web console, 167
Web developer tools, 39

X

XMLHttpRequest, 99
XML Model, 169

XML View, 129
XS
    project, *389*

Y

Your own control, 278

- Learn how you can integrate SAP with non-SAP UIs and applications

- Create OData services for UI and application development

- Get step-by-step instructions on using Gateway and OData to connect UIs, mobile, web, and enterprise applications to SAP

Carsten Bönnen, Volker Drees, André Fischer, Ludwig Heinz, Karsten Strothmann

OData and SAP NetWeaver Gateway

Facebook uses OData, Netflix uses OData—and now, with SAP NetWeaver Gateway, so does SAP. In this comprehensive guide, learn everything you need to know about how to use Gateway to make SAP system data accessible from any device, platform, or environment. Familiarize yourself with the concepts of OData and REST, get step-by-step instructions on developing services, and learn how to administer a Gateway system.

666 pp., 2014, 69,95 Euro / US$ 69.95
ISBN 978-1-59229-907-2
www.sap-press.com

Galileo Press

■ Understand the impact of SAP
HANA on ABAP application
development

■ Learn how to develop applications
for SAP HANA with SAP NetWeaver
AS ABAP 7.4

■ Work with advanced functions
such as fuzzy search and predictive
analysis

Thorsten Schneider, Eric Westenberger, Hermann Gahm

ABAP Development for SAP HANA

They say there's nothing new under the sun—but every once in a while,
something novel comes along. With SAP HANA, even the most seasoned ABAP
developers have some learning to do. Newbie or not, this book can help: install
the Eclipse IDE, brush up your database programming skills, perform runtime
and error analysis, transport old ABAP applications to HANA—and more.
Expand your horizons!

609 pp., 2014, 69,95 Euro / US$ 69.95
ISBN 978-1-59229-859-4
www.sap-press.com

Interested in reading more?

Please visit our website for all new
book and e-book releases from SAP PRESS.

www.sap-press.com